British Folk Customs

Hutchinson of London

British Folk Customs

Christina Hole

By the same author

E. & M. A. Radford
Encyclopedia of Superstitions
edited and revised by Christina Hole

Hutchinson & Co (Publishers) Ltd
3 Fitzroy Square, London W1

London Melbourne Sydney Auckland
Wellington Johannesburg and agencies
throughout the world

First published 1976

Set in Monotype Baskerville
Printed in Great Britain by litho by
The Anchor Press Ltd and bound by
Wm Brendon & Son Ltd
both of Tiptree, Essex

ISBN 0 09 127340 4

CONTENTS

FOREWORD

In this book certain traditional customs and ceremonies of Great Britain have been briefly described. Of these, some are still alive today and can be seen by anyone, at least in the modern form to which the changing years have brought them. Others have vanished now, but flourished until fairly recently, and did not disappear until some time, early or late, in the last century. The accounts here given are arranged in alphabetical order, for convenience, but the book itself does not attempt to be anything like an encyclopedia. Rather, it is a more or less random collection of customs, chosen for their intrinsic interest, or their beauty, their importance, former or present, in the lives of the people and, in many cases, for the length of their history and their faraway beginnings in pagan or early Christian times. Much that is, or was, important, or beautiful, has been left out for reasons of space, since to include everything would need a book of enormous size, or more than one. Thus, the ancient Mummers' play has been mentioned only slightly and occasionally, and so too, Morris and Sword Dancing, though a great deal of space could rightly be devoted to the growth and history of both dancing and play. Similarly, and for the same reason, only three or four out of our many fairs, surviving or otherwise, have been included, and these chiefly because of some particular oddity of custom or tradition attaching to them.

Folk-custom ranges freely through countless centuries, and carries us back to our earliest recorded beginnings, and beyond. May Day retains its essentially pagan character today, as in the past, in spite of the new accretions of political processions and the like which have been imposed upon it. The people who burn the Clavie at Burghead on Old New Year's Eve are doing what their Stone Age ancestors did, just as, farther south and in a milder season, the inhabitants of Helston continue to bring home the Summer in the Furry Dance, like their far-off forefathers before them. Many still existing customs have their roots in the Middle Ages, like the Tichborne Dole, or the Lot Meadow Mowing at Yarnton, or the horseshoe tribute paid by peers coming to Oakham Castle for the first time. And there are some which are comparatively new in time, but have already acquired the status of fixed customs, such as the Christmas card, which only came into general use in the middle of the nineteenth century, or the still more modern Oranges and Lemons ceremony, which dates from 1920.

Yet, if some of our surviving customs can trace their ancestry a very long way back, and have hitherto resisted all attempts to uproot them, many others have vanished for ever. Especially, they disappeared during the last hundred and fifty years or so, for this was a period of great change everywhere, affecting traditional customs as much as anything else. Shifting populations, new building spreading over lands long dedicated to festival games, or dances, or the holding of unofficial fairs, new methods on the farm that have done away with ancient harvest or sheep-shearing ceremonies – all this, and much more, has contributed to the steady decline of old ways, and so, of course, has the incidence of the two great wars of this century. Even while this book was being written, that lively, noisy pre-dawn parade of young people known as Teddy Rowe's Band, which is thought to be at least five hundred years old, and perhaps older, and regularly ushered in Pack Monday Fair at Sherborne, has sunk beneath the weight of a police ban, and is not very likely to rise to the surface again.

Within the text itself I have ignored the county boundary changes which have taken place since the Second World War, since the old counties represented historic areas significant in the study of folk customs. However, for the convenience of those wishing to visit the places concerned today, the new county locations are indicated in the Calendar and map.

'The present generation', wrote P. H. Ditchfield in 1896, 'has witnessed the extinction of many observances which our fathers practised and revered, and doubtless the progress of decay will continue. We have entered upon a diminished inheritance.'[1] Yet it was then, and it still is, an inheritance full of life and vigour. More than seventy years after he wrote, a host of living customs still flourishes in different parts of Great Britain. Some have greatly changed in detail and in date. Some have lost much of their old meaning and significance; many that had been allowed to lapse have been revived, like the Pancake Race at Olney, or the dancers' visit to Salisbury Cathedral during the Grovely ceremonies. And some that P. H. Ditchfield[1] recorded in his book have disappeared. Of these survivals and revivals, and of their nineteenth-century predecessors which did not survive, a few are hereafter described.

Oxford CHRISTINA HOLE

1. P. H. Ditchfield, *Old English Customs* (1896).

SELECT CALENDAR

JANUARY	New Year's Day		January 1st
	Last Part of Twelve Days of Christmas		1st week of January
	Mari Lwyd visits	South Wales	1st week of January
	First Footing		January 1st
	Street Football	Kirkwall, Orkneys	January 1st
	Needle & Thread Ceremony	The Queen's College, Oxford	January 1st
	Baddeley Cake Ceremony	Drury Lane Theatre, London	January 6th
	Haxey Hood	Haxey, Lincolnshire (Humberside)	January 6th
	Royal Epiphany Gifts	Chapel Royal, London	January 6th
	Plough Sunday Services & Blessing of Ploughs	Many parishes	Sunday following January 6th
	Burning the Clavie	Burghead, Morayshire (Grampian)	January 11th, New Year's Eve, Old Style
	Hunting the Mallard	All Souls College Oxford	January 14th – every 100 years. Next due, 2001
	Wassailling Orchards	Roadwater and Carhampton, Somerset	January 17th Old Twelfth Night
	Up Helly-aa	Lerwick, Shetland	Last Tuesday in January
	Maids Money diced for	Guildford, Surrey	End of January
FEBRUARY	Candlemas Day		February 2nd

Cradle-Rocking Ceremony	Blidworth, Nottinghamshire	Sunday next February 2nd
Forty Shilling Day	Wotton, Surrey	Candlemas Day (or later if weather very bad)
Carlow Bread Dole	Woodbridge, Suffolk	February 2nd
Jethart Ba'	Jedburgh, Roxburgh (Borders)	Candlemas Day, (Also Fastern's E'en)
St Valentine's Day		February 14th
Blessing the Salmon-Net Fisheries	Norham-on-Tweed, Northumberland	February 14th
Shrovetide and Lent		*See Movable Feasts p. 15*
Whuppity Stourie	Lanark (Strathclyde)	March 1st
Tichborne Dole	Tichborne, Hampshire	March 25th
Oranges and Lemons Ceremony	St Clement Danes, London	March 31st, or near
All Fools' Day		April 1st
Candle Auction	Tatworth, Somerset	Tuesday after April 6th
Holy Week and Easter		*See Movable Feasts p. 15*
May Day		May 1st
Garland Dressing Day	Charlton-on-Otmoor, Oxfordshire	May 1st
Hobby Horse Day	Padstow, Cornwall	May 1st

MARCH

APRIL

MAY

Hobby Horse Day	Minehead, Somerset	May 1st
Singing on Magdalen Tower	Oxford	May 1st
Singing on Bargate	Southampton, Hampshire	May 1st
Furry Dance	Helston, Cornwall	May 8th
Garland Day	Abbotsbury, Dorset	May 13th Old May Day
Lilies and Roses Ceremony	Tower of London	May 21st
Arbor Tree Day	Aston on Clun, Shropshire (Salop)	May 29th
Garland King Day	Castleton, Derbyshire	May 29th
Grovely	Wishford Magna, Wiltshire	May 29th
Neville's Cross Commemoration	Durham Cathedral	May 29th
Oak Apple Day (or Royal Oak Day)		May 29th
Founder's Day	Chelsea Royal Hospital, London	May 29th or near
Oak Apple Day Celebrations	Leycester Hospital, Warwick; Northampton; and Worcester	May 29th, or near May 29th, or near May 29th, or near
Ascension and Whitsuntide		*See Movable Feasts p. 15*

JUNE

Midsummer Bonfires	Cornwall (various parishes)	June 23rd, Midsummer Eve
Knollys Rose Ceremony	Mansion House, London	June 24th

Peace & Good Neighbourhood Dinner	Kidderminster, Worcestershire, (Hereford and Worcester)	June 24th (or near)
Well-Dressing	Buxton, Derbyshire	Thursday nearest Midsummer Day
Well-Dressing	Youlgreave, Derbyshire	Saturday nearest Midsummer Day
Rushes strewn in Church	Barrowden, Rutland (Leicestershire)	June 28th
Rushbearing	Warcop, Westmorland (Cumbria)	June 29th
Rushbearing	Great Musgrave, Westmorland (Cumbria)	June 29th
Hay strewn in Church	Wingrave, Buckinghamshire	Sunday after June 29th

JULY

Lot Meadow Mowing	Yarnton, Oxfordshire	Early in July
Midsummer Bonfires	Whalton, Northumberland	July 4th Old Midsummer Eve
Bawming the Thorn	Appleton Thorn, Cheshire	July 5th, Old Midsummer, Intermittent
Tynwald Ceremonies	Isle of Man	July 5th, Old Midsummer
New-mown Hay in Church	Glenfield, Leicestershire	Thursday after July 6th
Hay strewn in Church	Old Weston, Huntingdonshire (Cambridgeshire)	Sunday nearest July 15th

Knillian Games	St Ives, Cornwall	July 25th. Every five years. Next due 1981
Horn Fair, Ebernoe	Ebernoe, W. Sussex	July 25th
Rush-bearing	Ambleside, Westmorland (Cumbria)	Last Saturday in July
Swan-Upping	On R. Thames, London to Henley	End of July

AUGUST

Lammas Day		August 1st
Doggett's Coat & Badge Race	London	August 1st – or near
Minden Day		August 1st
Clipping the Church	Guiseley, Yorkshire (W. Yorkshire)	August 5th
Rushbearing	Grasmere, Westmorland (Cumbria)	Saturday nearest August 5th
Woodmen of Arden, Grand Wardmote of	Meriden, Warwicks (West Midlands)	Early August
Well-Dressing	Barlow, Derbyshire	Wednesday after August 10th
Burning Bartle	West Witton, Yorks	Saturday nearest August 24th St Bartholomew's Day
Preston Guild	Preston, Lancashire	Week following August 29th, or near. Every 20 years. Next due – 1992

Plague Memorial Service	Eyam, Derbyshire	Last Sunday in August	
Burryman's Parade	S. Queensferry, W. Lothian (Lothian)	c. 2nd week in August	
St Giles' Day		September 1st	*SEPTEMBER*
St Giles' Fair	Oxford	Monday and Tuesday after first Sunday after St Giles' Day	
Oyster Season, Opening the	Colchester, Essex	September 1st	
Horn Dance	Abbots Bromley, Staffordshire	Monday after the first Sunday after September 4th (Wakes Monday)	
Sheriff's Ride	Lichfield, Staffordshire	September 8th	
Clipping the Church	Painswick, Gloucestershire	Sunday next September 19th	
Bellringers' Feast	Twyford, Hampshire	October 7th	*OCTOBER*
Lion Sermon preached	St Katharine Cree Church, London	October 16th	
Oyster Feast	Colchester, Essex	October 20th, or near	
Punkie Night	Hinton St George, Somerset	Last Thursday in October	
Horseshoe and Faggot-cutting Quit Rents	London, (Royal Courts of Justice)	During October	
Hallowe'en		Oct. 31st – Nov. 2nd	
Soul-Caking Play	Antrobus, Cheshire	November 2nd	*NOVEMBER*

Souling	Cheshire, Shropshire (Salop)	Occasional November 2nd
Guy Fawkes Night	General	November 5th
Bonfire Night	Ottery St Mary, Devon; Edenbridge, Kent; Bridgwater, Somerset; Battle, Lewes, Newhaven, Rye, E. Sussex; and elsewhere	November 5th
Turning the Devil's Boulder	Shebbear, Devon	November 5th
Mischief Night	Yorkshire and other parts of Northern England	November 4th Guy Fawkes' Eve
Martinmas (St Martin's Day)		November 11th
Firing the Fenny Poppers	Fenny Stratford, Buckinghamshire	November 11th
Wroth Silver paid	Knightlow Cross, Warwickshire	November 11th

DECEMBER

First Part of Twelve Days of Christmas		Last Week of December
Christmas Day customs & ceremonies	General	December 25th
Ringing the Devil's Knell	Dewsbury, Yorkshire (W. Yorkshire)	December 24th
Boar's Head Ceremony	Queen's College, Oxford	December 25th, or near
New Year's Eve	General	December 31st
Burning the Old Year Out	Biggar, Lanark (Strathclyde); Wick, Caithness (Highland)	December 31st

Flambeaux Procession	Comrie, Perthshire (Tayside)	December 31st
Fireball Parade	Stonehaven, Kincardineshire (Grampian)	December 31st
Tar-Barrel ceremony	Allendale, Northumberland	December 31st
MOVABLE FEASTS		
Shrovetide		February or March
Shrove Monday		Monday before start of Lent
Hurling	St Ives, Cornwall	Shrove Monday
Shrove Tuesday or Fastern's E'en		Tuesday before start of Lent
Hurling	St Columb Major, Cornwall	Shrove Tuesday
Football	Alnwick, Northumberland; Ashbourne, Derbyshire; Atherstone, Warwickshire; Sedgefield, Durham	Shrove Tuesday
Skipping	Scarborough, Yorkshire (N. Yorkshire) on beach	Shrove Tuesday
Pancake Greeze	Westminster School	Shrove Tuesday
Pancake Race	Olney, Buckinghamshire	Shrove Tuesday
Ash Wednesday		1st Day of Lent
Start of Marbles Season		Ash Wednesday

Mothering Sunday, or Simnel Sunday		Fourth Sunday in Lent
Palm Sunday		1st Day of Holy Week
Pax cakes, Distribution of	Hentland and Sellack, Herefordshire (Hereford and Worcester)	Palm Sunday
Royal Maundy Distribution	Westminster Abbey in years of even date: other churches or cathedrals in those of odd date.	Maundy Thursday
Travice Dole	Leigh, Lancashire (Greater Manchester)	Maundy Thursday
Good Friday		Friday before Easter
Burning Judas	Liverpool, Lancashire (Merseyside)	Good Friday
Skipping	Alciston, S. Heighton, E. Sussex	Good Friday
Pace-Egg Play Acted	Midgley, W. Yorkshire	Good Friday
Marbles Championship Match	Tinsley Green, W. Sussex	Good Friday
End of Marbles Season		Good Friday
Football	Workington, Cumberland (Cumbria)	Good Friday (Also Easter Tuesday and Easter Saturday)
Maidservants' Charity	Reading, Berkshire	Good Friday

Borrington Dole	Ideford, Devon	Good Friday
Butterworth Dole	St Bartholomew the Great, London	Good Friday
Candle Auction	Aldermaston, Berkshire	Eastertide – every 3rd year
Clipping the Church	Radley, Berkshire (Oxfordshire)	Easter Sunday
Biddenden Dole	Biddenden, Kent	Easter Monday
Hare-Pie Scramble and Bottle-Kicking	Hallaton, Leicestershire	Easter Monday
Egg-rolling	Preston, Lancashire; Edinburgh, Midlothian (Lothian); Derby; Penrith, Cumberland (Cumbria) etc.	Easter Monday
Riding the Black Lad	Ashton-under-Lyne, Lancashire (Greater Manchester)	Easter Monday (Intermittent)
Running Auction	Bourne, Lincolnshire	Easter Monday
Hocktide Ceremonies	Hungerford, Berkshire	2nd Monday & Tuesday after Easter
Blessing Crops, Ships, etc., and Beating the Bounds	Many parishes	Rogationtide
Midsummer Tithes	Wishford Magna, Wiltshire	Rogation Monday
Planting the Penny Hedge	Whitby, Yorkshire (N. Yorkshire)	Ascension Eve
Well-Dressing	Tissington, Derbyshire	Ascension Day
Bread and Cheese Distribution	St Briavels, Gloucestershire	Whit Sunday

Rushes strewn in Church at Lord Mayor's Visit to St Mary Redcliffe	Bristol, Gloucestershire (Avon)	Whit Sunday
Cheese-rolling	Cooper's Hill, Gloucestershire	Whit Monday
Dicing for Bibles	St Ives, Huntingdonshire (Cambridgeshire)	Whit Monday
Dunmow Flitch Trial	Great Dunmow, Essex, (usually) or elsewhere	Whit Monday
Corby Pole Fair	Corby, Northamptonshire	Whit Monday. Every 20 years, next due – 1982
Greenhill Bower & Court of Array	Lichfield, Staffordshire	Whit Monday, or near
Ramroasting Fair	Kingsteignton, Devon	Whit Monday
Well-Dressing	Wirksworth, Derbyshire	Whit Monday or some other day in Whit week
Grass-Strewing	Shenington, Oxfordshire	Trinity Sunday & following Sunday
		N.B. Events formerly held on Whit Monday are often transferred to the new Spring Holiday (May 28th), and should be checked by those wishing to see them.
DAILY or OCCASIONAL CUSTOMS		
Ceremony of the Queen's Keys	Tower of London	Nightly

Oakham Horseshoe, given by Peer on first visit	Oakham Castle, Rutland, (Leicestershire)	On the occasion of a Peer's first visit
Horn-Blowing	Ripon, Yorkshire (N. Yorkshire)	Nightly
Horn-Blowing	Bainbridge, Yorkshire (N. Yorkshire)	Every night between Michaelmas Eve and Shrove Tuesday
Searching the Houses of Parliament	London	Before State Opening of Parliament
Wayfarers' Dole,	St Cross, Winchester, Hampshire	Daily

THE TRADITIONAL COUNTIES

1 Cornwall
2 Devon
3 Somerset
4 Dorset
5 Wiltshire
6 Hampshire
7 Sussex
8 Kent
9 Surrey
10 Berkshire
11 Essex
12 Middlesex
13 Hertfordshire
14 Bedfordshire
17 Buckinghamshire
16 Oxfordshire
17 Gloucestershire
18 Warwickshire
19 Northamptonshire
20 Cambridgeshire
21 Suffolk
22 Norfolk
23 Herefordshire
24 Shropshire
25 Worcestershire
26 Leicestershire
27 Nottinghamshire
28 Lincolnshire
29 Staffordshire
30 Derbyshire
31 Cheshire
32 Lancashire
33 Yorkshire
34 Durham
35 Northumberland
36 Cumberland
37 Westmorland
38 Rutland
39 Huntingdon & Peterborough
40 Glamorgan
41 Caernarvon
42 Merioneth
43 Flint
44 Denbigh
45 Montgomery
46 Radnor
47 Brecknock
48 Pembroke
49 Carmarthen
50 Cardigan
51 Monmouth

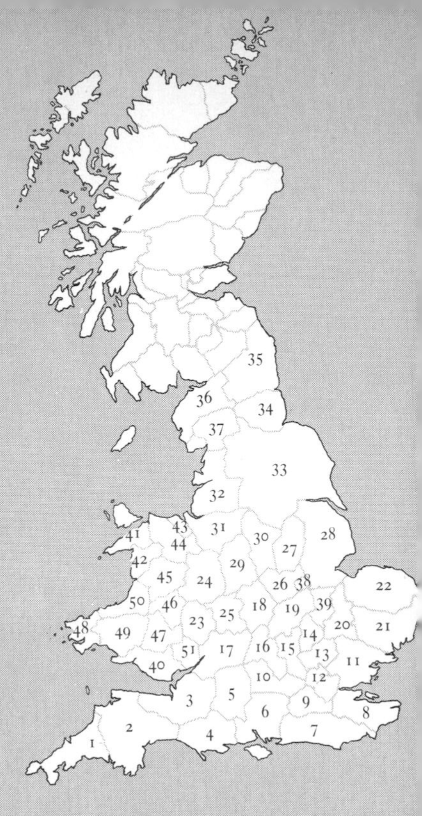

THE MODERN COUNTIES

1 Cornwall
2 Devon
3 Somerset
4 Dorset
5 Avon
6 Wiltshire
7 Hampshire
8 Isle of Wight
9 West Sussex
10 East Sussex
11 Kent
12 Surrey
13 Berkshire
14 Essex
15 Hertfordshire
16 Bedfordshire
17 Buckinghamshire
18 Oxfordshire
19 Gloucestershire
20 Warwickshire
21 Northamptonshire
22 Cambridgeshire
23 Suffolk
24 Norfolk
25 Hereford & Worcester
26 Leicestershire
27 Nottinghamshire
28 Lincolnshire
29 Salop
30 Staffordshire
31 Derbyshire
32 Cheshire
33 Humberside
34 Lancashire
35 North Yorkshire
36 Cleveland
37 Durham
38 Cumbria
39 Northumberland
40 Gwynedd
41 Clwyd
42 Dyfed
43 Powys
44 West Glamorgan
45 Mid Glamorgan
46 South Glamorgan
47 Gwent
48 Tyne and Wear
49 Merseyside
50 Greater Manchester
51 West Yorkshire
52 South Yorkshire
53 West Midlands
54 Greater London

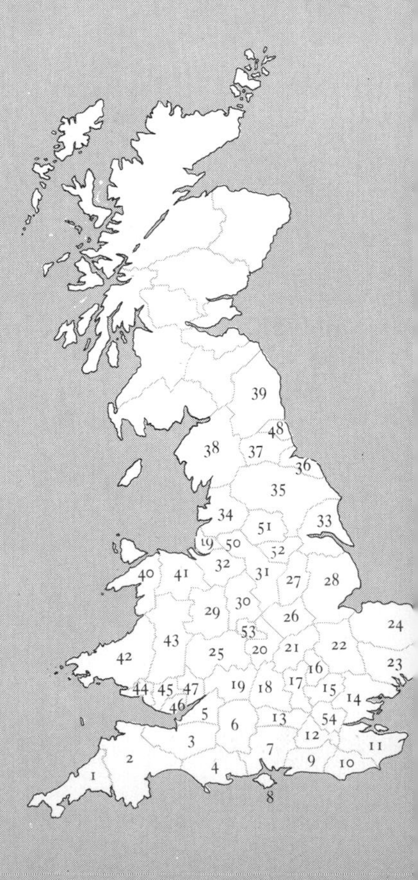

Warrington
Manchester
Appleton
Whitley
Antrobus
Castleton
Great Budworth
Knutsford
Tideswell
Buxton
Great Hucklow
Bakewell
Youlgreave
Parwich
Wirksworth
Tissington
Ashbourne
Norham-on-Tweed
Kirkwall, Orkneys
Wick
Lerwick, Shetland
Alnwick
Burghead
Whalton
Cullercoats
Newcastle-upon-Tyne
North Shields
Allendale
Balmoral
Durris
Stonehaven
Chester-le-Street
Hebrides
Durham
Aberfeldy.
Penrith
Sedgefield
Dunkeld
Dundee.
Workington
Warcop
Connel Ferry
Comrie
Brough
St Andrews
Grasmere
Great Musgrave
Bannockburn
Ambleside
Far and Near Sawrey
Whitby
South Queensferry.
Edinburgh
Bainbridge
West Witton
St John's
Glasgow
Tynwald Hill
Ripon
Scarborough
Douglas
Lanark
Biggar
Jedburgh
Scotton
Barton-le-Street
Skipton
York
Guiseley.
Kirkmaiden
Morley
Kirkham
Bradford
Barwick-in-Elmet
Preston
Calder Valley
Hedon
Dewsbury
Midgley
Pontefract
Barton
Leigh
Hooton Pagnell
Epworth
Broughton
Little Crosby
Ashton-under-Lyne
Grimsby
Appleton
Stockport
Doncaster
Haxey
Liverpool
Anglesey
Caistor
Prestatyn
Heswall
Mobberley
Neston
Comberbach
Glentham
Knutsford
Barlow
Horncastle
Chester
Tarvin
Congleton
Blidworth
Eyam
Barthomley
Belper
Eardington
Abbots Bromley
Duffield
Nottingham
Oswestry
Derby
Ellesmere
Enville
Rippingale
Frisby-on-the-Wreak
Darlaston
Llanfyllin
Shrewsbury
Bilston
Bourne
Lichfield
Pontesbury
Oakham
Wellington
Glenfield
Wichnor
Barrowden
Wisbech
Norwich
Longnor
Leicester
Bridgnorth
Walsall
Atherstone
Peterborough
Stretton Valley
Hallaton
Coleshill
Hinckley
Corby
Whittlesey
Kempton
Halesowen
Glatton
Coventry
Ramsey
Aston on Clun
Meriden
Knightlow Cross
Ludlow
Old Weston
St Ives
Kidderminster
Kenilworth
Ellington
Godmanchester
Warwick
Dunchurch
Wootton Wawen
Eynesbury
Northampton
Worcester
Bascote
Hildersham
Golden Valley
Welford-on-Avon
Stratford-on-Avon
Ampthill Park
Woodbridge
Olney
Linton
Llanwenog
Peterchurch
King's Caple
Overbury
Fenny Stratford
Edlesborough
St Davids
Shenington
Sellack
Hentland
Somerton
Baldock
Great Dunmow
Spelsbury
Kirtlington
Drayton Beauchamp
Cooper's Hill (Brockworth)
Witney
Colchester
Brightlingsea
Randwick
Dunstable Downs
Painswick
Little Waltham
St Briavels
Headington
Kingscote
St Albans
Epping
Dursley
Rochford
Tetbury
Whitchurch
Henley-on-Thames
Rayleigh
Kingston St Michael
Harlington
Bristol
Woolwich
Eton
Wargrave
Chelsea
Silbury Hill
Windsor
Hungerford
Charlton
Rochester
Broadstairs
Reading
Congresbury
Aldermaston
Camberley
Kingston-on
Mitcham
Chatham
Reculver
Bradford-on-Avon
-Thames
Minehead
Combe Martin
Guildford
Charing
Wishford
Exmoor
Carhampton
Stourton
Dorking
Magna
Chilbolton
Edenbridge
Roadwater
Chedzoy
Wotton
Mere
Biddenden
Bridgwater
Winchester
Tinsley Green
Folkestone
Clovelly
Motcombe
Salisbury
Tichborne
South Molton
Langport
Martock
Shaftesbury
Morwenstow
Cheriton
Hinton St George
Twyford
Battle
Rye
Sherborne
Ebernoe
Lewes
Shebbear
Henscott
Tatworth
South Petherton
Hastings
Southampton
Durweston
Ottery St Mary.
Brighton
Whitchurch Canonicorum
Alciston
Exeter
Mudeford
Newhaven
Powerstock
Northleigh
South Heighton
Padstow
Buckland-in-the-Moor
Kingsteignton
St Columb Major
Bishopsteignton
Tavistock
Holne
Torwood Manor
Little Colan
Ideford
St Blazey
Brixham
Ives
Woodstock
Kidlington
Yarnton
Eynsham
Burford
Charlton-on-Otmoor
Wilcote
Oxford
Headington
Helston
Bampton-in-the-Bush
Cumnor
Radley
Scilly Isles
Uffington
Drayton
East Hendred

Advent Images. *(See Wassailing.)*

All Fools' Day. The first day of April is known in England as All Fools' Day, or April Fool's Day or, in some northern districts as April Noddy Day. In Scotland and along the Border it is Huntigowk Day or Gowkin' Day. Other countries have other names for this cheerful anniversary[1] on which, by time-honoured and widespread custom, any person, young or old, important or otherwise, may be made an April Fool between the hours of midnight and noon.

Children are, of course, very keen supporters of the tradition although some of the more elaborate practical jokes perpetrated on this day cannot be laid at their door. Their victims are of all types and ages – other children, parents, schoolteachers, tradesmen, friends, or any one else unwary enough to fall into their well-laid traps. Most of their tricks are far from original, and many have been used so often that they have now become traditional, yet they succeed again and again, and will probably go on doing so for a long time to come. One is to tell someone that his shoelace is undone, or his tie is crooked, or that something else is wrong with his dress, when in fact all is in order. As long ago as 1825, William Hone recorded how, thirty years before he wrote, boys would stop a man in the street and say, 'Sir, if you please, your shoe's unbuckled', and then joyously shout 'April Fool!' when he looked at his feet. When buckles went out of fashion, the joke was transferred to laces.[1]

1. Making fools of people on April 1st, or near it, is a custom known in France, Sweden, Germany, Portugal, and elsewhere in Europe, in the United States of America, and in other English-speaking countries. In India, Huli Fools are made on the last day of the Huli Festival in late March.

Other 'stock pieces' are the false summons to the door or, nowadays, to the telephone, the urgent call to deal with a domestic disaster that has not occurred, or the sharp warning that an insect is crawling over the victim's clothes or neck. Nearer to the true practical joke is the empty eggshell set upside down in the cup at breakfast, the basin of water placed where someone will step into it, the sleeve or trouser-leg sewn up, or the letter that either mocks its recipient with the words 'April Fool', or contains some deceiving message or invitation. One of the earliest known English examples of this last trick is recorded in Drake's *News-Letter* for April 2nd, 1698, where we read that a number of people received invitations to see the lions washed at the Tower of London on April 1st, and duly went there for the purpose. Precisely the same trick was played with equal success by some unknown person in 1860.

Best-loved of all is the bootless errand. The young and innocent may be sent to fetch a pint of pigeon's milk, a pennyworth of strap-oil or elbow-grease, a guttering-peg, or some other non-existent commodity. Apprentices and juniors in factories and offices are despatched by their straight-faced elders to buy a pot of striped paint, or a soft-pointed chisel, or a box

1. William Hone, *The Everyday Book*, 1826.

of straight hooks.[1] In Scotland, people are sent upon a gowk's errand. A gowk is properly a cuckoo, but the word also means a fool. The victim is sent out with a note which, unknown to him, contains the words 'Hunt the gowk another mile', or some other message showing what is afoot. When the recipient reads this, he tells the messenger that the answer must be sought at another house. Off goes the poor Huntigowk, only to be told the same thing at the second place. So he goes on, hunting the gowk another mile, and then another, until he finally realizes what is happening, or some kinder-hearted person tells him.

On the stroke of noon, all ends. This rule is rigidly observed everywhere, because to break it causes the mockery to recoil upon the joker's own head. If any one attempts a trick after midday, the intended victim retorts,

> April Fool's gone past,
> You're the biggest fool at last,

or

> April Noddy's past and gone,
> You're the fool and I'm none,

or in a Northumberland version of the couplet,

> The gowk and the titlene sit on the tree,
> You're the gowk as well as me.

A variety of theories have been put forward to account for these lively and persistent customs, but their origin still remains obscure. The fact that they are attached to a date in Spring falling close to the Vernal Equinox, and that they must cease at a fixed hour, suggests that their roots lie deep down in something more than mere outbursts of exuberance. In spirit they are akin to those licensed buffooneries, jests, and extravagances that were once associated with certain religious festivals, like the Saturnalia of ancient Rome, or the mediaeval Feast of Fools, or Feast of Asses. At such festivals, the utmost freedom of speech and action was tolerated, with open mockery of respected persons and institutions, and even burlesques of sacred ceremonies. These odd and often unedifying antics may have been survivals of very ancient rituals, but it was a deep-seated human instinct that made and kept them popular. In all ages, men have loved to mock and deride their fellows, and especially their superiors, whenever it could be done in safety; and it is perhaps the perennial upspringing of that derisory spirit that has kept the fooleries of April 1st alive in so many regions long after their original and deeper meanings have been quite forgotten. *(See May Goslings.)*

Arbor Tree Day. An early Summer custom which is clearly very much older than it is locally supposed to be is the Arbor Tree ceremony at Aston-on-Clun in Shropshire. The Arbor Tree is a large black poplar, standing on the roadway in the centre of the village. Once a year, on May 29th, it is dressed with flags suspended from long poles which are fixed to the main branches. These flags are left hanging during the year, and are then renewed when Arbor Tree Day comes round once more.

It can hardly be doubted that this ceremony, like the somewhat similar ritual at Appleton Thorn in Cheshire (*see Bawming the Thorn*) has its roots in ancient tree-veneration, but local tradition explains it as a commemoration of the

1. In many trades and industries, the fooling of apprentices and novices by their seniors is a traditional custom not confined to April 1st.

wedding of John Marston, then Lord of the Manor, to Mary Carter on May 29th, 1786. The tree was dressed for the occasion, and it is said that the bride was so delighted by this pleasant sight that she gave a sum of money to enable the dressing to be repeated annually on the same day forever. No doubt the Squire's marriage, which did in fact occur on that date, would be celebrated in the village with rejoicing and display, but it is hardly likely that the Arbor Tree custom began as a Georgian wedding compliment. What is more probable is that the bride's gift served to endow, and so to preserve a ceremony that was already firmly established at Aston-on-Clun when she first saw it. How long it had been observed there is, of course, uncertain; but it is perhaps significant that it was then, and is now, associated with Oak Apple Day, that anniversary which has, in the course of time absorbed so many traditional customs older than itself.

Another local tradition, not often spoken of now but apparently remembered by some of the older villagers, is that the flags are put out 'to keep the witches away'. This belief may have some connection with another tree-custom which formerly flourished in Herefordshire. There, a tall birch-sapling, locally called a Maypole, used to be ceremonially brought in on May Day, adorned with red and white streamers, and set up outside the stables. It was left standing all through the year as a protection against witchcraft and misfortune, and to save the horses from being 'hag-ridden' at night. These 'maypoles' are now rarely seen, but in a letter published in *Folklore* (Vol. 70. 1959), it is stated that on one or two farms the old custom is still kept up 'for luck'.

A few years ago it was reported in some newspapers that the twigs of the Arbor Tree were believed to have fertility powers and were much sought after by women desiring children. The twigs, it was said, were asked for, and sent to, brides in many parts of Britain and even farther afield. How this curious idea arose is not clear. It was certainly not supported by any old tradition that could be traced, and was probably one of those spurious pieces of so-called folklore which do spring up from time to time. Nevertheless, it was the cause of good deal of undesirable publicity which, in the short time that it lasted, even endangered the survival of the Arbor Tree ceremony itself. The latter was already threatened by proposals to remove the tree because, standing as it does at a crossroads, it was thought to be an obstacle to traffic. Fortunately, however, no permanent harm was done, and the Arbor Tree still stands and is ritually dressed with its flags as of old.

Armistice Day. *(See Martinmas.)*

Ashen Faggot. The Ashen Faggot was a West-country substitute for the Yule Log which was once very well-known in Devon and Somerset, and is still to be seen there occasionally in houses which have fireplaces wide enough to accommodate it. Instead of the great single log used in other places (*see Yule Log*), a thick faggot of green ash-sticks, firmly held together with bands of ash, or hazel, or bramble-canes, was brought indoors with ceremony on Christmas Eve.[1] Its size varied with that of the hearth on

1. In Somerset, an Ashen Faggot was sometimes burnt on St Catherine's Eve (November 24th), as well as at Christmas. The same cider-drinking customs on the breaking of the bands were observed on both dates. (R. L. Tongue *Somerset Folklore* ed. K. M. Briggs, 1965).

which it was to be burnt, but it was customary to make it as large as possible, and very thick in the centre, to ensure that, once alight, it would go on slowly burning all through the Twelve Days of Christmas. In a house with a really deep open hearth, it could be both huge and heavy, needing to be secured in its place by two stout chains. A faggot of this type was burnt in 1952 in the New Inn at Northleigh in Devon, where the hearth is seven-and-a-half feet wide and three feet deep; it weighed about a hundredweight, was five feet long and eighteen inches thick, and bound with five strong bands of hazel.[1] Many old farmhouses and inns once had immense hearths of this sort, needing faggots of similar majestic size. When grates came into fashion, smaller bundles sufficed, and these are still used in some houses today. Even the difficulty of narrow, modern fireplaces is occasionally overcome by the use of miniature faggots.

An important part of the Ashen Faggot ritual was watching for the breaking of the bands in the heat of the fire. These bands varied in number, sometimes four or five, often nine, and sometimes many more. Their bursting one by one, was a signal for cheerful toasts and renewed drinking by all present, and also for a form of marriage-divination. Young people would each choose a band beforehand and then watch carefully to see how it fared. He or she whose band was the first to break would be the first to marry. An eye-witness' account of the celebrations in 1836 at Torwood Manor, near Torquay, says that the faggot there was drawn to the house-door by a team of four oxen, not so much because the load was more than one ox could manage as because custom required that there should be four. As many bands as possible had been tied round it in its making, and as each one broke in the flames, the assembled company demanded, and received a fresh gallon of cider.[1] This tradition still survives, though the response is not always quite so generous today. In some country inns where the Ashen Faggot still appears, the landlord provides a free round of cider, or ale, when the first (or the last) band breaks.

1. J. R. W. Coxhead *Old Devon Customs*, 1957.

1. *Transactions of the Devonshire Association*, Vol. 6. 1873.

Baddeley Cake. (*See Twelfth Day Revels.*)

Barring-Out the Schoolmaster. Barring-out the Schoolmaster was a lively custom once enthusiastically observed by the scholars of numerous old-established schools on certain traditional dates which varied in different districts. Of these, the most usual seem to have been Shrove Tuesday, or St Nicholas Day, or the last day of the Christmas term, but the practice has also been recorded on St Andrew's and St Thomas' Days, at the beginning of Harvest, or just before Easter.

On the appointed morning, the children locked the master out of his own school, and refused to let him in until he had granted a holiday for that day, or according to some of the earliest accounts, had promised a number of holidays during the coming twelve months. All his attempts to enter were fiercely resisted, and while the siege continued, the defenders shouted or sang traditional barring-out rhymes. There were many versions of these. At Frisby-on-the-Wreak in Leicestershire, on Shrove Tuesday, the children sang:

> Pardon, master, pardon,
> Pardon in a pin;
> If you don't give us a holiday,
> We won't let you in.

A Scottish ditty for St Thomas' Day ran:

> This is the shortest day,
> An' we maun hae the play,
> An' if ye wunna gies the play,
> We'll steek ye oot a' the day.

In some cases, 'a' the day' was an understatement. Brand says in his *Popular Antiquities* (1849 edition) that if the scholars could hold out for three days, they were automatically victorious, and a treaty was then made with the master, in which he granted them at least some of their demands and exempted all concerned from punishment. In the *Denham Tracts*, however, it is recorded that one famous barring-out at Alnwick Grammar School lasted for a week, beginning on St Andrew's Day. But if the master somehow managed to effect an entry, or the scholars were unable to hang out for as long as three days, through lack of food or adequate preparations then the victory was his, and he was entitled to make his own terms with his unruly scholars.

In *The Captain's Wife*, Eiluned Lewis relates how barring-out was observed, though in a mild form, when her mother was a child at St Davids. In the school she attended, the summer holiday date was fixed by the needs of the local farmers, who wanted their children home to help with the harvest. On a certain day, therefore, some ripe ears of corn were brought to the school, and laid upon the mistress' desk. Then, at the first opportunity provided by her temporary absence, the door was locked against her, and the room barricaded with benches pulled from their places. When she returned, and demanded to be let in, a month's holiday was at once asked for, and granted. No Summer Term ever ended without this traditional uprising of the pupils.

At Tideswell, in Derbyshire, the schoolmaster was barred out on Shrove Tuesday until at least as late as 1938. The children rode to school on long poles, carrying each other in turn, and having arrived there, hastened to lock the door against the headmaster. They demanded a holiday in exchange for admission, and eventually, with some show of reluctance, the master gave way, and was let in. The children would, in fact, have had their holiday anyway, as Shrove Tuesday is so observed in that district; but the old tradition of barring-out seems to have persisted in this village until long after it had died out almost everywhere else.

Bawming the Thorn. Bawming the Thorn is a custom once regularly, but of late years somewhat intermittently, observed at Appleton Thorn, in Cheshire, on or near July 5th (Old Midsummer Day). *Bawming* is a dialect word meaning *adorning*, or according to some authorities, *anointing*; the thorn in this case is a living tree growing in the centre of the township, from which the village takes the second part of its name. Tradition says that the first thorn on this site was planted by Adam de Dutton in 1125, and that it was an offshoot of the Holy Thorn of Glastonbury. The present tree dates only from 1967. Its immediate predecessor was blown down in 1965, and was replaced two years later by a thorn-sapling planted on October 25th, 1967.

The full ceremonies of Bawming Day include a procession through the village, the decoration of the tree's branches with flower-garlands, red ribbons, posies, and flags, and dancing round the thorn in a wide ring, together with the singing of the Bawming Song, a rather uninteresting ditty written about 1870 by R. E. Egerton-Warburton, of Arley, which may possibly have replaced something older and more vigorous. Afterwards, there is a festival tea for the dancers, and the rest of the day is filled with sports, games and amusements of various kinds. In 1967, the new tree was too young to bear the weight of the garlands and flags, and so could not be bawmed properly; but this essential part of the old ceremony was preserved by decorating the iron railings surrounding it.

Children are now the principal performers in this Midsummer ritual, but formerly, everyone in the village took part. William Beamont described how, in the nineteenth century, and earlier, the thorn was regularly honoured every year, 'the neighbours paying respect by bawming and adorning it with flowers and ribbons, and holding a rural fete round it.'[1] Many people, he says, came from elsewhere to see the garlanded tree and share in the merriment – too many, in fact, because the great influx of strangers led to rowdiness and damage to property. For this reason and others, the custom was allowed to lapse, but it was revived, in a slightly altered form, about 1906, and again, after another lapse, in 1930. In spite of its intermittent performance in modern times, this is a most interesting ceremony, as it appears to be a relic of ancient tree-worship, and of the reverence once paid to the 'guardian trees' of early settlements.

Bell Belt Day. The Town Clerk of Congleton in Cheshire, has in his keeping, along with the seventeenth-century Mace and the other Borough insignia, three broad leather belts of considerable age, on which spherical, loose-clappered, metal bells are fastened, five on one belt and seven on the other two. Each of these bells has a different tone, and gives out a strong deep note on the slightest movement. They are now known as the Sweeps' Bells, though that was not their original name, and they preserve the memory both of a mediaeval religious custom, and of the curious history of that custom in post-Reformation times.

The Parish Church of Congleton is dedicated to St Peter. The Patronal Festival, which was once the town's chief holiday, is held on Lammas Day (August 1st), the Feast of St Peter-in-Chains. On that anniversary, during the Middle Ages, three acolytes used to run through the streets at midnight, wearing the belts and jangling the bells to represent the clanking of chains that bound St Peter when he was in prison. As they ran, they called upon the faithful to remember what day it was, to rise and pray, and later to assemble at the Market Cross to listen to a homily. After the Reformation, this pious custom ceased, but August 1st

1. William Beamont, *An Account of the Cheshire Township of Appleton*, 1877.

remained the day of the annual Wakes (*see Wakes and Feasts*), until the calendar was changed in 1752, after which the holiday was held on the Sunday nearest August 12th, Old Lammas Day.

Somehow or other, the bell-belts passed into the hands of a family of chimney-sweeps named Stubbs. Exactly how or when this happened is not clear. T. A. Coward, in his *Cheshire* (1932) suggests that the Stubbs who originally acquired them may have been a town official in Henry VIII's time – perhaps the chimney-looker who was an important officer when timber buildings were common and the danger of serious fires was constant. One William Stubbs was Queen's Bailiff in Elizabeth I's reign and Mayor of Congleton in 1595, so presumably the family was of some consequence in the town at that

time. Later, however, they appear as simple chimney-sweeps, with no pretensions to social importance except as the hereditary possessors of the bell-belts. By virtue of that ownership, they claimed the right to perambulate the streets on Wakes Sunday, or Bell-Belt Day as it was frequently called, in accordance with ancient custom.

Needless to say, their version of the ritual did not greatly resemble its mediaeval beginnings, though St Peter's bells were duly rung as of old. The Belts were worn by two of the more lively members of the clan, who ran through the town, making as much noise as they could, and followed by a cheerful, shouting, and often drunken crowd. At the Market Cross, they stopped to make speeches urging all the citizens of Congleton to drink as much ale as possible, and generally to enjoy themselves to the full on Wakes Day. In the nineteenth century, the multiplication of the family led to disputes between two different branches each of whom claimed possession of the belts. These differences between kinsmen often resulted in free fights during the perambulations, in which the spectators vigorously joined in support of one side or the other. By the middle of the century, the whole thing had developed into a serious nuisance, and finally John Wilson, the Town Clerk at that time, took steps to end it for good and all.

After a day of the usual wild brawling and disturbances, he arrested the leaders of both the fighting factions and left them to cool down in the town gaol for the night. In the morning, when they were sober once more he offered to release them if, in return for ten shillings each, they would relinquish 'all their rival claims, rights, titles and interests in the ancient Chains of Peter.'[1] This they agreed to do, and the historic belts passed into the possession of Congleton Corporation, where they still remain. So perished the last traces of an ancient religious ceremony, and of the noisy customs that grew out of it in later times; and no doubt, Congleton Wakes has since been a pleasanter and more peaceful holiday for the majority of the townspeople.

Bellringers' Feast. (*See Wayfarers' Charities.*)

Biddenden Dole. The Biddenden Dole is a charity of uncertain age which is annually distributed on Easter Monday at Biddenden in Kent. It is said to have been founded in the twelfth century by twin sisters named Eliza and Mary Chulkhurst, who left twenty acres of land,

1. Letter from John Wilson to *The Cheshire Sheaf*, 1st Series. II.

still called the Bread and Cheese Lands, to provide an annual dole of bread, cheese, and beer at Easter for the poor of Biddenden parish. Tradition says they were born in 1100, and that they were joined together by ligaments at the shoulders and hips. When they were thirty-four years old, one died. The friends of the survivor besought her to save herself by having the ligaments cut, but she refused, saying that as they had come together, so they must go together and six hours afterwards she too died.

How much truth is contained in this odd tale is very uncertain. The famous Biddenden Cakes, which form part of the Dole, appear at first sight to support it. Impressed upon them are the figures of two women standing so close together that they might well be united on one side, and having, apparently, only one arm apiece. The names of the Chulkhurst sisters are inscribed above their heads, and that of the village under their feet. On the apron, or

A

skirt, of one is stamped 34, their age at death,

Y

and on that of the other, 'in 1100'. But this imprint, though it looks old, is not so in fact. Edward Hasted, the Historian of Kent, says that no figures appeared on the cakes until about fifty years before he wrote in 1790, and that when they did, they were not intended to represent the donors, but two poor widows who would be among those entitled to benefit by the charity. He dismisses the story of the joined twins as a tale without foundation, and adds that the givers of the land were 'two maidens of the name of Preston.'[1]

It is now fairly widely agreed that, whether the other details of the legend are true or not, the dates are wrong, and that the charity was more probably founded in the sixteenth than in the twelfth century. However that may be, the parish records show that the Biddenden Dole has been regularly distributed, at first on Easter Sunday and now on the following day, for more than three hundred years. In 1646, and again in 1656, William Horner, the Puritan minister appointed in place of the sequestered Anglican Rector, attempted to claim the Bread and Cheese Lands as part of the Glebe lands, but on both occasions his claim was defeated. Originally, the distribution was made inside the Church, but in 1682 the Reverend Giles Hinton, then Rector of the parish, complained to Archbishop Sancroft that the custom 'even to this time is with much disorder and indecency observed and needs a regulation by His Grace's Authority.'[1] Thereafter, it took place in the church porch until the end of the nineteenth century, when it was transferred to the Old Workhouse, built on the Bread and Cheese Lands in 1779 and now used as two cottages, which is still the site of the ceremony. A part of the Lands is now covered by a housing estate known as the Chulkhurst Estate.

One of the original gifts has disappeared from the Dole. The distribution of beer is mentioned in the records of the mid-seventeenth century, but after that no more is heard of it. The bread and cheese survive, however, and are still annually given to genuine claimants. Each person receives in addition a Biddenden Cake in memory of the donors, and these cakes are also freely given to the many visitors who come to see the ceremony. Although they are always called cakes, they are really biscuits, and are decidedly more valuable as memorials than as food, since they are extremely hard, long-lasting, and practically uneatable.

Blessing the Salmon Net Fisheries on the Tweed. The thirty-eight salmon net fisheries on the River Tweed are annually blessed at Norham-on-Tweed, at the beginning of the fishing season on February 14th. A short open-air service is held just before midnight at the ancient fishery of Pedwell, and to it, in the darkness of the February night, often in wild or snowy weather, come fishermen and others from both sides of the Border. The Vicar of Norham calls down a blessing upon the river itself, and upon all the boats, nets, fishermen, and all concerned with the thirty-eight fisheries.

1. Edward Hasted, *History and Topographical Survey of the County of Kent*, 1790.

1. *The Story of Biddenden*, published by the Biddenden Local History Society, 1953.

The service is timed to allow the first boat of the season to be launched immediately after midnight.

In its present form, this ceremony is hardly a century old, but it is locally believed to be derived from earlier usage. It conforms to an ancient tradition, once very common amongst fishermen everywhere at the start of their season; and in view of the known antiquity of the Pedwell fishery, it is not unlikely that this comparatively modern rite is the successor of some older and now forgotten ritual once held in the same place and for the same purpose.

Blessing the Throat. *(See St Blaise's Day.)*

Blood-Letting on St Stephen's Day. The blooding of horses and oxen on St Stephen's Day (December 26th), or near it, was formerly a widespread farming practice in England and Wales, and also in Austria and Germany. It was done for the good of the animals' health, and was believed to increase their strength and staying-power and to protect them from sickness during the coming year. Tusser, in his *Five Hundred Points of Husbandrie*,[1] directs that

> Yer Christmas be passed, let horsse be let blood,
> For manie a purpose it dooth them much good.
> The day of S. Steeven old fathers did use;
> If that do mislike thee, some other day chuse.

The reason why Tusser's 'old fathers did use' that date may have been mainly practical, inasmuch as it fell in the Christmas holidays, when the animals could be sure of at least three or four days of rest after the operation. Mrs Leather, writing in 1912, mentions an old man of Peterchurch who could remember horses and oxen being regularly blooded then on his uncle's farm, and afterwards being allowed to rest and do no work until Twelfth Night was past.[2] Nevertheless, there was also a traditional reason for the choice of date, since in legend St Stephen was often closely associated with horses, and in many regions he was regarded as their patron.

1. Thomas Tusser, *Five Hundred Points of Good Husbandrie* ed. Dorothy Hartley, 1931.
2. E. M. Leather, *The Folk Lore of Herefordshire*, 1912.

In some parts of Germany and Austria, his anniversary used to be marked by a kind of horse-festival, during which races and ceremonial rides were held, and the horses, as well as being blooded for their health's sake when the ridings were over, were blessed by the parish priest and given consecrated food to eat. In Sweden also, there were races, and a pre-dawn cavalcade in which young men rode at speed from village to village to waken the sleeping inhabitants with songs and shouts, and to receive from them gifts of ale or spirts. These riders were known as 'Stephen's men', and were supposed to represent St Stephen and his followers.

It is not, however, altogether clear whether it was originally the first Christian martyr who was thus honoured, in spite of the fact that the celebrations took place on his feast-day. The saint intended may have been another St Stephen, he who first brought the Gospel to Sweden and was martyred there at some time in the eleventh century.[1] Legend says he was a great lover of horses, and had five of his own – two red, two white, and one dappled, on which, riding each in turn until it was tired out, he was able to cover immense distances on his missionary journeys through what must then have been a wild and dangerous countryside. He was murdered in the forest by heathen men, and the unbroken colt upon which they bound his body carried him straight back to his home at Norrtalje. His grave thereafterwards became a shrine to which sick horses and other animals were brought for healing. Later tradition seems to have given his five horses to the earlier St Stephen; but since there is nothing in the brief account of the latter in the *Acts of the Apostles*[2] to connect him in any way with horses, it is possible that the two saints have become confused in Swedish belief, and that both have inherited something from pre-Christian midwinter rituals.

A curious custom which was observed in parts of Wales until about the middle of last century, or a little later, seems to associate the proto-

1. St Stephen of Corvey, believed to have been martyred *c.* 1075. His feast-day is on June 2nd.
2. *Acts.* Chapters VI and VII.

martyr with the shedding of human as well as animal blood. This was known as Holming, or Holly-beating. Men and boys beat each other fiercely on the legs with branches of prickly holly until they drew blood. They also attacked women, and in some areas the latter appear to have been their principal victims. M. H. Mason records that at Tenby, on Holming Day, furious onslaughts were made 'on the naked and unprotected arms of female domestics and others of a like class.'[1] A holly branch used with vigour draws blood very quickly, and to do so was in fact the object of the proceedings.

A local explanation of the custom was that St Stephen's cruel death by stoning was thus commemorated on his feast-day. In the Scottish Highlands, however, something of the same sort took place on New Year's Eve without any Christian explanation to account for it. Boys beat each other with holly branches then, believing that for every drop of blood lost in this way, a clear year of life was assured to the loser. Similarly, in many parts of Ireland and Scotland, it was once thought essential that the blood of some animal, bird or fish should be shed on New Year's Day, or at Martinmas, otherwise misfortune would follow in the coming year. Holming probably had its origin in primitive notions of the same sort. It also seems to have been considered, at least by some people, to be good for the victim's health, through the actual loss of blood, just as the blooding of the animals at the same season was thought beneficial to them. It will be remembered that periodical blood-letting was, during many centuries, esteemed by people of all classes as a sovereign remedy for all sorts of ills.

Boar's Head Ceremony. Of all the splendid dishes which appeared on the tables of the wealthy at Christmas, the boar's head was the chief throughout the Middle Ages, and it continued to be so until at least as late as the beginning of the seventeenth century. Swans and bustards, venison, and peacocks glorious in their feathers, with their tails spread and their beaks gilded, were all acceptable Christmas fare

1. M. H. Mason, *Tales & Traditions of Tenby*, 1858.

in mediaeval great houses;[1] but it was the boar's head, decorated and garlanded, that was brought in with high ceremony. Its entry into the hall was often heralded by the sound of trumpets, and it was carried to the table processionally, upon the finest dish available.

It is still so served at Christmas-time at the Queen's College, Oxford, as it has been for centuries. The ceremony can be traced back in the archives as far as the late fourteenth century, when the College itself was still young.[2] In those days, and for long afterwards, University students rarely returned home more than once a year, in the Long Vacation. The other vacations were too short to allow them to do so, when travelling speeds were limited by the pace of the horse, unless their homes were very near. Normally, therefore, their Christmases were spent, with all the customary festivities, in college. Eventually the Christmas vacation was lengthened, but for the Queen's College men,

1. The turkey, which is now the principal English Christmas dish, did not appear until about 1542, and did not achieve its present supreme position until much later. It is said to have been first made popular, or at least, acceptable in Great Britain by James I, who did not like pork in any form.

2. R. H. Hodgkin, *Six Centuries of an Oxford College*, 1949.

who were mostly north-countrymen from Cumberland and Westmorland, the winter journey remained formidable for a long time thereafter. It is perhaps for this reason that the mediaeval custom has survived there until now.

When the Provost and Fellows have taken their seats at the High Table and Grace has been said, the boar's head, adorned with springs of rosemary, bay and holly and with an orange fixed in its teeth, is carried into the Hall upon a silver dish. Before it goes the chief singer, and behind come choristers. On its way up the to High Table, the procession halts three times to allow the chief singer to sing one of the verses of the ancient Boar's Head Carol, which was old when Wynkin de Worde printed it in 1521. It runs,

> The Boar's Head in hand bear I,
> Bedecked with bays and rosemary,
> And I pray you, my masters, be merry,
> *Quot estis in convivio.*
>
> The Boar's Head, as I understand,
> Is the rarest dish in all this land,
> Which thus bedecked with a gay garland
> Let us *servire cantico.*
>
> Our steward hath provided this,
> In honour of the King of Bliss,
> Which on this day to be served is,
> *In Reginensi atrio.*

In between each verse, and also before the procession enters the hall, the choristers sing the refrain,

> *Caput apri defero,*
> *Reddens laudes Domino*

As they do so, the whole company moves forward; after the fourth repetition, the High Table is reached, and the boar's head is laid upon it. The Provost takes the orange from between the teeth and gives it the chief singer, and the green sprigs, some of which are gilded, are distributed among the guests and spectators.

A pleasant story is told to account for the ceremony. One, Copcot, a scholar of the Queen's College, met a wild boar on the heights of Shotover and, being unarmed, thrust the copy of Aristotle he was carrying down its throat, crying 'Swallow that if you can!' The boar replied '*Graecum est*', and thereupon expired. The ceremonial bringing-in of the head at the Christmas banquet was supposed to commemorate this unusual contest. Yet this explanatory legend, if it was ever more than a joke, is hardly necessary, since similar customs prevailed elsewhere, in a great variety of places where Copcot and his singular presence of mind in the face of danger were quite unknown.

A Boar's Head feast with more boisterous preliminaries took place at Hornchurch in Essex until well into the nineteenth century. The lessee of the tithes was required to provide a dressed and garlanded boar's head on Christmas Day. In the afternoon, it was carried into the Mill Field, near the church, upon a pitchfork (or according to the *Daily News* of January 5th, 1852, upon a pole) and was wrestled for there. The winner and his friends afterwards took it to an inn and feasted upon it, 'with all the merriment peculiar to the season.'[1]

Bonfire Night. (*See Guy Fawkes' Day.*)

Borrington Dole. (*See Graveside Doles.*)

Boxing Day Gifts. December 26th, the 'morrow of Christmas', is the Feast of St Stephen, but in England it is far better known as Boxing Day. This is an example of an ancient festival acquiring a popular name from one of its own lesser customs. On this anniversary formerly, the generosity of Christmas spilled over from the family and friends of almost every household into a much larger circle of beneficiaries to whom gifts, commonly known as Christmas-boxes, were given. Why they were so-called is not altogether certain. According to one theory, the name was derived from the alms-boxes, of churches which were opened on St Stephen's Day for the relief of the poor. According to another, it sprang from earthenware boxes, with a slit on top for coins, which were sometimes carried round by hopeful collectors as they went from house to house.

Until very recently, the postman, the dustman, and a few other public servants used to call on

1. W. Hone, *The Every-Day Book.* Vol. II. 1827.

December 26th at the houses they had served during the year to collect their Christmas-boxes.[1] They were the last of a once considerable company. Formerly, errand-boys also, lamp-lighters, turncocks, journeymen and itinerant tradesmen, and many other workers expected to receive presents, usually in the form of small sums of money, at this time. Apprentices received them from their own master, and then went hopefully round to his customers for further contributions. Domestic servants usually had their gifts with the rest of the family on Christmas Day itself, but if not, they looked for them on Boxing Day, and so did clerks in offices, shop-assistants, road-sweepers, watchmen, and sometimes bellringers and the sexton of the parish. Even inn-keepers at one time gave their customers a kind of Christmas-box by remitting part of the charge for any meal served on December 26th.

If all this giving of miscellaneous gratuities tended to become a trifle automatic, or even, as Robert Chambers rather sourly described it in 1864, 'a great nuisance',[2] there is no doubt that the custom sprang originally from a real and deep-seated desire to share the joys of Christmas with those who were less fortunate. From time immemorial, food, money, or clothing had been given to the poor on St Stephen's Day, either from Church funds or directly by individuals. Farmers' wives normally made large pies, which they cut up and sent round to the cottages of their husbands' labourers. Rich people sometimes gave the remains of their own Christmas dinner, which in an age of lavish meals was probably well worth having. At Bampton-in-the-Bush, in Oxfordshire, the three Vicars of the parish provided a breakfast of boiled beef and beer, known as St Stephen's Breakfast, to all who came for it. The Vicar of Cumnor, in Berkshire, entertained his tithe-payers to bread, cheese and beer on the evening of Christmas Day, and then gave what was left of the feast to the poor next morning. For this purpose he was required to provide four bushels of malt for ale and small beer, half a hundredweight of cheese, and two bushels of wheat in the form of bread. These pleasant practices have ceased now in both places, but at Cumnor, 'loaves are still given on New Year's Day to such as care to receive them.'[1]

Stephening was the name given to a rather similar Boxing Day custom at Drayton Beauchamp in Buckinghamshire. The villagers went to the Rectory, where they expected to be given as much ale, bread, and cheese as they could consume. This they regarded as their right though why they did so is not at all clear. According to local tradition, one Rector was bold enough to refuse their demands, whereupon they broke into the house and helped themselves to the entire contents of larder and cellar. Whether this tale is true or not, Stephening seems to have been accompanied by a good deal of noise and rowdiness, and in the early nineteenth century, another incumbent managed to persuade the people to accept an annual distribution of money instead of the traditional food and drink. Eventually, in 1827, this too was given up because, as the population of the village increased, the Rector found he was no longer able to meet the cost from his own purse, and there was no fund upon which he could draw. Some years later, when the Charity Commissioners were enquiring into the origin and history of various old charities, they heard many statements from Drayton people concerning the antiquity of Stephening and the Rector's clear duty in the matter; but no legal rights could be proved, and after 1834 the ancient dole disappeared for ever.

Boy Bishops. An ancient legend made St Nicholas the patron saint of children, especially schoolboys, as other legends made him the patron of sailors, captives, bankers, and pawn-

1. Within the last twenty years or so this friendly custom has declined considerably. In some towns, the postmen, dustmen, and others have altogether ceased to call for the Christmas-boxes, and elsewhere the once general habit has become more or less intermittent. Soon, perhaps, it will have vanished entirely, and the time may come when the majority of Englishmen will have forgotten why the day after Christmas was called Boxing Day.

2. *The Book of Days*, ed. R. Chambers, Vol. II. 1864.

1. *The Berkshire Book*. Berkshire Federation of Women's Institutes, 1950.

brokers. During the Middle Ages, his feast-day on December 6th was an important anniversary for many children because it was the day on which the Boy Bishop's term of office normally began. The boy-choristers of numerous British and European cathedrals, collegiate and parish churches, and some schools, elected one of their number to be their bishop from St Nicholas' Day until that other great festival of children, Holy Innocents' Day on December 28th. During that period, the chosen boy performed, so far as that was possible, the duties of a real bishop. He wore episcopal robes and mitre, carried a pastoral staff, and was attended by other children who acted as his chaplain, dean, canons, and lesser clergy, and wore the vestments appropriate to these offices. He sang Vespers and played a principal part in all the services of the Church, except, of course, those which could only be celebrated by an ordained priest. On the last day of his term, he was required to preach a sermon, and to go in solemn procession through the city to bless the people. While his short reign lasted, he was treated with respect by everybody, feasted, entertained, and showered with gifts; and if he died in office, he was entitled to be buried with all the honours due to an adult prelate.

All this is so alien to our modern ideas that it is not always easy to see the custom in its true perspective as a serious rite. It has often been described as a juvenile counterpart of the disorderly Feast of Fools, but in fact, though there are some resemblances in detail the two celebrations seem to have been very different in spirit and practice. The Feast of Fools, which took place in early January, was a riotous and sometimes blasphemous revel, very popular in France, but less so in England, though it was known here. The adult clergy of the lower ranks chose a bishop, or 'lord of the feast', under whose leadership they usurped the functions of their superiors, burlesqued some of the Church services, and ran about in masks, singing lewd songs, dancing, and indulging in all sorts of unedifying antics. While the Feast lasted, a state of topsy-turveydom prevailed, with the lowly exalted above the great, and there is no doubt that the proceedings were strongly tinged with pagan notions derived from the Roman Saturnalia and Calends of January. This fantastic celebration flourished from the twelfth to the fifteenth century, in spite of the Church's efforts to suppress it. In 1434, it was sternly prohibited by the Council of Basle, but even after that, it lingered on for a long time, and is said to have been observed at Amiens as late as 1721.

The Boy Bishop custom also had its mock-prelate and its temporary rise to importance of unimportant people, but during most of its history it seems to have been generally free from objectionable elements. The children took their duties seriously and performed them efficiently and with reverence. Until the Reformation, the custom was not frowned upon by the authorities, though from time to time, particular ceremonies were reformed and creeping abuses corrected. With the laity, high or low, it was always very popular. Generous gifts were made to the little Bishop and his retinue, both by wealthy individuals and as a result of collections from the townspeople. In 1299, Edward I gave 40s. 0d. to the child-bishop who sang Vespers before him in his chapel at Heaton. At York, in 1396, presents to the value of £77 were collected for the Boy Bishop of that year. On Holy Innocents' Day, the faithful of all ages flocked to hear his sermon, including, in London, the scholars of St Paul's School. In 1518, the Statutes of that school required that the pupils should 'every Childermas Daye, come to Pauli's Church[1] and hear the Childe-Bishop sermon; and after be at hygh masse, and each of them offer 1d. to the Childe-Bishop, and with them the maisters and surveyors of the scole.'

By 1518, however, the ancient custom was nearing its end. After the Reformation, it was quickly abolished in most Protestant countries, and in Catholic lands, it died out gradually, and was gone by the end of the eighteenth century. In England, it was suppressed by royal proclamation in 1541. Mary I restored it in 1554, but in her successor's reign it was once again forbidden.

1. St. Paul's Cathedral.

In spite of its former great popularity, it seems to have been very quickly forgotten, except in a few places where dim memories of it lingered in the form of local games or customs.[1] Yet within the last forty years or so, there has been a kind of partial revival in some English parishes, where a greatly modified version of the custom is practised. One of the choir-boys is chosen as Boy Bishop, sometimes, rather curiously in conjunction with a May Queen. He is but a shadow of his splendid mediaeval predecessors, and needless to say, his duties do not include officiating in the services of the Church or preaching a sermon. Nevertheless, he does, as a rule, have definite duties and responsibilities, which he is expected to take seriously and in some parishes he acts as the children's leader in Church matters throughout the following year. It remains to be seen whether this rather pale modern version of a colourful mediaeval ceremony (which incidentally is sometimes seen in churches which never had a Boy Bishop in the Middle Ages) will take root and grow, and become once again a genuine and living tradition.

1. It is often said that the famous Eton Montem directly derived from the Boy Bishop ceremonies. Some historians of the School have denied or questioned this statement. Montem consisted of a colourful procession to Salt Hill, near Slough, during which some of the boys collected money (known as 'salt') from all and sundry. The money was given to the Captain of the School, who was Captain of Montem, and out of it he paid for a grand breakfast in Hall, various other entertainments and charges, and fees and presents for his followers. The earliest account of the custom was written in 1560, when the procession took place on or about January 25th (Conversion of St Paul); later, the date was fixed as the first Tuesday in Hilary Term, and in 1759, as Whit Tuesday. Subsequent accounts at different times show that Montem changed in detail during the centuries, but remained constant in general character until it was abolished in 1847. Eton was one of the schools which in the Middle Ages annually elected a Boy Bishop.

Bread and Cheese Distribution, St Briavels. At St Briavels in Gloucestershire, small pieces of bread and cheese are distributed every year to the inhabitants of the village on Whit Sunday, immediately after the Evening Service in the parish church is ended. The food is carried in baskets to a narrow lane near the church, along which runs a high stone wall. From the top of this wall, the pieces are flung to the people waiting in the roadway below, and as they fall, they are scrambled for with a great deal of lively pushing and laughter. At one time, the distribution took place in the church itself. A writer in the *Gentleman's Magazine* in 1816 records that 'after the service, bread and cheese is flung from the galleries inside the church among the congregation, the parson coming in for his share as he left the pulpit.' After 1857, the scramble was transferred to the churchyard, the baskets being emptied from the top of the tower; but as this practice resulted in some damage to the graves, the ceremony was eventually moved once more, this time to its present site in the nearby lane.

The due observance of the custom is said to be necessary to maintain the commoners' rights of grazing, and of cutting timber in Hudnall's Wood. These privileges appear to be of considerable age. The liberty to take wood from 'the Wood of Hodenhales' was evidently enjoyed by the men of St Briavels in the late thirteenth century, for it is mentioned in the record of a perambulation of the Forest of Dean in 1281–2;[1] and probably it was already in existence in King John's reign, when Humphrey de Bohun, son of the Earl of Hereford, ceded all his rights in the Forest to that monarch. The commoners' rights, however, appear to have been specially safeguarded in the transfer. They survived all the changes of later centuries, including an attempt by Cromwell to usurp them during the Commonwealth, and after the Restoration of Charles II, they were confirmed by Act of Parliament.

Exactly how, or when, they were first acquired is not now known. In his *New History of Gloucestershire*, published in 1779, Samuel Rudder refers to a tradition that they were won for the people by some undated Countess of Hereford who rode naked through the parish, as Lady Godiva did for a similar good cause through the streets of Coventry. This unlikely legend, which Rudder himself did not believe, and for which there is no evidence of any sort, is still occasion-

1. *Bristol and Gloucestershire Archaeological Society Transactions* Vol. XIV.

ally repeated, but it is improbable that anyone has any real faith in it today.

Burning Bartle. The custom known as the Burning of Bartle is observed at West Witton, in Wensleydale, Yorkshire, on a Saturday near St Bartholomew's Day, August 24th. Formerly the ceremony took place on St Bartholomew's Day itself, which is the patronal festival of the parish, and was at one time the beginning of a week-long feast and holiday. The transfer to a varying Saturday date is a matter of modern convenience.

A large effigy, usually more than life-size, is carried in procession round the village. If any car or bus is encountered on the way, Bartle is lifted up to the windows, so that the passengers may see him. Similarly, if any house-door is left open, the procession halts outside it, the effigy is displayed to those within, and the following rhyme is declaimed by one of the bearers:

> At Pen Hill crags he tore his rags,
> At Hunter's Thorn he blew his horn,
> At Capplebank Stee he brak his knee,
> At Grassgill Beck he brak his neck,
> At Waddam's End he couldn't fend,
> At Grassgill End he made his end.

In another recorded version of this ditty, the place-name Briskill is given instead of Grassgill, but whichever is correct, it is at the bottom of Grassgill that Bartle now makes his end. When that point is reached, he is soaked in paraffin and thrown on to a large bonfire, and there he burns, while hidden fireworks explode all round him, and the watching crowds cheer, shout, and sing the popular songs of the moment at the tops of their voices.

Who or what Bartle represents is uncertain. His name and the date both suggest that he is St Bartholomew and, according to Edmund Bogg,[1] who wrote in the 'nineties of last century, that is whom he was then supposed to be. But nothing in the history of that great saint and apostle provides any reason for such a celebration, and although the custom is sometimes vaguely associated with the Masssacre of St Bartholomew's Day in 1572, the local legends of Bartle himself have no ecclesiastical or saintly connections. One is that he was a robber who, at some unspecified period, raided the swinepens of the district, and was eventually captured on Pen Hill. Another says he was a cattle-stealing giant, killed by a band of farmers. A third theory is that he was not mortal at all, but a spirit of the forest that once stretched from Middleham to Bainbridge, and that he was associated with fertility and the harvest. The fact that the modern effigy evidently has some luck-bringing qualities, as shown by the displays to passers-by and householders, may have some bearing on this last explanation. If so, it is possible that Bartle began life as some sort of harvest deity, to whom St Bartholomew's name was subsequently given because of the coincidence of dates.

Burning the Bush. The ceremony of Burning the Bush was observed on most Herefordshire farms until the 'seventies of last century, and in some parts of the county it survived until just before the 1914 War. The Bush was a globe made of twisted hawthorn twigs which, together with a branch of mistletoe, hung in the farm-

1. Edmund Bogg *From Eden Vale to the Plains of York* n.d.

house kitchen all through the year. Very early on New Year's morning, usually about five o'clock, it was taken down by the farmworkers and carried out to the first-sown wheatfield. There it was burnt on a large straw fire, with customary ceremonies that varied a little in different districts.

At Brinsop, the globe was filled with straw and set alight, and a man ran with it over the first twelve ridges of the field. Evil spirits were said to be caught in its convolutions and so destroyed, always provided that the rite was performed at the proper time, that is, between the hours of midnight and six o'clock in the morning. Elsewhere, a bundle of flaming straw was taken from the bonfire and carried part of the way; then another bundle was lit from it and a third from that, and so on until the twelfth ridge was reached. At Birley Court, near Leominster, two globes were used, 'one for the Master and one for the eldest born.'[1] These were thrown on the fire together, the smaller inside the larger, and then one of the men took burning straw on his pitchfork and ran over the field, dropping a little straw on each ridge as he ran. Whichever method was followed, it was considered an extremely bad omen if the flames failed before the end of the run.

When this part of the ceremony was over, all present stood in a ring round the fire and cried 'Auld Cider!', very slowly, with long-drawn-out syllables ending in a sort of growl, bowing low on each note. This was repeated three times, after which there was cheering and feasting on cider and cakes provided by the farmer, either then and there on the field, or subsequently in the farmhouse kitchen. At Birley, the men used to march round the fire singing a Christmas carol.

While all this went on outside, a new Bush was made at home to replace the old one. The hawthorn twigs were twisted together and their ends were scorched in the fire. Mrs Leather records that one old man from Shobdon told her that cider was poured over the globe when

1. E. M. Leather, *The Folk-Lore of Herefordshire*, 1912. She remarks that she knew of no instance of the two-globe custom elsewhere.

it was complete, 'to varnish and darken the bush like.'[1] It was then hung up in the kitchen, with a new bunch of mistletoe, and left in place for the following twelve months.

The explanation usually given for this custom was that the Bush represented the Crown of Thorns, and that when it, or the straw from the bonfire, was carried flaming over the fields, it fertilized and purified the soil and drove out the Devil and other evil spirits. At Brinsop, it was said to protect the wheat from the disease known as 'smut'. At one time it was firmly believed that without the performance of this ceremony the crops would not flourish. Inside the house, the Bush seems to have been regarded as a protection against fire and misfortune. It was considered very unlucky for it to be absent from the homestead for a single night, which was the reason given in one instance for fetching it at five o'clock on New Year's morning and not, more conveniently, on the previous evening.[2]

In Worcestershire, a variant of the custom consisted in making a crown of blackthorn before daylight on January 1st and baking it in the oven. It was then carried out to the first-sown, or on some farms, the last-sown wheatfield and burnt there, after which the ashes were strewn over the ridges to fertilize them. In this county, blackthorn was believed to blossom on Old Christmas Eve, like the Holy Thorn, and to have been the tree from which the Crown of Thorns was made. In some West Midland and Welsh Border houses, where mistletoe was commonly kept for luck during the year, a new bough was ceremonially hung up on New Year's morning. The old one was then taken out and burnt in the fields, though without the more elaborate ceremonies of the true Burning the Bush rite.

Burning the Clavie. The Burning of the Clavie is an old fire-ritual connected with the New Year, which is still anually performed at Burghead in Morayshire on January 11th (New

1. E. M. Leather, *op. cit.* Concerning the cider-pouring at Shobdon, she observed that 'the practice strongly suggests a survival of primitive ritual.'

2. *Ibid.*

Year's Eve, Old Style). How old it is is uncertain, but some of its details show signs of very considerable age, with roots running backwards into pagan antiquity. Moreover, although the custom is now confined to Burghead, the evidence of various Presbytery and Kirk-session Records of the seventeenth and eighteenth centuries show that something very like it once took place in several other East Coast fishing-ports, and even as far inland as Inveravon in Banffshire, where flaming 'torches of firr' were carried, 'superstitiouslie and Idolatrouslie' about the folds and fields at New Year.

On the afternoon of January 11th, the Clavie is prepared according to certain time-honoured and inflexible rules by a band of young men whose leader is known as the Clavie King. Tradition demands that they should all be members of long-established local families. No stranger may take part in the work, or handle the tools used. Everything needed for the construction of the Clavie must be given or borrowed; nothing must be bought, for that would be very unlucky. An Archangel tar-barrel is sawn into two unequal parts. The upper, and larger portion is broken up, to serve as fuel later. The bottom half is fixed on to a salmon-fisher's stake, about six or eight feet in length and known as the Spoke, by means of a single long nail which has been specially forged for the purpose by the blacksmith. This nail has to be hammered in with a smooth, round stone, for the use of a metal hammer is strictly forbidden.

A herring-cask is then broken up, and its staves are fastened at two-inch intervals round the bottom of the half-barrel, with their lower ends firmly fastened to the Spoke, leaving a space large enough to admit the head of the Clavie-bearer. The completed Clavie is propped against a wall, and two young men, standing on the latter, fill it with dry, tar-soaked wood, piled up in the shape of a pyramid. At about six o'clock in the evening, when everything is ready, the King sends one of his helpers to fetch a burning peat from a nearby house, and with this, thrust into a hollow left for it in the pyramid, he sets the whole mass of fuel ablaze. No modern matches may be used for this purpose, and the peat itself has to be already burning on the household fire before the messenger comes to receive it. Tar is poured over it, and with flames shooting high from its top, the Clavie is raised aloft by the first of the bearers amid loud cheers from the onlookers, and the procession starts on its way.

It goes all round the old town, following the old boundaries, but leaving out the modern town which has grown up outside them. On the way, burning faggots are thrown from time to time for luck through the open doors of houses. To be the first to carry the Clavie is an honour, but no man could support the heat and the weight for long, and so, at certain points along the route, another takes on the burden. If the Clavie-bearer stumbled or fell, it would be a very bad omen, both for the man himself and for the whole town.

Eventually, the procession arrives at a mound on the headland which is known as the Doorie Hill, and here the Clavie comes to rest on an altar-like stone pillar with a socket in its top, into which the Spoke is fitted. Formerly, a cairn of stones was prepared for it, but in 1809, the pillar was specially built for it, and has been used ever since. As soon as the Clavie is in position, more wood is thrown on to it, and fresh tar poured over it, making the flames shoot up in a blaze that can be seen from a very long way off. Once it was kept burning all night, with constant additions of wood and tar, but now it is allowed to burn only for a certain time, after which it is hacked to pieces by the King and his men. Burning fragments fly out in all directions, streams of flaming tar pour down the hill, and everyone scrambles for bits of wood, regardless of scorched fingers. These, like the faggots thrown into the house-doors, are luck-bringing and are treasured throughout the following year, as a protection against evil, or are sent to Burghead men, or their descendants, now living overseas.

Burning Judas. As soon as it is light on Good Friday morning, little groups of children appear on the streets in the South End of Liverpool, near the docks. Each small band carries a straw-stuffed effigy, dressed in an old suit of men's clothes and having a comic mask over its face. It looks very much like the traditional guy of November 5th (*see Guy Fawkes Day*), but it is supposed to represent Judas Iscariot. When the sun rises, the leader of a group hoists the figure on a pole and knocks with it upon the upper windows of the houses, while the rest of the children shout, 'Judas is short of a penny for his breakfast!' If the householders are wise, they throw out their pennies at once; certainly, they will get no peace until they do so, and most realize this fact only too well from past experience.

When they have visited as many houses as possible, the children set about the business of 'burning Judas'. Wood, straw, and other fuel have been patiently collected in the preceding weeks, and this is now brought out. A fire is made and lit in the middle of the street and the effigy is thrown on it. While it burns, the children shout, dance round the fire, and throw more fuel on the flames. This rather dangerous proceeding is not liked by the police, and before long, a policeman usually appears, scatters the bonfire, and carries off the effigy to the police-station, closely followed by its indignant owners. 'It is comic', says a writer in *Folk-Lore* (Vol. 65, 1954) 'to see a policeman with two or more "Judases" under his arm striding off to the Bridewell and thirty or forty children of all ages crowding after him shrieking "Judas", and by this time the youngest children are thinking the policeman is Judas. . . . For a few days when a policeman is seen the cry of "Judas" is shouted after him, but it dies away after less than a week, only to be revived again next Good Friday'. Tradition demands that the burning must take place by eleven o'clock in the morning. By noon, the fires are all out, any effigies, that have escaped the police have been consumed, and all that remains to be done is the counting and spending of the collected pennies.

No other part of Liverpool's wide dockland area celebrates Good Friday in this way. The custom is said to have begun in the South End in the days when Spanish sailing-ships came there to discharge their cargoes of fruit or wine. If the ships were in dock on Good Friday, the sailors could be seen vigorously flogging a Judas-effigy round the decks, and afterwards throwing it overboard.

Punishing Judas was once a widespread, and is still quite a well-known Good Friday practice in Spain, Portugal and some Latin-American countries. Life-sized figures of wood or straw are, or were until recently, dragged about the streets of towns and villages, beaten, kicked, cursed, spat upon and finally destroyed. On board ship, similar figures were thrashed, drowned or hanged. In April, 1874, a report in *The Times* described how on the Good Friday of that year, a crowd of curious Londoners gathered to watch the flogging of effigies on Portuguese and South American ships in the London docks. Another newspaper account of about 1810 records the solemn hanging of Judas on board some Spanish and Portuguese men-of-war then at Plymouth. Each ship had its own Judas-figure which was left hanging until sunset (or in one case, until Easter Sunday evening), and was then cut down, ripped to pieces, and thrown into the water.

The same idea of punishment appears elsewhere in other forms. In Corfu, crockery is violently hurled down a steep hill, and as each person throws his piece, he calls down curses on the arch-traitor. In the West of England, formerly, it was considered meritorious to break at least one piece of pottery on Good Friday, because the jagged edges were supposed to pierce the body of Judas. The Jack-o-Lent figure that used to be dragged about in many districts at the beginning of Lent, and was then shot to pieces on Ash Wednesday evening or on Palm Sunday, was sometimes said to represent Judas also, though in fact this custom is more likely to have been associated, at least originally, with the age-old ritual of Driving Out Winter.

Burning the Old Year Out. A custom so named is still observed at Biggar, in Lanarkshire, on New Year's Eve. This is a survival of an ancient and once very widespread practice of lighting communal bonfires on this, or some other date near the Winter Solstice, in order to drive out old evils, and bring fertility to the crops and cattle in the year that is coming. At Biggar, a huge bonfire, containing many fireworks as well as fuel, is slowly built up during the three or four weeks beforehand, on a convenient piece of ground not far from where the now-vanished Mercat Cross once stood. At about half-past nine on the night of December 31st, a man specially chosen for the task sets light to it with a torch. Cheers and shouts greet the flames as they leap up, and for the next two-and-a-half hours, the night is filled with sounds of crackling wood, snapping fireworks, and general human rejoicing. Then, as midnight strikes, silence falls on the noisy crowd, the church-bells ring out, and *Auld Lang Syne* is sung by all present. Thereafter, a sort of 'Mischief Night' begins, and pranks of all kinds are played by young people of both sexes, including the time-honoured antic of removing gates and hiding them in inaccessible places. Finally, men and boys go out first-footing until well into the small hours of the morning.

Wick, in the Far North of Scotland, also burns the Old Year out with a great bonfire, and formerly, farmers in Angus used to shoot it out, with shotguns fired into the air at midnight. At Comrie, in Perthshire, there is a very colourful Flambeaux Procession on December 31st, when men in strange and exotic costumes carry immense torches round the village in a parade led by pipers, and followed by a lively crowd of people, many of whom are in fancy dress. The procession starts from the Square on the last stroke of midnight, and there, after circuiting the village, it returns. The flambeaux, still alight, are thrown in a pile on the ground, and round this pile, people and flambeaux-bearers together dance until it is burnt out.

At Stonehaven, in Kincardineshire, it is not bonfires or torches that burn the Old Year out, but fireballs. These are round balls of inflammable material soaked in tar, and held in wire-netting cages on the end of long pieces of wire-rope. They are carried by young men who appear at midnight and parade up and down the main street of the Old Town, swinging the blazing balls in great fiery arcs round their heads. The effect is both startling and exciting, but the whirling fireballs are not as dangerous as they look because of the practised skill of the performers in the manipulation of their long ropes. Another interesting New Year's Eve fire-ceremony takes place at Allendale, in Northumberland. Here the Guisers go on their rounds from about half-past eight onwards, while a band plays in the Square, near a central bonfire as yet unlit. As midnight approaches, a procession is formed outside the Dale Hotel, and the Guisers appear, carrying blazing half-barrels filled with tar and other combustible materials on their heads. They have to walk very quickly, for obvious reasons. When the bonfire is reached, it is circuited, and then each Guiser hurls his blazing headgear on to it, thus setting it alight. Immediately after midnight, they set off first-footing all round the parish. New Year's Eve is a great night for hospitality offered to friends and relatives by the people of Allendale.

Formerly, open house was kept for all and sundry, but so many strangers now come to witness the fire-ceremony that is no longer possible. *(See Burning the Clavie.)*

Burryman's Parade. On the day before the Ferry Fair at South Queensferry, on the Firth of Forth, the Burryman perambulates the town, visiting the houses and receiving cheerful greeting and gifts of money from the householders. No one knows how, or when, this custom began, but it is obviously much older than the fair with which it is now associated. The latter is not very old, as fairs go, dating only from 1687; it was originally held on St James' Day, July 25th, and now takes place in the second week of August.

The Burryman is a man who needs to be of robust physique because his annual task is an arduous one. He is dressed from head to foot in white flannel so closely covered with the adhesive burrs of the burr thistle (*Arctimus bardana*) that the total effect is that of a suit of chain armour. Arms, legs, body, and face are all hidden by this prickly material, so that the wearer is altogether unrecognizable, only his eyes being visible through holes cut in the cloth to enable him to see. On his head, he has a cap, or helmet, of roses, and in each hand he carries a staff profusely decked with flowers.

At about nine o'clock in the morning of

Ferry Fair Eve, he starts out on his slow perambulation of the burgh, which does not end until well towards evening. He is accompanied by two attendants who wear ordinary, undecorated clothes, and usually followed by a lively company of children and young people. He walks with his arms outstretched sideways, carrying the flower-staves, and his attendants, one on each side, help him to bear the weight by supporting the staff-ends. He goes from house to house along the seven-mile route, and as he comes to each one, a shout is raised, and those within run out to greet him and bestow their gifts upon him. During all this, the Burryman does not speak at all, but stands in silence before the door, while the money given is collected in a can carried by his attendants.

Various theories have been put forward to account for this curious ceremony. One is that it commemorates the landing at South Queensferry of Queen Margaret, the saintly wife of King Malcolm Canmore, from whom the town derives its name. This was an important event in the history of the burgh, and is recorded on its seal. But the peculiar nature of the Burryman himself suggests that he is far older than the eleventh-century Queen, and is quite probably a relic of some pre-Christian figure connected with the harvest, or perhaps one transferred from the vegetation-rites of May to a later date in the year. It is clear that his visits are still felt to be in some way luck-bringing, and there is, or was, a tradition that if the custom was ever abandoned, it would bring misfortune to the town.

It is possible that he may once have played the part of the Scapegoat. There is no record that he was ever driven out, or sacrificed, but Marian McNeill[1] records that he was formerly believed to carry away the evils afflicting the community as he passed. At Buckie, on the Moray Firth, when the fishing-season was bad, a man wearing a flannel shirt stuck all over with burrs was paraded through the village in a hand-barrow, to bring better luck to the fishing. At Fraserburgh also, until the middle of last century, the fishermen chose one of their number to act as Burryman and 'raise the herring', when ordinary luck failed. He too wore garments covered with burrs, and a hat with herrings hanging head downwards all round the brim. Thus attired, he rode on horseback through the streets, preceded by a piper, and followed by a large and noisy crowd of fishermen and townspeople.

Butterworth Dole. *(See Graveside Doles.)*

1. F. Marian McNeill, *The Silver Bough* Vol. IV. 1968.

Caistor Gad Whip. A very curious tenure-custom, of which neither the beginning nor the meaning have ever been exactly explained, used to be regularly observed at Caistor, in Lincolnshire, until about the middle of last century. Certain lands at Broughton, near Brigg, were held from the Lord of the Manor of Hundon by a service rendered every year on Palm Sunday. A man came from Broughton to the church at Caistor during the time of Divine Service. He carried a large whip, known as a gad-whip, which had a handle of ash-wood, bound round with white leather, and a thong of very considerable length. Four pieces of wych-elm fixed lengthwise on the stock were sometimes said to represent the four Gospels.

While the Vicar of Caistor was reading the first lesson inside the church, the messenger from Broughton stood in the porch outside, and cracked his whip loudly three distinct times. He then entered the church and sat down, still holding the whip, to the end of which a purse containing twenty-four silver pennies had now been affixed. When the time came for the second lesson to be read, he knelt before the clergyman on a cushion, and first waved the purse on the end of the whip three times round the cleric's head, and then held it over him until the lesson was finished. After the service, the whip and the purse were taken to the manor-house at Hundon and left there.

The rendering of this peculiar service on Palm Sunday still seems to have been required of the Broughton tenant in 1845, when the property was sold, for it is mentioned in the particulars of sale circulated at that date. However, it does not appear to have continued long afterwards. The writer of an article on the custom published in the *Archeological Journal* for 1849, refers to it as 'recently discontinued.'[1]

Candle Auctions. Candle Auctions were well-known and popular in the seventeenth and eighteenth centuries, and still exist in a few places today. A piece of land, often belonging to the parish church, or connected with some charity, is let for a given period by the burning of a candle. Thus, at Aldermaston in Berkshire, a meadow known as the Church Acre is auctioned every third year at Easter-tide. A pin is thrust into a tallow candle, about an inch below the flame, and bidding goes on until it falls out. The last man to make his bid before this happens becomes the lessee of the land for the next three years.

At Tatworth, in Somerset, an auction takes place every year on the first Tuesday after April 6th, Old Lady Day. About twenty-five people, who together constitute Stowell Court, meet to take part in auctioning a piece of land called Stowell Mead, which includes a watercress bed, and also to share a supper of bread and cheese and watercress. A tallow candle is used, (this time without the pin), and the last bid made before it burns out secures the use of the Mead for a year. Chedzoy, in the same county, has a traditional candle-auction which is said to date from the fifteenth century, and

1. Quoted by T. F. Thistleton Dyer, *British Popular Customs*, 1876.

to be one of the oldest in the country. Here again, there is a piece of land called Church Acre and, as at Aldermaston, the money obtained from it goes to the Church. It is said to have been given by Sir Richard Sydenham. The auction is held, and apparently always has been, every twenty-one years, the next one falling due in 1988.

Collinson, in his *History of the County of Somerset* (1791), gives an account of a custom formerly observed at Congresbury in that county on the Saturday before Old Midsummer Day. Two pieces of common land called the East and West Dolemoors were divided into single acres, each having a distinctive mark cut upon the turf for the occasion. Corresponding marks were cut upon a similar number of apples, and these were put into a bag and distributed by a young lad, one to each of the commoners present. The acre so obtained was then claimed by the individual concerned. Afterwards, four remaining acres were auctioned in the usual way, by inch of candle, in order to pay the expenses of the apple-distribution and the subsequent festivities. (*See Midsummer Tithes: Running Auction.*)

Candlemas Day. The second day of February is the Feast of the Purification of Our Lady and of the Presentation of Christ in the Temple, and it is also Candlemas Day because then the candles used in the churches are blessed and distributed and carried round in procession. This festival has taken the place of the pre-Christian Feast of Lights, which fell on February 1st, when blazing torches were carried about the streets, and also, to some extent, of the Roman *Lupercalia* on February 15th. It has been an important Christian feast since at least as early as the fifth century, and is traditionally associated with Simeon's words in the Temple, when he spoke of Christ as 'a light to lighten the Gentiles, and the glory of thy people Israel.'[1]

After the Reformation, the custom of consecrating the candles on February 2nd was condemned by many as 'popish', but the use of the candles themselves never completely ceased, and Purification services continued to be lit by candleshine in spite of disapproving reformers. The Puritans of the seventeenth century detested the custom, but they could not obliterate it altogether. In 1628, one Peter Smart, a prebend of Durham, preached an angry sermon in that Cathedral, in which he referred to 'some notorious acts' of John Cosens, the Bishop's chaplain who, 'on Candlemas Day last past . . . in renuing that Popish ceremonie of burning candles to the honour of our Ladye, busied himself from two of the clocke in the afternoone till foure, in climbing long ladders to stick up wax candles in the said cathedral church: the number of all the candles burnt that evening was two-hundred and twenty, besides sixteen torches; sixty of those burning tapers and torches standing upon and near the High Altar (as he calls it), where no man came nigh.'[1]

All this indignation, and the reiterated disapproval of other preachers, was more or less wasted, for the old candle-tradition persisted, at least in part, in most Protestant, as well as Roman Catholic, countries. In some parts of Europe, the candles distributed to the congregation in church were carefully kept afterwards at home, because they were deemed to have curative powers, or to act, when relighted, as a protection against storms and earthquakes. In many English houses, a specially large candle was prepared for Candlemas night, round which all the family gathered and feasted until it finally burnt itself out.

A Scottish Candlemas custom was the presentation of gifts to the schoolmaster in the grammar or village school, and the subsequent acclamation of the Candlemas King. At one time it was usual for the pupils to provide money to buy candles to light the schoolroom, but later these gifts were made for the master's own benefit. The children brought whatever their parents could afford as a Candlemas offering, and presented it to the schoolmaster, who sat in state to receive it. The amounts varied from about five shillings to as much as a guinea, or even more. The boy who gave the largest sum

1. Luke, II, 32.

1. Quoted in Brand's *Observations on the Popular Antiquities of Great Britain*, ed. Sir Henry Ellis, 1849.

became the Candlemas King; in a mixed school, there was also a Candlemas Queen, chosen in the same arbitrary fashion. The King reigned for six weeks, and while his reign lasted, was entitled to demand an afternoon's play for the whole school once a week, and had 'also the royal privilege of remitting all punishments.'[1] *(See also Christmas Greenery: Cradle-Rocking: Yule Log.)*

Care Sunday. Passion Sunday, the fifth in Lent, was formerly known as Care Sunday, and sometimes as Carle, or Carline, or Carling Sunday. The origin of the word 'Care' in this connection is uncertain, but the most usual explanation is that it refers to the care, or sorrow, of Our Lord's Passion, the commemoration of which in the ceremonies of the Church begins on this first day of Passiontide. The name is rarely used now, but Carling Sunday is still a quite well-known title for the anniversary in northern England and in Scotland.

On that day it was customary for housewives to provide carlings at the family dinner, and for innkeepers to supply their customers with them as a free gift. Carlings are grey parched peas, which presumably took their name from Care Sunday, the day on which they were most commonly eaten. They were soaked in water overnight, seasoned with pepper and salt and sometimes with vinegar, and fried in butter; in some areas they were served with sugar and rum. In Northumberland, a form of marriage-divination was practised with them during the family meal. Each person helped himself in turn from the dish until only a few peas were left, and these were then taken one by one. Whoever got the last pea would be the first to marry. Another method was to hide a bean among the peas; the person who found it in his or her helping was the lucky individual.

In many north-country villages, a little festival was held at the local inn on Care Sunday, where all the men of the parish came to spend their 'carling groat' on beer, and were given free carlings by the landlord. Brand says that in Yorkshire it was believed that if any man failed to observe this cheerful custom, he would be unsuccessful in most of his enterprises during the following year.[1] The provision of free carlings at public-houses on this day survived until very recently. The custom is still kept up in some northern districts even now, though it is not as widespread as it was before the last war.

A highly-spiced pancake, called a Car Cake, was a traditional offering to mothers in Scotland, where a family feast, similar to the Mothering Sunday feasts in England, was often held on Care Sunday. In the Wisbech area of Cambridgeshire, the day was once known as Whirlin' Sunday, and special cakes, called Whirlin' Cakes, were made in almost every household.

Carlow Bread Dole. *(See Graveside Doles.)*

Cattern Day. The Feast of St Catherine of Alexandria on November 25th was, until well towards the end of last century, a festival occasion for young people, and for the workers in the several trades of which St Catherine was the patron. In England, it was commonly called Cattern, or Cathern Day, and in the main lacemaking districts, it was observed as a

1. *County Folk-Lore: Fife*, Vol. VII, 1914.

1. J. Brand, *Observations on the Popular Antiquities of Great Britain*, Vol. I, ed. Sir Henry Ellis, 1849.

holiday, both for the children in the Lace Schools and for the adult workers. Women went about during the day, often dressed in men's clothes, singing their traditional working-songs, and visiting their neighbours' houses, where they were entertained with cakes flavoured with caraway seeds, and known as wiggs, and a drink made of warm beer, beaten eggs, and rum. At night they had a feast, let off fireworks, especially catherine-wheels, and played Leap-candle and a variety of other games. It was never altogether clear whether all this merriment was in honour of St Catherine herself, or of a rather vaguely identified Queen Catherine, who may perhaps have been Catherine of Aragon. There is a Bedfordshire tradition which says that the latter introduced bobbin-lace into England by teaching the local girls how to make it when she was living at Ampthill Park. In fact, this type of lace seems to have been known in Edward IV's reign, for a manuscript of that time describes how it is made.[1] Queen Catherine may, however, have encouraged a small country industry by her patronage, and probably she is the original heroine of a Buckinghamshire legend which relates how a certain Queen Catherine, undated and unidentified, burnt all her lace when trade was poor and ordered more to be made in its place.

Confusion between the saint and the queen would be quite easy because in one version of her tradition, St Catherine is described as a princess, and in Church art she is often depicted wearing a crown. The more usual story is that she was a young girl of high rank and considerable learning who was martyred at Alexandria for her Christian faith in or about A.D. 310. She was condemned to be broken upon a spiked wheel, but as soon as she was bound to it, the wheel miraculously broke and the spikes, flying in all directions, killed several people in the crowd which had assembled to see her die. She was then beheaded with a sword, and in later years the sword and the wheel became her two principal emblems. Because of the latter, she is the patron saint of spinners, ropemakers, wheelwrights, carters, millers, and others whose work is connected in some way or other with wheels.[1]

Carters used to honour her anniversary with merry-making, and by fashioning miniature wheels with a woman's figure upon them which they set up on the doors of their sheds. At Chatham, the ropemakers held a torchlight procession, headed by a drum-and-fife band. Here the ropery was said to have been founded by Queen Catherine, and she was represented in the procession by a young girl who wore a gilt crown, and was carried in a chair of state by six ropemakers. Cattern Day was also a spinners' holiday in some areas, and probably no one looked forward to it with greater excitement than the little girls of Peterborough Workhouse, whose normal work was spinning. On that day they walked in procession round the city, wearing white dresses and scarlet ribbons, with the tallest girl among them representing the Queen, crowned and sceptred. They called at all the larger houses and received gifts of food or money, and as they went along they sang:

Here comes Queen Catherine, as fine as any queen,
With a coach and six horses, a-coming to be seen,
  And a-spinning we will go, will go,
  And a-spinning we will go.

Some say she is alive and some say she is dead,
And now she does appear with a crown upon her head.

Old Madam Marshall, she takes up her pen,
And then she sits and calls for all her royal men.

All you that want employment, though spinning is but small,
Come list, and don't stand still, but go and work for all.

If we set a-spinning, we will either work or play,
But if we set a-spinning, we can earn a crown a day.

1. Margaret Brooke, *Lace in the Making*, 1923.

1. St. Catherine is also the patron saint of unmarried girls. Generations of young maidens have sought her aid in finding a husband. 'Sweet St. Catherine, send me a husband', runs one traditional prayer, 'A good one, I pray; but arn a one better than narn a one. Oh St. Catherine, lend me thine aid, and grant that I may never die an old maid.' In modern France, she is the patron of old maids also; and if any girl reaches the age of twenty-five unmarried and unbetrothed, she is mockingly said to 'do St. Catherine's hair'.

And if there be some young men, as I suppose there's some,
We'll hardly let them stand alone upon the cold stone,
And a-spinning we will go, will go,
And a-spinning we will go.[1]

In Worcestershire, youth rather than membership of a particular trade or craft was a reason for celebrating Cattern Day. Young people used to go round begging for apples and beer, and singing a song of which there were several versions. One of these began,

Cattern and Clement come year by year,
Some of your apples and some of your beer,
Some for Peter and some for Paul,
Some for Him who made us all.

Another version was more ambitious in its demands. It ran,

St. Clement! St. Clement! A Cat by the ear!
A good red apple, a pint of beer,
Some of your mutton, some of your veal,
If it is good, give us a deal,
If it is naught, give us some salt.

Butler, butler, fill the bowl,
If you fill it of the best,
God will send your soul to rest,
But if you fill it of the small,
The Devil take butler, bowl and all!

The reference to St Clement in these ditties, and in many other variants of the Catterning song, was due to the fact that his festival is only two days earlier, on November 23rd, and that some of the customs of both anniversaries were very similar. In some districts, the young people went round collecting and singing on the earlier date, in which case they were said to go a-Clementing, or Clemenssing. In others, they went a-Catterning on St Catherine's Day instead; but the object of their visits and the general pattern of the proceedings was the same on both occasions. *(See St Clement's Day.)*

A pleasant custom was observed by the Dean and Chapter of Worcester Cathedral on St Catherine's Day. This was the last day of their annual audit, and the work being completed, they celebrated the occasion by offering to all the inhabitants of the College Precincts wine mixed with ale and spices in a bowl known as the Cattern Bowl.

1. A. E. Baker, *Glossary of Northamptonshire Words & Phrases*, 1854.

Ceremony of the Keys. On every night of the year a ceremony, now nearly seven hundred years old, takes place in the Tower of London when the gates of that fortress are locked against all enemies and intruders. This is the Ceremony of the Keys, or more correctly, of Her Majesty's Keys.

At 9.53 p.m. the Chief Warder, wearing his long scarlet coat and Tudor bonnet, comes from the Byward Tower, carrying a candle-lantern and the keys of the gates. He goes to the Bloody Tower Archway, where he is met by a sergeant and four guardsmen who form the Escort to the Keys. He hands the lantern to the Drummer or Bugler of the Escort, and then joins the ranks. On the command of the sergeant, the whole party marches down Water Lane towards the Byward Tower Archway, where they are joined by the Watchman, also scarlet-coated, who accompanies them as far as the Middle Tower and there falls out to prepare the gates for locking. The rest go on to the West Gate, where the Chief Warder, lighted by the Drummer holding the lantern, locks the gate, and the Escort present arms. The Middle and Byward Tower gates are locked in turn with the same ceremony.

The company then return to the Bloody Tower Archway, where they are challenged by the sentry on duty with the words, 'Halt! who comes there?' The Chief Warder replies, 'The Keys', and is asked 'Whose Keys?' He replies 'Queen Elizabeth's Keys', and the sentry then says, 'Advance Queen Elizabeth's Keys. All's Well'. The party passes on through the Archway to a position opposite the Main Guard; the Guard and Escort present arms, and the Chief Warder, taking two steps forward, doffs his bonnet and says 'God preserve Queen Elizabeth!', to which all reply 'Amen'. Then, at the precise moment that the barrack clock strikes ten o'clock, the Bugler sounds the Last Post, and the Chief Warder, taking back the lantern, carries the Keys to the Queen's House, where they are left in the custody of the Resident Governor for the night.

Charlton Horn Fair. *(See Horn Fair, Ebernoe.)*

Cheese-Rolling. Cheese-rolling on Cooper's Hill, in the Gloucestershire parish of Brockworth, is an old Whit Monday custom which has now, like so many others, been transferred to the newly established Spring Bank Holiday. In the evening of that day, the youth of the neighbourhood run races down the precipitous hillside for the prize of a cheese. The necessary decked with coloured ribbons, hands a cheese to the person who has been chosen to act as Starter for that year, and slowly counts four. At the word 'three', the Starter sends the cheese rolling and bouncing down the slope; at 'four', the competitors rush after it. Since the ground is rough and the gradient extremely sharp, most of the runners measure their length more than once on the tussocky grass, and some roll a good part of the way, like their quarry, before the bottom of the hill is reached. The winner keeps the cheese, which is protected on its headlong flight by a strong wooden casing, and there are money prizes for the competitors who finish second and third. When the first race is over, other cheeses are released for the following races, of which there are sometimes as many as five or six, including one for girls.

Cheese-rolling on this site is said to run back to a very remote period, and to be a necessary performance for the maintenance of grazing rights on the common. Tradition says that there cheeses for these sports were formerly given by individual parishioners, and sometimes they still are; but nowadays a collection is usually made beforehand to pay for them, and to provide money for other prizes and the general expenses of the festivity.

The course to be run is down that part of the very steep hill which is free from trees. At the head of it there is a tall standing maypole which is decorated with flowers for the occasion. Before each race begins, the Master of Ceremonies, wearing a white coat[1] and a top hat

1. Until fairly recently, the Master of Ceremonies wore a white smock and tall grey, beribboned hat. The last Master to wear a smock was Tom Windo, who retired about 1955. His predecessor, William Brookes, who was Master for fifty years, was buried in his smock and hat, which were symbols of his office.

has never been a break in the annual ceremony. Even during the last war, when food-rationing made the provision of several whole cheeses quite impossible, continuity was preserved by using a wooden dummy together with a very small piece of real cheese.

When the White Horse of Uffington was ceremonially scoured at intervals by the local people, cheese-rolling is said to have been included in the many cheerful sports that accompanied the work. A cheese was rolled down the side of the coombe known as the Horse's Manger, and pursued by energetic young men who must have had even greater difficulty in keeping erect than do the competitors of Cooper's Hill today. Whether this was a regular or merely occasional feature of the celebration is uncertain. The handbill advertising the Scouring in 1776 mentions 'A Cheese to be run for down the White Horse Manger', along with various prizes for other races and events on less precipitous parts of the hill. Thomas Hughes[1] was told by an old man who could remember the 1785 Scouring that cheese-rolling (which he described) took place then. The 1857 handbill also advertised 'Races down the "Manger" (for cheeses)', but in that year it was a cartwheel which was pursued down the hillside, and the cheeses served only as prizes.

Another interesting cheese-custom, now quite obsolete and forgotten, used to be observed on May Day at Randwick in Gloucestershire. Three cheeses, garlanded with flowers, were carried on a litter to the churchyard, and solemnly rolled three times round the church. They were then replaced on the litter and carried in procession to the village green, where they were cut up and distributed to the assembled parishioners.

Christmas Bull. Going about in animal-disguises at the Winter festival, or at other significant seasons, was a pagan ritual practice that was already hoary with age when the Christian Church tried to suppress it in the early centuries by forbidding the faithful to take any part in it. 'The heathen . . .' wrote Caesarius of Arles in the fifth century, 'and what is worse,

1. Thomas Hughes, *The Scouring of the White Horse*, 1858.

some who have been baptised, put on counterfeit forms and monstrous faces. . . . Some are clothed in the hides of cattle; others put on the heads of beasts, rejoicing and exulting that they have so transformed themselves into the shapes of animals that they no longer appear to be men. . . .' Some four hundred years later, in the *Penitential* of Pseudo-Theodore, it is written: 'If any one at the Kalends of January goes about as a stag or a bull, that is, making himself into a wild animal, and putting on the heads of beasts; those who in such wise transform themselves into the appearance of a wild animal, penance for three years, because this is devilish.'[1] Other churchmen at various times condemned the custom in the strongest terms, but their reproaches and prohibitions were largely disregarded. All over Europe, these strange horses, bulls, stags, goats, or bears continued to appear for centuries, working their seasonal magic long after their ancient religious or sacrificial significance had been forgotten. Some, indeed still do; and others lingered on in numerous countries, including Great Britain, until almost within living memory.

One such survival in England was the Hodening (or Hooden) Horse (*see Hodening*). Another was the Christmas Bull. The latter was a man wearing, or supporting on a pole above his own head so that he seemed to be wearing, a hollowed-out bull's head, complete with horns and glaring eyes of bottle-glass. His human body was concealed in some cases by the animal's hide, with the tail hanging down behind, and in others by rough sacking, or a long white sheet. Thus disguised, the Bull went round the parish at Christmas-time, usually at dusk, with a man who acted as his keeper, and an attendant band of men and boys. According to an account quoted by a contributor to *Dorset Up Along and Down Along*,[1] he often arrived unexpectedly at some Christmas gathering. 'None knew when he might or might not appear. He was given the freedom of every house and allowed to penetrate into any room, escorted by his keeper. The whole company would flee before his formidable horns, the more so as, towards the end of the evening, neither the Bull nor his keeper could be certified as strictly sober.'

1. This *Penitential* has been ascribed to Theodore of Tarsus, who was Archbishop of Canterbury in the sixth century; but in *The Mediaeval Stage* (1903), Vol. II, Appendix N., Sir E. K. Chambers states that it was really a nineth-century Frankish document, based in part on Theodore's genuine *Penitential*, but not so far as the words quoted above are concerned.

2. Women's Institute Publication, ed. M. R Dacombe, n.d.

The Christmas Bull was known in Wiltshire and Gloucestershire as well as Dorset. At Kingscote in Gloucestershire, he was known as the Broad, and was accompanied by young people carrying a wassail-bowl. About sixty years ago, a slightly different form of the custom was still in existence at Tetbury, in the same county. There, a bull's head, made of wood, with long, curving horns, black shiny eyes, and a white face was taken round in the Christmas season by three or four men, one of whom carried a small Christmas tree in a pot decorated with red and white rags. They visited houses in the town, and also in the surrounding villages, and stood outside singing carols. When the door was opened to them, the head, which had previously been covered with sacking, was unveiled and displayed to the householders. One interesting point about this Tetbury custom was that the head belonged to a family living in a poor part of the town, who claimed to have owned it for at least three or four generations.[1] At Stourton, in Wiltshire, another head of the same type was said to have been the property of one family for more than a century.

Christmas Cards. Christmas cards are now so essential a part of the Christmas festivities that they can hardly be omitted from any list of established customs. Nevertheless, they are little more than a hundred years old, and were unknown before Victorian times. In the late eighteenth and early nineteenth centuries, it was a pleasant, though by no means universal, custom to send complimentary verses, often of the sender's own composition, to particular

1. Information given to the Editor by Mrs Knight, formerly of Doughton, a village one-and-a-half miles from Tetbury, who, as a child, saw the Christmas Bull there several times.

friends at Christmas, or on other great occasions. For this purpose, specially prepared sheets of paper, with engraved headings and ornamental borders, were frequently used. Similar, but less elaborate sheets were used by schoolboys for the 'Christmas pieces' given to their parents at the end of the winter term. These consisted of two or three sentences, very carefully written, which served both as a greeting and as a proof of progress in the art of writing, the latter, no doubt, being the more important from the schoolmaster's point of view. Ornamental stationery for these two purposes was sold in considerable quantities in the first half of last century, and from it the true Christmas card, with its printed message and pictorial decoration, seems to have developed.

More than one person has claimed the honour of inventing the new form of greeting, or has had it claimed for him in later years. A boy named William Egley may have designed the first card as early as 1842. This is now in the British Museum, but unfortunately, the date written upon it is not clear enough to show whether the last figure is a 2 or a 9. Edward Bradley, a clergyman of Newcastle, sent out lithographed greetings in 1844, and in the same year, W. A. Dobson, head of the School of Design in Birmingham, used hand-painted cards for his friends, to save himself the trouble of writing individual letters. Probably, however, the strongest claim to be the inventor is that of J. C. Horsley. In 1846, a pictorial card designed by him in 1843 at the suggestion of Sir (then Mr) Henry Cole, was published by Summerly's Home Treasury Office, and about a thousand copies were sold.

This was the small beginning of a fashion which has never since looked back. By about 1870, the Christmas card had become really popular in England, and a few years later it reached the United States. As for the designs, these have naturally varied considerably in the course of a century, ranging from simple sprigs of holly and mistletoe and homely family scenes to really fine work by established artists. In our own time, the search for novelty has sometimes resulted in the appearance of pictures that are quite irrelevant to Christmas, and some that seem completely unsuitable for the feast of peace and loving kindness. But one familiar figure has remained constant from the beginning until now – the robin, friend of man and symbol of life-giving fire, who still appears on countless cards every year.

By one of those pleasant exchanges of custom which sometimes occur, the United States, which acquired the Christmas card from England in the first place, have now lent us a design that is essentially American. This is the poinsettia, the accepted Christmas flower of North America, which is now often seen on English cards and wrapping papers. It received its name from Mr Poinsett in 1828, but in Mexico, its country of origin, it has another and older name. There it is called the 'Flower of the Holy Night', and has long been closely associated with Christmas, perhaps because its vivid scarlet colour marks it as specially appropriate to that feast of fire and light.

Christmas Crib. The Christmas Crib, with its model figures of the Holy Family in the stable at Bethlehem, the attendant animals, and shepherds kneeling in adoration, is known under different names in many European countries, and in lands beyond Europe to which migrating Christians have carried it. In France, it is called the *Crèche*, in Germany, the *Krippe*, in Italy, where it is the best-loved of all Christmas symbols, the *Presepio*. Large or small, with life-sized figures in an imposing grotto, or with little clay images in a pasteboard stable, it is made every year with infinite care in churches or at home, and stands with candles burning round it throughout the Twelve Days of Christmas. Until comparatively recently, it was to be found mainly in Roman Catholic churches and homes, and only rarely elsewhere. Of late years, however, it has spread to churches of many denominations, as well as to some non-Catholic households, and even, somewhat unexpectedly, to shops and business houses.

It is commonly believed that the custom was first started by St Francis of Assisi who, at Greccio in 1224, caused a *presepio* to be prepared with an ordinary manger filled with hay, and a real ox and ass standing beside it. This was evidently something quite new in that district. Some fifteen days before Christmas, St Francis gave detailed instructions concerning what was to be done to a friend, one, Messer John of Greccio. On the holy night, when all was ready, the brethren from the nearby religious houses were summoned, and with them came a great concourse of the townspeople, carrying lighted torches and tapers, and singing hymns of praise. In a *Life* of the saint, we read that 'the night was lit up as the day . . . the woodland rang with voices, the rocks made answer to the jubilant throng.'[1] Mass was sung over the manger, and then St Francis, himself moved to tears, preached to the assembled people of Christ's birth in a humble stable, reminding them how, for love of them, the King of Heaven had been laid in just such a simple manger as they now saw before them.

This touching and impressive ceremony, however, was not the first of its kind. From as far back as the eighth century, a permanent *presepio* had stood in the Church of St Maria Maggiore in Rome. Here, in the Middle Ages, the Pope himself celebrated Mass at Christmas, with the manger serving as an altar. There was also a liturgical drama known as the *Officium Pastorum* which was performed in many churches from at least as early as the eleventh century. For this, a *presepio* was erected behind the altar, and to it came five cantors, representing the shepherds searching for the Christ-Child. They were met by two priests who asked them, in song, Whom it was they sought, and after the dialogue of question and reply, and the singing of hymns and the *Gloria in excelsis*, the Shepherds knelt before the *presepio* in adoration, and so the drama ended.[2] Nevertheless, if St Francis did not really invent the cult of the Crib, there is little doubt that he and his followers were responsible for at least the beginnings of the great popularity which that cult was afterwards to achieve.

In modern churches, where Midnight Mass is sung, the figure of the Infant Jesus is carried in procession and solemnly laid in the manger before Mass begins. At Epiphany, the figures of the shepherds are usually removed, and those of the Three Kings are substituted. This is often done in private houses also, where small models of the Crib are set up on Christmas Eve in the living-room or in the hall. In some, the rather charming custom is observed of re-enacting the long journey to Bethlehem by placing the images of the Kings in some remote corner of the room on Christmas Eve, and bringing them a little nearer each day until at last, at Epiphany, the Crib itself is reached.

In Austria and southern Germany, where boys go about singing traditional songs known as star-songs during the Octave of Epiphany, they sometimes carry a small Crib with them, and leave it in any house that has not got one already. They come in bands of four, the leader carrying a pole with a gold star upon it, and the other three being dressed as the Three Kings. One always has a soot-blackened face, to represent Balthazar of Saba. After they have sung some of their star-songs outside a house, they are admitted, to sing more songs indoors, wish good fortune to the inmates of the house and, if necessary, set in place the little Crib they have brought with them. They are then rewarded with gifts of food and money.

Christmas Gifts. The giving of presents at Christmas-time has a long pre-Christian ancestry. Before Christianity was known in the world, gifts of various kinds used to be exchanged at some of the pagan religious festivals of mid-winter. In ancient Rome, it was usual for wealthy men to give money or clothing to their poorer neighbours during the seven-day celebrations of the Saturnalia and to receive garlands, or tapers, or a few grains of incense in return. At the Kalends of January, the Roman New Year feast beginning on January 1st, there was another exchange of gifts, in which friends, relatives, children and dependants, all shared. The presents then given were known as *strenae* because, according to tradition, they had originally been simple twigs or branches of greenery gathered in the groves of the goddess Strenia. In later times, they took many different

1. Thomas of Celano, *Lives of St Francis*, trans. A. G. Ferrers Howell, 1908.

2. E. K. Chambers, *The Mediaeval Stage*, Vol. II, 1903.

forms, varying from humble to quite valuable offerings, according to the means of the giver. Since they were given at New Year, when almost everything was regarded as an omen of good or evil fortune to come, they were often carefully chosen for their luck-bringing properties. Thus, sweets or honey might be given to ensure a year full of sweetness and peace, lamps to fill it with light, and gold, silver, or money to bring prosperity and increasing wealth.

These pleasant customs prevailed all over the Roman Empire in the days when Christianity was still a young and growing religion. Because they were connected with the pagan New Year, the early Church frowned upon them, as it did upon all the other celebrations of that lively festival. Devout Christians did not exchange gifts at this season, as the pagans did, or at least, they were not supposed to do so. Yet it is difficult to believe that they never did. Old ways die hard, and to be generous in a season of happiness is a natural human instinct that will keep breaking out, notwithstanding all prohibitions. Certainly, gift-giving at New Year, or on some other day in the Christmas period, never seems to have vanished completely from the European scene; and today, the custom flourishes in every part of the world where Christ's Nativity is honoured.

Because of the widespread tradition of the Gift-bringer, Christmas presents are never quite the same as those given at any other anniversary. Almost everywhere, there is a legend that on Christmas Eve, or whenever the customary present-giving day is kept, the Gift-bringer comes, sometimes at night, secretly and unseen, sometimes openly by day, in the form of a man dressed to represent him. In many parts of Europe, it is St Nicholas, that kindly Bishop of Myra in the fourth century A.D., who visits the houses on his own festival-eve (December 5th), or on Christmas Eve, or some day in Advent, wearing episcopal robes and mitre, and often accompanied by a train of strange, masked followers of terrifying aspect. Elsewhere, it may be St Martin, or a mysterious character known as Knecht Rupprecht, who is dressed in skins, or straw, and looks very fierce. In some German regions, it is the Christ-Child Himself for whom the children leave letters of request on the window-sills during the days before Christmas. In France, where adult gifts are mostly exchanged on New Year's Day, children often leave their sabots in the hearth on Christmas Eve to be filled by the Infant Jesus or, in some districts, Father Christmas. In Italy, Befana, a female visitant of uncertain lineage, brings gifts on Epiphany Eve. Presents are given at Epiphany in Spain also, and there shoes are put out on balconies and window-sills on Epiphany Eve, for the Three Kings to fill as they ride past. Legend says that every year, on that night, they repeat the journey to Bethlehem which they first made nearly two thousand years ago.

Children in the British Isles, the United States and elsewhere in the English-speaking world, look to Father Christmas (or Santa Klaus) for their gifts on Christmas Eve. Or at least, they still do so in the early years of their lives until the multiplication of 'Father Christmasses' in shops, or the detection of some adult in disguise begins to sow doubt in their young minds. In England, Father Christmas was certainly known as far back as the fifteenth century, for he is named in a carol of that period beginning 'Hail, Father Christmas, hail to thee!' He appears also in many versions of the traditional Mumming Play, and in *Christmas His Masque*, which Ben Jonson wrote for King James I. Then, in the nineteenth century, he borrowed some of the attributes of the Teutonic Santa Klaus, who was once Odin, riding through the Yuletide nights to distribute rewards and punishments to his worshippers, and only later a Christian bishop. In the modern version of his legend, Father Christmas has become a very old but never-ageing man, dressed in red robes and furs, who comes from the Far North in a sleigh drawn by reindeer, and deposits his gifts by night in the houses, unseen and unheard.

Christmas Greenery. Bringing in greenery for the decoration of buildings at the midwinter festival is a custom of extreme antiquity. Long before the Christian era began, evergreens, which flourish when everything else in nature is withered and dead, were regarded as symbols

of undying life, and used in magical rites to ensure the return of vegetation. The sacred buildings of Europe and Western Asia were decked with them for the Winter Solstice rituals. In ancient Rome, houses were adorned with laurels and bay at the Kalends of January, and green garlands were worn and given as presents during the week-long celebrations of the Saturnalia in December. Because these were heathen practices, the early Christian Church condemned them, and forbade the faithful to take any part in them. They were not to burn candles at midwinter, as the pagans did, nor yet to fix on their doorposts laurels destined soon to be burnt. 'If thou hast renounced temples', wrote Tertullian in his *De Idolatria*, 'make not a temple of thine own house-door.' But time, and the innate conservatism of ordinary people, gradually softened these harsh views, and eventually not only the houses of Christians, but their churches also, burst into a permitted splendour of greenery at Christmas, as they still do today.

Laurel and bay, rosemary, ilex, box, fir, and pine-twigs, have all been used as decorations from very early times. Cypress and yew have been recorded sometimes, though cypress is a funeral plant, and yew rightly belongs to Easter. Best-loved of all, now as in the past, are holly, ivy and mistletoe. For our forefathers, they were strong life-symbols, not only because they are ever-green, but also because, unlike most plants, they bear fruit in winter. The prickly holly, with its bright red berries, is traditionally masculine and therefore lucky to men, as the smooth variegated she-holly and the trailing ivy are to women. It is still a widespread custom in England to lay holly wreaths on the graves of the family dead at Christmas, and in the United States, similar green circles, tied with red ribbons, are hung upon the front doors of houses.

All these plants can be, and frequently are, included in the Christmas decorations of churches, with one exception. This is the mistletoe which, by long tradition, is never allowed inside a church at any time.[1] This ancient ban is still very widely observed. In most parishes, if a branch of mistletoe is accidentally introduced with the rest of the Christmas greenery, it is removed as soon as it is noticed. Occasionally a bunch is allowed to hang in the porch, but not in the body of the church. Unlike other evergreens, which also had their heathen significance once, mistletoe has never quite lost its pagan and magical associations. It was the Golden Bough of classical legend. It was sacred alike to the Celtic Druids and to the Norsemen. For the latter, it was the small and deadly weapon, overlooked by the gods, by which Baldur the Beautiful was slain. It was also the plant of peace, under which enemies had to cease their warfare, at least for the time being. In most places where it grows, it was associated with thunder, and was therefore regarded as a protection against fire and light-

1. The most notable exception to this rule was the custom, observed in York during the Middle Ages, of ceremonially laying a branch of mistletoe on the high altar of the Minster on Christmas Eve and leaving it there throughout the Twelve Days of Christmas. A universal peace and pardon was proclaimed at the city gates for so long as it remained in position. Similarly, at Wolverhampton, mistletoe was placed on the altar of the Collegiate Church, blessed, and distributed to the people. Entries in the churchwarden's accounts of Bilston, Staffordshire (1672) and Darlaston in the same county (1801) show purchases of mistletoe along with other greenery for church decorations at Christmas.

ning for any house that contained it. One of its names was All Heal, because it was commonly believed to cure many diseases, promote fertility, avert misfortune, and nullify the effects of poison.

In some parts of England, it is considered unlucky to cut it at any time except Christmas. Until very recently it was customary (and perhaps still is in some households) to keep a bunch in the house from one Christmas to the next as a protection against evil. If a sprig from such a bunch was given to the cow who calved first after New Year's Day, the prosperity of the herd was thought to be assured. In Herefordshire formerly, mistletoe was not brought in with the rest of the Christmas decorations. The old bunch from the previous year remained hanging, but it was not replaced by a new one until New Year's morning, when the Bush was burnt. *(See Burning the Bush.)*

Kissing under the mistletoe seems to be an entirely English custom, only found in other countries when English settlers have carried it there. Its long-lived popularity may be partly due to the fact that, until at least as late as the early seventeenth century, the English were much given to kissing as a form of greeting. Various foreign visitors noted with surprise and pleasure how freely men and women kissed each other on meeting and parting, and how even strangers, on their first introduction into a family, were permitted, and indeed expected, to kiss the host's wife and daughters on the lips. 'Wherever you go,' wrote Erasmus in the sixteenth century, 'everyone welcomes you with a kiss, and the same on bidding farewell. You call again, when there is more kissing . . . in short, turn where you will, there are kisses, kisses everywhere.' Times have changed since then, and manners with them; but even today a girl who stands under mistletoe must expect to be kissed and, by custom, has no real right to refuse.

It is traditionally ill-omened to bring Christmas greenery into the house before December 24th, or to leave it hanging after the festival season has ended. Nowadays, the former belief seems to have faded in most places, and it is quite usual for decorations to appear a week or ten days in advance. The rule about taking them down is, however, still remembered. Many people believe it essential to remove them at the end of the Twelve Days, either on Epiphany Eve or at the close of the following day. Formerly, they were often left until Candlemas Eve, which marks the end of the ecclesiastical Christmas season. Herrick, describing Candlemas ceremonies in his *Hesperides*, wrote:

> Down with the Rosemary and Bayes,
> Down with the Mistletoe;
> Instead of Holly, now up-raise
> The greener Box for show.

Along the Welsh Border, when the Christmas decorations had been taken down, a bowl of snowdrops was sometimes brought in, to drive out evil at the beginning of the Spring season, and give to the house what was known as 'the white purification'. Snowdrops are the special flower of Candlemas, variously known in different districts as Purification Flowers, or Candlemas Bells, Mary's Tapers, or February Fair Maids. Although, even today, they are often thought to be ill-omened if brought indoors at any other time, their presence in the house just as the year turned from Winter to Spring was, in that part of Great Britain, held to confer a blessing.

The disposal of Christmas greenery after its removal also has its traditional customs, though these are less carefully observed now than they once were. It was once generally considered very unlucky to throw them away carelessly, like any other rubbish, for the luck of the house went with them. Farmers sometimes gave them to cows to eat, as a charm against calf-slipping. In some districts, the dead branches used to be ceremonially burnt; in others, this was thought unlucky, and instead, they should be left in some part of the garden to wither quietly away. A belief still quite often encountered is that no branch, and particularly, no holly branch, which has remained green and alive should ever be burnt. To do this is supposed to bring death or some other grave misfortune into the family. *(See Christmas Tree.)*

Christmas Tree. The Christmas Tree that now spreads its lighted and decorated branches every year in so many different countries came originally from Germany. How long it has been known there is uncertain. The first definite mention of it dates only from the early seventeenth century, but it is probable that it existed in some form or another well before that time. According to one legend, it was introduced by Martin Luther who, walking at night in the woods and seeing the winter stars glittering through the branches, conceived the idea of having a candle-lit tree in his home, as an image for his children of the starry heavens from whence Christ came to this world. There are, however, other legends which connect the tradition with St Maternus or St Boniface, and so carry it back to the fourth or the eighth century. What is perhaps more likely is that no saint or hero was needed to introduce a ritual which, in that land of forests may have developed gradually and naturally from the age-old custom of decorating houses with evergreens at the midwinter festival, as a symbol of continuing life and a magical rite to ensure the return of vegetation. *(See Christmas Greenery.)*

We know that Christmas trees existed in recognizable form at Strasbourg in 1605 because in that year an anonymous writer recorded how the citizens of that town 'set up fir trees in the parlour . . . and hang thereon roses cut out of many-coloured paper, apples, wafers, gold-foil, sweets etc.'[1] These early trees apparently had no candles; but from the middle of the following century onwards, candles are frequently mentioned, and it is hard to believe that so lovely an adornment could ever have been omitted once it had been introduced. In some parts of Germany, small pyramids of green brushwood and coloured paper on a wooden frame were used instead of real trees, and these too, were often, though not always, candle-lit. Both forms flourished mainly in Protestant districts, for the traditional association with Luther's tree made them slightly suspect in Roman Catholic areas; and when in the course of time the custom spread to other countries, it was in Protestant lands that it took root first and most firmly.

1. A. Tille, *Die Geschichte der deutschen Weihnacht*, 1893: quoted by C. A. Miles, *Christmas in Ritual and Tradition*, 1912.

Christmas trees reached America before they came to England, carried there by German settlers, and by the Hessian soldiers in George III's army, who are said to have set them up in their camps during the American War of Independence. The first English example of which we have a precise record was one arranged by a German member of Queen Caroline's household for a children's party in 1821. This, although the giver called it a tree, was actually a branch of evergreen fixed on a board, decorated with gilt oranges and almonds, and having a model farm, complete with animals, round its base.[1] The three little trees at Panshanger, which Princess Lieven gave in 1829 for another children's party, were more like the ones we know. They were then still sufficiently novel for Charles Greville, a guest in the house, to describe them fully, and thus we know that they were set in pots on a table covered with pink linen, that red, blue, green, and white candles burnt on their branches in three circular rows, and that gifts of various kinds were piled up in front of them. 'It was very pretty', says Mr Greville, and he adds: 'Here it is only for the children; in Germany the custom extends to persons of all ages.'[2]

In 1841 Queen Victoria and Prince Albert had a lighted tree, the first of many, at Windsor Castle. The event was widely reported, naturally. In the next few years, accounts and pictures of successive royal trees in the Castle appeared in newspapers and journals, and doubtless helped to make the custom better known. But even before 1841, Manchester people were well acquainted with it, for the many resident German merchants in that town had introduced it to their English neighbours. 'It is spreading fast among the English there', wrote William Howitt in 1840,[3] and probably the same was true of other towns where Germans had settled. The royal trees at Windsor made the Christmas tree fashionable; and if for a few years still,

1. *The Losely Manuscripts and Other Rare Documents*, ed. A.J. Kempe, 1836.

2. Charles Greville, *The Greville Memoirs*, ed. R. Fulford, 1963.

3. William Howitt, *The Rural Life of England*, 2nd ed. 1840.

ordinary people tended to think of it as a foreign importation – 'the new German toy', as Dickens called it in 1850 – by the late 'sixties it was already a familiar sight in most parts of the country, and was slowly but surely replacing the older, native Kissing-Bough.

This was a garland of greenery which hung from the middle of the ceiling in the main living-room. It was shaped like a double-hooped May-garland, or like a crown, and it was adorned with candles, red apples, rosettes of coloured paper, and ornaments of various kinds. The most important item was a bunch of mistletoe suspended from the centre. In some districts, where the plant was scarce, the bunch was omitted, and the Bough itself was called 'the mistletoe.'[1] The candles were ceremonially lit on Christmas Eve and every night thereafter during the Twelve Days of Christmas. Throughout the festival, the Kissing-Bough was the glowing centre of the family rejoicings, under which carols were sung, games were played, and kisses were exchanged in the mistletoe's shadow. These lovely garlands are still to be seen in some English homes, either as an ornamental accompaniment to the Christmas tree, or instead of it.[2] They are, however, fairly rare now, and in the majority of households the Teutonic tree has gained so firm a hold that its native predecessor has been almost entirely forgotten.

In recent times the Christmas tree has spread outwards from the home into the churches and the streets. Tall fir trees, ablaze with lights that are now usually electric, can be seen in churches of many different denominations, standing in the nave or at the west end, and sometimes outside in the churchyard. Anonymous gifts are often piled up round them for the inmates of hospitals and orphanages. Many towns also have a communal tree, round which carol-services are often held, in some square or park, or outside the Town Hall. This custom began first in America, where an illuminated tree was set up in 1909 at Pasadena in California. From thence, it spread to New York and elsewhere in the United States, and onwards to Europe and various other parts of the world. Many English towns now have these communal trees, the most famous being that which, since 1947, the citizens of Oslo regularly give to the citizens of London. Immensely tall and brilliantly illuminated, it stands every year in Trafalgar Square, close to Nelson's monument. A charming allied custom that is becoming increasingly common is the setting up of small decorated and lighted trees in the gardens of roadside houses, where they can be seen and their beauty shared by all who pass by.

1. A Lincolnshire contributor to *Notes & Queries* in 1911 said: 'The Christmas bough . . . has always been called "the mistletoe" as long as I can remember, and is supposed to convey the same kissing privileges as the mistletoe itself, which was never seen here before the days of railways.' *Notes & Queries*, XI, 3, 1911.

2. In parts of Northumberland, until quite recently presents were suspended from the Kissing-Bough at the end of long ribbons, and there was no Christmas-tree.

Clipping the Church. Clipping the Church is a dance-like ceremony in which the people of the parish 'clasp' or 'embrace' their church by joining hands and moving round it in a wide ring. It is really a Spring ritual, usually associated with Easter, or Shrove Tuesday, but in some parishes it is, or was, performed at the Patronal Festival, or on some other appropriate date. At Guiseley, in Yorkshire, where the church is dedicated to St Oswald, it takes place on St Oswald's Day, August 5th. At All Saints' Church, Hastings, the old ceremony was revived in 1952 on Mid-Lent Sunday; at Radley in Berkshire, there was a similar revival in 1965, on Easter Sunday, after a lapse of about two hundred years. An account of the latter event in the local paper records that 'the intention was to dance gaily round the church to express the joy of Easter Sunday, but the quickest were confined to the pace of the slowest, and it resolved itself into a happy but orderly procession.'[1]

At Painswick, in Gloucestershire, the church is clipped on the Sunday nearest September 19th, the Feast of the Nativity of Our Lady (Old Style). The children of the parish walk in procession to St Mary's Church, and there, holding hands, they encircle the building, advancing towards it and retreating three times,

1. *Oxford Mail*, 19th April, 1965.

while the Clipping Hymn is sung. Afterwards, a special sermon is preached from a small doorway in the tower to a large crowd gathered outside to hear it. Formerly, when the service was over, the children used to rush down the road towards the old Vicarage, shouting 'Highgates!', a word of which no one knew the meaning, and for which a variety of interpretations have been suggested, but this part of the celebration is now obsolete.

In 1897, the Revd. W. H. Seddon, then Vicar of the parish, published a pamphlet called *Painswick Feast*, in which he suggested that the clipping ceremony was a direct descendant of the ancient *Lupercalia* festival which the pagan Romans observed on February 15th, and which included the sacrifice of goats and a young dog, and a wild rushing through the streets of scantily clad youths armed with goatskin thongs. Mr Seddon believed that the children's flight down the road might have sprung from some vague folk-memory of this part of the pagan ritual, and that the mysterious word 'Highgates' was probably a corruption of the Greek *aig-aitis*, derived from *aig*, a goat, and *aitis*, an object of love.

He also considered that the curious custom of making 'puppydog pies' at Painswick Feast had its roots in the dog-sacrifice of the *Lupercalia*. These pies are really round cakes, crowned with almond paste, and containing a small china figure of a dog; but tradition has it that originally they were genuine pies filled with the cooked flesh of puppies.

A contributor to Hone's *Every Day Book* (Vol. 1, 1826) described how, when a child, he was taken every year to see the children of the local charity schools clip Birmingham's two churches on Easter Monday. The first to arrive stood with their backs to the building, holding hands, and the rest, as they appeared, joined the ring until the church was entirely surrounded. There is no mention of any movement round or towards it, but, says the writer, 'as soon as the hand of the last of the train grasped that of the first, the party broke up, and walked in procession to the other church (for in those days Birmingham boasted but of two), where the ceremony was repeated'.

At Bradford-on-Avon, and South Petherton in Somerset, as well as at Wellington and Ellesmere in Shropshire, the clipping ceremony used to be preceded by the game known as Thread the Needle. This was a very old Springtime game, played on Shrove Tuesday or at Easter. Children or young people ran through the streets in a long double line made up of handfast couples, weaving in and out under arches formed by the uplifted arms of the leaders. As soon as all had passed through the first arch, the next pair raised their arms to make another arch, and so on until every couple had had their turn. While this was going on, a traditional rhyme, varying in different localities, was sung or chanted. At Bradford-on-Avon, this was a Shrove Tuesday pastime, beginning at dusk and continuing until about seven or eight o'clock, when the players ran into the churchyard and clipped the church. At South Petherton, on the same day, young people of both sexes gathered in the market-place, and then played Thread the Needle through the township, adding to their numbers as they went. Finally, when practically every available young person had been swept into the moving line, they all ran to the church, joined hands round it, and clipped it three times in the traditional manner.

Corby Pole Fair. The Pole Fair, or Charter Fair, at Corby in Northamptonshire takes place once in every twenty years, on Whit Monday. It was last held in 1962 and falls due again in 1982. This lively celebration, which has survived not only the natural changes of nearly four centuries, but also the transformation of a village into a 'new town', is called the Charter Fair because it commemorates a charter granted to Corby by Elizabeth I in 1585 and confirmed by Charles II in 1682. By it, exemptions from various toll-payments, and from some jury- and militia-services, were conferred upon the people. Local legends say that these privileges were given to Corby by Queen Elizabeth in gratitude for the prompt help rendered to her by certain villagers when she was in difficulties. During a visit to the nearby Kirby Hall as the guest of Sir Christopher Hatton, she went out riding.

Her horse bolted with her and threw her into a bog, and from this awkward predicament she was rescued by some men working in the fields.[1] What she did not bestow upon them, for this or any other reason, was the right to hold a fair; but custom has added that name to the Whit Monday celebrations which, like many other country festivals, have long outlasted a number of true fairs in the neighbourhood.

The name Pole Fair has a far more interesting origin. It is derived from a custom which clearly has nothing to do with any privileges granted by visiting royalty, and of which the age and history are obscure. Before the festivities begin, the roads leading into the town are closed by strong barriers, and all travellers wishing to enter are required to pay a toll. If any one refuses, he or she is carried off – astride a pole if it is a man, in a chair if it is a woman – to one of the town's three surviving stocks, and made to sit in them until payment is forthcoming. From this cheerful custom, there is no appeal. Corby people stand firmly on their 'immemorial right' to act thus on Fair Day. Usually, it is true, recalcitrant captives are given a second chance to pay on arrival at the stocks, and before they are actually set in them, but this is the only concession allowed.

Nor is it only visitors from outside who are so treated. Any one in the streets, male or female, old or young, is liable to be seized and similarly imprisoned unless due ransom is paid. Unwarned strangers may find it a little startling to be thus precipitated into the middle of a centuries-old frolic, but they can always escape a pole or chair-ride by paying up promptly. Most people, whether visitors or townsfolk, enter freely into the spirit of the thing, and it is by no means unknown for potential 'victims' to put themselves deliberately in the way of capture, for the thrill of sitting in the stocks, as their forefathers so often had to do for more serious reasons, and perhaps getting some friend to photograph them in that unusual position. Those who really object to such antics are well advised to keep away altogether on the one day in twenty years when Corby remembers its ancient privileges.

The Charter, with its list of benefits (but of course, with no mention of a fair, since none was granted) is always read at the Opening Ceremony, to which the Rector and the Town Officials are carried solemnly and with dignity, in chairs.

Corn-Showing. Corn-showing was an old semi-magical farming custom which survived in some districts along the Welsh Border until just before the end of the nineteenth century. On the afternoon of Easter Sunday, the bailiff and the farmworkers, with their families and some of their friends, went to one of the wheatfields, and feasted there upon plum cake and old cider. Then they joined hands and walked over the field, saying,

> Every step a reap, every reap a sheaf,
> And God sent the master a good harvest.

In the Golden Valley, in Herefordshire, where the custom seems to have persisted longest, a small piece of plum cake was buried in the ground, and a little cider was poured over it, after which everyone wished the farmer a good crop. Probably this rite, with its suggestion of an offering to the Corn Spirit, was once

1. A somewhat similar story of courtesy rewarded is told in connection with the Haxey Hood Game in the Isle of Axeholme. *See Haxey Hood.*

observed wherever Corn-showing was usual; but when Mrs Leather wrote about it in 1912, she remarked that 'the burying of the cake is not remembered now in any part of the county except the Golden Valley.'[1] On some farms, a similar ritual was performed in the orchards as well as in the wheatfield, for the benefit of the fruit-crop.

In his *Ariconensia* (1821), T. D. Fosbroke described Corn-showing as a practical custom designed to rid the field of corn-cockles. Parties were made up for the purpose of picking the cockles. Cake, cider, and 'a yard of toasted cheese' were provided for the feast, and he who picked the first cockle from the wheat had the right to the first slice of cake, and a kiss from one of the girls.

Corn-showing died out gradually during the 'eighties and early 'nineties of last century. One of Mrs Leather's informants told her that it was discontinued in the Golden Valley because 'owing to the importation of wheat from abroad, the crop had no longer so much importance, and also it gave rise to a noisy assemblage on Easter Sunday.'[1]

1. E. M. Leather, *The Folk-Lore of Herefordshire*, 1912.

Cradle-Rocking. On the Sunday nearest Candlemas Day, the ancient and lovely ceremony of Cradle-Rocking is held in the parish church of Blidworth in Nottinghamshire. An old wooden rocking-cradle, decorated with flowers and greenery, is brought in and placed in the candle-lit chancel, near the altar. The boy-baby most recently baptized in the parish is presented by his parents to the Vicar, who lays him in the cradle and, during the service that follows, blesses the child and gently rocks the cradle for a few moments. Then the baby is restored to his parents, and the short rocking-service ends with the singing of the *Nunc dimittis*.

This charming ceremony commemorates the Presentation of Our Lord in the Temple, which is remembered in the liturgy of the Church on Candlemas Day. It is said to have been held in Blidworth as far back as the thirteenth century. It lapsed after the Reformation, but was revived in 1923, since when it has taken place regularly every year.

Dice and Lot Charities. Three charities curiously decided by dicing or casting lots still survive in modern England. Two are concerned with rewards for industrious and faithful maidservants, the third with the gift of bibles to children. All were founded in the seventeenth century, the oldest being the Maidservants' Charity in Reading.

By his will, dated June 30th, 1611, John Blagrave, the mathematician, provided for the payment of twenty nobles to 'one poor maiden servant who should have served dwelt, or continued in any one service within any of the three parishes of Reading, in good name and fame five years at the least, for her preferment in marriage'. To be sure of fairness in awarding the money, three duly qualified girls were to be chosen to compete by the casting of lots, 'yearly, for ever, upon Good Friday'. This is still done annually, though not now upon Good Friday, nor in the Town Hall, the original place of the lot-casting. The girls now go to St Mary's Church House on the Thursday after Easter, and cast their lots there for the prize.

In 1674, John How, of Guildford, left £400 for the benefit of a charity since known as Maids' Money. The interest was to be diced for by two maids who had qualified by remaining in service in the same Guildford household for two clear years, provided only that the house in question was neither an inn nor an alehouse. The full amount was to go to the girl who threw the highest number; there was no provision for a second prize. Now, however, there is one. In 1702, John Parsons, another Guildford man, left £600, with directions that the interest should go to some poor young man at the end of his seven-year apprenticeship, who was willing to swear before a magistrate that, at that time, he was not worth twenty pounds. Should no young man present himself in any one year, the money was to go to a maidservant 'of good repute' who had served in a private house for three years together. In the course of time, applications from apprentices failed, and the bequest became permanently attached to John How's Maids' Money. The girl who comes second in the dicing competition receives John Parson's award, with the rather singular result that, as his original gift was greater than that of How, she, as loser, gains rather more than the winner. The competition takes place every year in January, in the Guild Hall.

At St Ives, in Huntingdonshire, six bibles are annually diced for by twelve children, according to the will of Dr Robert Wilde. In 1675, he left £50, the income from which was to be spent upon bibles, which were then to be diced for at Whitsun by poor children 'of good report . . . and able to read the Bible'. A piece of land, still called Bible Orchard, was bought and the rent used to buy the books. The contest takes place in the presence of the Vicar, six of the competitors belonging to the Church of England, the other six being Nonconformists. Originally the dice were thrown upon the altar of the parish church, but this ceased about 1880, and a table near the chancel steps was used instead. After 1918, the custom was transferred to the local Church school until 1963, when the Revd. R. O.

Jennings restored it to its earlier form, and the table by the Chancel steps was (and is) once again used.

Doggett's Coat and Badge Race. The oldest sculling-race in the world is the Thames Watermen's Race for Doggett's Coat and Badge, which is rowed annually on August 1st, or as near as possible to that date, from London Bridge to Chelsea. This race was founded in 1715 by Thomas Doggett, a well-known actor-manager of that time, who held strong political views and was a firm supporter of the Hanoverian dynasty. To mark the anniversary of George I's accession to the throne, he gave an orange-coloured coat and a silver badge embossed with the White Horse of Hanover (or as he preferred to call it, 'a badge representing Liberty'), to be competed for on August 1st by six young watermen who had finished their apprenticeship during the previous twelve months. It was his wish that the race should 'be continued annually on the same day for ever', and to ensure this he left funds in the hands of the Fishmongers' Company which is still responsible for all the arrangements.

Thomas Doggett died in 1721, but his race still goes on though not always on the date he chose. Being an actor and not a waterman, he made no allowance for the state of the river, and this oversight had subsequently to be rectified by fixing the event 'as near to August 1st as the tides allow'. The boats now used are racing out-riggers instead of the heavier craft of his day, and the colour of the coat is now scarlet instead of orange. The Fishmongers' Company have added other awards to the original bequest so that now the winner receives £10 as well as the Coat and Badge, and every competitor who actually reaches the winning post, even if belatedly, receives a prize. Eliminating heats are rowed before the event, for the race is very popular, and there are usually many more entrants than the six permitted by the bequest. Except for these changes, and for the fact that probably few, if any, of the competitors realize that they are supposed to be honouring the memory of George I, this strenuous and testing race against the tide is just as it was when it was first rowed more than two hundred and fifty years ago.

Dunmow Flitch. The Dunmow Flitch is a flitch (or sometimes a gammon)[1] of bacon which has been awarded at intervals during the past six centuries, and possibly for an even longer period, to claimants stating upon oath that, having been married for at least a year and a day, they have never once, 'sleeping or waking', regretted their marriage or wished themselves single again. This award is still made, though by now what was originally a serious ceremony has degenerated into little more than an hilarious entertainment, usually held on Whit Monday

at Great Dunmow in Essex, though sometimes elsewhere.

The mediaeval home of the custom was Little Dunmow, where a Priory of Augustinian Canons existed before the Reformation. Exactly when it began is unknown. It is often said to have been instituted by a member of the Fitzwalter family in the thirteenth century, but of this there is no clear proof. Philip Morant suggests that it may

1. A flitch is the whole side of a pig, and must have been a valuable addition to a poor man's larder. A gammon is rather less so, being only the pig's thigh, but even so, a welcome prize.

run back to Saxon or Norman times as 'a burthen upon the estate, as the same custom was at Wichenor in Staffordshire.'[2] The first award of which there is a definite record was made in 1445, but long before that date, the custom had been mentioned by William Langland in *The Vision of Piers Plowman*, and by Chaucer in the Prologue to *The Wife of Bath's Tale*. Both poets refer to it quite casually, without explanation, and evidently expect their readers to know all about it.

The applicant was required to go to Little Dunmow Priory and there, kneeling upon two sharp stones, to make the necessary sworn statement in the presence of the Prior and the assembled monks and people. 'The Ceremony being long', says Dugdale in his *Monasticon Anglicanum*, 'it must be painful to him', and probably it was; but he had his moment of triumph afterwards, when having won the flitch, he was carried in procession in the Prior's Chair. This was an ancient wooden stall, with holes under the seat to allow for carrying. It is now kept in Little Dunmow Church. Modern applicants are still 'chaired', but today a newer, and wider, seat is used.

Only three awards are known to have been made before the Reformation, though there may possibly have been others of which we have no record. In 1445, Richard Wright of Bawburgh won the flitch. In 1457, Stephen Samuel of Little Easton received a gammon, and in 1510, 'Thomas the fuller of Coggeshall' did the same. Twenty-six years later, the Priory was dissolved, and we hear no more of the Dunmow Flitch for nearly two hundred years.

Nevertheless, the manorial obligation to provide the bacon for legitimate claimants still existed, and in 1701 it was honoured at a Court Baron presided over by Thomas Wheeler, Steward of the Manor of Little Dunmow. A gammon was then awarded to John and Anne Reynolds, who had lived together in wedded harmony for ten years, and another to William and Jane Parsley, who had done so for three years. This was the first time that the wife was definitely included in the award. Hitherto it had been the husband alone who made the claim, and what his wife thought about her married life was not stated or considered. It was also the first time that a jury was recorded as sitting to decide upon the truth of the claims. It consisted of five young women, the Steward's daughter and the four daughters of the Lord of the Manor. In 1751, when Thomas and Ann Shakeshaft received a gammon, six bachelors and six spinsters formed the jury, and this has been the custom ever since.

The 1751 ceremony was the last of the true manorial awards. Thereafter successive Lords of the Manor showed themselves unwilling to continue the ancient custom, probably because of the large and often destructive crowds it attracted. Applications were made, and refused, in 1772, 1832, 1836, and 1851. A gammon was given to Samuel and Mary Blomfield at Saffron Walden in 1837, and another to a man named Hurrell at Little Easton in 1851, but these were private awards made by individuals unconnected with Little Dunmow. In 1885, Lord Northwick claimed a flitch, for the usual reasons, from the Reverend James Hughes-Hallett, then Lord of the Manor. The latter sent him one as a private gift, but stated in an accompanying document that the custom had 'become obsolete and disused in the Manor, and it appears undesirable to renew it.'[1] It had, indeed, already been renewed elsewhere and in more frivolous manner when he wrote, but its manorial associations had ended with the prize won by the two Shakeshafts.

What may be regarded as the beginning of the Flitch ceremony in its modern form was the revival of 1885, which was largely due to the enthusiasm of William Harrison Ainsworth, the novelist. This revival took place at Great Dunmow, and was a very lively affair, with a splendid procession after the examinations of the claimants in the Town Hall, a fête, sports, and other amusements. Harrison Ainsworth presented two flitches, and these were won by James and Hannah Barlow, and Jean Baptiste and Clara de Chatelain. In the following years, several more such celebrations were held, and

1. Philip Morant, *History and Antiquities of the County of Essex*, 1768.

1. F. W. Steer, *The History of the Dunmow Flitch Ceremony* 1951.

now the custom is kept up more or less as an annual event. Little remains of its former serious character. The 'trial' has become a sort of facetious parody of court proceedings, with a robed and bewigged judge taking the place of the old Manor Steward, counsel for the claimants, counsel 'for the bacon', witnesses, court officials, and a jury. The applicants have to face a searching cross-examination in a room full of hilarious spectators, and those who win the prize certainly deserve to do so, if only for the amusement they provide. Yet, in spite of the general atmosphere of merriment, serious claims are still sometimes made, and probably few who were not completely callous and insensitive would care to come forward if their married lives were not in fact peaceful and happy.

A prize of bacon for wedded contentment was not peculiar to Dunmow. In Vienna formerly, a flitch hung on the Red Tower, and any man who did not rue his marriage or fear his wife could cut it down if he could prove his claim. Tradition says that there was another, obtainable on similar conditions, at the Abbey of St Melaine in Brittany. One of the services by which the Manor of Wichnor in Staffordshire was held from Edward III's time onwards was the provision of a bacon flitch, which had to be kept hanging in the Hall, 'ready arrayed, all times of the year but Lent'. This was to be given to any married man or woman 'after the day and year of their marriage be passed', and to any archbishop, bishop, monk or priest who demanded it 'after the year and day of their profession finished or their dignity received.'[1]

The demand had to be made in due form, and that form was somewhat elaborate. The claimant had to apply in person or by deputy, to the Bailiff or Porter of the Manor, and then to return upon a day agreed, bringing with him two neighbours who could swear to his truthfulness. On the appointed day, he was met by the tenants of the Manor, and led by them with music, and all wearing chaplets, to the door of the Hall. There he was met by the Lord of the Manor, or the Steward, and asked certain questions; after which the flitch was

1. Dr R. Plot, *The Natural History of Staffordshire*, 1686

laid in the doorway upon a measure of wheat and another of rye. A book was laid upon the bacon and the corn, and on this the claimant laid his right hand while he knelt and solemnly swore that, having been married for a year and a day to his wife (whom he named), he 'wold not have chaunged for none other, farer ne fowler; rycher ne powrer; ne for none other descended of gretter lynage; slepyng ne waking, at noo tyme'; and also that if he and she were both single, he 'wolde take her to be my wyfe before all the wymen of the worlde, or what condiciones soever they be, good or evylle, as help me God and hys Seyntys, and this flesh, and all fleshes.'[1]

The neighbours who had accompanied the claimant then testified that 'verily he hath said truly', and the bacon was given to him. If he was a freeman, he received, in addition, the wheat and a cheese, if a villein, the rye but no cheese. Then, on his own horse if he had one, but if not, on one lent to him for the occasion, he was escorted to the boundaries of the Manor by all the free tenants of Wichnor, and minstrels playing upon trumpets and other instruments. At the Manor limits, this gay company left him (and the borrowed horse had to be returned); but one man had still to go with him as far as the county border, and there see him and the flitch safely across it. The arrangements for this last part of the ceremonial journey were a service due from the Lord of the Manor of Rudlow, who had to provide whatever was necessary at his own costs and could be fined one hundred shillings if he defaulted.

Although so much is known concerning the details of the Wichnor ceremony, no reliable record of its ever having been carried out seems to have survived. If any one did claim and win the bacon in the course of centuries, we do not know his name, or whether he was priest or married man, or in what year he came. Even the approximate time when the custom finally fell into disuse is unknown. Unlike the Dunmow celebration, it has no modern form, and all that now commemorates it is a wooden flitch hanging over the main fireplace at Wichnor Hall.

1. Dr R. Plot, *op. cit.*

Easter Eggs. Wherever Easter is celebrated, there Easter eggs are usually to be found. In their modern form, they are frequently artificial, mere imitations of the real thing, made of chocolate or marzipan or sugar, or of two pieces of coloured and decorated cardboard fitted together to make an egg-shaped case containing some small gift. These are the Easter eggs of commerce, which now appear in shop-windows almost as soon as, and sometimes even before, Ash Wednesday is past, and by so doing lose much of their original festival significance. They are, however, comparative newcomers, hardly more than a hundred years old. Artificial eggs do not seem to have been used before the middle of last century, and popular as they are today, they have not yet entirely displaced the true Easter egg of tradition.

This is a real egg, hard-boiled, dyed in bright colours, and sometimes elaborately decorated. It still appears upon countless breakfast-tables on Easter Day, or is hidden about the house and garden for the children to find.[1] It is used in games like egg-rolling and egg-shackling (*see Easter Games*), and in places where the old customs of pace-egging or egg-clapping are kept up, it is begged from householders by visiting youngsters. Like its artificial counterpart, it is one of the most widespread of Easter gifts, and it is also the oldest, with an ancestry running far back into pre-Christian times.

Because eggs are obvious symbols of continuing life and resurrection, the pagan peoples of ancient China, Egypt, Greece, and Persia used them, centuries before the first Easter Day, at the great Spring Festivals, when the revival of all things in Nature was celebrated. The early Christians saw them as emblems of Christ's Resurrection, and adopted them as holy and appropriate gifts for Eastertide. Eggs were brought to church to be blessed at the beginning of the festival, given to the parish priest and to kinsmen, friends and neighbours, and used in some of the rituals of the season. A form of words appointed by Pope Pius V for use in Great Britain and Ireland at the blessing ceremony runs: 'Bless, O Lord, we beseech Thee, this Thy creature of eggs, that it may become a wholesome sustenance to Thy faithful servants, eating in thankfulness to Thee, on account of the Resurrection of Our Lord.' Eaten in thankfulness they probably were in more ways than one, for eggs were forbidden food all through Lent, and their reappearance on the table after so long an absence must have been one of the minor joys of the Easter feast.

Colouring and decorating the festival eggs seems to have been customary since time immemorial. An old Polish legend says that Our Lady herself painted eggs red, blue, and green to amuse the Infant Jesus, and that since

1. In some European countries, including England, the Easter Hare is said to bring the Easter eggs, and to conceal them in odd corners of the gardens, stables, or outbuildings. (*See Easter Hare Customs*). In France, and often in Roman Catholic households elsewhere it is the bells that bring them. During the 'Still Days', that is, between Maundy Thursday and the celebration of the Easter Vigil Mass, there is no bell-ringing in the churches, and the children are told that the bells have gone to Rome to fetch the eggs.

then all good Polish mothers have done the same at Easter. A Roumanian tale says that the vivid red shade, which is a favourite almost everywhere, represents the blood of Christ. On Calvary, Our Lady gave a basket of eggs to the soldiers in the hope that they might treat her Son more kindly, and His Blood, flowing down over the eggs as they lay in the basket at the foot of the Cross, dyed them scarlet. Roumanian women believe that this is why Easter eggs are so often painted red; but since the Chinese are known to have exchanged scarlet eggs at their Spring Festival as far back as B.C. 900, it is perhaps more likely that red was originally preferred to other colours because, like the egg itself, it is an emblem of life.

There are many ways of tinting and decorating the eggs, some simple and some requiring a high degree of skill. They can be dipped into a prepared dye or, more usually boiled in it, or they may be boiled inside a covering of onion-peel. In the household accounts of Edward I for 1290, there is an entry of eighteenpence spent upon 'four hundred and a half of eggs', which were to be covered with leaf-gold, or else 'stained' by boiling, and then distributed to members of the Royal household.[1] Ordinary commercial dyes are often used today for colouring, but originally only natural ones, obtained from flowers, leaves, mosses, bark, wood-chips, or other sources, were employed. In England, gorse-blossom was commonly used for yellow, cochineal for scarlet, and logwood-chips for a rich purple. Spinach leaves gave a fine green, and so did the petal of the purple anenome called the Pasque-flower. The outer skin of an onion, wrapped round an egg and boiled with it, is still very often used to obtain a delicate mottled yellow, or a pleasant brown. Similarly, if strips of coloured rag or ribbon are bound on, a marbled effect is produced. In the northern counties, and also in Switzerland, minute flowers and leaves are sometimes laid on the egg underneath the onion-peel to make a white flower-pattern on the yellow or brown surface. Other designs or mottoes, can be traced on the shell before it is dyed with a white wax pencil, or a piece of candle shaved to a point. Another method is to colour the eggs first, and then to trace a white design upon them by scraping away the dye with an engraving tool or a stylus.

The decoration of Easter eggs is a traditional peasant art in Eastern and Central Europe. Favourite designs vary in different regions. In Hungary, red flower-patterns on a white ground are often seen; sometimes the decorated eggs are fitted with tiny metal shoes, with minute spurs attached, and curious little metal hangers. In Jugoslavia, the letters XV usually form part of the design. They stand for *Christos Vaskrese*, meaning 'Christ is risen', which is the traditional Easter greeting of Eastern Europe. Russian eggs are sometimes elaborately decorated with miniature pictures of the saints, or of Our Lord. Polish designs are often geometrical, or abstract, or they may include Christian symbols, like the Cross or Fish, mixed with pagan emblems of new life. Painted eggs of this type, known as *pisanki*, always appear on the Easter Table which, in many households, is adorned with green leaves and spread with the finest foods that the family can afford.

Until just before the first World War, Polish girls often sent large numbers of decorated eggs – sometimes as many as a hundred to a favoured suitor. These, carefully wrapped in a fine lawn kerchief on which the young man's initials had been embroidered, were carried to his house by an elderly female friend of the girl's family usually with some small gift added, such as a posy of flowers, some nuts, or a packet of tobacco. In return, he was expected to send her a piece of dress-material, or a kerchief, or a bunch of many-coloured ribbons. It was customary for the girl to decorate the eggs herself, but if she lacked the requisite skill, she went to some local woman who specialized in the art. Such specialists were to be found in most Polish villages, and also in Hungary and Czechoslovakia. Some were renowned over a wide area for the variety and beauty of their designs. They were paid for their services in money or in kind, or sometimes, if a girl was very poor, by help given in the house or garden.

In some East European countries, scarlet eggs,

1. John Brand, *Observations on the Popular Antiquities of Great Britain*, Vol. I, ed. Sir Henry Ellis, 1849.

as symbols of resurrection, are placed on, or buried in, the graves of the family dead. In the Balkans, they are sometimes buried in the fields or the vineyards to protect the crops from thunder and hail-storms in the coming year. A few also are kept in the house to bring good luck. The latter custom was known in northern England until about the middle of last century. One or two of the most beautifully ornamented Pace-eggs – the name by which Easter eggs are still most commonly called in the northern counties[1] – would be saved and kept in tall ale-glasses in a corner cupboard, or some other place where they could be easily seen. An egg that is boiled really hard will last for years; some very fine specimens, originally decorated for the poet's children, are still preserved in the Wordsworth Museum at Grasmere. Here and there also, in cottages or farmhouses, others have survived as relics of Easters long gone by. But naturally, they are scarce, since only a very few eggs, cherished for superstitious or sentimental reasons, ever survived the first year. The majority were either eaten during the festival, or broken to pieces in the vigorous egg-games that were played at this season. *(See Easter Games: Pace-Egging.)*

Easter Games. Easter, like Shrovetide, was formerly a season when many lively and energetic games were played. In Oxfordshire, even now, older people sometimes refer to Easter Monday as Ball Monday, because of the numerous ball-games that used to be played on that day. Stoolball, knurr-and-spell, trapball, ninepins, handball, bowls and football were all customary pastimes of the Easter holidays. So was tipcat, which is not a ball-game, but is played by striking in mid-air a piece of wood called a cat with a stick, or catstaff. Another favourite was prisoners' bars, which we now think of as a children's game only, but which was quite commonly played by adults until about the middle of last century. It was specially popular in Shropshire and Cheshire, where

1. In Scotland, Easter eggs are often called Peace or Paiss eggs. 'Pace', 'Peace' and 'Paiss' are all corruptions of Pasch, or Paschal, of which the original root is the Hebrew word *pesach* meaning Passover.

matches between rival townships were often arranged. In 1856, the Rector of Barthomley[1] called it one of the traditional sports of Cheshire, and complained that, though it was still very popular there when he wrote, it was being slowly but steadily superseded by that 'innovation from the south of England' cricket.

All these games flourished at Easter, and many made their first appearance then, but they were also played at other times of the year. There were, however, some, like the Bottle-Kicking contest at Hallaton (*see Easter Hare Customs*), and various games played with eggs, that were peculiar to Eastertide. Since eggs have always been symbols of renewed and continuing life, alike in pagan and Christian times (*see Easter Eggs*), it is likely that these egg-games once had a religious or magical significance, though in their later forms they often appear as pastimes of the simplest kind. In one which was formerly popular both in France and in Great Britain, eggs were tossed into the air and caught again as they fell. The player who dropped one had to pay a forfeit. Another, which still survives is egg-shackling. In it, a hard-boiled egg is firmly grasped in the right hand and used as a weapon to strike the eggs of other players, the object

1. Revd. E. Hinchcliffe, *Bartholmley*, 1856.

being to break these whilst keeping one's own intact. The winner of each round keeps the broken egg for himself. Since hard-boiled eggs often prove unexpectedly tough, one boy may acquire a number of these forfeits before his luck deserts him, and his own egg goes down at last before some as yet undamaged specimen. Thomas Hyde, in his *De Ludis Orientalibus* (1694), says that the game was played by the Christian children of Mesopotamia during the whole of the forty days between Easter Sunday and Ascension Day. It is still a popular Easter pastime in several European countries and in the northern English counties.[1]

Egg-shackling is often associated with the Polish custom known as *Dingus*, or *Smigus*. This takes place on Easter Monday, or Ducking Monday,[2] as it is often called in Eastern Europe. Young men and girls splash each other vigorously with water, and it is after this proceeding, when both sides are thoroughly wet, that the egg-contest begins. In Hungary, unmarried girls used to be seized by the local young men at daybreak on Ducking Monday, dragged off to some pond or stream, and thrown in bodily. This was supposed to make them good wives in the future. Nowadays, the ritual, where it survives, is not quite so drastic. The girls are no longer ducked, but buckets of water are emptied over them, or they are generously sprinkled or splashed with water from the well. They are, of course, expected to submit with good grace, and even, in some areas, to pay for the privilege with gifts of painted eggs, or glasses of brandy. No doubt they do this the more willingly, since to be left out of these lively sports would be a sure sign of unpopularity, and to be well and truly ducked or splashed in the early hours of Ducking Monday, is therefore a real, if somewhat uncomfortable, compliment.

1. Egg-shackling in England was always mainly a northern sport, but a milder game, bearing the same name and usually played on Shrove Tuesday instead of at Easter, has been recorded during the nineteenth century in the south-western counties. At Powerstock school, in Dorset, a game so-called consisted of shaking eggs gently in a sieve; as each one was cracked, it was removed until only the strongest remained. The owner then received a prize (*Dorset Up Along and Down Along*, ed. M. Dacombe, n.d.) In her *Somerset Folklore* (1965) Miss R L. Tongue mentions a similar game at Martock, where the winner took all the cracked eggs, one played at Langport until 1870, where the schoolmaster had them, and others of the same sort in Exeter. At Langport, the winner wore a patchwork fool's cap in token of victory, and afterwards headed a procession of schoolchildren round the village. At St Columb Major, about 1820, children in a dame school struck unboiled eggs together at noon on Shrove Tuesday the schoolmistress holding a plate beneath to catch the contents, with which she subsequently made pancakes for her own dinner. The battle continued until only one sound egg remained, its owner then being acclaimed the winner. (F. W. P. Jago, *Western Antiquary*, March, 1884).

2. In Devon and Cornwall, May 1st used to be known as Ducking Day, or Dippy Day, because boys claimed the right to throw water over any person encountered in the streets who was not wearing a sprig of hawthorn.

Egg-rolling is a traditional Easter pastime which still flourishes in northern England, Scotland, Ulster, the Isle of Man, and Switzerland. It takes place on Easter Sunday or Monday, and consists of rolling coloured, hard-boiled eggs down a slope until they are cracked and broken after which they are eaten by their owners. In some districts, this is a competitive game, the winner being the player whose egg remains longest undamaged, but more usually, the fun consists simply of the rolling and eating. This is evidently the older form of the custom, since egg-rolling does not appear to have been originally a game to be lost or won. In the Hebrides, formerly, it provided an opportunity for divination. Each player marked his or her egg with an identifying sign, and then watched to see how it fared as it sped down the slope. If it reached the bottom unscathed, the owner could expect good luck in the future, but if it was broken, misfortune would follow before the year was out. Similarly, at Connel Ferry in Argyllshire, where it was customary for young men to roll their eggs in one place, and for young women to roll theirs in another, the man or girl whose egg went farthest and most smoothly would be the first person to marry in that particular group.[1]

Any handy bank, or hillock or slanting lawn may be used for egg-rolling but in some districts there are traditional sites. Thus, at Penrith, the rolling takes place in the Castle moat, at Derby, on Bunker's Hill, at Edinburgh, on

1. Dr Maclagan's MS. Collection, quoted in *British Calendar Customs: Scotland*, Vol. I, ed. M. M. Banks, 1937.

Arthur's Seat. The customary ground at Preston, in Lancashire, is Avenham Park where, on Easter Monday, very large crowds of adults and children annually congregate, and thousands of gaily-coloured eggs can be seen rolling and bouncing down the steep grassy hillside towards the River Ribble. Here it is usual to bring oranges to eat with the broken eggs, and sometimes these are rolled as well. This, of course, is a purely modern innovation, intended simply to add to the fun; but perhaps the addition of these golden, sun-like globes is not altogether inappropriate in a custom which is sometimes said to have been originally a solar rite.

Egg-rolling is known in at least one city in the United States of America, though it was not one of those traditional customs which crossed the Atlantic with the early settlers. It was introduced in 1877 by Mrs Madison, the wife of the President of that time, who taught the children of Washington D.C. how it was done, and opened the grounds of the White House to serve as their Easter Monday rolling-ground. Since then the game has been regularly and enthusiastically played there every year, except in times of war, and by now it has almost become a traditional American custom in its own right. It has been estimated that as many as 100,000 eggs are annually rolled on Easter Monday over the White House lawns.[1]

A very curious game, half pastime and half ritual observance, used to be played at Whitchurch, near Cardiff, until at least as late as the latter half of the eighteenth century. Every childless married woman in the parish was expected to go to the churchyard on Easter Monday, taking with her twenty-four tennis balls of which twelve were white and the rest covered with black leather. These she threw from the rear part of the graveyard, right over the church, to be scrambled for as they fell by a crowd of people waiting in front of the building. 'So imperative was this custom', says a writer in *Bygones* (19th October, 1892), 'that neither rank nor age were excused, until they were relieved, by the birth of a child, from its annual performance.' By the late eighteenth century, doubtless, this practice had come to be regarded as a sort of frolic; but it seems very probable that it began life as a magical fertility rite, the due performance of which in the burgeoning Spring season was expected to result in the longed-for childbirth.

Easter Hare Customs. The hare was the sacred beast of Eastre (or Eostre), a Saxon goddess of Spring and of the Dawn, from whose name as the Venerable Bede tells us, the English word Easter is derived.[1] A widespread European tradition makes it the bringer of Easter eggs. In England, children in many families search in the garden, or in nooks and crannies of the house, for the eggs that the hare has concealed there. In Jugoslavia, they go to the stables to find the hare's nest in the hay. The little baskets in which German and Hungarian children collect their Easter gifts are often adorned with the figure of a hare, and so are Easter cards in many parts of Northern Europe. In the United States of America, the Easter Rabbit has taken the place of the European hare, but this is simply a variant of the same tradition. Rabbits and hares are often confused in folk-belief, especially in regions where the former are better known.

Thomas Blount[2] mentions a manorial custom at Coleshill in Warwickshire connected with hares. The young men of the parish used to go out early on Easter Monday morning to catch a hare. If they succeeded in doing so, and could take the animal to the Rector before ten o'clock, they could by immemorial right, claim a calf's head and a hundred eggs for their breakfast,

1. Although egg-rolling has been so enthusiastically accepted in Washington, it does not seem to have spread to other parts of the United States. In 1947, a sophisticated variant was started for New York children, with wooden eggs rolled by wooden spoons along a set course in Central Park. Since there are no real eggs to be eaten when the game is over, the children are rewarded with toys and other prizes. But this sport, unlike the lively White House celebration, has come so far from its simple traditional origin as to be hardly recognizable as the same custom.

1. Another theory is that the name is derived from *oster*, to rise.

2. Thomas Blount, *Fragmenta Antiquitatis, or Ancient Tenures of Land and Jocular Customs*, ed. Joseph Beckwith, 1784.

and a groat in money. A similar custom existed at Wooton Wawen in the same county.

In Leicester, until towards the end of the eighteenth century, one of the principal festivities of Easter Monday was that known as Hunting the Hare. The Mayor and Corporation officials rode in their scarlet robes, accompanied by a great crowd of townsfolk, to Black Annis' Bower, a cave on the nearby Dane Hills. This cave was a place of sinister reputation, supposed to be inhabited by a terrifying creature called Black Annis, or Anna, who had sharp teeth and long nails, and devoured human beings when she could catch them. From what ancient hill-

spirit, local deity, or perhaps human cave-dweller, her legend sprang has long since been forgotten, and the cave, which she was traditionally said to have dug out of the solid rock with her finger-nails, has now been filled in. Until well into the nineteenth century, however, she was remembered as a kind of bugbear, or as a witch who once lived under the Castle and used to run along secret underground passages from its cellars to her Bower on the Dane Hills. Leicester children were often warned not to go too near her cave, for if they did, she would seize them, scratch them to death, suck their blood, and hang their skins up to dry on an old pollard oak growing nearby.

The Easter Monday revels opened with games and sports on a piece of land called the Bower Close. Then, at noon, began what had probably been a real hare-hunt originally, though in the later years of the custom it had degenerated into a drag-hunt in which the corpse of a cat soaked in aniseed-water was used. The trail was laid on a zigzag course running from the cave-mouth downwards into the town and ending outside the door of the Mayor's house. Hounds and horsemen poured down the hill, through lanes and alleyways and streets, leaping fences and cutting off garden-corners on their way, cheered on by crowds of shouting spectators, and followed by large numbers of foot-runners. When the hunt was over, the Mayor provided a feast for his friends, and so the cheerful, noisy celebration ended.[1]

It is not known when this Easter hare-hunt began. It is mentioned in the Town Records in 1668 as an 'ancient custom', and probably it had existed for a considerable time before that date. In the second half of the eighteenth century it began to decline, and finally it ceased altogether. The last trace of this time-honoured festivity, lingered on for some years after the disappearance of the Hunt in the form of an annual gathering known as Dane Hills Fair.

The Hare-Pie Scramble, which still takes place on Easter Monday at Hallaton in Leicestershire, is probably of mediaeval origin, though no one now knows when it actually began. It is followed immediately by a strenuous inter-parish game known as Bottle-Kicking, which may well be very much older. The Scramble is connected with a piece of land which, at some date now unknown, was settled upon the successive rectors of the parish, on condition that each in his turn provided every year, at Easter, two hare pies, a quantity of ale, and two dozen penny loaves, to be scrambled for on the rising ground known as Hare-Pie Bank. The special mention of hares for the pies at a time when they are out of season suggests that this bequest may have absorbed some older custom associated with the ancient concept of the Easter Hare. In this connection it is interesting to note that in

1. J. Throsby, *History of Leicester*, 1791.

some years a figure of a sitting hare, mounted upon a pole, has been carried in the procession to the Bank. It is hardly necessary to say that the modern pies (or now, more usually one very large pie in place of the original two) do not contain hare, but are made of beefsteak, or some other meat.

They are cut up by the Rector, and the resulting small pieces are then put into a sack and ceremonially carried to Hare-Pie Bank. A long procession winds round the village, and in it march three men carrying the so-called bottles that will be used in the following game. These bottles are, in fact, small wooden barrels, strongly made and hooped with iron. Two contain ale; the third is a dummy. During the parade they are held in high in the air, balanced upon the flat of the bearer's hand. When the procession reaches the Bank, the sack is emptied, and the pieces of pie are scrambled for by the waiting crowd with as much energy and excitement as might be shown if the Easter Monday dinner depended upon them. Formerly, the loaves were scrambled for also, but these have now vanished from the proceedings, an equivalent, and perhaps more useful gift for the aged poor having been substituted for them at the end of last century.

After the Scramble is finished, the Bottle-Kicking begins. One of the full barrels is thrown into a circular hollow on top of the Bank, and a strenuous contest then follows between two teams of players, the men of Hallaton on one side and the Medbourne men on the other. Medbourne is the adjoining parish, but the team bearing its name does not necessarily consist only of its inhabitants. It may include 'strangers' from another village, or indeed, any one who is not a Hallatonian. There is no limiting of numbers, and as many as will can play on either side.

The object of the game is to get the bottle away from the Bank and over the boundary in one direction or the other. Whichever team succeeds in kicking it over their own line has won that round and can claim the contents of the barrel. Much fierce struggling, however, is needed before this can be achieved, and the contest usually lasts for a considerable time. When it is over, the dummy bottle is fought for with even greater vigour and enthusiasm. Finally, the second full barrel is carried in triumph at the game's end to the old Market Cross on Hallaton Green, where it is broached with full honours, and its contents shared by both sides. The leader of the winning team is hoisted on to the top of the Cross and, in that rather uncomfortable position, he takes the first drink. The barrels used in this boisterous game are carefully kept from year to year, repainted and decorated for each occasion, and only replaced when they have become too battered to be of further service.

From time to time, attempts have been made to suppress both parts of this cheerful celebration, usually on the grounds that the Bottle-Kicking is too rowdy and the money needed for the Hare-Pie Scramble might be better employed. One Rector in the eighteenth century tried to divert the funds to other charitable uses, but he met with so much opposition that he had to abandon the idea. 'No pie, no parson, and a job for the glazier!' was chalked all over the Rectory doors and walls and on the outside of the Church. In 1878, when the railway was being built and Hallaton was feeling 'modern', it was proposed to substitute other and quieter sports for the wild Bottle-Kicking. But this proposal failed like the other, and today, notwithstanding two wars and some local difficulties, Hallaton's annual Easter Monday festival still preserves its ancient two-part form, and is celebrated with as much vigour as in the past.

Easter Lifting. Lifting, or Heaving, at Easter was a very popular custom, particularly in north-western England and on both sides of the Welsh Border, until the second half of the nineteenth century. On Easter Monday, parties of young men visited the various houses of the parish in which they lived, carrying a stout chair that was decorated with greenery, flowers, and ribbons. In this chair, the women of each house were made to sit in turn, young and old alike, and were hoisted three times into the air and turned round. The lifters were then entitled to claim a kiss and a small gift of money as their reward. On the Tuesday, the women went round with the chair and lifted the men. In some places, this day-order was reversed, so that the women went out on the first of the two 'Heaving Days', and the men followed on the second. On both days, lifting ceased punctually at noon.

This custom was observed as part of the traditional Easter merrymakings in both rural areas and towns.[1] In the country parishes, where all concerned were known to each other, it was a cheerful and often very charming rite, in which everyone knew what was expected of him or her, and willingly took part. In Shropshire and Herefordshire, the feet of the person lifted were sprinkled with water from a wet bunch of flowers carried by one of the visiting party. F. T. Havergal records that in the latter county the lifters, as they entered the house, sang 'Jesus Christ is risen again!'[2] In his *Bartholmley* (1856), E. W. Hinchcliffe, the Rector of that Cheshire parish, speaks with approval of what he considered a pleasant and harmless custom, and relates with evident pleasure how his parishioners came with their decorated chair to lift his wife on Easter Monday, and returned on the following day to do the same for him. At Neston, in the same county, it was customary for girls to feign terror on Heaving Monday and, when they saw the young men approaching, to rush to their houses and bar the doors. It was, however, understood that if the lifters could make their way in by any other entry they would do so, and usually they had little difficulty in finding a window 'accidentally' left open in some part of the house.

In the larger towns, the proceedings were frequently far more rough and ready. The house-to-house visits were often omitted, and the lifters did not always burden themselves with a be-ribboned chair. People on the streets were liable to be seized without warning by noisy bands of men or women, hoisted, kissed and made to pay ransom before they were released. Respectable girls stayed at home behind genuinely locked doors and windows until noon was past, but travellers and strangers had no such protection. At Kidderminster, ropes were stretched across the roads, and any one of the right sex (male on Monday, female on Tuesday) who came too near them was seized, thrust into a chair, and lifted without further ado. Elsewhere, even the convenience of a chair was lacking. Baring-Gould records how a school-inspector of his acquaintance, a rather timid clergyman, came to Warrington on Easter Monday, and was set upon by a company of mill-girls, unceremoniously lifted in their brawny arms and, in spite of all his protests, carried in triumph through the town. Another friend of his was lifted on another occasion at Wednesbury, 'and kissed till he was black in the face by a party of leather-breeched coalpit women.'[1]

If these two men escaped with only one hoisting, they were more fortunate than some others. An angry letter published in *Adams Weekly Courant* in 1771 declared that individuals coming to Chester on serious business were likely to be thus inconvenienced and delayed, not once but several times in the course of the morning. The writer demanded the immediate suppression of the custom by the magistrates, but evidently this was not as easy as he supposed. Thirteen years later, the *Gentleman's Magazine* for February, 1784, reported that the Manchester justices annually forbade the practice, sending the bell-man round to proclaim the ban well in advance, but still it went on, there as elsewhere.

Time and changing ideas, however, were more successful than the magistrates. By the mid-'seventies of last century, Lifting had died out naturally in most places, or was dying out. Here and there it survived a little longer. In 1883, a man living at Heswall in Cheshire brought an action against three men who came to lift his wife. They pleaded immemorial custom, and

1. According to a record ,dated 1290, communicated to the Society of Antiquaries in 1805, and quoted by Brand in *Popular Antiquities* (Vol. I), Edward I was lifted on Easter Monday by a party of ladies of the court, to whom he gave a reward of £14.

2. F. T. Havergal, *Herefordshire Words & Phrases*, 1887.

1. S. Baring-Gould – footnote to William Henderson's *Folk-Lore of the Northern Counties* (1866 edition, p. 64). In this note he adds: 'The same custom prevails in the Pyranees, where I have been lifted by a party of stout Basque damsels.'

the case was dismissed after apologies and the payment of costs; but the fact that such an action was ever brought at all shows how far this ancient rite had declined in popularity, even in a county that had formerly been one of its strongholds.[1]

Lifting was often explained as a commemoration of Our Lord's Resurrection at Eastertide. Doubtless it was so for many in its hey-day, though the rowdy celebrations of the towns can hardly have had much religious significance. Even in the villages, it is probable that most people thought of it as something lively and pleasant that had always been done at that season, and needed no further explanation. It is, however, likely that it was derived from a far older agricultural and magical custom, and that the origins of Lifting are to be found in a pre-Christian Spring rite once performed to foster the growth of the crops.

1. Lifting does not seem to have been customary in north-eastern England; but in Northumberland, Durham, and Yorkshire, young men used to snatch the shoes (or buckles) from the feet of girls on Easter Sunday, or Monday, and the girls retaliated by seizing the boys' caps or hats on the following day. Shoes and headgear were afterwards redeemed by a kiss and a few coins.

Eating a Rose. *(See Minden Roses.)*

Egg Rolling. (*See Easter Games.*)

Fig Sunday. Figs, both uncooked and in the form of boiled puddings or small pies, used to be eaten in large quantities on Palm Sunday. Hence, in many parts of England,[1] the day was known as Fig Sunday. The puddings or pies were served at the midday meal, and children were also given little packets of the fruit in the early morning, to remind them what day it was. Grocers and fruit-merchants expected to sell more figs in the preceding week than at any other time in the year, and in some places special Fig Fairs were held to cope with the demand. A traditional explanation of the custom was that it commemorated that barren fig-tree to which Our Lord, being hungry, came on the morning after the first Palm Sunday, and found no fruit upon it.[2]

Fig-feasts were annually held on Dunstable Downs, at Kempton in Hertfordshire, and on the top of Silbury Hill in Wiltshire. People came in considerable numbers from all the nearby villages and sometimes from farther afield, to eat figs in the open air, to toast each other in ale or cider, and generally to make merry. These cheerful gatherings ceased about the end of the last century, but figs remained a traditional Palm Sunday dish in many households until shortly before the first World War. Since then, the custom has almost entirely died out, and today the old name of Fig Sunday is rarely used, except occasionally by elderly people remembering the vanished ways of their childhood.

1. Particularly in the Midlands, the Home Counties, Wiltshire, and Yorkshire.
2. *Mark* XI, 12–14.

In some areas, the traditional day for eating figs was not Palm Sunday, but Mid-Lent Sunday or Good Friday. In Lancashire the customary Good Friday dish was fig-sue. This was made of ale, bread, figs, and nutmeg, all boiled together to a soup-like consistency, and eaten hot.

Fireball Parade, Stonehaven. *(See Burning the Old Year Out.)*

Firing the Fenny Poppers. At Fenny Stratford in Buckinghamshire, a ceremony known as Firing the Fenny Poppers takes place every year on St Martin's Day (November 11th). This is not a traditional Martinmas custom, though it has now been observed on that date for some two hundred years. It forms part of the celebrations of the Patronal Festival of the parish, and it is also a tribute to the memory of Dr Browne Willis, the man who was mainly responsible for the building of the church.

The Fenny Poppers are six miniature cannon, curiously shaped and believed to be of considerable age, which are normally kept in the belfry of St Martin's Church. On the festival day, they are brought out to the churchyard and solemnly fired, first at eight o'clock in the morning, then at noon and at two o'clock, and finally at six o'clock in the evening. It is customary for the Vicar to fire the first Popper.

This queer little ceremony has its roots in the history of the church itself, originally a chapel-of-ease of Bletchley parish. Before the eighteenth century, Fenny Stratford had no church of any kind, and that it has one now is due to the enthusiasm and generosity of Dr Browne Willis, who was patron of the living of Bletchley. He felt that a chapel-of-ease was necessary for Fenny Stratford people and started a subscription for this purpose, contributing generously himself, and encouraging the local gentry by selling space on the ceiling of the church for the display of the arms of all those who gave ten pounds or upwards. These heraldic signs can still be seen, stretching from end to end of the ceiling. In 1730, when the church was finished and dedicated to St Martin, he arranged for a special sermon to be preached every year on the dedication anniversary, and for a parish feast to be held in the evening. Soon after his death in 1760, the firing of the old cannon which he had presented to the church, was added to the other celebrations of the festival, and this custom has been kept up ever since.

First Foot. The first visitor to enter a house on New Year's morning is commonly known in Great Britain as the First Foot. In Yorkshire he is sometimes called the Lucky Bird, in the Isle of Man, the *Quaaltagh*. Elsewhere in Europe he has other names, but wherever he appears, he is a personage of great importance. He may be a chance caller, or a man on some errand unconnected with the anniversary or he may be the ceremonial First Foot who comes on purpose to let the New Year into the house and bring good luck to the family. Whichever he is, he is traditionally supposed to influence the fortunes of the householders in the following twelve months, both by the gifts he brings and by his own character and appearance. Hence it is essential everywhere that he should be an individual with certain definite qualities, though what these are varies a little from one region to another.

In Scotland and northern England, the custom of First-footing in the early hours of January 1st is still kept up with great vigour. The First Foot comes as soon as possible after midnight has struck. He brings symbolic gifts of food or fuel or money as tokens of prosperity in the year that has just begun. Sometimes, instead of these presents, or in addition to them, he carries a bunch of evergreens as a promise of continuing life. Nothing must be taken out of the house before these gifts have been brought in, nor should any one go outside until he has arrived. He must be admitted by the front door and, since he is a luck bringer, he must be hospitably entertained with food and plentiful supplies of wine or spirits.

Usually, the First Foot greets all within as he crosses the threshold, and is at once loudly welcomed in return. In some parts of Scotland, however, he does not speak until he has laid a peat or a coal upon the fire. This silent entry and first concern with the hearth, the life-centre of the house, has been recorded in other regions also, and may perhaps represent an older form of the rite. Charlotte Burne relates how, at Longnor in the nineteenth century, the New Year was let in by an old man who came in without knocking or speaking, and stirred the fire before he offered any greeting.[1] In his *English Festivals* (1947), Lawrence Whistler describes an impressive version of the ceremony, in which the First Foot carried an evergreen branch in one hand and a sprig of mistletoe in the other. He entered in silence, crossed the room to the hearth, and there laid the green branch upon the flames and the mistletoe on the mantelpiece above. No one spoke while he did this, and only when he turned to wish the assembled company a happy New Year was the general silence broken.

The ceremonial First Foot may be one of a band of young men going round from house to house, or a friend of the family who has arranged to let the New Year in for them. Sometimes a man of the right type will undertake to visit every house in a given street or district. Strictly speaking, the First Foot should always be someone from outside the home, but occasionally, when no such early morning visitor is expected, a male member of the household will go out just before midnight and be ceremonially let in again as soon as the hour has struck, with the appropriate gifts in his hand. These, in England, are usually a piece of bread

1. C. S. Burne, *Shropshire Folk-Lore*, 1893.

and a piece of coal, as symbols of food and warmth and a coin or a little salt to ensure wealth in the coming year. In Scotland, a bottle of whisky is often included, or a compound of spirits, beer, sugar and eggs known as a Het Pint. Round Dundee, and in the fishing villages of the East Coast, a red herring is a lucky gift, as a promise of good fishing to come; and in some Scottish rural areas a sheaf of wheat, symbolizing a good corn-harvest, is often carried. For the First Foot to come empty-handed is a very bad omen, for this means losses and poverty before the year's end.

To be a true luck-bringer, the First Foot should be vigorous and healthy and, if possible, young and good-looking. If he is flat-footed, or cross-eyed, or lame, if his eyebrows meets across his nose[1], if he is dressed in black, or appears to be ailing, the omens for the coming twelve months are bad. In most areas, a dark-haired or dark-complexioned man is lucky, though there are local exceptions to this rule. In some east Yorkshire districts, for instance, and in parts of Lincolnshire and Northumberland, the First Foot must be fair. Red hair is very widely disliked.[2] In some counties, a bachelor is best, in others, a married man. Children and adolescent boys are usually popular first visitors, and so in some regions is, a man known to be a footling, that is, one who was born feet foremost, and who is consequently supposed to have magical powers of healing.

In the Isle of Man, the *Quaaltagh* may be of either sex, though a man is usually preferred.

1. Meeting eyebrows are usually considered a bad sign. In England, it is said that those who have them 'will not live to wear wedding clothes'. which may denote either an early death or misfortune in love. In Scotland, meeting eyebrows are supposed to mean that their owner is immoral, or born to be hanged. In Greece, a man so marked is suspected of being a vampire, in Germany, Denmark and Iceland, of being a werewolf. An Old Icelandic name for such a man was *hamrammr*, meaning one able to change his shape.

2. Very occasionally, red hair has been noted as lucky, e.g. in part of Aberdeenshire and the West Riding of Yorkshire. A contributor to *Folk Lore* (Vol. 5, 1894) stated that round Bradford and Huddersfield, a red-haired man was sometimes paid to go round to various houses, if a First Foot of the colour could not be relied upon to come in the ordinary way.

Similarly, in Scotland a woman can be a lucky First Foot in some areas, though not in all. But in England a female First Foot is a disaster almost everywhere. In the northern counties, where the ceremonial letting-in of the New Year is most widely observed, no woman would ever dream of presenting herself for this purpose. Along the Welsh Border formerly if a woman had occasion to call at a house on January 1st, she was expected to enquire first whether a man had been there before her; if she failed to do this, and came nevertheless, she was suspected of deliberate malice towards the family concerned. Charlote Burne says that in the Stretton Valley, a female visitor arriving before noon on that day was considered unlucky, even if the New Year had already been let in by a male First Foot.[1] In Wales generally, a woman was sometimes a permissible first-comer and sometimes not, according to district; but in Montgomeryshire she was so unlucky in that capacity that, after her ill-omened visit, little boys were sometimes marched all through the house 'to break the witch.'[2]

Until about sixty or seventy years ago, it was customary in some parts of England[3] for Christmas, as well as New Year to be ceremonially let in by a First Foot, or Lucky Bird. The same rules as to sex, colouring, and appearance were observed on both occasions. Thus, no woman was ever allowed to perform this office in any of the counties, where the custom was kept up. If she did so inadvertently, by coming before the male Lucky Bird, it was an omen of misfortune. Mrs Leather records that in some Herefordshire parishes only women who had slept in the house on the previous night were allowed to enter during the whole of Christmas Day, and even girls who came round singing carols were unwelcome and usually sent away unrewarded.[4]

The accepted First Foot of Christmas was a man, or a boy, of the right type, who came very

1. C. S. Burne, *Shropshire Folk Lore*, 1893.

2. *Bye-gones*, 17 January, 1900.

3. This custom, now almost entirely forgotten, was once well-known in Yorkshire, Derbyshire, Nottinghamshire and Lincolnshire, and also in part of Staffordshire, Shropshire, Herefordshire and Worcestershire.

4. E. M. Leather, *The Folk-Lore of Herefordshire*, 1912.

early on Christmas morning. He entered by the front door and, in many places, walked right through the house, going into every room, and leaving finally by the back door. Unlike the New Year counterpart, he brought no symbolic gifts, though he usually carried a sprig of evergreen. It was, however, essential that something should be given to him. In East Yorkshire, he was sometimes given bread, salt, and a small coin as soon as he crossed the threshold. Elsewhere, the customary gifts were sixpence or a shilling, and a generous portion of Christmas cake, or cheese, with cider, ale, or home-made wine. Unless these, or other gifts were made to the Christmas luck-bringer, very bad luck would follow during the coming year.

Flambeaux Procession, Comrie. *(See Burning the Old Year Out.)*

Flowering Sunday. In Wales Palm Sunday is called *Sul y Blodau*, or Flowering Sunday, because of the custom, once widespread in the Principality, of dressing family graves with flowers and greenery on that day. In preparation for Eastertide ,every grave was carefully trimmed cleaned, and adorned. All weeds were removed, the sides were raised with new turf, the stones freshly whitewashed, and the surface strewn with Spring flowers and evergreens. Sometimes friends as well as kinsmen were thus remembered and, in urban districts especially, large crowds came annually to the churchyards and cemeteries, to leave their flowers on the graves of those they had known in former years. A writer in *Bye-gones* (September 9th 1896) records how in Cardiff, 'thousands wend their way to the Cemetry, the roads thereto presenting an appearance like unto a fair.'

Although the name of Flowering Sunday is applied now only to Palm Sunday, grave-flowering seems to have occurred in some Welsh areas on other days. Easter Day is mentioned in some early nineteenth-century accounts; so is Easter Eve. In Glamorgan formerly, graves appear to have been regularly dressed at Easter, Whitsuntide and Christmas, perhaps as a means of allowing the loved dead to share in the joys of the three greatest festivals of the Church's year. By the end of the nineteenth century, however, these variations had faded away, and the custom had become almost entirely fixed upon Palm Sunday.

Graves are still dressed on that day in parts of Glamorganshire, particularly in and around the towns. Unlike most traditional customs, this one declined first in country districts, where it might have been expected to survive longest, and lived on, or sprang up anew, in the industrialized areas. It was never an English custom, though it has been recorded in a few villages in the counties of Gloucestershire and Staffordshire.

Football. *(See Shrovetide Football.)*

Forty Shilling Day. *(See Graveside Doles.)*

Founder's Day. *(See Oak Apple Day.)*

Furry Dance. The Furry Dance at Helston in Cornwall is one of the most interesting, and probably one of the oldest, examples of a communal Spring festival dance still surviving in Great Britain. It has been performed there for centuries, and the local people claim that this has been done without a break, except in times of war or pestilence. At one time, similar dances took place at the Lizard on May 1st, at Penrhyn on May 3rd; but these have vanished now, while the Helston custom is as fresh and vigorous today as ever it was in the past.

Furry Day falls on May 8th, the Feast of the Apparition of St Michael the Archangel, who is the patron saint of the parish. Various local legends are told to explain its ceremonies. One is that St Michael and the Devil fought for the possession of the town, and that the people danced in the streets for joy when the battle was won by the Archangel. Another says that the fight took place at Mont St Michel in Brittany, and that the result was somewhat less definite. St Michael was forced to take refuge on St Michael's Mount, near Marazion, but fortunately Satan feared to cross the sea, and contented himself with removing the great stone that sealed the mouth of Hell and throwing it after his enemy. It fell short by nine miles, and landed in the yard of the Angel Hotel in Helston. So huge a block of granite might have done immense damage, but St Michael protected his people, and no one was hurt. So on that day they danced, as they have done on the anniversary ever since; and in proof of the veracity of the legend, the stone, or part of it, may still be seen, built into the west wall of the hotel.

In the course of centuries, the festival has been variously called Flora, Faddy, or Furry Day,[1] the last being now the most usual name. Today, as in the past, it is the great holiday of the town's year. For two or three weeks beforehand, everyone is busy painting, whitewashing, and generally smartening up the houses and gardens. On May 1st there is a sort of preliminary canter. The Town Band parades through the streets at six o'clock in the morning and seven o'clock at night, playing the Furry Dance

music. It is followed by hundreds of dancing children whose performance, unlike that of a week later, is entirely spontaneous and not in any way organized.

On the great day itself, houses and public buildings are decorated with branches of sycamore and beech, flowers, and evergreens. The church-bells are pealed, and a special early morning service, is held in St Michael's Church. At seven o'clock the Early Morning Dance, the first of the day, begins. This is for the young people who, like their elders later on, dance through the narrow streets and in and out of gardens and houses, all of them wearing lilies-of-the-valley, the particular flower of the festival.[1] While this is going on, other young people are out in the woods gathering yet more green branches. With these they perambulate the town, accompanied by young men dressed as St Michael and St George, Robin Hood, Friar Tuck and Little John. At certain fixed points, they stop to sing the ancient Hal-an-Tow song, one verse of which shows very clearly what it is that they are really celebrating. It runs:

> With Hal-an-Tow! Jolly Rumble, O!
> For we are up as soon as any day, O,
> And for to fetch the Summer home,
> The Summer and the May, O,
> For Summer is a-come, O,
> And Winter is a-gone, O.

At ten o'clock the children dance, all in white and wearing the traditional lilies. Each school sends a contingent. Then, exactly at noon, the principal dance begins. The Mayor goes first, wearing his chain of office, and behind him come men and women in couples, the men in morning coats and top hats, and the women in their prettiest summer frocks. They dance through all the main streets, and into gardens, shops and houses, in at one door, and if possible out through another, to bring the luck of Summer to the owners and tenants, and drive out the darkness of Winter.

The last dance begins at five o'clock, led by the young people who danced in the first. In

1. 'Furry' is sometimes said to be derived from the Latin *feria*, or (more probably) from the Cornish *feur*, or *fer*, a fair or jubilee, and 'Faddy' from an old English word, *fade*, meaning to go, and especially to go forward in a dance.

1. In Paris, lilies-of-the-valley are a customary gift on May Day, and large quantities of these flowers are annually sold for the purpose.

this the spectators may join, and most of them do, so that at the end of the day the whole town seems to be dancing. Formerly there was a ball at night, but nowadays this is not always held. There is, however, a civic luncheon after the noon dance, and a breakfast at the Guildhall for the early morning dancers.

Like all long-continued customs, this one has changed a little in the course of time. Formerly, the young people who went to gather greenery at daybreak had the right to demand a toll from every stranger entering the town on Furry Day. Any person found working on this general holiday used to be carried on a pole to the River Cober and ordered to leap across it, or else pay a fine. The victim usually chose the latter alternative, since the river's width made it almost impossible to jump over it without falling into the water. At one time, the children carried willow-branches in their dance, which now seem to have disappeared and obviously the rigidly enforced top-hat-and-morning-coat uniform of the noon dance cannot be very old, though probably 'best clothes' were always worn then.

Nevertheless, what is really remarkable about Helston's Furry Day, is its essentially unchanging character. In spite of the thousands of visitors who come to see it, it has never been commercialized, or used to raise money for charitable or other ends. It remains a communal festival in the true sense, a celebration in which everyone, from the Mayor down to the youngest schoolchild takes part. It is considered a great honour to be chosen to lead any of the dances, and by a firm rule, only those born in the town may be leaders. The ancient origins of the festival show clearly in the green boughs gathered so early and carried about, in the words of the traditional song, and in the never-omitted luck-bringing visits. If any pre-Christian ancestor of today's dancers could return on Furry Day now, he would probably have little difficulty in recognising the descendants of those rites by which he, too, once brought the Summer home, and carried luck and fertility to every homestead.

Garland Day, Abbotsbury. May 13th, which is Old May Day, is Garland Day at Abbotsbury in Dorset. For some days beforehand, the children go round collecting flowers which are then woven into garlands of traditional shape and mounted upon short poles. On the day itself, the children carry the garlands about the village, stopping outside the houses to show them as luck-bringers to the householders, and receiving gifts of pence or small silver in return. At the end of the day, the money is shared out, and the garlands are laid round the War Memorial as an offering to the memory of those whose names are inscribed upon it.

This is all that now remains of a ceremony, undoubtedly of considerable age and locally said to run back for a thousand years, which was connected with the start of the fishing-season. When Abbotsbury had its own fishing-fleet of a dozen boats or more, each manned by a local crew and owned by local men, Garland Day marked the formal opening of the season. Every boat had a garland in the bow, made from flowers gathered by the seamen's children. At noon, all the garlands were carried to the parish church, where there was a service, and afterwards they were taken back to the boats. In the afternoon, the whole village made merry on the beach, and played games and danced on the green below the Castle. Then, towards evening, the boats put out to sea, and when they were some way from land, the garlands were thrown overboard. As they floated away, or sank, a song was sung, or according to some accounts, a prayer was said. All this was done to bring good luck to the fishing. The ceremony was never omitted, and only after it had been duly performed by the crews of all the boats was the new season considered to have been really started.

Now the fishing-fleet has gone, and the garlands are no longer carried out to sea. They are still made, however, in the old way and on the old date, and this custom is likely to continue for some time yet. In 1954, the whole village sprang to its defence when the untimely zeal of a new policeman, a stranger to the district, suddenly threatened its existence. On the grounds that the children's house-to-house visits with the garlands amounted to begging, he stopped the parades and confiscated the money already collected. The immediate reaction of practically all the adults in the parish was openly expressed rage, culminating in a procession of protest and a strong complaint to the Chief Constable of Dorset. As at Hinton St George, where much the same thing had happened some years before (*see Punkie Night*), the protests were successful. Garland Day was officially acknowledged as an established and valued part of the Abbotsbury year, and since then the custom has been annually kept up without let or hindrance.

Garland Dressing, Charlton on Otmoor. In the parish church of Charlton-on-Otmoor, in Oxfordshire, a large wooden cross covered with clipped yew and box stands above the rood-screen. It is locally known as The Garland, and twice in the year it is taken down, dressed with flowers and fresh leaves, and then replaced. The first of these renewals takes place on May Day, the second at the village Feast on September 19th. On the May anniversary, little wooden, flower-covered crosses are made by the children of the parish, and taken by them to a service in the church and round about the village.

These customs have their roots in mediaeval times. Before the Reformation, two images, one of Our Lady and the other of St John, stood above the rood-screen, and on May Day, the former used to be carried in procession across the moor to the Benedictine Priory at Studley. During the upheavals of the Reformation, the statues were destroyed, and the people of Charlton erected two green garlands in their place. An illustration in Dunkin's *History and Antiquities of Bullingdon and Ploughley* (1823) shows two hooped garlands, decked with evergreens and surmounted by a cross of slightly irregular shape, one larger than the other, and both curiously suggesting a roughly-shaped human figure. By 1840, one of these had evidently disappeared, for in J. H. Parker's *Glossary of Architecture*, published in that year, a similar illustration shows only one. This remained in position until 1854, when the Reverend George Bliss, then Rector of Charlton, had it taken away. That this was an unpopular move with his parishioners is proved by the fact that, as soon as he left the village, the garland, or another like it, was replaced.

Until the middle of the nineteenth century, both garlands, while there were still two, and later the remaining one, used to be taken down for re-dressing on May Day and carried into the churchyard. From thence, preceded by Morris dancers and a musician, they were taken into the open fields and about the village. The greater garland was carried, as the statue had been before it, across Otmoor to Studley Priory, by then a private house and now an hotel, while the smaller one was borne through the parish by women and girls. Dancing and singing made up the rest of the festival celebrations until 1857, when the processions and dances finally ceased, though the ceremonial garland-dressing still went on, as the dressing of the garland-cross does today.

In an account published in 1903,[1] a former Rector of Charlton, the Reverend C. E. Prior, recorded that many of his older parishioners could still remember the green cross being carried over the moor, with six Morris-dancers in attendance. In his time, the task of re-decorating the garland was in the hands of one woman who would never allow any one else to help her. She always spoke of the garland-cross as though it was a person, calling it 'My Lady', and referring to 'her dress', 'her arms', and to the flowers newly set down the front as buttons on 'her bodice'. This may have been simply a personal idiosyncrasy; or it may possibly have been due to an unconscious memory of the time when her mediaeval ancestors dressed, not a garland or a wooden cross, but a statue of the Virgin Mary, in whose name the church at Charlton-on-Otmoor is dedicated.

Garland King Day. On May 29th (Oak Apple Day), the people of Castleton in Derbyshire, remember the Restoration of Charles II in 1660 by a ceremony which is obviously much older in origin than the happy event it

1. *Oxfordshire Archaeological Society Reports*, 1903.

commemorates, and is probably a transferred May-Day rite. At about six o'clock in the evening, a procession sets out to the music of a brass band, and goes all round the village. It is led by the Garland King, a man riding a cart-horse, and wearing over his head and shoulders a large wooden frame completely smothered in flowers and greenery. This is the Garland, which weighs about sixty pounds, and hides its wearer so effectually that only his legs are visible. On its top a separate posy of specially fine flowers is fixed, and is known as the Queen. Following the King in the procession is another rider, who is also called the Queen now, but seems originally to have been referred to simply as 'the Woman'. Until 1956, 'she' was always a man in female dress, veiled and riding side-saddle – the Man-Woman of tradition. In that year, however, the man who normally played the part withdrew, and his place was taken by a girl, as it has been ever since. Only time will show whether this break with long-established custom is permanent, or whether, on some future Garland King Day, the Man-Woman will be seen once more in his/her old form.

At various points along the route, including the six inns of the village, the procession stops, and the dancers perform. These are now schoolgirls dressed in white, but formerly it was the bell-ringers of the parish who danced, carrying oak-sprays in their hands in honour of the King who hid in an oak tree. Before the present Garland Committee was formed at about the turn of the century, the ringers not only provided the dancers, but were also responsible for organizing and running the whole ceremony.

The procession ends at the church gates. The King rides into the churchyard, where the great Garland is lifted from his head, and the Queen-posy is detached from its place at the apex. Then the Garland is hauled by ropes to the top of the tower and fixed to one of the pinnacles. Once, it used to be left hanging there for the rest of the year, or until it was destroyed by the wind and the rain, but nowadays it is taken down after a short time and stowed away until next Garland Day comes round. Finally, the Queen-posy, which in the years before the Great War, would have been offered to some admired local personage as a mark of honour, is deposited by the King at the foot of the village War Memorial.

Grass-strewing. (*See Rushbearing.*)

Graveside Doles. A number of ancient charities were, and some still are, distributed beside or across the graves of the original donors. Usually this was because the giver stated in his will that he wished his gifts to be so made, sometimes as a kind of *memento mori*, or in the case of pre-Reformation bequests, to obtain the prayers of the beneficiaries for his soul.

In 1585, Bartholomew Borrington, of Ideford in Devon, charged certain lands with an annual payment of £1.0.0., which, in the form of twenty new shillings, was to be laid upon his tomb every Maundy Thursday and given to twenty poor people of the parish. This is still done, although in the course of time, the day has been changed to Good Friday. The Rector and churchwardens stand at one end of the tomb in the churchyard and lay the coins upon its flat top, and the beneficiaries come one by one to the opposite end and pick up their money.

The Butterworth Charity in London also involves the placing of coins upon a tombstone. On Good Friday morning, twenty-one sixpences are laid upon a flat stone in the churchyard of St Bartholomew-the-Great in Smithfield for the benefit of as many poor widows. Each woman kneels in turn to pick up a sixpence, and then steps across the stone and is given half-a-crown in addition and a hot cross bun. The payment of this dole is first mentioned in the churchwardens' accounts for 1686, and the charity itself is often said to derive from a bequest of that year. In fact, there is nothing in the entry, or in any other parish record, to show whether the custom was old or new then, or how it came into being. The original documents relating to it have all been lost, and now the date of the bequest, the donor's name, and the position of his (or her) grave in the churchyard are all alike unknown. In the late nineteenth century, it seemed probable that the charity would fail for lack of funds; but in 1887 it was saved by the generosity of Mr Joshua Butterworth, who gave a sum of money as a perpetual endowment. It is for this reason that it is now known as the Butterworth Charity.

The Travice Dole is distributed on Maundy Thursday at Leigh, in Lancashire, in accordance with the will of Henry Travice, who died in 1627. Forty poor people come to the donor's tomb in the parish church and there receive five shillings each. On Candlemas Day, loaves of bread are distributed from the stone covering George Carlow's grave at Woodbridge in Suffolk. He died in 1738, leaving directions that bread was to be given to the poor from the gravestone (on which these instructions are inscribed) on the same anniversary 'for ever'. Peter Symonds was another who used the hopeful words 'for ever' when he drew up his will in 1587. He was a London merchant who left money for various Good Friday donations to the local poor, and also for a packet of raisins and a new penny to be given to sixty of the younger boys of the Blue Coat School (Christ's Hospital). These gifts are still made, but not, as was formerly the custom, across his tomb in All Hallows, Lombard Street, for time, change, and rebuilding have obliterated it.

Another charity, of a homely type and apparently dictated by a real affection for young people, formerly existed at Barton-le-Street in Yorkshire. There, on Ascension Day, the children of the parish were given bread, cheese, and beer, which they were required to consume inside the church, close to the tomb of the testator. No one saw anything unsuitable or irreverent in this when the bequest was made in the seventeenth century; but ideas change as time goes on, or perhaps the children were too noisy, or left too many crumbs in the sacred building. At all events, the little feast was transferred to the churchyard in William IV's reign, and finally, about 1840, it disappeared altogether. The money that paid for it was given instead to the aged poor, which was doubtless much more sensible, but not, perhaps, quite what the child-loving giver would have wished.

In 1717, William Glanville, of Wotton in Surrey, provided in his will for the payment of forty shillings each, to five poor boys, aged sixteen or less, who fulfilled the conditions that he laid down. On the anniversary of his death, whenever that should occur, they were to go to his tomb, lay their hands upon it, and recite from memory the Lord's Prayer, the Apostles' Creed and the Ten Commandments. They were also to read aloud the fifteenth chapter of the First Epistle of St Paul to the Corinthians, and write two verses of the same chapter in a clear and legible hand. This curious bequest is still honoured in full on what is now locally known as Forty Shilling Day. This should be, and usually is, February 2nd, because that is the anniversary of the day on which William Glanville died; but occasionally, if the Winter is severe, it is postponed to a later date in Spring. The weather matters in this case because the tomb on which the boys have to lay their hands is in the churchyard, and in some years it has been necessary to enclose it in a tent to save those concerned from being drenched by rain or snow.

An odd little ceremony known as Washing Molly Grime's Grave used to be performed on Good Friday at Glentham in Lincolnshire. By a bequest, of which the date and history are uncertain, a rent-charge of 7s. od. was laid upon a local estate for the payment of one shilling each to seven poor spinsters of the parish who, on Good Friday, came to wash a stone effigy, called Molly Grime, on a tomb in the church. The terms of the bequest required that they do this with water fetched from Newell Well, a spring about two miles away from the village. Exactly what the connection was between Molly Grime and this well, or why the women had to trudge so far with their heavy buckets of water, is not now known. In his *Collection of Old English Customs* (1842), Edwards says that the effigy was regularly washed, and the money paid to the spinsters, until 1832. After that time, the necessary funds for the maintenance of the charity disappeared because, the owner of the estate having become bankrupt, 'the property was sold without any reservation of this rent-charge.'

Greenhill Bower & Court of Array. Lichfield's Greenhill Bower and Court of Array is a combination of two ancient customs, one social and religious, and the other purely military in origin. No one knows how old the Bower is, or what its precise form was originally though it always seems to have been connected with flowers and processions, as it still is. It is said to run back to the time of King Oswy, who founded a bishopric in Lichfield in A.D.656. Some believe it to be much older, and to be the direct descendant of some pagan floral festival, perhaps associated with Midsummer. In the Middle Ages, all the guilds of the city assembled on Whit Monday, at Greenhill, carrying statues or other signs of their patron saints and, later, emblems of their trade and garlands of flowers. The modern ceremony, which takes place on the new Spring Holiday instead of on Whit Monday, has now developed into a sort of pleasure-fair and carnival, with processions through the streets, bands, tableaux on wagons, and similar attractions.

There is, however, one part of the programme which makes Lichfield's annual festival quite different from any other. This is the Court of Array, which is said to date from 1176, and the parade and inspection of the town's ancient suits of armour. 'A Court', wrote Thomas Harwood in 1806,[1] 'is annually held by the Bailiffs on Whit-Monday, in the Guild-Hall, which is immediately adjourned to an open mount, called Green-Hill, in the parish of St Michael . . . where the names of all the householders of the twenty-one wards of the city are called over; as owing suit and service to this Court, who are required to appear, or are liable to the payment of a small fine.' By a statute of Henry II's reign, enacted in 1176, and by the Statute of Winchester in 1285, every freeman in the country between fifteen and sixty years of age was obliged to equip himself with weapons and armour, according to his position in the community, and to keep these in good order and ready for immediate use. To ensure that he did so, every county had its Commissioners of Array, whose duty it was to hold periodical inspections of the bows and arrows, axes, pikes, swords, and suits of armour provided, according to the Law, by the freemen of his district. In Lichfield, this Court of Array seems to have been combined at an early date with the city's old Bower festival.

1. Revd. Thomas Harwood, *History and Antiquities of the Church and City of Lichfield*, 1806.

In the fifteenth century, the town itself became responsible for the provisions of twelve suits of chain-armour and two suits of knight's armour as a contribution to the defence of the country. Of these, some still survive, and are paraded annually at Greenhill. The legal necessity to hold Courts of Array ceased in James I's reign; but in Lichfield, the old Court was kept up, and is still formally held in the Guildhall and associated with Greenhill Bower.

Grotto Day. The Feast of St James the Great on July 25th is sometimes known as Grotto Day because, on that anniversary children make little grottoes of shells and other materials, and set them out on street pavements, against the walls of buildings. This was once a very popular custom, especially in London and in the ring of villages which were formerly outside and are now part of the metropolis,[1] and it is not altogether forgotten there yet. It is still possible to see in some streets small grottoes constructed of scallop- or oyster-shells, stones, earth, and sometimes clinkers from the gasworks, and ornamented with flowers, moss, and bits of glass and coloured china. There may be a little forecourt outlined by a half-circle of stones, and usually a lighted candle burns inside the finished tunnel. The proud builders stand beside their handiwork cap in hand, asking largesse from the passers-by. The usual form of request is 'Please sir, remember the Grotto' or 'A penny for the Grotto', or occasionally, with a nicer regard for tradition, the words of an old rhyme that begins:

1. Camberwell, Leytonstone, Chelsea, Islington, etc. In the *Sussex Archeological Collections*, Vol. 33 (1883), it is recorded that grottoes were made on Old St. James' Day (August 5th) 'within the last twenty years'. A letter to *The Times* of November 26th, 1957 said that the custom was still very much alive at Mitcham in Surrey at the time of writing.

Please to remember the Grotto,
Its only once a year.
Father's gone to sea,
Mother's gone to fetch him back,
So please remember me.

In this children's custom we have, perhaps, the last faint memory of the great mediaeval pilgrimages to the shrine of St James of Compostella at Santiago. That shrine was the traditional burial place of St James the Apostle, who, according to legend, brought the Gospel to Spain after the Ascension of Our Lord. He returned eventually to Jerusalem where, as we know from the *Acts of the Apostles*,[1] he was beheaded by Herod Agrippa. A further tradition relates that his disciples took his body back to Spain and there, guided by various miracles, they buried him in the place afterwards called Santiago in his honour.

Many thousands of pilgrims travelled to his shrine during the Middle Ages, and having done so, they were entitled to wear his badge, which was a scallop-shell. Exactly how this shell became his emblem is uncertain. One legendary explanation is that as the boat containing the saint's remains neared the coast, a horseman plunged into the sea and swam towards it, either from excessive devotion or, as another version of the tale has it, because his horse bolted with him into the water. In either case, the result was the same. Man and horse were saved from drowning by the power of the Apostle, and when they emerged from the sea, both were seen to be thickly covered with scallops. Henceforward, the shells of these creatures became the emblems of St James.

This odd story does not seem to have been recorded until about the middle of the fifteenth century, but long before that time, pilgrims to Santiago were wearing scallop-shells upon their cloaks or hats. The author of *Liber Sancti Jacobi*, a book written about 1130, states that they were sold for this purpose in booths outside the Cathedral. He also relates how, in 1106, a certain knight of Apulia was miraculously healed of a goitre by being touched with one of these shells, brought home by a pilgrim. Thus, from at least as early as the twelfth century, the scallop-shell has been recognized as the badge of St James, appearing in statues, carvings, and embroideries everywhere, and finally in the folk-tradition preserved by the children's grottoes.

These last are not now, nor were they formerly always made of scallop-shells. A writer in *The Times* for November 21st, 1957, says that when he was a boy in the Old Kent Road, he and his companions always insisted on having scallop-shells for their grottoes; but in the account of the custom given in *The Book of Days*, (Vol. II, 1864), only oyster-shells are mentioned. Probably most children were content with these, if only because they were easier to obtain. One of the reasons why Grotto Day flourished so long in London may have been because in the nineteenth century, Old St James' Day, August 5th, coincided with the opening of the oyster season there. 'He who eats oysters on St James' Day will not want during the year', says an old proverb, and very large quantities used to be eaten by Londoners then and in the following few weeks. Discarded shells could be begged from fishmongers and restaurant-cooks, and from these most of the grottoes were probably made. The true Grotto Day is, of course, July 25th, but a natural confusion between the Old and New Style calendar, allied to a plentiful supply of shells, would be enough to explain its celebration on the later day. In 1944, when several letters about the custom appeared in *The Times*, more than one writer said he remembered seeing the grottoes in early August, rather than on the New-Style festival. Now, the July date, or near it, is the usual time for the celebration, though it must be added that oyster-shells are still far more often seen in the modern grottoes than the true shell of St James.

Grovely. At Wishford Magna, in Wiltshire, a custom connected with the maintenance of wood-gathering rights in Grovely Forest is annually kept up on May 29th. Although the Wishford celebrations have now been held on Oak Apple Day for a very long time, they have no real connection with that festival, except in so far as they appear to have been transferred

1. *Acts*, XII, 2.

to it from their original Whitsuntide date as an expression of loyalty. The forest privileges which are preserved by the observance of the Grovely custom are far older than the Restoration, and were described in a document drawn up in 1603 as having existed 'ever by auntient custome and tyme out of mind'.

This document, sometimes referred to as the Book of Rights, is a record of the proceedings of a Court held in Grovely Forest on March 15th, 1603. It sets forth all the 'olde auntient and laudable customes' then enjoyed by the manors of Wishford and Barford St Martin, and is signed by ten local men, one of whom bears the curious name of Catkat. Some of the privileges listed therein have now disappeared, or have been exchanged for money payments by various owners of the woodlands, but the right to gather 'all kinde of deade snappinge woode Boughes and Stickes' for firewood still remains. Such wood can be gathered at any time; and once a year (now on Oak Apple Day), green boughs are cut and brought in. These boughs have to be 'drawen by strength of people', without mechanical aids. Hand-carts may be used, but horse-drawn carts are not allowed, nor, of course, is any form of motor-transport. When bicycles were invented, there was some debate about them, but finally it was decided that, since human strength is necessary to move them, their use could be permitted.

The modern Grovely ceremonies begin about three o'clock in the morning, when the local young men march through the village with drums and bugles, shouting 'Grovely, Grovely, and all Grovely!' and stopping outside the houses to greet, and be greeted by, those whom they have awakened by their noisy passage. They go to Grovely Woods, and there they cut their green branches, some of which are set before the doors of houses in the village, and others carried in a grand procession held later in the day. Practically every house and cottage sports its oak-bough on this anniversary, and every man, woman, and child wears a sprig of oak-leaves or oak-apples. One large branch known as the Marriage Bough, is decorated with ribbons and hauled to the top of the church-tower, there to bring good luck to all who are married in the church during the following year.

One of the most interesting ceremonies of this crowded day is the visit to Salisbury Cathedral. In the 1603 document it is recorded that 'the lords, freeholders, Tennants and Inhabitance of the Mannor of greate Wishford . . . have used to goe in a daunce to the Cathedrall Church of our blessed Ladie in the Cittie of newe Sarum on Whit Tuesdaie in the said Countie or Wiltes, and theire made theire clayme to theire custome in the Forrest of Grovley in theis wordes; Grovely Groveley and all Groveley'. It is said that formerly those taking part in this ritual, dressed all in white and carrying oak-branches, danced along the whole six miles between the village and the city. On arrival, they first danced before the Cathedral and then, entering and standing before the High Altar, made public claim to their rights by shouting the historic words. This custom continued until the beginning of the nineteenth century, by which time a kind of unofficial fair had grown up round it. Stalls and booths were erected in the Close, and a general revel took place. Eventually this became offensive to the Cathedral authorities and was suppressed. The dancing and claim-shouting was then transferred to the village and was enacted in front of the Rectory. For some years it was customary for two women, representing the bough-gatherers, to go alone to Salisbury and reverently lay oak-sprigs before the altar, but in time, even this ceased. In 1951, however, this ancient and important part of the Grovely ceremonies was revived, and now, during the morning of Oak Apple Day, four women carrying sprigs of oak and accompanied by numerous villagers, travel to the city, where they dance upon the Cathedral Green. This being done, the whole company goes into the Cathedral to make their claim in the traditional form by standing before the altar and crying 'Grovely! Grovely! and All Grovely!', after which all return to Wishford to take part in the remaining celebrations of the day.

A procession is formed at the Town-End Tree at the south end of the village. In it walk the same four women who danced at Salisbury, now carrying faggots of snap-wood on their heads, schoolchildren carrying flowers and led by their May Queen, men and women in fancy-dress of all kinds, and the male and female members of the Oak Apple Club,[1] carrying oak-boughs and a banner, and preceded by bandsmen. The handcarts used for gathering the wood in the Forest also appear, now decorated in various ways. After the procession has marched all round the village, there is a ceremonial lunch in a marquee erected in a field, and the rest of the day is spent in a variety of amusements and gaieties, cheerfully enjoyed in the certain knowledge that the wood-gathering privileges of the community have been safely preserved for another year.

Guy Fawkes' Day. Guy Fawkes' Day is the anniversary of the discovery of the Gunpowder Plot in 1605, or more precisely, of the arrest of Guy Fawkes, since the Government had already received warning of the Plot itself through an anonymous and obscurely worded letter addressed to Lord Monteagle. As a result of this warning, Lord Monteagle and the Lord Chamberlain made a search through the cellars under the Palace of Westminster on November 4th. In one of these cellars they found a great stack of wood, and a man who said his name was Johnson. They passed on then, but in the small hours of November 5th, just after midnight, the cellar was visited again by a small band of men led by a magistrate. Outside it they encountered 'Johnson' once more and took him into the cellar where, tearing down the pile of wood, they found thirty-six barrels of gunpowder hidden underneath it. Their prisoner, whose real name was Guy Fawkes, was the man chosen by his fellow-plotters to set fire to this powder later in the day, and so destroy King, Lords and Commons assembled together in the building above for the Opening of Parliament. For this purpose he had with him a slow fuse which, when lit, would give him time to escape before the explosion to a waiting boat on the river. Thereafter the conspirators intended to seize power and set up a new Government under which Roman Catholic grievances would be redressed and England would return to the Old Faith.

By the timely arrest of Guy Fawkes, the failure of the Gunpowder Plot was assured. A thankful Parliament ordered that November 5th should henceforth be observed as a holiday, with general rejoicings, the pealing of bells, the firing of cannon, and a special service to be held in all churches.[1] The ordinary people responded to this mandate with an enthusiasm that sprang partly from genuine relief and indignation, and partly from the natural love of a jollification. A wave of loyal rage swept over the whole country, intensifying anti-Catholic feeling everywhere, and especially in those areas where, for one reason or another, it was already very strong. In Lewes, where seventeen Protestants were burnt as heretics in the reign of Mary I, traces of ancient hatreds can still be faintly seen in the Bonfire Night celebrations, where an eighteenth century 'No Popery' banner is often carried in the processions and until very recently, an effigy of the Pope was burnt along with that of Guy Fawkes.[2] Yet religious zeal and fury was not the only reason for the immediate popularity of this holiday imposed by authority. The early seventeenth century was a period when rising Puritan influence tended rather to the suppression of old festivals than to the institution of new ones, and any additional excuse for merriment was likely to be welcomed, especially by the young. Moreover, for many who remembered the old celebrations of Hallowtide, the lighting of bonfires in early November was nothing new, even if the reason for doing so was now different.

Lighted they were, in towns and villages and hamlets, for fun, as a demonstration of Protestant loyalty, and because those who shared in the work felt that by so doing they were some-

1. The Oak Apple Club was founded in 1892 to ensure the preservation of Wishford's rights and privileges, as these were stated in the document of 1603. Only men and women genuinely resident in the parish are entitled to be members.

1. This service remained in the English Prayer Book for more than two centuries, and was not deleted from it until 1859.

2. At Bridgwater in Somerset also, signs of old religious enmities coloured the Guy Fawkes celebrations until a very late date because of bitter memories of Monmouth's rebellion and the Bloody Assizes.

how striking a blow at England's enemies. Torchlight processions wound through the streets, or flaming tar-barrels were rolled along them, and in countless parishes, Guy Fawkes was ceremonially burned in effigy. Out of all this spontaneous rejoicing, once so topical and full of political meaning, grew the modern Guy Fawkes' Day which has now become the principal fire-festival of the year in most parts of England. It has long outlived the old fears and religious animosities that gave it birth; and the fact that it flourishes today, more than three centuries after the event, is almost certainly due to its having absorbed, as time went on, most of the far older fire – and mischief – customs that rightly belong to Hallowtide. *(See Hallowe'en Fires: Mischief Night.)*

Whether the average Bonfire Night reveller, young or old, now gives more than a passing thought to the original conspirators and their murderous plans is very uncertain, but some of the traditional rhymes chanted by children keep the memory of the Plot green.

> Remember, remember the Fifth of November,
> Gunpowder Treason and Plot;
> I see no reason why Gunpowder Treason
> Should ever be forgot.

is a ditty commonly heard in many districts. Nottingham children sing:

> Gunpowder Plot shall never be forgot
> While Nottingham Castle stands on a rock,

and so do Edinburgh boys, only substituting the name of their own castle for that of Nottingham. So, too, when the effigy burns on the fire, the cry goes up,

> Guy Fawkes, Guy, poke him in the eye.
> Stick him up the chimney-pot,
> And there let him die.

More seriously, at Lewes, the proceedings begin with the marching of each of the six Bonfire Societies in turn to the War Memorial, where wreaths are laid, hymns are sung, and there is a short sermon in which England's deliverance long ago is remembered. The Bonfire Societies, here like the Committee in Bridgwater, are responsible, not only for the organization of the festivities, but also for the maintenance of good order and the prevention of damage while they last. In the mid-nineteenth century, when huge fires were lit in the heart of the town, and lighted tar-barrels were rolled through the streets, the danger of fire was very great, and the authorities made more than one attempt to suppress the celebrations altogether. The only result was serious rioting, in which many people were injured. Finally, as a compromise, the Lewes Societies and the Bridgwater Committee undertook the duty of keeping order if the festival was allowed to continue, and this arrangement has worked very admirably ever since.

Very imposing Guys are often constructed in places where the arrangements are in the hands of adult committees. These may be life-sized, or larger, black-clad, holding the traditional three fuses in one hand and a dark lantern in the other, and with the body stuffed with fireworks that go off with an exciting roar when the figure is caught by the bonfire's flames. But a far more familiar Guy is the one carried about by bands of children when they go round collecting money for fireworks and materials for their bonfires in the two or three weeks before November 5th. It is usually made from an old suit of clothes, padded out with straw and stiffened by a pole thrust up the back, with a mask for a face and old hat crowning all. It bears little resemblance to the seventeenth-century Yorkshire gentleman it is supposed to represent, but it is satisfyingly hideous, as befits the image of one who has become the very symbol of treason.

At various times, effigies of other individuals have been dragged about and finally burnt as well as, or occasionally instead of, Guy Fawkes. Pope Paul IV was one of these because of his supposed encouragement of the Gunpowder Plot. Napoleon I was another; so was Cardinal Wiseman in the nineteenth century, when the fuss about the Catholic bishops was raging, and the Sultan of Turkey at the time of the Armenian atrocities. Kruger appeared thus during the Boer War, and so, inevitably did the Kaiser and Hitler during the two wars of 1914 and 1939. Even local hatreds were sometimes expressed in this simple and unmistakeable manner. In Oxford, at the end of last century, a quite recognizable figure of an unpopular Alderman was carried about for several days, and then burnt in the presence of a large and jeering crowd. Nevertheless, Guy Fawkes has always been, and still remains the most usual victim, even though, for the majority of people today, he has become a more or less symbolic figure, and is hardly remembered as a once living person.

In some districts, the Guy is the central feature of the celebrations; in others, it is of secondary importance, or does not appear at all.[1] The true essential of the festival today is fire. On this night the sky is bright with fireworks everywhere. Bonfires, large or small, blaze in private gardens, in back streets, on wastelands near the edges of towns, on village greens, and high upon hill-tops and open moorlands. At Rye, the Bonfire Boys drag a boat through the streets and burn it with great ceremony on the Town Salts, along with numerous Guys, and torn-down official notices prohibiting this or that. Lewes has splendid torchlight processions which continue from dusk until nearly midnight, and there are similar fire-parades at Bridgwater, Battle, Edenbridge, Newhaven, and some other places.

Until well into the second half of last century, blazing tar-barrels were rolled through the streets of many towns, a Bonfire Night practice not unnaturally disliked by most civic authorities but dearly loved by those who took part in it. At Burford in Oxfordshire, two such barrels were sent hurtling down the long steep High Street at midnight, rolling and bouncing downwards in a whirl of sparks and flame, like two small suns suddenly fallen from the night sky. Not far off, at Witney, there was a lively contest between the Up-street men and the Down-street men, each side, armed with long poles, trying to push a series of burning barrels up or down the road against the defensive efforts of their opponents. At Torquay, young men carried the barrels on their heads for as long as it was safe, and then rolled them on the ground until they fell to pieces. Similar customs flourished in several West-country towns, and one of a very spectacular kind is still kept up at Ottery St Mary.

1. In two of the places where Guys do not appear, there is a good reason for the omission. One is Scotton, near Knaresborough, where Guy Fawkes lived as a boy. The other is St Peter's School, York, where he was once a scholar.

Here nine burning tar-barrels are carried and rolled along defined routes through the town at stated intervals during the evening, each one starting from a different point. The first is lit outside the Factory at 8.15 p.m. As soon as it is well alight, a man with his hands and arms swathed in stout sacking picks it up and, holding it above his head, runs with it as far as he can down the street. When the heat becomes unbearable, he sets it down and lets it roll along the ground. Another man then picks it up and carries it onwards until he too can do no more. This goes on until the barrel becomes impossible to hold, after which it is rolled until it finally disappears in a sheet of flame. The same process is repeated with the other barrels in turn. The last of the nine is timed to reach the end of the course at about 11.45 p.m., when the lively celebrations, which also include the burning of a Guy upon a huge bonfire, come to an end.

In his account of the custom, J. R. W. Coxhead remarks that the performers frequently suffer burns, but they do not mind them, since they regard the danger as part of the fun. 'They like', he says, 'to be able to prove that the men of Ottery St Mary are still as tough and hardy as they were centuries ago.'[1] There is also a 'junior' barrel-rolling at four o'clock in the afternoon, when four or five smaller barrels are lighted and carried by boys whose hands and arms are protected in the same way as those of the young men in the evening.

1. J. W. R. Coxhead, *Old Devon Customs*, 1957.

Hallowe'en Fires. Hallowe'en, or All Hallows Eve, is the beginning of Hallowtide, that brief winter season which consists of the Vigil and Feast of All Saints on October 31st and November 1st, and the Feast of All Souls on November 2nd. From time immemorial, this has been a period associated with ghosts and spirits and with death. The Christian dead have been commemorated then by the Church since the ninth century,[1] and remembered all over Europe in a variety of curious folk-customs down to our own day; but long before the coming of Christianity, what we now call Hallowtide was a holy season when the barriers between this world and the next were believed to be down, the dead returned from the grave, and gods and strangers from the Underworld walked abroad. It was also a time of beginnings, with all the dangers and protective rituals that belong to beginnings. Among the pagan Celts, the year began on November 1st, when the Feast of *Samhain* was celebrated. This was the great festival which marked the end of summer and of the late northern harvest, the day on which winter and the new year started together. On it, beginning on the Eve, which coincides with our Hallowe'en, the dead were honoured, divination was practised to see what the year would bring, harvest-end ceremonies were performed, games were played, and ritual fires were kindled upon hill-tops and open spaces for the purification of the people and the land, and the defeat of the powers of evil, which were then at their strongest.

If Christianity sanctified the pagan season with new names and feast-days, it did not put out the Hallowe'en fires, which continued to blaze upon countless hills and cairns until almost the end of the nineteenth century. They still survive in England, though now they burn there five days later, on November 5th (*see Guy Fawkes' Day*), and for another reason. Unlike those of Beltane, which were kindled at dawn, the Hallow fires were lit at dusk – for luck, for the saining of the fields, for protection against the fairies and witches who had taken the place of forgotten pagan spirits, and very certainly, for the sake of fun and merriment. They were lighted with ceremony, sometimes to the noise of blowing horns, circuited by dancers, and generally made the occasion of great festivity. About 1840, Sheriff Barclay, travelling from Dunkeld to Aberfeldy, saw no less than thirty bonfires on the surrounding hills, 'each having a ring of people dancing round it.'[1] Young men used to leap through the flames, or run through the hot embers. In some districts, bands of lively youths would set out to attack and scatter someone else's bonfire. They came suddenly out of the darkness, armed with sticks and stones, and fell upon the guardians of the fire, who were usually well prepared and gave

1. The Feast of All Saints was established to honour the saints in Heaven as early as the seventh century, when it was observed on May 13th. It was transferred to November 1st in A.D. 835. The commemoration of all the faithful departed on November 2nd (All Souls) began in A.D. 988.

1. A. D. Cummings, *Old Times in Scotland*, 1910.

as good as they got. The ensuing fight was often really fierce; if the attackers nevertheless succeeded in scattering their opponents' fire, they returned home in triumph with burning peats fixed like pennants on the top of pointed sticks.[1]

In Scotland, the main purpose of the Hallowe'en bonfires was often said to be to destroy witches. It seems clear that here the word 'witches' was stretched to cover far more than mere human practitioners of magic, however dangerous, and that it stood rather for all those ancient malevolent forces that threaten mankind at all times, and never more so than on this most perilous night of the year. In Aberdeenshire, boys went about beforehand collecting fuel and crying 'Gie's a peat t' burn the witches!' While the bonfire blazed, it was constantly stirred and tossed to increase the volume of purifying flame and smoke, and when it had died down, the ashes were kicked and scattered as far as possible.

At Balmoral, in Queen Victoria's time, a huge bonfire used to be lit in front of the Castle, opposite the main door. A procession of clansmen marched to it, to the sound of bagpipes, bringing with them a trolley on which was an effigy of an old witch known as the Shandy Dann, and also a man whose duty it was to keep the figure erect. A long indictment of the witch was solemnly read, with reasons why she should be burnt. No one spoke for her, naturally, since she represented all the evils that afflicted or might afflict, the clan; and being duly condemned, she and the trolley that contained her were hurled into the flames. Her human guardian leapt to safety at the last possible moment, and stood with the rest of the company, laughing and cheering as the ancient enemy was consumed in the fierce heat. An account of this ceremony, contributed to *Scottish Notes and Queries* by a man who had often seen it, throws a pleasant, if somewhat unexpected, light upon Queen Victoria herself. One does not usually associate her with a keen interest in folk-custom, but the writer informs us that the people in the Castle came to watch the rite, 'and no one there entered more heartily into it than the head of the Empire herself'.[1]

In Wales, great quantities of straw, gorse, thornwood, and other easily ignited materials were carried up to a hill-top, and there set alight at dusk. Potatoes and apples were roasted and eaten; the people danced and shouted round the bonfire, and the bolder spirits leapt through it. The end of the ceremony was usually a headlong flight down the hill to escape the *hwch ddu gwta*, the tailless Black Sow who was one of the terrors of Hallowe'en. Out of the shadows of the pagan past she came at the moment when the flames died down, and all fled before her, crying 'May the tailless Black Sow take the hindmost!' She might sometimes be encountered elsewhere on All Hallows Eve, and always, like the other strange wanderers of that night, she was dangerous.

Both in Wales and in Scotland, it was customary for each person present to mark a white stone and throw it to the Hallow Fire. On the following morning, he or she returned to search for it in the ashes. If it was still there, and unharmed, all was well, but if it was missing, or found to be cracked in the heat, or otherwise damaged, the omen was very bad; the owner would not live to see the next Hallowtide fires lighted. In some Scottish districts, the stones were not thrown into the bonfire, but were placed in a circle round it. Here again, one cracked or injured foretold an early death and so also if it was displaced, or if a footprint was seen near it.

Hallow Fires were known as Teanlas or Teanlay, or Tandles in Lancashire and Westmorland, and as Tindles in Derbyshire. Sometimes a farmer would light a small fire in one of his own fields, and carry flaming straw from it upon a pitchfork to the highest point of the ground. There he would throw it as far as it would go over the land. While he did so, his household knelt round the bonfire and remembered the dead of the family. Whether they actually prayed for the departed souls probably depended upon whether they were Catholics or

1. *Scottish Notes and Queries*, Vol. IV. 1891.

1. Alexander Macdonald, *Scottish Notes and Queries* 2nd Series III, 1901.

Protestants, but that such prayers once formed part of the custom is shown by the fact that on many northern farms certain fields where this rite used to be performed are still known as Purgatory Field. Bunches of blazing straw were also carried about the cornfields to bless and fertilize them. In Scotland, torches, or lighted fir-splinters were used for this purpose, or failing these, bundles of heather-stalks tied together. The bearers circuited the boundaries of the farm, going the way of the sun. In some districts a faggot on a pole was carried by a running man all round the village. As one faggot burnt out, another was attached to the pole in its place, and so on until the full circuit had been completed.

A ceremony known as Lating the Witches used to be performed on Hallowe'en in North Lancashire. Large candles, each one representing a single person, were carried over the hills between eleven o'clock and midnight. If any candle burnt steadily all the way, the person it was lit for would be safe for that year from witchcraft, but if it went out for any reason, misfortune might be expected. A man (or woman) could carry his own candle on this nocturnal quest, or he could ask someone else to do it for him, or the enquiry into the future might be made on behalf of some individual without his knowledge. It was thought very unlucky to cross the threshold of any person whose candle was being so carried before the ritual journey was quite ended, or to do so at all that night if his candle had gone out.

Hallowe'en Games. Hallowe'en is known as Nutcrack Night in some districts, or as Crab Apple Night, or Apple and Candle Night, or by other names referring to the traditional games with nuts, apples, and fire that are played then. Most of these games are cheerful, noisy, by no means easy to play and, where water is involved, decidedly messy, but like the Hallowe'en fires, they have a very long history, running back to the pagan Winter's Eve. Bobbing or Ducking for apples is one that is still very well known. It requires a tub filled with water, with apples floating in it. The players, with their hands tied behind their backs, kneel in front of the tub and try to grasp an apple with their teeth. Sometimes this is done with nuts or a silver coin instead of apples. Ducking for money, which does not float, means that the whole head has to go under water, and the lips not the teeth, have to be used. The player who succeeds in securing the coin is allowed to keep it, and has the additional satisfaction of knowing that he will be lucky in money matters during the coming year. A variant of the apple-game is to hold a fork between the teeth and try to spear the bobbing fruit with it.

Another form of Bob Apple is to suspend an apple from a beam or a cord stretched across the room, and for the player to attempt to bite it as it swings. Here he does not get wet, but he is liable to be hit in the face by a hard apple on the return swing if he does not succeed in getting his teeth into it. In Scotland, a bannock smeared with treacle is sometimes used in the same way, and this, of course, is a gloriously messy game, providing much entertainment for the onlookers. In the Apple-and-Candle game, a short rod or board with an apple at one end and a lighted candle at the other is hung from the ceiling and rapidly whirled round. Each player in turn leaps upwards and tries to catch the fruit in his teeth without getting

burnt by the candle-flame or spattered by the grease.

Many Hallowe'en games are divination-rites, mostly practised today with a kind of joking half-belief, but once with genuine and serious faith. On this night, the old New Year's Eve, when supernatural beings are abroad and everything is touched with strangeness, young people try to ascertain the future, particularly where love and marriage are concerned. Two nuts may be placed on the bars of the fire, or in the embers, one named for a young man and the other for a girl. If they burn away quietly together, the couple will marry, but if they flare up fiercely, or explode, or start away from each other, the courtship is doomed. To discover the initial of the future mate's name, an apple is peeled very carefully, so that the peel comes off in one long unbroken strip. At midnight preferably, but if not, at some other time during the evening, the peel is thrown over the enquirer's left shoulder, and the initial of the lover's name is read from the form it takes as it lies on the floor. Or a piece of lead may be melted over the fire in an iron spoon and poured into cold water. The future partner's trade is indicated by the shape that it assumes.

Another apple-rite requires the performer to stand at midnight in front of a mirror, eating an apple and at the same time, brushing or combing the hair. The form of the future husband or wife will appear in the mirror, looking over the person's left shoulder. In its modern form, this is usually a game which girls play in company, each one taking her turn before the looking-glass amid much laughter and jollity. Originally, however, it was a secret and rather alarming ceremony, performed alone at midnight in the privacy of the bedroom by the light of a single candle. A more elaborate method required that the apple be cut into nine pieces, of which eight had to be eaten by the performer, who stood with her back to the mirror. She then threw the ninth piece over her left shoulder, and turning swiftly, saw the face of her future husband looking at her from the glass.

In some parts of Scotland, charms are concealed in a dish of mashed potatoes which is passed round to all present. Each person takes a spoonful, and according to the charm which he finds in his portion, so will the coming year be for him. If he finds a coin, he will have plenty of money, if a wishbone, he will achieve his heart's desire, if a ring, he will be the first to marry, and so on. In Wales, a ring is used to be concealed in a mash made from several different vegetables mixed with raw milk, which was a customary Hallowe'en supper-dish.

Another traditional game, less popular in these more careful times than it once was, is to place twelve lighted candles in a fairly wide ring on the floor. Each candle represents one month of the year, and the players take it in turn to leap over them in due chronological sequence. For every clear leap achieved, a successful and happy month may be expected; but if a candle is knocked over, or the flame is blown out by the draught of the player's passage, the omen for that month is bad. A more private form of enquiry connected with fire consists of writing a wish on a piece of paper which is then rolled up and thrown into the hearth-fire. If it burns away quickly and is destroyed, all is well, but if it remains half-burnt or merely charred, the wish will not be granted. A great variety of other divination-games, too numerous to list here, are, or were until fairly recently, played on this night.

Hallowe'en was, and still is in some places, a time when mischievous pranks of many kinds are played and tolerated. *(See Mischief Night.)* It was also one of the anniversaries on which the Guisers appeared. They still do so in some parts of Scotland and Ireland, although nowadays the old ritual is mainly in the hands of the children. Formerly, it was more often young men, and sometimes young women as well, who went about the parish in disguise, fantastically dressed, or wearing the clothes of the opposite sex, with their faces blackened by soot or covered by grotesque masks. They went, as the child-Guisers still do, from house to house, collecting money or gifts of food. At Ballycotton in Co. Cork, a procession of horn-blowing youths used to be led by a man called the *Lair Bhan*, whose body was covered by a white sheet, and who carried, or wore, the skull of a mare, in much the same way as his Welsh kinsman, the *Mari Lwyd*, still does in some parts of the Principality at Christmas time. *(See Mari Lwyd.)*

They visited the various houses of the district and demanded largesse in the name of the Muck Olla, a legendary boar of monstrous size who was said to have been slain by one of the Geraldines.

In England, Guy Fawkes Day has absorbed most of the customs of Hallowtide, and in many parts of the country Hallowe'en is almost entirely neglected as a festival night. Where it is remembered, it is associated chiefly with witches, from a vague memory that this was one of the traditional occasions of the Witches' Sabbat. In the north west, some of the old games are still played, though with rather less vigour than in Scotland and Ireland. The customary disguises appear mostly at organized indoor parties, but children still go about in some areas with blackened or masked faces, and carrying turnip-lanterns. The latter are made by scooping out the inner pith of a large turnip or swede. On the front of the shell thus left, holes are cut out to represent eyes, a nose, and a mouth, or else a skull-and-crossbones, or some other alarming device is carved upon the rind. A lighted candle is set inside, and the finished lantern is carried about at dusk on a pole, or a long wire, or a forked stick. It provides light for the little groups who go round soliciting gifts or it can be used to frighten people by jumping out upon them and thrusting the strange mask into their faces, or by lifting the lantern high on its pole and knocking upon the windows of houses. This, of course, is great fun, but it also has a deeper meaning; for though the children are unaware of the fact, the origin of their custom, like that of the Hallowe'en Guisers, was the impersonation of the returning dead and still stranger spirits then abroad, and by that impersonation, the protection of themselves and others from the power of these spectres. In this connection, it is interesting to note that in some Somerset and Welsh districts, turnip-lanterns are hung upon gateposts on October 31st for the express purpose of protecting the house from evil spirits.

Handsel Monday. The first Monday after Old New Year's Day (January 12th) is known in Scotland as Handsel Monday. Until nearly the end of the nineteenth century, it was a recognized holiday for farm labourers and other workers, and a day for feasting and jollifications of all sorts. It was called Handsel Monday because those who were employed expected to receive handsel from their employers in the form of money-gifts, in much the same way as their English brethren did on December 26th (*see Boxing Day Gifts*), and poor people expected to receive it from their wealthier neighbours. Schoolmasters were sometimes handselled also. The children brought whatever their parents could afford to present to the master, and the boy and girl who brought the largest sum became King and Queen for the occasion. The King had the right to claim a holiday for the whole school in return for the gifts.

Some customs that rightly belong to New Year's Day or Eve were kept up on Handsel Monday, including first-footing, torchlight parades, and the kindling of bonfires. Boys went about blowing horns, and often indulged in pranks of the Mischief Night variety. *(See Mischief Night.)* A number of traditional games were played, and there were foot-races along the high roads, shooting matches, wrestling, and cockfighting until (and probably after) it became illegal.

Raffles for shortbread, buns or fruit, and sometimes more valuable commodities, were very popular, and large quantities of gingerbread, oranges, treacle-ale, and sweets were sold on booths set up in the streets of small towns. At home, special foods were eaten, including pies and plum pudding, a goose, or a pig's head. Whisky flowed freely everywhere. Farmers often began the day by providing a large breakfast of roast and boiled meats, cakes, and ale for all their workers. In Islay, the tacksmen entertained the cottars and their own servants to a supper of *Buntat' Breac*, or mutton stewed with potatoes and onions, and a liberal allowance of whisky or porter. This was a day of general hospitality, on which neighbours visited each other, dances were held in barns and halls, and young married couples returned to their old homes for a family celebration.

In some parts of Scotland, the festivities continued over the following day, which was known as Handsel Tuesday.

Harvest End. Before the farms were mechanized, the end of the corn harvest was, for all who took part in it, the splendid crown of the farming year. It still is, of course, since here something is achieved that has been planned, worked for, carried against odds through all the hopes and harassments of the long months before it. Now it is accomplished, and the triumph is not only that of the farmer, but also of every man and woman who shared in the work both before, and at the time of the actual harvest. But it is no longer the joyous festival of the ingathering that it used to be not so very long ago. Most of the people who once played their necessary part on the field are not seen there any more, and for the two or three who are, theirs is a task well done, and satisfactory, but not very much more. And only very little now remains of the time-honoured customs which formerly lent colour and a half-remembered meaning to the activities of all concerned.

As long as hand-reaping lasted, so long did the significant ceremonies of the Last Sheaf endure. Anciently, it was believed that the Last Sheaf embodied the Corn Spirit, and that the man who cut it killed her, and long after this archaic belief had been forgotten, the remains of the old fear and reverence still lingered in men's minds. It was considered, sometimes vaguely, sometimes definitely, to be unlucky to be the cutter of the Sheaf. On some farms, when the last field of harvest was nearly finished, it was customary for a little of the uncut corn to be left standing, with the stalks tied or plaited together. The reapers stood round it in a fairly wide half-circle, and threw their sickles at it, one by one. Thus the Last Sheaf was, as it were, cut in common, and the responsibility was spread. But if it was one man's sickle which was clearly seen to give the last cutting stroke, then what happened to the man concerned varied very considerably from district to district. Sometimes he was rewarded with a small sum of money, or given certain privileges, sometimes – and this was certainly the more ancient custom – he was swathed in the corn he had cut, jostled, bumped upon the field, and generally roughly handled by his mates. Like many other customs with ancient roots, this had become a frolic by the time it died out, but in pre-Christian times, it had a serious and sinister meaning. The unfortunate sheaf-cutter – or some unhappy stranger in his place – was killed there and then on the field, to restore life to the Corn Spirit who had died when the Last Sheaf was cut.

When all the reaping was ended, the custom of Crying the Neck, or Crying the Mare, was observed on many farms. The last ears of wheat were gathered into a carefully shaped bundle, known as the Neck (or the Mare), and lifted high into the air by the Harvest Lord (if there was one), or by the oldest reaper, or by some old and respected man who still had a strong voice, easily heard at a distance. Holding the Neck above his head, he cried out, 'I havet! I havet! I havet!' All the men in the field shouted in return 'What havee? What havee? What havee?', to which he replied 'A Neck! A Neck! A Neck!' The words and some of the details of this custom varied a little from one area to another, but the underlying pattern was always the same, that of a triumphant announcement to all within earshot that here, on this farm, all the corn was safely cut, and the main part of the harvest over. Shouts and cheers greeted the final Crying, and sometimes one of the younger men would seize the Neck and make off with it, as fast as he could run, towards the farmhouse. There one of the maids stood on guard with a bucket of water which she threw over him as he arrived, breathless, at the door; but if he managed to elude her and get into the house still dry, then he could claim the right to kiss her.

In Hone's *Every-Day Book* (Vol. II, 1826), a correspondent describes how he heard the farm people Crying the Neck more than once in North Devon. He says 'I have once or twice heard upwards of twenty men cry it, and sometimes joined by an equal number of female voices. About three years back, on some high grounds, where our people were harvesting. I heard six or seven "necks" cried in one night, although I knew that some of them were four miles off. They are heard through the quiet evening air, at a considerable distance sometimes'. Although, at the beginning of his letter, he remarks that the custom 'is never omitted on any large farm in that part of the country', he now adds a little sadly, 'But I think that the practice is beginning to decline of late, and many farmers and their men do not care about keeping up the old custom. I shall always practise it myself, because I take it in the light of a thanksgiving.'

In some regions, a dilatory farmer who was behindhand with his cutting was often mocked by the men of a nearby farm where the harvest was ended. They went to some high ground over-looking the other farm and, standing in a circle, shouted at the tops of their voices 'Oyez! Oyez! Oyez! This is to give notice that Mr . . . . (their master), has given the old sack a turn, and sent the Old Hare into Mr . . . . . (the neighbour)'s standing corn!' Then they joined hands, and bowing down low, cried out 'Wow! Wow! Wow-w-w-w!' as loudly as they could.

This, of course, was a sort of joke in most places, a way of boasting by one set of reapers, and of 'crowing over' others. But it was not always quite so harmless or so amiable. In some parts of Scotland, there was no shouting from high ground, no cheers and laughter, but instead, a quieter, and often more resented form of insult. A part of the last sheaf was twisted into the form of the Auld Wife (or Cailleach), and sent by the hands of a swift horseman to a farm where the harvest was not finished. As he rode past one of the uncut fields, he flung the wheaten figure into it, and then fled as fast as his horse could carry him. He did well to fly, for the angry fieldworkers often gave chase at once; and if they caught him, he was liable to be very roughly handled.

From the corn of the Last Sheaf was made the figure variously known as the Corn Dolly, or the Kern Baby, or in Scotland, as the Maiden if the harvest is early, or the Cailleach, or Carlin, meaning an Old Woman, if it is late. The figure was usually, though not always, made in human form. It could be a spiral pyramid, a miniature sheaf, or an intricate design of plaits and hanging ears; but often it was a female doll, dressed in white or coloured paper and tied with ribbons, with hair (and sometimes hands also) made of wheat-ears. It was carried home in triumph to the farmhouse, where it presided over the Harvest Supper in the kitchen or the barn, and was then kept all the year until it was replaced by the Corn Dolly from the next harvest. In some parishes, a communal Corn Dolly was made and taken to the church. This is still done at Whalton, in Northumberland, and at Little Waltham, in Essex, where it is fixed to a pew during the Harvest Festival. At Overbury, in Worcestershire, a pyramid made of twisted corn, with wheat-ears hanging from its base, hangs in the church porch, and is renewed, not every year, but as it becomes necessary.

The making of corn-dollies as ornaments has now become a country craft, practised by skilled men and women who produce very interesting and attractive figures of intricate design. But the old corn-dollies, fashioned in haste and in triumph on the field at harvest end are now only a memory.

Harvest Home. When the reaping was finished, in the pre-mechanization harvest, the Last Load and the Corn Dolly were brought home in triumph, in a great harvest-wain decorated with flowers and boughs of oak and ash, and drawn by four or six garlanded horses. The men rode on top of the load, shouting, singing, and

blowing horns. Sometimes the man driving the wagon, or men riding on the horses, wore female dress. One of the songs they sang was:

> Harvest Home! Harvest Home!
> We've ploughed, we've sown,
> We've ripped, we've mown,
> Harvest Home! Harvest Home!
> We want water and kain't get none!

In some districts, girls following the load threw water over the singers on the last line.

That evening the Harvest (or Mell, or Kern) Supper was held for all who had taken part in the harvest. It consisted usually of roast beef, or other meat, plum puddings, apple-pies, and unlimited supplies of ale or cider. After the meal had been eaten, there were toasts to the farmer and his family, the singing of old songs, and in due course, dancing. The harvest-home songs varied a little in different districts; here is the beginning of one from Berkshire and Oxfordshire that was still in use wherever the Harvest Supper survived at the end of last century:

> Here's a health unto our master,
> The founder of our feast;
> We hope his soul to God will go
> When he do get his rest.
> May everything now prosper
> That he do take in hand;
> For we be all his servants
> As works at his command.
>
> So drink, boys, drink,
> And see you do not spill,
> For if you do you shall drink two,
> For that be master's will.

The excitement and colour of Harvest Home has vanished now, and the Last Load comes in without noise or acclamation, and without any decorated wain, or garlanded horses, or young girls with their bowls of water. There are, however, still some farms where a Harvest Supper is held, though this is usually a much quieter entertainment than it used to be, with fewer toasts and far fewer traditional songs. Nevertheless, it is often the last of the old Harvest customs to be kept up. The Harvest Festival, which is celebrated today in parishes all over England and is so well-liked that there are some people who go to church only then and at Christmas, is quite modern. It began in 1843, when the Revd. R. S. Hawker, Vicar of Morwenstow, in Cornwall, revived in that parish (though later in the season), the ancient thanksgiving and service of Lammas, long faded from the Church's liturgy. From that local beginning, the custom spread widely, and is now an established part of the liturgical and agricultural year. It has become an occasion for the offering of harvest gifts, and the decoration of the church with fruit and vegetables, bread and corn, all of which afterwards go to the hospitals, or to local charities. And as we have seen (*see Harvest End*), in a few parishes, the ancient Corn Dolly, is included on a pew-end, or in some other prominent position in the church.

Haxey Hood. The old and unusual game known as the Hood Game, or Throwing the Hood, is played every year on Old Christmas Day, January 6th at Haxey in north Lincolnshire. On this date, Haxey Hood, one of the two annual Feasts of the parish, is held. The other, Haxey Midsummer, falls on or near July 6th, and is much like other village feasts elsewhere; but Haxey Hood has a character all its own. It is the great festival occasion of the parish year, when everyone keeps holiday, and some very interesting traditional customs are observed.

The ceremonies of Haxey Hood begin in the early afternoon with the procession of the Fool and his twelve Boggans up the village street to a small green outside the parish church. The Boggans are the official team of players in the Hood Game and play against all comers; they are, and need to be, vigorous young men who are often useful members of the local football team. Chief among them is the King Boggan, or Lord of the Hood, who carries a wand, or roll of thirteen willows bound with thirteen withy-bands as a badge of office. Tradition demands that he and all his team should wear scarlet flannel coats and hats wreathed with red flowers. The Lord usually does so, though his coat is not always made of flannel now. So do some of his men, but quite often a red jersey or shirt replaces the coat. A few Boggans may turn out in their ordinary clothes, but invariably the ritual red appears somewhere in their dress, if only in the form of an armband or some fluttering scarlet ribbons.

The Fool, who leads the procession and has the right to kiss any woman he chooses throughout the day, also has a good deal of red about him. His face is smeared with soot and red ochre, and his sackcloth trousers are patched with pieces of red cloth cut in a variety of shapes. His shirt, or coat, is red, and so are the flowers that adorn his fine feathered hat. In his hand he carries a whip with a sock filled with bran at the end of the thong, and this he uses for the time-honoured purpose of belabouring those who are unwary enough to come within reach.

During the week before Old Christmas Day, the Fool and the Boggans go round to all the nearby villages, singing *John Barleycorn, The Farmer's Boy*, and *Drink England Dry*, and inviting all and sundry to come to the Hood-throwing. At the same time, they collect money for the festival expenses. All wear full ceremonial attire, except that the Fool's face is not smeared. On the day itself, when the procession reaches the green by the churchyard, the Fool mounts upon a stone which once formed the base of a tall Cross. There he makes a speech, welcoming all present and inviting them to join in the game, and mysteriously stating that two bullocks and a half have been killed, but the other half had to be left running about the field, and can be fetched if it is wanted. Finally, he reminds his hearers that the order of the day is:

> Hoose agen hoose,
> Toon agen toon,
> If tho' meet a man, knock 'im doon,
> But don't 'ut 'im!

While he is speaking, a small fire of damp straw is lit behind him, and a cloud of smoke pours out all round him. This is known as Smoking the Fool, and is a modern version of an ancient ceremony so called which formerly took place on the morning after the Hood Game. Some straw was set alight under a tree, and the Fool was tied to a branch above it; 'he was suspended over the fire and swung backwards and forwards over it until almost suffocated; then allowed to drop into the smouldering straw, which was well wetted, and to scramble out as he could.[1]' This custom, with its suggestions of ritual fumigation, had counterparts elsewhere; it persisted in the Haxey area until almost within living memory, but eventually it was abandoned because of its obvious dangers. It is often stated that all traces of it have vanished from the Haxey Hood celebrations today, but this is not the case. Before the last war, the modern form of the custom seems to have been only intermittently practised, but of late years it has become a usual part of the festivities. It is certainly safer than the old way, but even so, it has its perils. In 1956 an eye-witness recorded that 'someone forgot to damp the straw, and the Fool caught fire. However, many willing hands soon extinguished the blaze.'[2]

As soon as the speech-making and the Smoking are over, the Fool leads the way up the hill to a half-acre of ground near the top. Here the game begins. The Boggans stand in a wide circle and the Lord of the Hood and players

1. M. Peacock, 'The Hood-Game at Haxey, Lincolnshire', *Folk-Lore*, Vol. VII, 1896.

2. Mary Robinson, 'The Haxey Hood Game, 1956', *Folk-Lore* Vol. 67, 1956.

from Haxey, Westwoodside, and the other parts of the wide parish stand inside the ring so made. The Lord throws up the first Hood, one of several minor hoods which are played for first. These 'hoods' bear no resemblance to the headgear from which they are supposed to take their name. The lesser ones are tightly-rolled pieces of canvas, tied with ribbons, and the main, or Leather Hood, which is played for later in the game, is a two-foot length of thick rope encased in stout leather. As soon as the first Hood is thrown up, there is a fierce struggle for it, every man trying to seize it and carry it over the boundary to his own village. If any one manages to get it safely over the line and away, he can keep the Hood; but in order to do so he has to elude, not only the watchful Boggans, but all the other players who rush after him and try to wrest it from him. The function of the Boggans is to prevent the Hood from crossing the boundary. If one of them captures it, or even touches it, that Hood is 'dead', and is returned to the Lord to be thrown up again.

When all the minor hoods have been disposed of, the Sway, the really serious part of the game, begins. The Leather, or Sway Hood is produced, and is thrown straight up into the air, either by the Lord or by some prominent person present who has been invited to do so as a mark of honour. The ring of Boggans breaks up, and all semblance of orderly play disappears. Somebody seizes the Hood, but he does not run away with it because rapid independent movement has instantly become impossible. A solid compact mass of struggling humanity pours slowly down the hill, swaying backwards and forwards as the varying pressure of the pushing heaving crowd dictates. The Hood may not be kicked or tossed forward, but only 'swayed', that is, pushed, pulled, or dragged towards one of the three inns which serve as the 'goals' of this strenuous contest.

Every local man who is not too old to do so is expected to take part in the grimly earnest struggle. Stragglers are rounded up by the Boggans, and men on the edge of the watching crowds may be swept into the Sway as it moves slowly onwards. Everything in its path goes down before it, including hedges and sometimes even stone walls. Two hours or more may go by before one faction or another is finally victorious; but at long last, the contest does end, and the Hood is brought in triumph to the winners' inn. The landlord provides free drinks for all, and the Hood remains in his keeping until next Haxey Hood, except when it is needed for some reason and is fetched away by the Fool or the Boggans then in office. At one time, it used to be ceremonially roasted before the inn fire and doused with ale as it turned on the spit, the ale being then drunk by those present, but of this interesting custom no trace now remains.

Like many other ancient rituals of which the origin has been forgotten, the Hood Game is locally explained by a legend. This says that in the thirteenth century, Lady Mowbray, then Lady of the Manor, lost her scarlet hood in a high wind when she was riding from Haxey to Westwoodside. The flying hood was pursued and caught by twelve labourers who happened to be working nearby, though not without considerable difficulty because of the strength of the wind. As a reward for their help, she bestowed upon the parish thirteen half-acres of land, the rent of which was to provide a feast and a hood to be played for every year on the same day for ever. This tale is supposed to account for the number of the Boggans, their important duties in the ceremonies, and the red clothes that they wear, The piece of ground on which the Hood Game always begins is said to be the place where her hood blew off, and presumably it is also one of the half-acres that she gave. Exactly where the other twelve were is now unknown, for the deeds have all been lost.

It can, however, be quite safely assumed that whatever Lady Mowbray's real connection with Haxey Hood may have been, she did not originate its celebrations, as the story implies. It seems very likely that the roots run much farther back in time than the thirteenth century, and that what has now become a game and a village feast began as a pre-Christian fertility rite associated with the end of the midwinter festival and the beginning of Spring. The ferocity of the struggle for possession of the Leather Hood, the fact that the captured Hood was once roasted by the victors, the Smoking of the Fool, and the reference to bullocks in his speech, all point to such a beginning. Professor E. O. James[1] suggests that the game is a relic of ritual combat between different local groups, and that the Hood contended for was originally the half, or the head, of a bull sacrificed for the fertilization of the fields.

A form of Hood Game is also played at Epworth, close to Haxey, but the custom is not so regularly observed, and the method of play is somewhat different. Haxey people allege that the Epworth Hood is merely an imitation of their own game.

Hay-strewing. (*See Rushbearing.*)

Hiring Fairs. The Hiring, or Mop, or Statute Fair is not strictly a fair at all, but is derived from the mediaeval Statutes of Labourers, of which the first was enacted in Edward III's reign, in a time of shortage of agricultural workers. One of the clauses of such Statutes was that the magistrates were empowered to fix rates of wages, and to make them known at the Statute Sessions, which usually took place at Michaelmas or Martinmas, but sometimes at Whitsuntide, or on Old May Day. In due course, the Statute of Labourers was abolished by Queen Elizabeth I, but the Sessions had proved so useful that they were specially retained. Men and employers came together to the meeting-place to hear the rates of pay and conditions of service, and usually entered into hiring agreements then and there. Where people customarily gather in considerable numbers, sellers of food and drink quickly follow, and after them stall-holders who sell fairings of blue ribbon or gingerbread, and the providers of amusements. Before long, the sober Sessions had developed into a lively fair, enjoyed by everyone, which, if it had no charter, was none the worse for that.

Until fairly recent times, farm-workers were normally engaged by the year. If, as the year drew to an end, the farmer made no move to renew the engagement, or the man (or maid) wished to go elsewhere, then it was to the Hiring Fair that both parties repaired. Those seeking work stood in an allotted part of the street, or square, bearing the accepted signs of their calling – a crook, or a tuft of wool worn in the hat for a shepherd, a whip for a carter, a milking-pail for a dairymaid and so on. Once an agreement had been made with a farmer, the newly-hired worker received a 'fastenpenny' as an earnest of wages to come, and the rest of his day was spent in enjoying the delights of the Fair. Sometimes an agreement made at the Fair proved unsatisfactory, and either master or man, or both, wished to terminate it as quickly as possible. For them, there was in many places a Runaway Mop to which they could go a week or a fortnight later, to try their luck again.

Hiring at the Statute Fair lasted in many districts until the outbreak of the First World War and, in some places, for a few years after its end. There is, indeed, nothing to prevent a man from standing in the appointed place and offering himself for hire at any such fair today. He has a legal right to do so, but probably very few would care to attempt it now. Most of the surviving Mops or Hiring Fairs (of which there are still a good many in different parts of the country) are now straightforward pleasure-fairs. Stratford Mop, for instance, is one of the most famous pleasure-fairs of the Midlands, and attracts thousands of visitors to the town every October. But no one now comes there looking for work or service, and probably the majority of the visitors are unaware that any one ever did.

Hobby Horse Day. (*See May Hobby Horses.*)

Hocktide. The Monday and Tuesday after Low Sunday are together known as Hocktide. This short festival season is now almost forgotten, except at Hungerford, but before the Reformation, and in some areas until about the middle of the seventeenth century, it was an occasion for lively sports and games, and the collection of money for church and parish expenses. Hock Tuesday was also a recognized day for the payment of rents and other dues in those districts where the year was divided for land-tenure purposes into two halves beginning at Hocktide and at Michaelmas.

1. E. O. James, *Seasonal Feasts and Festivals*, 1961.

The customary celebrations were of a very boisterous nature, including much wild horse-play of which strangers and travellers were as likely to be the victims as the local people. In 1450, the Bishop of Worcester ordered the immediate suppression of 'the disgraceful sports and amusements practised on the days commonly called Hok-days'.[1] We do not know how far this order had the desired effect in his diocese, but it is clear from numerous records that the customs he condemned continued to flourish elsewhere for a long time thereafter. The two days were sometimes known as Binding Monday and Tuesday, because on the Monday the women of the township went out with ropes and bound any man they could catch, releasing him only when he had paid a forfeit. On the Tuesday, the men retaliated in like manner. In some districts, the order of the proceedings was reversed, the men going out on the first day and the women on the second. After the Reformation, the binding of passers by was forbidden, and instead, ropes were stretched across the road and lowered only when payment had been made.

As with Lifting in the previous week (*see Easter Lifting*), the central idea of the Hocktide custom was the capture and holding to ransom of women by men, and of men by women. Both customs appear to have their roots in ancient seasonal Spring rites connected with the need for a sacrificial victim; but just as Lifting was given a Christian meaning and was said to represent Christ's Resurrection, so Hocktide acquired an historical explanation. According to one legend, the festival commemorated the massacre of the Danes by King Ethelred's order on St Brice's Day,[2] 1002. In the Middle Ages, a play known as the Hock Play used to be acted at Coventry at this season. It was suppressed after the Reformation, but in July, 1575, it was revived for the entertainment of Elizabeth I at Kenilworth. 'Hither', says Dugdale in his *Antiquities of Warwickshire* (1656) 'came the Coventry men, and acted the ancient play, long since used in that city, called Hocks-Tuesday, setting forth the destruction of the Danes in King Ethelred's time, with which the Queen was so pleas'd that she gave them a brace of bucks, and five marks in money to bear the charges of a feast.' If she liked violent action, she had good reason to be pleased, for in Robert Laneman's account of this performance, we read that there were fierce mock-fights between actors representing Danes and Englishmen, in which the former were twice victorious, 'but at the last conflict, beaten down, overcome, and many led captive for triumph by our English women.'[1] Another tradition connected Hocktide with the sudden death of Hardicanute in 1042, and the subsequent delivery of England from Danish rule. However, neither of these stories need to be considered seriously for they are simply later legends invented to account for the existence of a custom of which the true origin and meaning had been forgotten.

It is probable that the ransom-money collected during the Hocktide sports once went to provide a feast for the captors; but in the course of time, it came to be used for parish expenses, and was often a very useful contribution to the church funds. Many churchwardens' accounts contain entries of sums acquired by such 'gaderyngs'. In 1497, 13/4d. was 'gathered by the women on Hob Monday' in the parish of St Mary-at-Hill in London, and five shillings by the men on the following day. In 1559, the men of St Mary's, Reading, collected 4s. od. and the women 22s. od. in Chelsea, 'the women that went a hocking' in 1607 brought in 45s. od. In most of the surviving accounts, the women are shown to have been better collectors than their husbands and brothers, though whether this was due to female ruthlessness or masculine chivalry it is now too late to determine. At St Peter-in-the-East, Oxford, the combined Hocktide gathering produced £6 in 1663 and £4 10s. od. in 1667. The latter entry is the last of its kind in the records of that parish. By then, the custom was already in decline, and little more is heard of it thereafter. It had vanished almost a century earlier in St Law-

1. J. Noake, *Worcester in Olden Times*, 1849. J. Brand, *op. cit.*, Vol. I.
2. November 13th.

1. *Robert Laneham's letter*, ed. F. J. Furnivall, New Shakespeare Society, 1890.

rence's parish, Reading, where it is noted in the churchwardens' accounts for 1573 that, 'The collections on Hock Monday and on the festivals, having ceased', it was agreed that women parishioners should pay for their seats in church at the annual rate of fourpence or sixpence, according to their position in the building.

Hocktide is still observed as a festival at Hungerford in Berkshire, but since it is also, and indeed primarily an important civic occasion there, the celebrations are not quite the same as those once found in other places. Unlike most English boroughs, Hungerford has no Mayor or Corporation. Instead, it has a governing body of Feoffees chosen from the commoners of the town, a High Constable, Bailiff, Portreeve, Tutti-men, and other officials. These officers are elected for the ensuing year at the Hocktide Court which, according to a document in the borough archives, 'is and time out of mind always hath been kept and holden on the Tuesday called Hockney-day', that is, on Hock Tuesday. The actual election is in the hands of a jury of twelve persons, but in theory at least, all the commoners are bound to attend this Court, and also the Court Baron on the following Friday when the newly-elected officials are sworn in, or else pay a fine of one penny. This is not, perhaps, a very serious penalty, though it once meant more than it does now, but there is also the further threat that if any one fails either to come or to pay, he may be 'deprived of his right of common or fishing for that year.'

The Tuesday Court now meets at nine-o'clock in the morning. Formerly it met at eight o'clock, and at that hour still, the Town Crier appears on the Town Hall balcony and blows a long blast upon a bugle-horn. This horn is a replica, made in 1634, of one far older which John of Gaunt gave to the townspeople in the fourteenth century, when he also bestowed upon them certain manorial privileges, including the right of free fishery in the River Kennet. These privileges and the horn still exist, but the latter is no longer sounded on Hock Day. Instead, the 'new' horn is used to open the proceedings, as it has been since it was first made. It bears the date 1634, and an inscription stating that:

JOHN A GAUN DID GIVE AND GRANT THE RIALL
OF FISHING TO HUNGERFORD TOUNE FROM
ELDRED STUB TO IRISH STILL EXCEPTING
SOM SEUEREAL MILL POUND
JEHOSOPHAT LUCAS WAS CUNSTABL.

After the horn-blowing, the Bellman parades the streets to remind the commoners of their obligations, and require them 'to attend your Court House at the Hall at nine o'clock this morning to answer your names on penalty of a fine. God save the Queen!'[1]

While the Court is sitting to elect its officers and deal with other manorial concerns, two Tutti-, or Tything-men, set out on their rounds, accompanied by an individual known as the Orange Scrambler, who carries a sack of oranges and wears cocks' feathers round his top hat. The Tything-men were originally officials whose duty it was to keep watch and ward over the inhabitants and their property during their year of office. On Hock Tuesday, they were entitled to demand a head-penny from every commoner in return for their services,[2] and this they still do, although their duties have long since ceased to be as onerous as they once were.

They go first to the Constable's house to receive their tutti-poles. These are two long staves, adorned with ribbons and a 'tutti', or posy of flowers, and surmounted by an orange. Armed with these, they visit every common-right house in the town to collect their dues. Women have the right to pay with a kiss instead of a coin if they so wish, and this has by now become the more usual procedure. For each kiss an orange is given, taken from the top of the tutti-pole, and every child in the house receives one as well. As each orange is removed from the pole, it is replaced by another from the Orange Scrambler's sack. The Tutti-men are also entitled to stop any woman they meet in the streets, whether she be resident, visitor, or simply passing motorist, and to demand from her the same payment of a penny or a kiss.

At the end of their morning round, they go to the Three Swans Hotel, where a civic

1. Walter Money, *An Historical Sketch of the Town of Hungerford*, 1894.
2. *Ibid.*

luncheon is held for Feoffees, officials, and local notabilities. Here the newly-elected Constable presides, and on either side of his chair the tutti-poles are set up. When the meal is over, the Tutti-men and the Orange Scrambler go outside and scatter oranges to be scrambled for by a joyous crowd of waiting children. Meanwhile, inside the hotel, the ceremony of Shoeing the Colt takes place. This is an initiation rite, rather like the 'shoeing' customs that used to be observed on farms at harvest and occasionally at other times.

The guests at the luncheon normally include a certain number of newcomers to the town and visitors from outside, and so, when the toasts have been drunk, the Constable rises to announce that there are 'strangers present', and that the colt must be shod. Two men then enter, one wearing a blacksmith's apron and carrying a hammer, and the other bearing a box of farrier's nails. By them each 'colt', or stranger, is seized in turn, and a pretence of driving nails into the sole of his shoe is made until he cries 'Punch!' and obtains his release by paying for a round of drinks. Thus he ceases to be a stranger, and is admitted to the company of Hungerford men. If he refuses to be shod, which he has the right to do, he must pay a fine of £1, but naturally, on so cheerful an occasion, very few people ever do refuse.

After the Friday meeting and swearing-in, the Constable usually gives a dinner, at which the health of John of Gaunt is drunk in silence; and finally the Hocktide ceremony comes to an end with the attendance of the newly-elected officials at the parish church on the following Sunday.

Hodening. The Hodening (or in Kent, the Hooden) Horse was one of that large company of strange animal-figures which from time immemorial and in many countries, have regularly appeared at certain critical seasons of the year, and especially at Midwinter. He came out at Hallowtide, or during the Twelve Days of Christmas, and like the Christmas Bull of Dorset and Gloucestershire (*see Christmas Bull*), he was a man disguised, more or less realistically, as an animal. He wore a stable-blanket or a sheet over his clothes, and carried a horse's head, with reins attached upon a pole about four feet long. This head was sometimes made of wood, but more usually, it was a real horse-skull, with hinged jaws that could be made to snap open and shut. Accompanied by a band of young men, the man-horse walked at night through the dark streets and lanes, with a crouching gait to make him look like a four-footed beast, and visited the houses as a luck-bringer. Nervous people were often alarmed by the sudden appearance of this weird-looking creature on their doorsteps; at Broadstairs, in 1839, one woman, coming face to face with him without warning, was so terrified that she died of fright, and the custom was consequently forbidden by the local magistrates. Nevertheless, startling though he might be upon occasion, he was usually recognized, even by those who had only the vaguest notions of his pagan origin, as a bringer of fertility and good fortune, and he and his companions were normally sure of a warm welcome at nearly every house on their rounds.

In East Kent, Hodening, or Hoodening, took place at Christmas. A wooden head was used for the Hooden Horse, with large iron nails for teeth and round holes for eyes. Here, too, the

jaws were hinged, a feature found in nearly all these heads, whether they were genuine skulls or imitations. Sometimes a lighted candle was set in the mouth, throwing eerie shadows and fitful gleams like those of a turnip-lantern. A group of farmworkers accompanied the Horse one leading him by a rope, or by reins, and carrying a whip, and another, chosen for his light weight, riding on his back. A third, known as Mollie, or Old Woman, was dressed in female clothes and carried a besom. The rest of the company bore handbells, or some other musical instruments.

On arrival at a house, the leader knocked loudly on the door. As soon as it was opened, the Horse kicked, reared, and gnashed his long teeth in as frightening a manner as possible, while the Old Woman swept the feet of the door-opener with 'her' besom. If the men were allowed to enter – and only very rarely were they refused – a red ribbon was tied to the Horse's head. Then followed music and carol-singing and general merriment, after which ale, cakes, and other refreshments were given to the visitors. At Reculver, only men who worked with horses during the year were allowed to go Hoodening, and this rule may perhaps have been observed in other parishes also. The strongest man among them was chosen to act the part of the Horse. As a widespread rural custom, Hoodening has now vanished from the Kentish scene, but within the last twenty years, modern versions of it have appeared, with heads copied from the old models, at Folkestone, Charing, and elsewhere.[1]

In the Doncaster district of Yorkshire, the Hodeners went round with the Christmas Mummers. A real skull was used, with a bar fixed beneath it to take the pole. One such skull, formerly in use at Hooton Pagnell, was lost for several years, and was then found in a pond and preserved as a relic of a custom now abandoned. In Wales also, the *Mari Lwyd*, a man wearing a natural or a wooden horse-skull, appeared in the Christmas season, and still does so in some parts of the Principality. *(See Mari Lwyd.)*

The Cheshire Hodening Horse appeared at Hallowtide, and accompanied the Soulers on their rounds on All Souls' Day or on the Eve of that festival (*see Souling*). This curious combination of two separate customs, one Christian and mediaeval, the other pagan and immensely old, survived in parts of the county till the turn of the century; some elderly people there can still remember seeing, as children, the frightening horse-figure rearing and prancing outside their homes in the November dusk, while the Soulers stood round and sang their ancient songs. He appeared also in the Soul-Caking Play, the Cheshire version of the Mummers' Play, which was acted on All Souls' night. This is the only version of that play which contains him, but in it he was a very popular character, known as Dick, or as Wild Horse. At Comberbach, local colour was added to his story by the lines:

> This horse was bred from Marbury Dun,
> The finest mare that ever run,
> Run fourteen mile in fifteen hours,
> And never sweat a hair.

Marbury Dun was a famous mare who really existed and, according to tradition, ran considerably more than fourteen miles in the time stated. Her owner, Lord Barrymore, is said to have wagered Marbury Hall against her ability to run there from London between sunrise and sunset. She did so; but she died after reaching home, and was buried in the park with silver horseshoes on her feet.

At Higher Whitley, also in Cheshire, when the Hodening-visits were ended and the Play had been acted, the horse's skull was buried by the Hodeners, and a mock funeral service was read over it. Rival gangs from a nearby village often tried to steal the head, and when this happened, there was a pitched battle in which very hard blows were exchanged. About 1935, one of the heads used at Whitley some forty

1. In Folkestone, the Hooden Horse, accompanied by handbell ringers collects for charity at Christmas. At Charing, since 1954, he appears at Whitsun, and is associated with the Morris Men who dance in the chancel of the Church and out into the Market Square. In 1956, the inn at Wickhambreaux, near Canterbury was renamed *The Hooden Horse*, and now forms the final point in a round of visits by Morris dancers and handbell-ringers, made in early September in connection with the hop-harvest. *Information supplied by Mr Barnett Field, of Folkestone, 1967.*

years earlier was rescued from imminent destruction by A. W. Boyd, of Frandley, and given to the Manchester Museum. It is a real skull, with white, red-ringed eyes painted upon it. It is somewhat battered after its long service, but it still has something strangely awe-inspiring about it, and would, perhaps, be capable of startling a good many people, if ever it was put to its old use again.

Holming Day. *(See Blood-Letting on St Stephen's Day.)*

Holy Innocents. On December 28th, the slaughter of the children by King Herod[1] is commemorated in the festival of Holy Innocents' Day. Although this anniversary falls within the festal season of the Twelve Days of Christmas, and is actually one of the Twelve, it was, for many centuries, believed to be the unluckiest day of the year. On it no one willingly began any new enterprise, or even did any ordinary work that was not absolutely necessary. Whatever was started then was believed certain to fail, or to have an unhappy ending. For this reason, Edward IV changed the date of his coronation, as soon as it was realized that the Sunday originally chosen coincided with Holy Innocents' Day. The notion of the feast's essential misfortune lingered on in some parts of Britain until as late as the beginning of the present century. Not only the festival day itself, but also the day of the week on which it fell was ill-omened all through the year, so that it was unwise to wash household linen or scrub floors then, and still more so to transact business, or set out on a journey, or get married.

The old name for Holy Innocents' Day was, and still is in many districts, Childermas. In Northamptonshire, it was known as Dyzemas Day, and in Ireland, 'the cross day of the year' because nothing attempted then ever prospered. In pre-Reformation times, it was the last day of the Boy Bishop's reign (*see Boy Bishop*). In many English parishes, a muffled peal used to be rung in memory of the martyred children. Gregorie, writing in 1684,[2] refers to the custom of whipping children on this day, so that they might remember more clearly Herod's crimes, and the sufferings of his victims. That, at least, is the theory he puts forward to explain the practice, but in fact, it seems more probable that it was connected with the many other whipping customs found all over Europe. These occur, or did occur, at different times of the year, not always on December 28th, nor are they invariably associated with children or with mourning. On the contrary, in many regions, they are extremely lively and hilarious, as in Hungary, where until quite recently, young people used to beat each other with willow-twigs, or with be-ribboned birch-twigs.[1] There can be little doubt that such beatings, including that at Childermas, are pre-Christian in origin, and are, or were originally intended to benefit the 'Victim' by driving away evil, and endowing him (or her) with health and fertility.

1. *Matthew*, II, 13–18.
2. *Episcopus Puerorum in Die Innocentium.*

Horn Blowing at Ripon. At Ripon in Yorkshire, the Mayor's Hornblower sounds the city horn every night at nine o'clock, four times in the market place and once outside the Mayor's house. This custom is locally believed to run back to Anglo-Saxon times. Before Ripon had a Mayor, it had a Wakeman, whose ancient office is commemorated in the city motto, painted in large letters across the front of the Town Hall: 'Unless Ye Lord Keep Ye Cittie, Ye Wakeman Waketh in Vain.' He was responsible for the preservation of good order, and the protection of the citizens against robbery and violence, from nine o'clock at night to sunrise. If any one during that time suffered loss or damage which could be proved to be due to lack of care on the part of the Wakeman and his assistants, compensation could be claimed. One of his duties, according to a document of 1400, was to sound the horn every night at the four corners of the Market Cross as a form of curfew, and also as a signal that his night-watch had begun. He had also to blow it on the five Horn Days. These were originally Candlemas Day, Easter, one of the Rogation-days, the Feast of St Wilfrid on October 12th, and the Feast of

1. Karoly Viski, *Hungarian Peasant Customs*, 1932.

St Stephen on December 26th. They are now celebrated on Easter Sunday, Whit Sunday, August Bank Holiday, Christmas Day and Mayor's Sunday.

When Hugh Ripley, the last Wakeman, became the first Mayor of Ripon in 1604, an official Hornblower was appointed, and by him and his successors the horn-ritual was, and still is, performed. In 1955, the office was duplicated, so as to allow the holders to leave the city for an occasional holiday if they so wish. Previously this had been impossible, since the horn had to be blown on every night of the year, and only the official Hornblower was permitted (and perhaps only he was competent) to blow it.

Ripon has had three horns during its long history. The one now used is not very old, dating only from 1864, when it replaced another that had been in continuous use since 1690. The oldest of the three, which is said to have been first blown in A.D. 886, is preserved among the city's treasures, and brought out only on ceremonial occasions, and on the five Horn Days. At such times, it is not sounded, but is carried in procession by the Sergeant-at-Mace, attached to a magnificent baldric adorned with heavy silver medallions showing the coats-of-arms and badges of former Wakemen and Mayors.

Horn Dance, Abbots Bromley. The Abbots Bromley Horn Dance, which Violet Alford has called 'The most primitive dance in Europe',[1] is annually performed in that Staffordshire village on the Monday of the local Wakes Week which is the Monday following the first Sunday after September 4th. But if this date is now constant, it appears to have been otherwise at one time, for Robert Plot, who described the dance briefly in his *Natural History of Staffordshire* (1686), says it was performed 'within memory' at Christmas, New Year and Twelfth Day. This suggests that it was originally a Winter Solstice custom, and also that Plot did not see it himself, perhaps because it had temporarily lapsed at the time he wrote. It is not known when the celebration was shifted to the Wakes date. Nor is it known how old it is, for its age and origin are alike very uncertain.

One explanatory theory places its beginning in the reign of Henry I, after the granting to Bromley of some forest rights in Needwood. These rights are commonly said to have concerned hunting, and the Horn Dance is said to

have been evolved as an expression of communal rejoicing in consequence. There is, however, no evidence that any such hunting privileges were ever given to the people at this time. From a marginal comment, in a Cartulary of Burton Abbey, dated 1125, it appears that five men then farming Abbots Bromley Manor asked for and obtained grazing rights in the Forest, but nothing is said about the far more valuable hunting rights. The nature of the Horn Dance itself suggests a very much earlier beginning, in pre-Christian times and associated with either hunting – or fertility – magic. It seems, in any case, to have been danced continuously for many centuries in this area, with only occasional lapses, such as that which occurred during the Civil War.

The horns used have their own mystery. They

1. Violet Alford, 'The Abbots Bromley Horn Dance', *Antiquity*, June, 1933.

are undoubtedly reindeer-horns, mounted upon carved wooden deer-heads, to which short poles are attached for convenience in carrying. There are six pairs, of which three are painted white, and the other three blue. The largest pair has a span of thirty-nine inches, and weighs over twenty-five pounds. It is always carried by the leader of the dance. The others vary somewhat in weight and span, the lightest being twenty-nine inches across, and weighing sixteen-and-a-half pounds. They are kept in the Hurst Chapel in the Parish Church, and are collected from the Vicar by the dancers on Wakes Monday morning.

No one knows where they came from, or when. Plot, in 1686, speaks of six 'Rain deer heads', which in his day were painted white and red, and had the arms of the three chief local families on them. The carving of the wooden heads on which the horns are mounted seems to be sixteenth-century work. At the extreme end of the seventeenth century, Lord Paget brought home from Turkey a set of elk-horns which have sometimes been confused with the dancers' horns. Unlike the latter, they were never kept in the Church, but in the now-vanished Town Hall. At some period, they seem to have been lost, and now no one can say where they are, or what became of them. Otherwise, nothing at all is known about the existing reindeer-horns, except that they are there, and are obviously very old. Perhaps some far-off Norse settler in the district brought them as reminders of his country, though it is difficult to see why he should have burdened himself with anything so cumbersome; or they may even be the horns of British reindeer, in which case they must run back till before the twelfth century, by which time our native deer are believed to have become extinct.

The dancing-team consists of twelve people. There are the six horn-bearers, the heart and core of the ancient ceremony, who carry their horns in such a way that they appear to be springing from their heads. There is also a man dressed as a woman, supposed now to be Maid Marian, though he/she may quite possibly be much older than that uncertain lady. She wears a long dress reaching to the ground and a floating white veil, and carries an ancient wooden ladle in which collections are taken, and a short stick, equally old, with which she beats it. Besides these, there are a Fool in conventional motley, a Hobby-horse, a Bowman, a boy with a triangle, and a musician who plays the accordion, as his predecessors played the fiddle and, earlier still the pipe-and-tabor.

With the exception of the Man-Woman and the Fool, the dancers wear a costume consisting of a flat cap, knee-breeches and knitted green stockings, and a coloured sleeveless jerkin, all in soft reds, greens, browns and gold. None of this is traditional. Formerly, the performers wore their own clothes, decorated with ribbons and patches of coloured cloth; but in the second half of last century, some local ladies designed a set of costumes, faintly reminiscent of the clothes worn by the Morris dancers in the famous Betley window, and perhaps inspired by them. The new garments proved very popular, and since then, they have been repeated and copied more than once. Although they are comparatively modern, they are very ornamental, and fit in admirably with the spirit of the dance itself, and with the woods and green fields through which it passes.

On Wakes Monday, when the dancers have retrieved the horns from the Church, they set off on a twenty-mile perambulation of the wide parish which takes them nearly all the day. On their way, they visit houses great and small, farmhouses and cottages, and dance outside them. It is said to be an omen of bad luck if they do not come. With the horn-bearers leading, they silently enter the farmyard or the front garden, and begin their ritual performance with a single-file circle. Then the leader breaks the ring by turning and passing between the second and third dancers, and the rest follow to form a loop. Then the six horn-bearers fall into two lines of three each, dancing face to face. They raise their antlers and advance upon each other, as if to fight; they retire, and advance again, and seem to lock horns; and after repeating this movement once or twice, they cross over, passing left shoulder to left shoulder, and turning, begin the whole thing again from the opposite side. Meanwhile, the boy with the triangle beats time with his instrument, the Hobby-horse rhythmically snaps his moveable jaws, and the musician plays the music of the dance on his accordion. The tunes he plays, like the clothes the dancers wear, are not old. One lovely old tune is known, but it is never played now. Two or three other customary melodies exist, but are of no great age, and unfortunately, there is a growing tendency to replace them with popular modern dance tunes.

When the set dance is over, the team quietly follows its leader away and on to the next port of call. Eventually, the long round, with its luck-bringing visits, comes to an end, and the dancers return to their home base, to dance again in the village street. And when that is over, the horns are returned to the Church's care until they are wanted again, and the rest of the evening is spent in well-earned revelry and feasting.

Horn Fair, Ebernoe. The Horn Fair at Ebernoe, in Sussex, takes place on July 25th, the Feast of St James the Great. It is locally said to have done so 'since time immemorial', and certainly though its history and origin are both obscure, it does seem, allowing for occasional lapses, to be several centuries old.

Its distinctive features are the roasting of a horned sheep, and a cricket match. Every year, Ebernoe challenges some other village to a match, and while this is being played, a horned sheep is roasted whole in a pit of embers on the edge of the common next to the cricket ground. The head projects well over the end of the pit, so as to prevent damage to the horns. The roasting begins early in the morning on Fair Day, and while it continues visitors to the Fair take it in turns to baste the meat, for this is supposed to be lucky. When the sheep is cooked, it is decapitated. The rival teams enjoy mutton for their lunch; and at the end of the match, the head and horns are awarded as a trophy to the member of the winning team who has scored the most runs.

A Horn Fair of a different sort used to be held at Charlton, in Kent, on St Luke's Day, October 18th. A local proverb declared that 'All's fair at Horn Fair', and this saying was used to cover all kinds of rowdy behaviour, horseplay, and general bawdiness. Horns were everywhere; men wore them on their heads, or carried a pair about, every stall was surmounted by them, even the gingerbread fairings were stamped with them. Men also quite frequently wore women's clothes, and amused themselves by striking women encountered on the fair-ground with sprigs of furze. 'I remember being there upon Horn-Fair Day', wrote William Fuller in his autobiography, 'I was dressed in my landladies best gown, and other women's attire and to Horn Fair we went, and as we were coming back by water, all the cloathes were spoiled by dirty water, etc, that was flung on us in an inundation, for which I was obliged to present her with two guineas to make atonement for the damage sustained.'[1]

A ribald and quite baseless legend ascribes the foundation of the Fair to King John's amours with a local miller's wife, and his subsequent bestowal upon the outraged husband of the right to hold an annual fair, which was at once nicknamed Horn Fair by the miller's envious neighbours. In illustration of this tale, a procession of horn-wearing merrymakers which, until about 1770, used to come from a Bishopsgate inn to Charlton, always contained people disguised as a king, a queen, a miller and his wife, and their attendants. However, history reveals that King John never granted a fair to Charlton, and that one granted by Henry III in 1268 took place at Trinity-tide, and in any case, had ceased before the middle of the seventeenth century. What does seem to be important is the fact that St Luke was the patron saint of the parish, and that the Fair was held on his feast-day, October 18th. Moreover, his emblem is a horned beast – an ox – which would account for the horns until popular imagination and legend-spinning lent them another meaning. It seems likely that the so-called 'fair' was really one of those charterless gatherings that sometimes grew up from the parish Wakes, and often lasted for a considerable time. Charlton's Horn Fair was not abolished until 1872.

1. *Life of Mr William Fuller*, 1703.

Horseshoe and Faggot-cutting Services, London. Two quit-rent services, dating at least as far back as the thirteenth century, are annually rendered by the City of London to the Queen's Remembrancer about the end of October, on a day falling 'between the morrow of St Michael and the morrow of St Martin'. They are rendered in respect of two holdings, one a piece of ground called The Moors at Eardington in Shropshire, and the other a tenement called The Forge in St Clement Danes parish. The exact site of the latter was uncertain for many years, a fact which did not prevent the annual discharge of the service relating to it. Now, however, the discovery of certain entries in the City's ancient documents has shown that the long-vanished Forge must have stood on, or near, the place where Australia House now stands. In the Great Roll of the Exchequer for 1235, it is recorded that one, Walter le Brun, a farrier, was granted land in St Clement's parish on which to build a forge. For this he paid yearly six horseshoes and sixty-one nails. A further entry in the Patent Rolls, 1258–60, mentions the grant of additional land to Walter the Farrier, perhaps the same man, or his son, in what was then known as The Gore, a triangular patch of ground now partly covered by Australia House.

The annual quit-rent ceremony, formerly held in the Court of the Exchequer, now takes place in the Royal Courts of Justice. It begins with the service rendered for The Moors. The 'tenants and occupiers of a piece of waste land called The Moors, in the County of Salop', are called upon to 'come forth and do your service', The City Solicitor, representing the Corporation of London, then cuts a faggot with a hatchet, and another with a billhook, and hands these implements to the Queen's Remembrancer, who acknowledges the work done with the words 'Good Service'. Originally, two knives had to be given, one strong enough to cut a hazel stick of one year's age in half at the first stroke, the other a 'weak knife' that could make little or no mark upon it. At what date, and why, the billhook and hatchet were substituted for these knives is not certainly known.

The tenants of The Forge are then summoned to do their service. The City Solicitor presents six immense horseshoes, pierced for ten nails each, and counts out sixty-one nails of appropriate size. The Queen's Remembrancer says 'Good Number', and the City being now confirmed in its tenancy of these two properties for another year, the ceremony ends. Like the custom itself the horseshoes and nails presented are of great age, perhaps running back to the days when Walter le Brun shod the heavy horses ridden by the Knights Templar at his forge, so conveniently situated near the Temple. They are kept during the year at the office of the Queen's Remembrancer, and are temporarily restored to the City of London representative in time for the October ceremony.

Hot Cross Buns. Eating hot cross buns at breakfast on Good Friday morning is a custom which still flourishes in most English households. Formerly, these round, spiced cakes marked with a cross, eaten hot, were made at home by housewives who rose at dawn for the purpose, or by local bakers who worked through the night to have them ready for delivery to their customers in time for breakfast. In towns, and especially in London, street vendors used to come out early in the mornings, carrying trays or baskets full of hot buns covered by a blanket and white cloth to preserve the heat, and crying as they went:

> Hot Cross Buns!
> One-a-penny, two-a-penny,
> Hot Cross Buns!

They made a cheerful noise which was one of the distinctive sounds of Good Friday. But they vanished from the streets when the bakers who supplied them with their wares ceased to work at night; and now that far fewer women than formerly do their own baking, the bun that appears on the Good Friday breakfast-table has usually been bought on the previous day, and simply re-heated for the meal.

There is an old belief that the true Good Friday bun – that is, one made on the anniversary itself – never goes mouldy, and in fact, if properly made in the traditional manner and kept in a dry place, it very rarely does so. It was once also supposed to have curative powers, especially for ailments like dysentery, diarrhoea, whooping-cough, and the complaint known as 'summer sickness'. Within living memory, it was still quite usual in country districts for a few buns to be set aside each year, hardened in the oven, and hung from the kitchen ceiling until they were needed. When illness came, as much as was necessary was finely grated and mixed with milk or water, to make a medicine which the patient drank. In some areas, powdered buns, mixed in a warm mash, were occasionally given to ailing cattle.

Hot Cross buns have a long ancestry, running backwards into pre-Christian times. Small cakes made of wheaten flour and marked with a cross were eaten in Spring by the pagan Greeks and Romans, particularly at the festival of Diana which was celebrated at the Vernal Equinox. The early Saxons also seem to have eaten similar cakes round about the same March date. The two petrified loaves with a cross on them discovered in the ruins of Herculaneum were almost certainly made for some pagan ritual purpose, for although by A.D. 79 – the year in which Herculaneum was destroyed by volcanic action – there may have been some Christians living in the doomed city, it is not very likely that the loaves were made for them. How soon after the general adoption of Christianity these festive little cakes became customary fare on what was always, and still is, one of the great fast-days of the Church's year is not certain. There is a tradition that something resembling them was given to the poor at St Alban's Abbey on that day in 1361, and that from thence, the custom of eating cakes on Good Friday spread to other places. However, that may be, it is certain that hot cross buns were popular in England[1] by the early eighteenth century, and they have remained so ever since.

1. M. H. Mason mentions hot cross buns at Tenby in the mid-nineteenth century (*Tales and Traditions of Tenby*, 1858), but they do not seem to have been known then in other parts of the Principality. They did not become usual in Scotland until comparatively recent times.

Hunting the Earl of Rone. Until 1837, a lively custom known as Hunting the Earl of Rone was observed on Ascension Day at Combe Martin in Devon. It was supposed to commemorate the capture, in the early seventeenth century, of the 'Earl of Rone', otherwise Hugh O'Neill, Earl of Tyrone. According to local tradition, that Irish nobleman, being outlawed for political offences, attempted to escape to the Continent. His ship was wrecked in the Bristol Channel, but he managed to reach the North Devon coast in a small boat, and landed near Ilfracombe. He then made his way secretly to Combe Martin and hid for several days in Lady's Wood, his only food being some ship's biscuits saved from the wreck. Eventually, however, his presence there became known, and a contingent of Grenadiers was sent to hunt him down. It was this search through the dense woods, and the Earl's subsequent capture, which was re-enacted every year on Ascension Day.

The historical basis of this curious legend is very uncertain. The true Hugh O'Neill, being suspected of treason, did in fact fly to the Continent in September, 1607, together with the Earl of Tyrconnell, who had similar reasons for leaving Ireland. They intended to sail for Spain, but their ship was driven out of its course by storms, and they finally landed in France. From there they went to Rome, where they found refuge. Hugh O'Neill was granted a pension by the Pope, and thereafter lived unharassed by his English enemies until his death in 1616. There is no evidence whatever to suggest that he ever came to Combe Martin, and certainly he was not captured there, or anywhere else. Perhaps some unfounded rumour that he had landed in Devon may have circulated at the time of his flight, or more probably, some other Irish fugitive may have been confused with him. What does seem clear is that his name somehow became entangled with a local festival custom already in existence, and thenceforward the chief figure in the Ascension Day celebration was known as the Earl of Rone.

His part was played by a man wearing a straw-stuffed smock, a grotesque mask, and a necklace of twelve hard sea-biscuits. He was mounted on a flower-garlanded donkey, which also had a string of sea-biscuits round its neck. With the Earl went the Fool and the Hobby-horse. These two were his faithful attendants throughout the day, as well as being the principal collectors of money for the expenses of the celebration, both on the day itself and during the preceding two weeks, when they went round the parish in full dress, visiting every house and gathering as much money as possible. The Fool was masked and gaudily clad; he carried a wet besom which he used for sprinkling water over the spectators. The Hobby-horse was gaily caparisoned, and provided with a formidable pair of snapping jaws, fitted with large teeth, and known as mappers. With these he seized unwilling contributors to the funds and held them until they paid up. The Grenadiers of the legend were represented by a band of men carrying fowling-pieces and wearing tall be-ribboned hats.

At about three o'clock in the afternoon, the Grenadiers marched to Lady's Wood, followed by hundreds of people in holiday clothes who came from all the surrounding parishes to see the fun. After a mock search, they 'discovered' the fugitive in his hiding-place, and fired a volley from their guns. Supposedly wounded by this, the Earl fell to the ground, but was helped up again and remounted, with his face to the donkey's tail by the Fool and the Hobby-horse, who loudly lamented his capture. A long procession of actors and spectators then started on its slow journey towards the sea-shore, about a mile and a half distant, stopping at every public house on the way. As there were a good many of these – in 1837, no less than nine – progress was far from swift. Every so often, the Grenadiers fired another volley, the Earl again fell from his steed, and was once more restored to the saddle by his two companions. Meanwhile, the Fool doused the crowd with water from his besom, and the Hobby-horse ran about, snapping and biting with his strong mappers. Eventually the shore was reached and there, at nightfall, the proceedings ended.

In its later days, this colourful mixture of Spring festival customs and confused history declined into rowdiness. Rough horse-play and a great deal of drunkenness became usual, and this undoubtedly hastened the final eclipse of the celebration. It was last held in 1837, when as a writer in the *Transactions of the Devonshire Association* records, 'there was so much mirth and wild conviviality during the strange procession . . . that most of the principal actors were pretty well done for by the time they had left the third public-house downwards . . .'[1] One man was 'done for' in a literal sense, for he fell from the steps of a house and broke his neck. This serious accident gave power to those who disapproved of the noisy celebration and enabled them to put a stop to it. After 1837, the Earl of Rone was never hunted again.

Hunting the Mallard. Hunting the Mallard is a traditional custom of All Souls' College, Oxford, which is now observed only once in every century, but was formerly an annual ceremony associated with the Feast, or Gaudy, on January 14th. It consists of a ceremonial hunt for the tutelary bird of All Souls, a mallard of great size which, according to legend, was discovered in a drain when the foundations of the College were being laid in 1437. One version of the tale says it was buried there, but another says it was very much alive and, being disturbed by the workmen flew away and was lost. Hence, on Mallard Night, after the feasting had ended, search used to be made for it by all the Fellows, led by an elected Lord Mallard and six officers appointed by him. These officers carried white staves in their hands, and wore medals struck for the occasion, depicting on one side the Lord Mallard and his attendants, and on the other, the Mallard on a long pole. At midnight, the whole company set off in procession, carrying lanterns and torches and singing the Mallard Song, to hunt diligently for their mythical bird in every part of the building, in and out of rooms and closets, along passages, up and down stairs, and out over the leads. The search lasted for several hours, and did not usually end until daybreak.

Exactly when the Mallard was first hunted thus is very uncertain. Tradition says that the custom is nearly as old as the College, and per-

1. *Transactions of the Devonshire Association*, Vol. 59, 1917.

haps it is, but we have no proof of it. The earliest known reference to the famous bird occurs in a letter written by Archbishop Abbot in 1632. In it he complains of a 'great outrage . . . last year committed in your College, where, although matters had formerly been conducted with some distemper, yet men did never before break forth into such intolerable liberty as to tear down doors and gates, and disquiet their neighbours as if it had been a camp or a town in war.' And he adds, 'Civil men should never so far forget themselves under pretence of a foolish mallard, as to do things barbarously unbecoming.'[1] Evidently the celebrations on the previous Mallard Night had developed into something more than ordinarily boisterous. It is clear from this letter that the custom was already flourishing in the early seventeenth century, but how old it was at that time is unknown.[2]

1. Andrew Clark (ed.), *The Colleges of Oxford*, 1892.
2. Montague Burrows, in his *Worthies of All Souls*, 1874, suggests that the whole tradition may not be much older than the late sixteenth or early seventeenth century, and may have sprung from the finding, in a drain on the site, of a thirteenth-century seal, marked with a griffin and the name of William Malard, clerk. He thinks that 'some wit of the College' may have been inspired by this discovery to invent a real Mallard, and a song praising it, and that the Hunt custom followed.

The song sung at the Gaudy and during the Hunt is said to date only from Jacobean or late Elizabethan times, but this proves little, since it may have replaced an earlier one. It has a rather odd chorus, which runs:

> O, by the blood of King Edward,
> O, by the blood of King Edward,
> It was a swapping, swapping Mallard!

No one knows which King Edward is meant, or how he comes into the tradition. Montague Burrows suggests that Edward I, who was honoured in several mediaeval songs is, the most likely. Perhaps this is the same unidentified monarch who is mentioned in a Cumberland wassailling-song wherein the singers ask for the gifts 'we were wont to have in old King Edward's time.' The verses of the Mallard Song make no reference to him and are as follows

> The Griffin, Bustard, Turkey, Capon,
> Let other hungry mortals gape on,
> And on their bones with stomachs fall hard,
> But let All Souls' men have their Mallard.
>
> The Romans once admired a gander
> More than they did their chief Commander,
> Because he saved, if some don't fool us,
> The place that's named from the scull of Tolus.
>
> The poets feign Jove turned a swan,
> But let them prove it if they can,
> As for our proof it's not at all hard,
> He was a swapping, swapping Mallard.
>
> Then let us drink and dance a Galliard
> Unto the memory of the Mallard,
> And as the Mallard doth in pool,
> Let's dabble, duck and dive in bowl.

Hunting the Mallard has had its ups and downs, like many other old customs. On January 18th, 1722, Thomas Hearne recorded in his *Diary* that:

'Last Monday, the 14th inst. (the 14th being always the day) was All Souls College Mallard, at which time 'tis usual with the Fellows and their friends to have a supper and sit up all night drinking and singing. Their song is the Mallard, and formerly they used to ramble about the College with sticks and poles, etc. in quest of the Mallard, and they had a Lord of the Mallard, but this hath been left off many years.'

However, the Hunt which was obsolete in 1722 must have been revived later, for in a letter dated January 15th, 1801, Bishop Heber, then in residence at Brasenose, described how he watched it from his window in the small hours of the morning. 'I write', he said:

'under the bondage of a very severe cold, which I caught by getting out of bed at four in the morning to see the celebration of the famous All Souls Mallard feast. All Souls is on the opposite side of Ratcliffe Square to Brazen Nose, so that their battlements are in some degree commanded by my garret. I had thus a full view of the *Lord Mallard* and about forty fellows in a kind of procession on the library roof, with immense lighted torches, which had a singular effect. I know not if their orgies were overlooked by any uninitiated eyes except my own; but I am sure that all who had the gift of hearing within half a mile, must have been awakened by the manner in which they thundered their chorus, "O, by the blood of King Edward".'[1]

Since then, it has become an established tradition that the Mallard is hunted with full ceremony only at the beginning of every century. The last occasion on which this took place was January 14th, 1901, and the next will be on the same night in 2001.

Hunting the Wren. The ritual hunting of the wren on a traditional day round about the Winter Solstice is a custom of great antiquity which still survives in Ireland and, in an attenuated form, in the Isle of Man. Until well into the nineteenth century, it also flourished in Wales, in some parts of France, and in a number of English counties, particularly in the south and west. It does not seem to have existed in Scotland, except at Kirkmaiden in Galloway, where a ceremony called the Deckan' o' the Wren took place on New Year's morning. Gangs of boys used to go out searching for wrens; when they caught one they adorned its neck and legs with ribbons, and then let it go free.[2]

1. *Life of Bishop Heber*, By his wife.

2. E. A. Armstrong (*The Folklore of Birds*, 1958) suggests that the Kirkmaiden custom was not native to that area, but had been imported at some time from the Isle of Man, a region with which the Galloway smugglers had close connections.

Elsewhere in Scotland, small birds and other wild creatures were often hunted at daybreak on January 1st, but this custom was not connected with the ceremonial Wren Hunt of other areas. It sprang from the once widespread Scottish belief that blood must be shed on the first day of the year, or bad luck would follow. The victim in this case did not have to be a wren. The first fish caught at sea, a domestic fowl killed for the festival dinner, or any bird, hare, or rabbit shot in the open would do, so long as its blood was shed early on New Year's Day. Walter Gregor records how, on the north-east coast, men and boys went out in large numbers, 'gun in hand, along the shore before daybreak, in search of some bird or wild animal, no matter how small, that they may draw blood and thus make sure of one year's good fortune.'[1]

The ritual nature of the true Wren Hunt is evident from the fact that its central feature was the ceremonial and public performance, in order to ensure good luck and avert evil, of an act which would have been thought extremely ill-omened at any other time. In folk-tradition, the wren was the King of the Birds, and like the robin and the swallow, it was sacred and must never be killed or harmed. It was widely believed and still is in some districts, that serious misfortune would befall any who injured these birds, destroyed their nests, or stole their eggs. In Cornwall it is said that whoever hunts the robin or the wren will 'never prosper, boy or man', and similar warnings exist elsewhere. Yet once a year, in the Christmas season,[2] the wren was vigorously hunted by men and boys armed with sticks or guns, and its corpse was afterwards carried about with ceremony upon a pole, or a garland, or a miniature bier, or inside a decorated and glass-ended box.

1. Revd. W. Gregor, *Notes and Queries*, Vol. IV, quoted in *British Calendar Customs*: Scotland, Vol. II, ed. M. M. Banks, 1939.

2. In Suffolk, the Wren Hunt took place on St Valentine's Day, and in Warwickshire, at any time during the winter. In France, at one time, wrens were sometimes caught alive for use as tribute during the *Bachelleries* held in early summer. Elsewhere, the hunt and procession usually occurred on various dates between Christmas Eve and Twelfth Night, often on St Stephen's Day, which in some areas was known as Wrenning Night.

The hunt did not end everywhere in the death of the bird. We have already seen that the Kirkmaiden wren was set free after being decked with ribbons. In Pembrokeshire, a caged bird was sometimes carried round on Twelfth Night by a boy who invited those to whom he showed it to 'make your offerings to the smallest, yet the king', and then released it. Or, in the same county, a living wren might be put into a small box with glass ends, called a Wren House, and taken to various houses, especially those of young couples who had been married during the previous year. In most districts, however, the bird was killed, and it was the carcase that was ceremonially paraded. Different versions of the song sung during the procession described how it must be slain 'with sticks and stones', or 'with great guns and cannons', and, in a Pembrokeshire Wren-song, how the little corpse must then be cut up 'with hatchets and cleavers' before it is boiled 'in brass pans and cauldrons'.

Round Tenby, the wren was sometimes carried in a Wren-house fixed by its corners to poles, and borne by four men who acted as though their minute burden was almost more than they could carry. In Devonshire, and at Le Ciotat, near Marseilles, the corpse was slung from the centre of a stout pole carried on the shoulders of two men who also walked as though overburdened by its weight. Elsewhere too, the idea of immense size and heaviness was conveyed either by action or by the words of the song. Harrison, writing in the middle of last century, remarks that 'it is a singular fact, that wherever we find this peculiar custom prevailing, it is always attended with appliances, as if the object sought for was one of extraordinary bulk or weight instead of being one of the most diminutive of our feathered tribe . . . it may, perhaps, be accounted for by the desire to render every homage to so important a personage as "the king of all birds" . . .'[1]

At Carcassonne, in France, where the Wren Boys went hunting during the last days of December, he who first killed one of these royal birds was himself hailed as King, and carried his victim home in triumph upon a pole. On New Year's Eve, a long procession, including the King and his fellow-hunters, torchbearers, and musicians, wound through the streets, halting every now and then to chalk *Vive le Roi* and the New Year date upon the doors of houses. At Epiphany, the King, robed, crowned, and bearing a sceptre, went in state to High Mass in the parish church, with the wren carried before him on a garlanded pole. Later in the day, he and his followers visited the Bishop and the town dignitaries, and received gifts of money to pay for a banquet and dance in the evening. These ceremonies, perhaps the most elaborate of all recorded Wren Hunt customs, were finally suppressed about 1830.

In the Isle of Man also, the first to kill a wren on St Stephen's Day was honoured, if not as a king, at least as leader for the time being, and as one who would have good luck throughout the year. The dead bird was carried round the township between the two hoops of a beribboned garland, or upon a long pole, also decorated with ribbons and sometimes with a fluttering handkerchief which served as a banner. Dr Clague says that the pole, or stick, was borne by two boys, and that there was a third lad in attendance who 'was covered with a net, and his face made black, and a bunch of leeks tied together to make a tail behind his back.'[1] The feathers were sold, or given away, as charms against evil. In coastal parishes, the bird was often taken on board the herring-boats to bring luck to the fishing, and single feathers were kept by the seamen to preserve them from shipwreck. At one time it seems to have been customary, at least in some districts to bury the denuded carcase at the day's end in the churchyard, or sometimes on the sea-shore. Now all that remains of the Manx ceremonies is the annual appearance of little bands consisting of three or four boys, who go from house to house, singing the Wren Song, and collecting coppers from the householders. One carries a green garland upon a pole, the others usually, though not always, bear staves adorned with leaves, flowers, and ribbons. But the wren which their garland ought to enclose is missing, and only the words of their traditional song indicate why

1. W. Harrison, Mona Miscellany No. 1, *Manx Society Publications*, Vol. XVI, 1869.

1. Dr John Clague, *Manx Reminiscences*, 1911.

they have come. It is a long time now since any bird was hunted on the island for the ritual of St Stephen's Day.

In southern Ireland,[1] the Wren Hunt still retains a good deal of its early vigour. The wren is hunted along the hedges by parties of boys and young men, armed with sticks, and is then carried about in a ribbon-trimmed bush, or a garland, or on a cross of sticks, and sometimes in a box or other container. Occasionally more than one wren is so paraded or, if none can be found, some other small bird may be caught instead; in a few districts, where bird-killing for this purpose is frowned upon, a potato carved to look like a wren and stuck with feathers may be substituted for the real thing.

The Wren Boys go round the village, dressed in grotesque costumes and fanciful head-dresses, singing or reciting a version of the Wren Song which, even in Irish-speaking areas, is almost always given in English. Other songs may be sung as well, and at some of the houses visited, the Boys dance. Music is supplied by two or three players upon the drum and the whistle. In some regions, the ritual is more elaborate, and a form of folk-play is, or was, acted. The Wren Boys are still regarded as luck-bringers, and as such they are usually welcome visitors. Food and drink are generously given to them at most houses, and also gifts of money which they spend on some sort of jollification In the evening of St Stephen's Day.

Various legends are told to account for the Wren Hunt in the places where this curious custom is, or was, known. Most are concerned with some sort of betrayal by the bird. When Our Lord hid in the Garden of Gethsemane, the wren revealed His whereabouts by its notes. Similarly when St Stephen was trying to escape the bird alighted on the gaoler's face and so aroused him. When the Irish were secretly converging on the Danes, or according to another version, upon Cromwell's forces, their enemies were awakened by a wren hopping on a drum. But these tales, and others like them are mere rationalizations of a ritual that appears to be older than Christianity, and probably originally from ancient notions connected with the periodic sacrifice of the divine king.

> The wren, the wren, the king of all birds,
> On St Stephen's Day was caught in the furze,

runs an Irish Wren-song, and it was perhaps because of this royal character that this little bird, which was sacred and protected at other times of the year, was thus ceremoniously slain and paraded on a date round about the ominous turn of the year in Winter.

1. The Wren Hunt appears to be unknown in Ulster today, and records of its existence there in the past are very few.

Hurling. (*See Shrovetide Football.*)

Jack-in-the-Green. Jack-in-the-Green is that very ancient figure who represents one aspect of the Summer, as the Lord and Lady, or the May Queen represents another. As Green George, or the Wild Man, his counterparts exist all over Europe. In England, he takes the form of a man encased in a high wickerwork cage which completely covers him, and is in its turn entirely smothered in green branches, leaves, and flowers. Only his eyes are visible, looking through a hole cut in the cage to enable him to see, and his feet below the level of the wickerwork. He is part of the traditional May procession, or was so once; he still is at Knutsford, in Cheshire, during their splendid celebration known as the Royal Festival May Day. Sometimes he used go to about alone, with only a few attendants and a musician or two, as he was still doing at Witney when P. H. Ditchfield wrote about him in 1896.[1] But wherever he is found, he is always the Summer itself, the very old bringer-in of the time of plenty, and as such he belongs to every part of the community.

In England, however, he has rather curiously become associated with the chimney-sweeps of London and the larger towns, so that his wide rural connections tend to be forgotten. In the latter half of the eighteenth century, the sweeps kept May Day as their holiday, and celebrated it by a street procession, of which Jack-in-the-Green was the principal character. There was also a Lord and a Lady, sometimes a Fool, or a Clown, black-faced boys carrying shovels and brushes, men carrying money-boxes, and dancers dressed in gaily be-ribboned clothes. These sweeps' processions were at one time very popular, but after 1840, when Parliament forbade the employment of young lads as chimney-climbers they began to decline, and slowly died towards the end of the century.

1. P. H. Ditchfield, *Old English Customs Extant at the Present Time*, 1896.

Jethart Ba'. Jethart Ba', the traditional handball-game of Jedburgh in Roxburghshire, is played every year on Candlemas Day and again on Fastern's E'en. The date of the Candlemas Ba' is, of course, fixed on February

2nd, but that of the Fastern's E'en game is variable. The name Fastern's E'en, meaning the Eve of the Lenten fast, is commonly applied to Shrove Tuesday throughout Lowland Scotland and the English northern counties; but in Jedburgh, the anniversary is not reckoned by the normal ecclesiastical calendar, but an old rhyme which says:

First comes Candlemas,
Then the new moon,
The First Tuesday after
Is aye Fastern's E'en.

Thus the second of Jedburgh's festival games may be played on Shrove Tuesday in some years, but in others it may take place on another date.

Jethart Ba' is a vigorous form of handball, played through the town streets between shop- and house-windows that have been carefully barricaded beforehand. It sometimes overflows into gardens, and usually reaches the River Jed, where a great deal of splashing and 'dooking' occurs. The balls used are decorated with coloured streamers, and are thrown, run away with, 'smuggled' from hand to hand, but never kicked. Originally the game was a wild type of football, but in 1704, the Town Council forbade 'the tossing and throwing up of the football at Fastern's E'en within the streets of the burgh' because this had 'many times tended to the great prejudice of the inhabitants . . . there have been sometymes both old and young near lost their lives thereby'. Football having been thus prohibited, handball was, after an interval, substituted for it.

There are two sides, the Uppies, or men born above the site of the Mercat Cross, who play towards the Castle Hill where they have their 'hail', and the Downies, or downwards men, who play towards the Townfoot. If of late years, it cannot be said that any have 'near lost their lives thereby', Jethart Ba' remains an extremely strenuous game, which cheerfully disrupts the life of the town on both the days concerned. In 1849, the Burgh authorities attempted to suppress it altogether by prohibiting the play and fining several of the most prominent players. But Jedburgh people were not to be so easily deprived of their traditional sport, and appealing to the High Court of Edinburgh, they secured a ruling that the right to play the game in the streets of the town was sanctioned by immemorial usage.

A local legend says that the custom began in the days of Border Warfare when, after a fight at Ferniehurst Castle, the victorious Scots played football with the severed heads of their English enemies. This is a fine bloodthirsty tale, still half-believed in the district. In fact, ball-games of various kinds have been played at Shrovetide from 'time out of mind', in England as well as in Scotland, and in the latter country, also at Candlemas and on the variable Fastern's E'en observed in Jedburgh. Jethart Ba' is now perhaps the best known of the northern celebrations because, as the Official Guide to the Burgh proudly states: 'Alone among the towns of Scotland, Jedburgh continues to celebrate the coming of Candlemas by the playing of the ba'; and at Fastern's E'en, Jethart Ba' possesses pride of place among the contests annually played at various places on the Borders'.

Kellums. In Kidderminster formerly, the election of the Bailiff on Michaelmas Day was marked by a very peculiar custom. This was the Lawless Hour, also known as Kellums, during which the whole town was given over to a wild sort of disorderly merriment. Between the end of the retiring Bailiff's term of office and the beginning of that of his successor, there was a kind of pause in government, and the townspeople took full advantage of it. The town bell was rung as a signal, and the streets filled with crowds of people, all engaged in the cheerful occupation of throwing cabbage-stalks at each other. Then the Bailiff-elect set out upon a ceremonial visit to his predecessor, accompanied by the rest of the Corporation and a drum-and-fife band, and also, less comfortably, by an unruly mob of hilarious citizens. These followed the procession, shouting, and pelting the Bailiff and the rest with apples. The *Gentleman's Magazine* for 1790 remarks that 'the most respectable families in the town' took part in this odd custom, apparently joining in the apple-throwing with as much vigour and enthusiasm as any one. 'I have known' says the contributor to the *Gentleman's Magazine*, 'forty pots of apples expended at one house.' The only explanation of this riotous custom known to the citizens of Kidderminster appears to have been that it had always been done, 'time out of memory of man'. It did not, however, survive the eighteenth century, and was abolished just before its end.

Kissing-Bough. *(See Christmas Tree.)*

Knillian. The Knillian (or Knillian-games, as it is sometimes called) is a celebration held every five years at St Ives in Cornwall on July 25th, the Feast of St James the Great. It was founded by John Knill, once Collector of Customs in that district, who in 1797 drew up a complicated deed of trust whereby certain monies were settled upon the Mayor and Burgesses of the borough for the provision of doles to various types of poor people at five-yearly intervals. The deed also provided for the perpetual upkeep of the Mausoleum, now known as Knill's Steeple, which he had built in 1782 on the top of Worvas Hill. This is a triangular granite pyramid, fifty feet high, which can be seen for miles and serves as a landmark for seamen. Knill intended it to be his tomb, but in the end he was not buried in it. Difficulties about consecration arose, and when he died in 1811, being then in London, he was laid by his own wish in St Andrew's Church, Holborn.

The trust provided for a number of different doles. £5 was to be divided among ten little girls, not more than ten years old and all children of seamen or tinners, who were to go on the appointed day to the Mausoleum and dance there for not less than fifteen minutes, and then sing the *Old Hundredth* to the tune used in the parish church in Knill's time. They were required to wear white cockades, and so was the fiddler who played for them and received £1 for his services. £2 was to be paid to two widows, aged sixty-four or upwards, who accompanied the children and had to 'certify to the trustees that the ceremonies have been

duly performed.' £5 went to the married couple, widow, or widower, sixty years old, or more, who had raised the largest family of legitimate children without receiving help from the parish, a like sum to the best knitter of fishing-nets, and to the best curer and packer of pilchards for export, and £2 10s. 0d. each to the two follower-boys judged to have behaved most excellently in the previous fishing-season. £10 was to serve as a wedding-portion for a girl whose marriage had taken place within a stated period,[1] and who was deemed by the trustees 'to be most worthy, regard being had to her duty and kindness to her parents, or to her friends who shall have brought her up'. There were also other gifts, including contributions to the funds of local Friendly Societies, and £10 to provide a dinner for the trustees.[2]

The Knillian was first celebrated in 1801, when its founder was still alive, and it has been kept up ever since. Certain alterations have had to be made in the payments, for the decline of the pilchard fishery has done away with the follower-boys, and the best packer of pilchards has had to be replaced by the best packer of any kind of fish. In general, however, the awards and the ceremonies remain more or less unchanged.

Knillian-day is a festival in St Ives. Hundreds of people come to see the children dance, and watch the presentation of the money to the various beneficiaries. Between ten and eleven o'clock in the morning, a long procession winds its way up the steep hill to the Mausoleum. In it walk the Mayor and town officials in their robes of office, the trustees, two sergeants-at-mace, the father of the longest family, and others who are to receive gifts, the white-cockaded fiddler, and the ten little girls in their white dresses and rosettes. The monument is danced round, the *Old Hundredth* and *Shall Trelawney Die?* are sung, not only by the children but by all present, and the Mayor calls upon the two widows to bear witness that everything has been done according to the founder's wish. When they have done so, the little girls receive ten shillings each, and the rest of the money is distributed. Then the procession re-forms and, led by the fiddler, goes down the hill into the town, not to be seen again for another five years. The last occasion on which the Knillian was held was in 1971 and it will be due again in 1981.

Knollys Rose Ceremony. An ancient quit-rent service, revived in 1924 by the Revd. T. B. Clayton, who was then Vicar of All-Hallows-by-the-Tower, Barking, is now rendered annually on Midsummer Day to the Lord Mayor of London. In the fourteenth century, Sir Robert Knollys (or Knolles), a distinguished soldier in his time, owned two houses standing opposite to each other in Seething Lane, a narrow thoroughfare in the City of London. To join these two properties together, he built a hautpas, or gallery, between them bestriding the street. A licence to do this was granted to him, and to his wife, Constance, by the City Corporation in 1381, in return for which he was required to render annually to the Mayor and Corporation one red rose at Midsummer.

This was clearly a straightforward rose-rent, of which many other examples can be found in different parts of the country. A curious legend

1. Between the previous December 31st and the day following the Knillian.

2. M. A. Courtney, *Cornish Feasts and Folk-Lore*, 1890.

seems, however, to have grown up about this perfectly ordinary transaction. It is quite often said that the rose was a penalty imposed upon Sir Robert for building the hautpas without prior permission given, and also, since there is nothing particularly onerous in producing one red rose in the middle of June, that the Corporation purposely made the penalty easy because of the very valuable services which Sir Robert had already rendered to his country in the wars. There does not seem to be any clear evidence for this tale, nor are its details very likely. The rose-payment was duly made for a number of years and then ceased at some uncertain date, as it may well have done if and when the houses concerned were demolished. Since it was restored in 1924, it is customary for the rose to be carried on a velvet cushion by the Churchwardens of All-Hallows-by-the-Tower (or sometimes by some other chosen person), and presented to the Lord Mayor at the Mansion House.

Lamb Ales. Lamb Ales were formerly held on Trinity Monday in the three Oxfordshire parishes of Kidlington, Eynsham, and Kirtlington. They do not seem to have been recorded elsewhere, though other customs are known in which a lamb played a principal part, nor were they celebrated in exactly the same way in all three places. In Blount's *Ancient Tenures* (ed. 1784), there is an account of the Kidlington ceremony, from which we learn that a live lamb was chased by the village girls, who had their thumbs tied together behind their backs and were required to catch their quarry with their mouths. She who succeeded in this rather difficult feat was proclaimed the Lady of the Lamb. The poor animal was then killed, and its dressed carcase, 'with the skin hanging on', was carried in procession on a long pole, followed by the Lady and her companions, musicians, and Morris-dancers. The rest of the day was spent in merrymaking and dancing, and on the morrow the lamb was eaten at a feast over which the Lady presided.

The Eynsham custom was much the same, except that there the Lady was chosen beforehand from among the prettiest girls of the village. She then had to catch the lamb; but the fact that she was apparently expected to do so without difficulty suggests that the thumb-tying may have been omitted. During the procession, the carcase was drawn by a team of horses, with the Lady riding on the foremost horse at the head of the parade.

At Kirtlington, the ceremonies were much more elaborate, and also more interesting. In his *History of Kirtlington*, H. W. Taunt says that the Lamb Ale there was originally held at Easter, or Whitsuntide, but was later transferred to Trinity Monday, which is still the day of the Village Feast. This was the beginning of a lively holiday lasting for eight or nine days, during which there were several processions, dancing, visits by the local Morris-Men to nearby villages, and a great drinking of ale which was sold without a licence in a shed constructed of green branches and known as the Bowery.

A popular young man was elected as Lord of the feast, and he and his friends chose the Lady, who was paid twenty-five shillings for her services during the first three days. Taunt says that as well as being pretty, she had to be of unblemished reputation, for 'only a good and modest girl was chosen for the very important office.'[1] On the Monday, Tuesday, and Wednesday of Trinity Week, she and the Lord took part in processions round the parish, their clothes decked with pink and blue ribbons, and both carrying a Mace as a badge of office. This was a short staff surmounted by a square board, from the four corners of which sprang two semi-circular hoops crossing in the centre. The whole Mace was covered with pink and blue silk, and adorned with rosettes and long ribbon streamers. Behind the Lord and Lady in the procession came the Fool, dressed in motley, who belaboured the bystanders with a bladder and a cow's tail fixed at opposite ends of a long pole, six Morris-men and their musicians,

1. H. W. Taunt, *op. cit.*

and two men carrying 'Forest Feathers', which were wooden clubs decorated with flowers, leaves, and ribbons.

The leader of the whole parade was the lamb, carried on a man's shoulders. It had to be the finest of the flock, and if possible, the first-born of the season. For three days, it was borne about the parish admired, and treated with the deference due to the traditional sacrificial victim; then, like its Kidlington and Eynsham fellows, it perished. That, at least, was the theory, and probably the fact also at one time, but in the later years of the custom, the lamb of the procession often escaped death precisely because it was the best in the village. It was quietly returned to the fold, and a less valuable beast was killed in its stead. The flesh was then cooked and made into pies, which were cut up and distributed to all and sundry as luck-bringers.[1] Only the Head-Pie, which contained the head with the wool left on it, was never given away. It was supposed to be a more powerful source of good fortune than the rest, and had to be bought, undivided, for not less than a shilling.

With the death of the lamb and the shared eating of its flesh in the pies, the main ceremonies of the Lamb Ale were over. The remaining five or six days were spent in dancing, drinking, and general merrymaking. The Morris-men went round each day to all the villages within reach, sometimes covering long distances, to perform and collect money, part of which was spent each night in the Bowery, and the rest used for the expenses of the feast and the upkeep of the Morris properties. The Lady's chief duties ceased with the processions, though she was still treated with the respect due to her exalted position, but the Lord continued to act as leader until the holiday ended, and the revellers returned at last to work.

1. Small 'Crown Cakes', made of rich currant dough, with a centre of minced meat and batter, were also luck-bringers. They were taken round during the feast by the Lord and the Morris-dancers, displayed to the people in return for a money-payment, or sold outright. The buyers often kept a slice throughout the year as a protective charm.
(Percy Manning, 'Lamb Ale at Kirlington', *Folk-Lore* Vol. 8, 1897).

At Kidlington and Eynsham, the Lamb Ales had gone by the beginning of last century, but the Kirtlinton Ale survived until 1958. Then it, too, ended; and today its memory is preserved only in the so-called Lamb Ale held in that village on Trinity Monday. It bears little resemblance to its colourful predecessors, and is in fact simply a modified version of the old Club Day. There is a morning service in the parish church, a dinner at which roast lamb is the traditional main dish, a cricket match in the afternoon, and games and dancing in the evening. But there is no dedicated lamb, no Morris-dancing, and no Lord and Lady, and only the name of the feast lives on, to remind Kirtlington people of their forefathers' ways, and to make this vestigial Club Day a little different from its surviving fellows.

Lammas Corn. On Lammas Day, August 1st, or on the Sunday nearest to it, new corn is once again brought into many parish churches, as it was into mediaeval churches before the Reformation. This is a revival of an ancient custom, long obsolete and forgotten until about thirty years ago, whereby the first new corn of the year, or bread made from it, used to be offered on the altar as a thanksgiving for the first-fruits of the harvest. It was not concerned with the splendid ingathering of later in the season, and indeed, nothing that we should actually recognize as a Harvest Festival in the modern sense seems to have been known in the Middle Ages. Rejoicing there was for corn saved and garnered, and plenty of it, but it was all very cheerfully pagan. It was at Lammas that Christian thanks began to be offered up. The word is said to be derived from the Anglo-Saxon *hlafmaesse*, meaning 'loaf-mass', the feast on which the bread of the Sacrament could first be made from the year's newly-ripened corn.

Lammas is a Quarter Day in Scotland and a cross-Quarter Day in England, and in both, at least in some districts, a day for the payment of half-yearly rents. It was also the day on which Lammas Lands, that is, those belonging to the community and let to individuals during the summer, reverted to the community. Before the coming of Christianity, it was the great feast of Lugh Long-hand, the sun-god of the Celts, when games, contests, marriages, fairs, and feasts of many kinds were celebrated and, coming full cycle through the changing religions, the beginning of the harvest.

Lawless Courts. A curious manorial custom survived at Rochford, in Essex, until nearly the end of last century. This was the meeting of the Court known as the Great Lawless Court, which belonged to the Honour of Rayleigh, and was originally held at Rayleigh before it was transferred to Rochford. It took place at cock-crow on the Wednesday morning following Michaelmas Day, in a field called King's Hill which was said to have been named after the original meeting-place at Rayleigh. The Steward and the tenants came in the morning darkness to a white-painted post in the field, round which the business of the Court was transacted. No one was allowed to carry a lighted lantern, but as much illumination as was absolutely necessary was provided by a single torch-bearer. The Steward called the tenants' names in a whisper and was answered in the same way, and the rents and other dues were paid in almost complete silence. 'They are all to whisper to each other', wrote Philip Morant in 1768,[1] 'nor have they any pen and ink, but supply that office with a coal.' Non-attendance was punished by severe fines.

The age and origin of this strange custom does not seem to be known. At one time, a similar meeting was held at Hocktide also, and was known as Little Lawless Court, but this vanished long before the Michaelmas gathering. Another Lawless Court existed formerly at Epping, and met under a maple tree between the church and Eppingbury. It has been suggested that the post at Rochford, and earlier at Rayleigh, may have preserved the memory of a tree round which the two Courts, Little and Great, may once have met. The term 'Lawless' in this connection is said to be due to the unlawful hour of meeting.

There is no doubt that in its hey-day, this Court, and the others like it, were entirely serious gatherings, as the Knightlow Cross pre-sunrise meeting at Martinmas is today. *(See Wroth Silver.)* But the Great Lawless Court seems to have lived a little too long, and in its last years, it degenerated into a mere revel, with cock-crowing and lantern-carrying, and little attempt to observe the old rules of darkness and silence. It was no longer taken seriously and finally lapsed, unregretted, by the end of the nineteenth century.

Lilies and Roses. On May 21st every year, Eton College and King's College, Cambridge, honour the memory of their founder, Henry VI, who died very suddenly, and was almost certainly murdered, in the Tower of London on that day in 1471. He is generally supposed to have been killed whilst at prayer in the Oratory of the Wakefield Tower, and here, on the anniversary, the Ceremony of the Lilies and Roses now takes place. Representatives of both colleges walk in procession with Beefeaters and the Chaplain of the Tower, and a short service is conducted by the latter, during which a prayer composed by Henry himself is said. A marble tablet in the Oratory marks the place

1. Philip Morant, *The History & Antiquities of the County of Essex*, 1768.

where the King is believed to have died, and on each side of it flowers are laid – lilies from Eton bound with pale blue silk, and white roses from King's College, bound with purple ribbon. They are left there for twenty-four hours, and then they are burnt.

Lion Sermon. On October 16th every year, a sermon known as the Lion Sermon is preached in the Church of St Katharine Cree in London, in accordance with the will of Sir John Gayer, who died in 1649. He was a London merchant who was Lord Mayor of that city in 1646 and 1647, and suffered imprisonmnent in the latter year for his bold refusal to subsidise Parliamentary troops from the City funds. The sermon commemorates his escape from deadly peril when on one of his trading expeditions into far countries, he somehow became separated from his companions and, alone and unarmed, suddenly came face to face with a lion. In this extremity, remembering Daniel, he fell on his knees and prayed earnestly for deliverance. His prayer was answered; the lion looked at him and turned away, leaving him unharmed. As a thank-offering for that miraculous escape, he afterwards gave money for a number of charitable purposes, and also provided for the annual preaching of a sermon in St Katharine Cree on the anniversary of his adventure. This sermon, now more than three hundred years old, is still regularly preached upon that date unless it falls on a Sunday, when it is transferred to the nearest weekday.

Lot Meadow Mowing. The custom known as Lot Meadow Mowing is an ancient method of apportioning strips of grassland which is still in use at Yarnton, in Oxfordshire, as it has been for centuries. Two meadows called West Mead and Pixey Mead are divided into lot-strips of varying size, and once a year, lots are drawn for them by freeholders of Yarnton, Wolvercote, and Begbroke who own the mowing-rights. Until a few years ago, another meadow, Oxhay, was similarly divided; but when the Witney by-pass was made, the various owners were bought out, (with some difficulty), to allow the passage of the road. What remained of the land was sold to the Lord of the Manor, and Oxhay is not now included in the annual lot-drawing.

The owners of the mowing-rights may, if they wish, sell their hay in advance, and for this purpose, an auction is held at the Grapes Inn on the Monday after St Peter's Day (June 29th), or as near to it as the state of the crop permits. In the following week, on a day fixed by the Head Meadsman, who is in charge of the proceedings, the lessees, or those who have bought the hay from them, go to the meadows, where they are met by the Meadsmen. All the strips are marked with stakes, with the exception of the Tydals, which are marked with stones. These are the portions that have been permanently assigned to the Rectories of Yarnton and Begbroke in lieu of tithes, and do not, therefore, change hands at the lot-drawing.

The Head Meadsman carries a bag containing thirteen very old wooden balls, known as Mead Balls. On each there is a name – Gilbert, Harry, White, Boat, William, Rothe, Walter Jeoffrey, Freeman, Green, Dunn, Perry, Boulton, and Watery Molly. Each ball represents a certain acreage, or a specified quantity of the whole acreage, reckoned by a complicated system of measurement in which the term 'a man's mowth', that is, as much as one man can mow in a single day, is used. The exact situation of the land so represented varies from year to year, in order that all shall take their turn with the poor as well as the better parts of the meadows.

The drawing begins at eight o'clock in the morning. For each lot, or part of a lot, to which a claimant may be entitled by the terms of his lease, or that of the man who sold him the mowing-rights for that year, a ball is drawn from the bag. Some of the grass is then cut with a few sweeps of the scythe, and the initials of the man to whom the lot has fallen are cut on the ground. This process is repeated until all the strips have been apportioned. Formerly a number of men used to 'run the treads', that is, mark the boundaries between strips by running quickly up and down them, shuffling their feet as they went. Today, this part of the work is done by tractors. As soon as the lot-drawing is ended, mowing begins.

Until the beginning of last century, it was customary to mow each meadow in a single day, and to celebrate the end of the work by general merrymaking. Farmers' wives provided their husbands' workers with specially-made plum puddings for a mowing-feast; there was a sort of unofficial 'fair', and various races, of which the most important was the race for the Garland. A garland of traditional type was annually provided to be run for; after the race, the winner placed it in the parish church, and it was allowed to hang there until the next Lot Meadow Mowing came round. These simple festivities eventually became rowdy and disorderly. In order to keep to the one-day time-table, labourers from elsewhere had to be employed in considerable numbers; in some years, as many as a hundred, or more, poured into the village, as well as idlers who came to drink and amuse themselves at the 'fair'. Fights and disturbances became common; and finally, in 1817, after a man had been killed in a riot, the mowing-time for each meadow was extended to three days, thereby eliminating the need for outside helpers, and reducing the size of the visiting crowds. In the course of time, the 'fair', the plum-pudding feast, and the race for the Garland all died out, and today, the Lot Meadow Mowing is a matter of straight farming business, without any general holiday associations.

Lucia Day. The Feast of St Lucia (or Lucy) falls on December 13th. In some parts of Europe, it is celebrated as a festival of light and fire, and as a day when young people practise divination to see what the year will bring them. It never seems to have been so observed in Great Britain[1], but in Scandinavian countries, especially Sweden, it marks the beginning of the Christmas season, and is known as Lucia Day, or as Little Yule. Except for the fact that her name means 'light', there is little or nothing in St Lucy's legend to account for the traditional customs of her feast. She is not, however, the only Christian saint who has been drawn, by a coincidence of dates, into the orbit of Yule and the pagan festival of the Winter Solstice; and in her case it is significant that, before the Gregorian reform of the calendar, her anniversary fell on the shortest day, a fact still remembered in the old jingle, 'Lucy-light, shortest day and longest night'.

In many Swedish villages still, a young girl is chosen to be the Lucia Queen, or Lucia Bride. She wears a white dress and a red sash, both symbolizing light and fire, and she is crowned before sunrise with a coronet of whortleberry-twigs containing seven or nine burning candles. Thus attired, she sets out while it is still dark to carry food and drink to every house in the parish, and also to visit stables and cow-byres, so that animals as well as human beings may share in the promise of lengthening days and greater plenty that she brings. With her goes a company of miscellaneous attendants. The procession is usually headed by a man on horseback who is supposed to represent St Stephen. The Lucia Queen herself follows next, on foot, and behind her come maids-of-honour bearing lighted candles, star-boys, lads dressed as old men with red beards, or as Biblical characters, and some masked trolls and demons of terrifying aspects who represent the evils of Winter, soon to be driven out by the reviving sun. Traditionally, the Lucia Queen's visits drive away misfortune and bring good luck and prosperity; and if, perhaps, this is not now quite as firmly believed as it once was, it is still considered a bad omen if any house is accidentally or deliberately omitted from her round.

Some families have their own Lucia Queen, who is often the youngest daughter. She, like her opposite number in the villages, is dressed in white and wears a flaming candle-crown. Very early in the morning – once at first cock-crow, between one and four o'clock, but now more usually at six o'clock – she wakes her sleeping relatives with coffee and the singing of a traditional song, and carries extra food to whatever animals may be attached to the household. Later, she sits in the place of honour at a special breakfast, served in a room as brilliantly illuminated as possible, and when she gets to school, she will probably find the same

1. Nevertheless, it has become familiar in some British cities because of the presence of Scandinavian settlers.

bright lights, for in many Swedish districts, the schools are illuminated on Lucia-morning as well as the houses.

In Sicily, St Lucy's Day is, or was, kept as a fire-festival also. Here the saint is at home for she was a Sicilian girl who was martyred at Syracuse in A.D. 304. There are no Lucia Queens or symbolic food-gifts for men and animals, but there are fire-bearing processions in which a statue of the saint is sometimes carried. Young men run through the streets with flaming brands; bonfires blaze in the by-lanes and gardens, and in some villages, a huge central mound of straw is set alight, and the people dance round it.

In Austria, formerly, witches were believed to be specially powerful on St Lucy's Eve, as they were in England on Hallowe'en and May Eve. Incense was often burnt in the houses to defeat them. A mysterious light, called the *Luzieschein*, was supposed to appear out-of-doors at midnight, and those who had the courage to watch for it could foretell the future from its varying forms. In Denmark, on the same night, young girls tried to induce dreams of their future husbands by saying, just before they went to bed:

> Sweet St. Lucy, let me know
> Whose cloth I shall lay,
> Whose bed I shall make,
> Whose child I shall bear,
> Whose darling I shall be,
> Whose arms I shall lie in,

and then retiring to bed without uttering any other word.

Maidservants' Charity. *(See Dice and Lot Charities.)*

Maids Money. *(See Dice and Lot Charities.)*

Making Christ's Bed. At Tenby, in Pembrokeshire, it was formerly the custom for young people to 'make Christ's bed' on or near Good Friday. For this they gathered long reed-leaves from the river-bank, and wove them into the form of a man. The figure thus made was then laid upon a wooden cross in a quiet corner of some field or garden, and there it was left. This custom, which does not seem to have been recorded elsewhere, was purely a folk-ritual, unconnected with any contemporary Church or chapel observances in the parish on that day. M. H. Mason, who described it in his *Tales and Traditions of Tenby* (1858), suggests that its origin perhaps lay in vague memories of a ceremony, long since obsolete but once sanctioned by the pre-Reformation Church, in which the burial of Christ was solemnly re-enacted on Good Friday.

Marble Day. Marbles, like Skipping, is one of the traditional Springtime games associated with Good Friday. In Surrey and Sussex, the anniversary was often called Marble Day because, formerly, it marked the end of the short Marble season. This ran from Ash Wednesday to Good Friday, and ended on the stroke of noon on the latter day. Marbles was essentially a man's game, and was very seriously played by men and youths in numerous parishes all through Lent. It is still played on Good Friday at Tinsley Green, near Crawley, where a championship match is held every year. It is said to have been held there for the last three hundred years. *(See Skipping.)*

Mari Lwyd. Just as in England the Hodening Horse went round at Christmas or at Hallowtide (*see Hodening*), so in Wales his near kinsman, the *Mari Lwyd*, did the same between Christmas and Twelfth Night, and sometimes for a longer period extending for two or three weeks after the latter date.

A horse-skull, usually a real one but occasionally a carved wooden replica, was decorated with coloured ribbons and draped with a long white sheet on which two pieces of black cloth were sewn to represent the horse's ears. It had a spring in the lower jaw to enable the mouth to open and shut, and eye-sockets filled with thick bottle-glass. A pole was fixed to its underside, and on this it was carried about by a man whose body was almost completely covered by a white sheet, so that only his feet were visible. A pair of reins with little bells attached to them was fixed to the skull, and with these the *Mari Lwyd* was led or driven by one of his attendants.

The latter consisted of five or six men and boys who wore coloured ribbons and rosettes stitched to their clothes, and sometimes a broad sash tied round the waist. In some districts, two of the band, known as Punch and Judy, had blackened faces. The Leader held the *Mari Lwyd*'s reins, and also a short wooden stick for knocking upon doors, The little group, with its awe-inspiring central figure swathed in white, started out at dusk and often continued on its rounds until far into the night. On arrival at a house, the Leader knocked on the door and, without waiting for it to be opened, asked 'permission to sing'. Then began a contest of rhymes and songs, some traditional and with many versions, and others made up on the spot. When 'permission to sing' had been requested the inmates of the house enquired in verse, and through the closed door, how many stood outside, what their names were, and whence they came. The reply was also in verse, and this interchange might go on for a long time, both sides making up impromptu verses which often included uncomplimentary references to the character or appearance of those of the opposing party. Eventually, however, inspiration failed. If the householders were the first to stop singing or reciting, then the door was opened and the visitors were admitted. If the *Mari Lwyd* party stopped first, they were supposed to go away and seek another house; but probably this was rarely allowed to happen, since if they did not come in, half the fun of the evening was gone, and so was the good luck they brought.

Once inside, the *Mari Lwyd* ran about, neighing and snapping his jaws, and chasing and biting the women, while the Leader pretended to restrain him, crying 'Whoa, there whoa!', and pulling on the reins. In Glamorganshire, each member of the party had a special name and separate task, including Merryman, who played the fiddle and indulged in all sorts of antics, Judy, who carried a broom and swept the hearth, and Punch, who kissed the girls and was noisily chased by Judy with her broom. Food and drink were provided by the hosts, and when the time for departure came, the visitors withdrew, singing a Welsh verse of which the translation runs:

> Farewell, gentle folk,
> We have been made welcome.
> God's blessing be upon your house,
> And upon all who dwell there.

or some other version of a traditional song calling down happiness and good fortune in the coming year upon the household.

This custom was once widespread throughout Wales, and it still survives in some parts of Glamorganshire and Carmarthenshire. In its present-day form, it is not quite so elaborate as it seems to have been in the past. The men who go round with the skull are usually content with their ordinary, unadorned dress now, and the different characters are not always so clearly defined. The *Mari Lwyd*, however, is still the same sheet-swathed and mysterious figure, and if this ancient character as a bringer of fertility is largely forgotten, his visits are still associated with good luck and merriment. The name *Mari Lwyd* is usually said to mean 'Grey Mare', or 'Grey Mary' though other meanings have been suggested by some scholars. Other names also have been used for this ancient custom in various districts, such as the Wassail, the Canvas Horse, or simply, the Horse.

Marling Customs. Marling was an ancient and long-lived method of fertilizing the land by spreading over it, at long intervals, marls of various kinds which were obtained from pits specially dug for the purpose. It was known to Pliny the Elder, who said it had been discovered before his time by the early Britons and Gauls, and it was intermittently practised until about the middle of the nineteenth century. It seems to have come into and gone out of fashion several times. In England, it was apparently used during the Roman period, and again in the Middle Ages. There are references to it in some mediaeval leases which required the tenant to keep the land well marled, and in a statute of 1225 which gave every man leave to sink a marl-pit on his own lands. Gervase Markham, in his *Inrichment of the Weald of Kent*, (1625), says it ceased during the Wars of the Roses, but was reintroduced about thirty years before he wrote, that is, about 1595. It is mentioned in various estate records and agricultural books of the seventeenth and eighteenth centuries, and it did not finally disappear until Queen Victoria had been upon the throne for some years.

Marling was a skilled craft which, in the course of time, evolved its own technical terms, songs, customs, and sayings. Its great agricultural value in the days before artificial manures were known is commemorated in a variety of old saws, like 'He that marls sand may buy the land', or 'He that marls moss shall have no loss', or 'He that marls clay flings all away'. The actual work was done by gangs of itinerant marlers who went from one farm or estate to another to sink the necessary pits, extract the marl therefrom and spread it on the fields. There were usually seven or eight men in a gang, one of whom was chosen as the leader, and was known as the Lord of the Soil, or Lord of the Pit. An old man named Lowndes who lived at Mobberley in Cheshire in the late nineteenth century, was always called 'Lord Lowndes' by his neighbours because, in his youth, he had been Lord of the Soil in a local marling-gang.

When the men were at work, it was their custom to hail any one who passed by and ask for money. If it was given, the Lord returned thanks by shouting, three times, 'Oyez! Oyez! Oyez! This is to give notice that Mr . . . has given us marlers part of £100, and to whomsoever will do the same, we will give thanks and shout'. If the gift was more than sixpence, the words were altered to 'part of £1,000'. Then the whole gang joined hands and, putting their heads close together, cried out 'Largesse! Largesse!' At the end of the week, the whole ceremony was repeated at the inn where the money was spent. Marling-songs were also sung, like that which runs:

> For them as grows a good turmit,
> We are the boys to fey a pit,
> And then yoe good marl out of it.
> When shut the pit, the labour o'er,
> He that we work for opes his door,
>
> And gies to us of drink galore,
> For this was allus marlers' law.
> Who-whoop, who-whoop, wo-o-o!

Since marling was a costly process, and its beneficial effects were expected to last for twenty years or more, it took place only at long intervals on any one estate. When it did, there was usually some sort of jollification at the end, with the 'drinks galore' of the song, dancing, and a feast in which marlers, farmworkers, neighbours and tenants shared. In his *Diary* for 1712, Nicholas Blundell, of Little Crosby, Lancashire, recorded how, when he had finished his marling, his marl-pit was flowered, there was a procession of young women carrying garlands, sword- and maypole-dancing, and a bull-bait in the bottom of the pit. These celebrations covered several days, and finally, on July 23rd, he wrote: 'I had my Finishing Day for my Marling and abundance of my Neighbours and Tennants eat and drunk with me in ye Afternoone . . . All my Marlers, spreaders, water-balys and carters dined here. We fetched home ye Maypowl from the Pit and had Sword dansing and a Merry night in ye Hall and in ye Barne.'[1]

Now these lively customs and the craft to which they belonged have vanished from country life and are almost forgotten. All that keeps their memory green for most people are a few place-names like Marlpit Lane or Marling Glen, some old pits full of water, and a Cheshire phrase, 'marling a man', which means cheering him loudly at dinners and other functions, as the marlers used to cheer those who gave them largesse.

Martinmas. Martinmas, the Feast of St Martin of Tours, falls on November 11th,[2] and sometimes comes in the middle of a short season of warm days known as St Martin's Summer. It was formerly one of the great feasts of the Church, made so by Pope Martin I in the seventh century; and like Hallowtide, it had a pre-Christian ancestry that associated it with the ancient New Year festivals of early November.[3] Some of its customs and traditions were very similar to those of Hallowtide, and an old Scots rhyme that used to be sung round the hill-top bonfires on October 31st links both together in a single season with the words:

1. *Blundell's Diary and Letter-Book* 1702–1728, ed. Margaret Blundell, 1952.

2. This November anniversary was sometimes called St Martin in the Winter, or St Martin in Yeme, to distinguish it from the Feast of the Translation of St Martin on July 4th.

3. The Germanic tribes of northern Europe appear to have celebrated their new year and beginning-of-winter festival on or about November 11th.

This is Hallaevan,
The Morn is Halladay,
Nine free nights till Martinmas,
An' sune they'll wear away.

For many centuries, Martinmas was an important day for the payment of rents and the beginning and ending of tenancies and engagements. It is still one of the Scottish term days. When farm-labourers were normally engaged by the year, or by the half-year, it was sometimes called Pack Rag Day, because on it servants packed their possessions and left the farm to find new employment elsewhere. Many Hiring Fairs were held about this time. In Scotland, the outgoing workers, and especially the ploughmen who often changed places then, entertained those who were staying on to a feast known as the Martinmas Foy. This was a simple repast of bread, cheese, and whisky which began after the horses had been 'suppered', that is, at about nine o'clock at night, and was followed by music, singing, and dancing until a very late hour. The Foy was held on the last night of the term, either on Martinmas Eve, or, where the Old Style calendar was adhered to, on Old Martinmas Eve, November 21st. On the following day, the outgoers departed to take up work elsewhere. The newcomers who took their places were usually welcomed about eight days after their arrival by a similar feast provided by those who were remaining on the farm for another year.

Martinmas was formerly a day for festive eating and drinking in many north-European countries, including Great Britain. From time immemorial, it had been the custom to slaughter large numbers of cattle and other beasts at this season for the simple economic reason that, before modern methods of farming were known, it was not possible to maintain them all throughout the Winter. The majority were therefore killed off, and their meat preserved by salting, pickling, or drying. In *Tusser Redivivus* (1744) we read that 'Martlemass beef is beef dried in the chimney, as bacon, and is so called because it was usual to kill the beef for this provision about the feast of St Martin.' But if most of the meat went into the winter stores, some of it was eaten fresh at the Martinmas feast. Everyone ate and drank as generously as he could then; even poor families, for whom meat of any kind was a rare luxury, hoped to enjoy a dish of beef or mutton or pork or, in some districts, roast goose. In Scotland, until comparatively recently, it was customary to kill an ox, known as the Mart, or some other animal at this time, eat a portion of it, and salt down the rest.

There were, however, other reasons for the slaughtering and feasting beside the purely practical ones. In some parts of Scotland and Ireland, it was considered essential that blood should be shed at Martinmas, as in some other regions, it was thought necessary on New Year's Day. If it was not done, the following twelve months would be unlucky. Some beast or bird from the farm was therefore ceremonially killed on St Martin's Eve, usually by the master of the household, and its flesh was eaten by all the family at the subsequent feast. A curious and elaborate ritual used to be observed in Ireland as late as last century. An animal, varying in kind with the means of the family, was slaughtered on Martinmas Eve – by the man of the house if it was a sheep or a lamb, by the woman if it was a bird from the poultry-yard. Its blood was then sprinkled over the house, inside and outside, and over the byre and all the outbuildings. The sign of the Cross was made in blood on both sides of the threshold and on the door, and also upon the foreheads of all the children and other members of the family. If a fowl had been killed, its head was sometimes thrown over the house-roof as a protection against evil in the coming year. When all this had been done, the flesh of the slaughtered creature was eaten, either on the same night or on the following day.[1]

In Ireland also, and in some Scottish districts, it was thought most unlucky if any wheel was turned on St Martin's Day. Carters and millers therefore had a kind of compulsory holiday, women could not spin, and even knitting, with its circular motions, was forbidden to them. This prohibition was usually explained by a legend that the saint had been killed by being thrown under a turning mill-wheel, just as the

1. R. H. Buchanan, 'Calendar Customs: Part 2. Harvest to Christmas', *Ulster Folklife*, Vol. 9, 1963.

killing of the Mart was sometimes explained by an even odder story that he had been cut up and eaten in the form of an ox.

After 1918, Martinmas took on a new significance as Armistice Day, the anniversary of the end of the First World War. The millions who died in that war were remembered on November 11th, not only by countless services in churches, cathedrals, and round outdoor War Memorials, but also in the Two Minutes' Silence which, at eleven o'clock in the morning – the hour at which the Armistice was signed – halted the life of the nation. Work ceased in offices and factories; men and women stood silent in the streets and the fields; cars, buses, and every kind of vehicle came to a stop wherever they happened to be when the sirens blew. This was a homage paid to the dead by everyone at the same moment, and few things were more impressive than the sight of an entire town frozen into sudden silence and immobility in the midst of its rushing work and business. The coming of the Second World War inevitably drained away some of the importance of the Armistice date; and now the silence and the services are no longer held on whatever day of the week November 11th happens to fall upon, but on Remembrance Sunday, the Sunday nearest to Martinmas, when the dead of both wars are honoured together.

May Birching. On May Eve formerly, at some time between sunset and dawn on the following morning, the May Birchers used to go on their secret rounds, to affix branches of trees, or plant-sprigs, on or before the doors of their neighbours' houses. What they left there depended upon their opinion of the householder, his wife, or his grown-up children. The trees or plants used were chosen either for their accepted symbolism, or because their names rhymed with whatever descriptive epithet the May Birchers considered most suitable. In either case, the message was clearly understood by all, and looking out next morning to see what, if anything, had been left in the doorway must sometimes have been rather nervous work.

A flowering branch of hawthorn was always a compliment, but any other thorn denoted that someone in the house was an object of scorn. Lime, which rhymes with prime, was another compliment, and so was pear, which meant fair either of face or of character. The rowan, or wicken, rhyming with chicken, was a sign of affection. It was otherwise with briar, holly, or plum, which stood respectively for liar, folly, and glum, and with alder, which is pronounced 'owler' in many country districts and so rhymes with scowler. A nut-branch outside a woman's door meant that she was a slut, and gorse in bloom that she was of doubtful reputation. Other indications of censure or unpopularity were nettles, thistles, sloes, crab-tree branches, and elders. In Lancashire, the worst possible insult on this night was the scattering of salt before a door.

Very often, this distribution of 'birches' represented the honest opinion of the villagers, and when it was uncomplimentary, it was intended to serve as a warning to the erring or the foolish. But it could all too easily be employed for purposes of spite or revenge, and in its more insulting forms, it could do lasting harm, especially where a girl was concerned. It frequently caused bitter ill-feeling, and sometimes resulted in violence if the aggrieved person,

or his or her relatives could discover the men actually responsible.

May Birching, which flourished chiefly in the north-western counties of England and in the Midlands, could only have existed in a small, closely-knit community, where all the inhabitants knew each other, and the good or bad opinion of neighbours really mattered. As the villages gradually grew larger and strangers came to live in them, it died out naturally, and in most places it had vanished by the 'eighties or 'nineties of last century. A custom akin to it lasted a little longer. On the eves of local weddings, hawthorn or some other friendly plant was set outside the bride's door, and sprigs of broom outside that of the bridegroom. On such occasions, uncomplimentary symbols were hardly ever used, unless there had been some sort of scandal about the marriage.

May Dew. Gathering dew in the early hours of May-morning and washing one's face in it is a centuries-old custom which is often said to be forgotten now, but which in fact lingers on in a great many places. Young girls in country districts still go out before sunrise on May Day, alone or in little bands, to collect dew from the grass and the bushes, and anoint their faces with it. They do this because they believe as their ancestors did before them, that it will make their complexions beautiful, or remove freckles and other blemishes, and also because the due performance of the rite is supposed to bring good luck in the following twelve months.

This is a very old belief. Queen Catherine of Aragon evidently held it, for it is recorded that she and twenty-five of her ladies went dew-gathering on May 1st in 1515.[1] Pepys noted in his *Diary* for 1669 how he was 'troubled, about three in the morning, with my wife calling her maid up, and rising herself, to go with her coach abroad to gather May-dew, which she did, and I troubled for it, for fear of any hurt, going abroad so betimes, happening to her; but I to sleep again, and she comes home about six, and to bed again all well.' This was on May 10th, which might seem to be the wrong day; but there is other evidence to suggest that the dews of the entire month were thought efficacious, though those of the first day were best. Pepys himself had recorded two years before how, on May 28th, 1667, his wife had gone to Woolwich to stay the night, 'and so to gather May-dew tomorrow morning, which Mrs Turner hath taught her is the only thing in the world to wash her face in.'

1. W. C. Hazlitt, *Faiths and Folklore*, Vol. II, 1905.

Long before Mrs Pepys' time, and long afterwards, May-dew was collected by people of all sorts, not only as a cosmetic, but also as a cure for consumption, goitre, spinal weakness, poor sight, and various other ills. Addy tells us that in Derbyshire delicate children used to be anointed with it. A sheet was spread out on the grass overnight, and the dew thus collected was rubbed next day into the child's loins.[1] In his *Natural History of Wiltshire*, Aubrey records that a man named William Gore, of Clapton, used to walk through the dew to cure his gout; and as a curious sidelight upon the grim history of his time, he adds that a friend of his told him that 'this was the very method and way of curing that was used in Oliver Cromwell, Protectour'.

Few people now remember this tradition of healing, but as a beautifying and luck-bringing agent, May-dew is still valued. Searching for it before dawn is, of course, mainly a country custom, but in Edinburgh, where the hills come close to the city, small parties of young people may still be seen walking through the King's Park to Arthur's Seat, once a famous rendezvous for this purpose, there to wash their faces in the dew, and to make a May-day wish by St Anthony's Well.

May Dolls. The May Doll still appears on May morning in some districts, seated in the centre of the garland or, though less frequently nowadays than formerly, carried about separately in a little flower-filled box or cradle. It is usually a quite ordinary girl-doll, dressed according to individual fancy, and with nothing

1. S. O. Addy, *Household Tales, with Other Traditional Remains*, 1895.

particular in its appearance to suggest its festival importance. It has been variously explained as a representation of the Blessed Virgin, to whom the month of May is dedicated, or of Flora, or of the May Queen. A few years ago an enquirer at Bampton in Oxfordshire was told by one group of young people that the doll in their garland was 'a goddess', and by another, more precisely but rather surprisingly, that it was Minerva. There can be little doubt that it was originally an image of the visible Summer, newly come back to the world, and a magical means of bestowing upon those who saw it all the blessings of fertility and plenty that belong to that season.

A custom once widespread, though never universal, was for the doll to be taken round from house to house with her face hidden by a piece of lace or a white handkerchief. The householders were asked if they would like to see the May Doll, or the May Lady, the Queen of May or, in some counties, the Maulkin. If they said 'yes', they were expected to pay for the privilege, and only after a gift had been made to the bearers was the covering removed, and the doll's luck-bringing face displayed to the givers. This was done at Eynesbury in Huntingdonshire until at least as late as the beginning of the 1939 War. Little girls went round the village in pairs, or in groups of three or four, carrying a garland with a veiled doll in the centre, and singing some verses of the traditional May-song of that district. Similarly, at Edlesborough in Buckinghamshire, until fairly recently, two dolls, one smaller than the other, and both together resembling the Mother and Child figures of the Vessel Cup custom, were taken round in a decorated chair covered by a white cloth. When a gift had been received by the bearers, the cloth was taken off.

This significant little ritual is now often omitted, either because it has been forgotten or because, in some places, it has never been part of local usage. At Bampton, for instance, a number of garlands, each containing a May Doll, are brought out every year on Whit Monday, and paraded through the streets. These dolls are not veiled and are visible to everyone from the beginning. So too, at Somerton, also in Oxfordshire, a single doll, set in a large garland, is carried in procession on, or near May 1st. Its face is not covered, and consequently there is no ceremony of revelation; nor does there appear to be any local tradition of such a ceremony having existed there in the past.

In 1927, an interesting letter appeared in *The Times*, describing the May Doll custom as it then was at Bishop's Teignton in Devon.[1] There boys and girls went round together, the girls carrying a doll in a be-flowered basket, and the boys carrying garlands in the form of short flower-wreathed poles, some of which were expanded into a fan shape. 'In one case', says the writer, 'a doll was tied to a boy's garland. No doubt this doll represented the King of the more formal celebrations'. He adds: 'The children have no idea of any meaning attaching to their action; but expectation is written on their faces, and pennies are exacted by each child. . . . So far as I can see, it is not etiquette to come out on this quest for pennies after 12 years of age for a girl or 14 for a boy'.

May Garlands. Garlands of flowers and green leaves have been made and carried about on May Day from time immemorial. They still appear in due season in a number of places, though now it is mainly children who carry them, instead of the young men and girls who were once the customary bearers. They are usually included in the pleasant, if slightly artificial, May celebrations staged by many local schools for the anniversary which is still often known as Garland Day. Here and there – in some country villages, or in the streets of Manchester, or Stockport, or Oxford – the old custom survives in a less formal manner. The children come out of their own accord in little bands of three or four, singing some version of the old garlanding-song, or as much of it as they can remember, and showing their home-made garland to householders at their doors, or to passers-by in the streets. They beg for coppers or other gifts in return and, in towns at least, they sometimes fall foul of the police for doing so. Yet even this clearly-voiced hope of

1. *The Times*, May 10, 1927. Letter from the Revd. J. McIntyre, of Bishop's Teignton.

reward is part of the old tradition; and it is perhaps these unsponsored little groups, rather than the carefully taught performers in the school celebrations, who are in the direct line of descent from the ritual garland-bearers of the past.

May Garlands have always been made in several different ways. Some are no more than simple posies tied to the tops of long wands, or flower-chains twisted round light staves. At Horncastle in Lincolnshire, until about the end of the eighteenth century, peeled willow wands were wreathed with cowslips. They were known as May Gads, and were carried by young boys in procession on May-morning from a place called the May Bank to a hill on the west side of the town where the Maypole stood on the site of a Roman temple. There they were struck together and their flowers scattered in honour of the First Day of Summer; and that night, as Dr Stukeley records, there was a bonfire 'and other merriment'.[1]

Some garlands are small wooden crosses covered with flowers and greenery, like those that are made every year at Charlton-on-Otmoor (*see Garland-dressing*). In Northumberland formerly, intricately patterned cushions of blossom were made by thrusting flowers of many colours up to their heads in a layer of soft clay spread upon the top of a short stool. These cushions were not carried about, but were displayed in the doorways of houses and at the ends of cross-lanes, and money for an evening feast was begged by their makers from those who passed by. A similar custom prevailed in Guernsey, but there it was observed at Midsummer instead of on May Day.

The hoop-garland is the one most usually seen in England today. It has a framework of two or more intersecting hoops of wire or thin wood, upon which the flowers are thickly massed to make a floral globe. Sometimes a May Doll is suspended or seated within it (*see May Dolls*). Crown-shaped garlands are fashioned from half-hoops of wood or wire attached to a circular base. Another variety, rarely seen now, was the pyramid contrived from parallel hoops supported and kept at the right distance from each other by upright poles. The traditional Huntingdonshire garland was of this form. It was often very tall, rising to a height of five or six feet, smothered in flowers, greenery and ribbons, and having a May Doll fixed upon its front. In the first half of the nineteenth century, such a garland used to be carried in the May Day procession round the village of Glatton. Afterwards, it was suspended on a cord stretched across the village street from the chimneys of two opposite houses, and the young people amused themselves by throwing balls backwards and forwards over it. The game of tossing balls over or through a suspended garland was played in other Huntingdonshire parishes also, and in some of them it outlived all the rest of the traditional May celebrations.[1]

Whatever its form, the May garland is a summer-emblem, and colour and gaiety are its essentials. Bright ribbons and fresh leaves have always been used in its making, and every sort of flower available at the season – cowslips, kingcups, polyanthus, crown imperials, tulips, wallflowers, early roses, and many more. Before the calendar reform of 1752, bosses of red and white may were regularly included, but nowadays they are absent more often than not. The hawthorn knows nothing of official calendars, and it is rarely in bloom in time for the New Style May Day, though it is usually faithful to the old date, our May 12th or 13th. Only one flower is customarily omitted of set purpose. This is the cuckoo-flower which, perhaps because it is a fairy plant, is supposed to be unlucky in May garlands. In some districts it is (or used to be) said that if a few sprigs are accidentally woven in with the rest, it is not enough to pull them out again; the whole garland must be taken to pieces and remade.[2]

An unusual type of garland, which died out

1. Dr William Stukeley, *Itinerarium Curiosum*, 1724.

1. C. F. Tebbutt, *Huntingdonshire Folk and Their Folklore*, 1951.

2. Although cuckoo-flowers are usually omitted from modern garlands with as much care as in the past, the rule is not observed everywhere. In Oxford, the cross-shaped garlands carried about the streets on May-morning by little bands of children almost always contain a profusion of these forbidden flowers, and no one seems to be aware that they are supposed to be unlucky.

in the early years of the nineteenth century, was that carried by the London milkmaids. This too had its flowers and ribbons, but its distinctive feature was silver, in the form of vases, tankards, cups, and anything else that could be borrowed for the occasion. 'On the 1st of May, and the five or six days following', wrote Henri Misson in 1698, 'all the pretty young girls that serve the town with milk dress themselves up very neatly, and borrow abundance of silver plate, whereof they make a pyramid, which they adorn with ribbands and flowers, and carry upon their heads, instead of their common milk-pails. In this equipage, accompany'd by some of their fellow milk-maids and a bagpipe or fiddle, they go from door to door, dancing before the houses of their customers, in the midst of boys and girls that follow them in troops, and everybody gives them something.'[2] In later years, it was usual for the heavy garland to be carried by a man, while the girls walked and danced in front of it. 'I really cannot discover', wrote Joseph Strutt in 1801, 'what analogy the silver tankards and salvers can have to the business of the milk-maids. I have seen them act with much more propriety upon this occasion when in place of these superfluous ornaments they substituted a cow. The animal had her horns gilt, and was nearly covered with ribbands of various colours, formed into bows and roses, and interspersed with green oaken leaves and bunches of flowers.'[1]

The milkmaids were not, however, the only people who decorated their garlands with silver. In Hone's *Every-Day Book* (Vol. I, 1826) there is an account written by a correspondent signing himself H.T.B., of the May dancers of North Wales, who also had a silver-bearing garland. These dancers were young men who went all round the neighbourhood on May Day and danced outside the farmhouses and other dwellings on their route. They wore be-ribboned shirts and hats, and carried a white handkerchief in one hand. Their leader was the *Cadi*, who planned the march, and acted as 'the chief marshal, orator, buffoon, and money collector'. He wore a man's coat and waistcoat and a woman's petticoats, and his face was either covered by a hideous mask, or else blackened, with the lips, cheeks, and eye-orbits painted red. On the march and during the dances, he made comic speeches, clowned, and flourished a ladle in which he collected money from all and sundry.

Next in importance to the *Cadi* was the garland-bearer who, during the week before the festival, went round the parish, accompanied by one of the dancers, to beg for the loan of silverware for the garland. The latter consisted of a long pole with a square or triangular frame fixed upon it. The frame was covered with strong white linen, and on it the silver was carefully arranged – spoons and small ornaments in circles, squares and stars, watches in rows between these figures and the finest and largest piece, usually a cup or tankard, at the top of the frame, opposite the pole in its centre. On May Eve, the garland was deposited, as a mark of respect, at the house of the farmer who had lent the most silver, or who was known to be a good and generous master; and next day, when the May-dancers set out on their day-long round, it was carried just behind the *Cadi*. Unlike most other garlands carried on that day, it does not seem to have had any flowers or leaves or ribbons, but it must nevertheless have been a very splendid summer-emblem, especially on a fine morning, with the sunlight gleaming and flashing upon its many silver ornaments.

May Goslings. In North Lancashire, Westmorland, Cumberland and the North Riding of Yorkshire, a custom similar to that already noticed on April 1st is kept up on May Day. The children who have already enjoyed all the delights of April Fool's Day have, in these areas, a second chance of showing their ingenuity in befooling their elders and each other. The tricks employed are much the same on both anniversaries, but the May Day victim is greeted with shouts of 'May Gosling!', or 'May Geslin!', or perhaps finds these words in a note left at his house, or enclosed in a sham parcel. As on the earlier date, the proceedings must cease punc-

1. H. Misson de Valbourg, *Memoirs and Observations of M. Misson in his Travels over England*, translated by J. Ozell, 1719.

2. Joseph Strutt, *The Sports and Pastimes of the People of England*, 1801, ed. J. C. Cox, 1903.

tually at noon. Whoever transgresses this rule lays himself open to the chanted retort of

> May Gosling's past and gone,
> You're the fool for making me one,

or some other variant of this derisory couplet.

The custom does not seem to have been recorded in southern England formerly, and it is not known there now. In its northern home, however, it has certainly flourished for nearly two centuries, and probably for a much longer period. A writer in the *Gentleman's Magazine* in 1791, tells us that a 'May Gosling, on the first of May, is made with as much eagerness in the North of England, as an April noddy (noodle) or fool, on the first of April.' *(See All Fools' Day.)*

May Hobby Horses. On May Day, the famous Hobby Horses of Padstow and Minehead come out to meet the Summer. That of Padstow, a Hobby of the 'horse and rider' type, locally known as Obby Oss, or Old Oss, is a very spectacular beast who attracts hundreds of people to the town every year. He wears a hoop-shaped frame, about six feet round and covered with black tarpaulin, which completely hides his human form. In front of the hoop is a small, wooden horse's head, with snapper jaws, but the horseman's own head is hidden by a ferocious-looking mask, surmounted by a tall, conical cap. Old Oss has a number of attendants who follow him about the streets, but the most important is the Teaser, or Club-man, who carries a padded club, and wears grotesque clothes which vary in pattern in different years.

The May festival at Padstow begins on the night before, when the Mayers go round the town singing the Night Song outside the principal houses. They stand outside the house, serenading the tenant and his wife by name, his sons and daughters, or his guests, and singing,

> Rise up, Mrs ——, all in your gown of green,
> For Summer is I-comen in today.
> You are as fair a lady as waits upon the Queen,
> In the merry month of May.

or

> Rise up, Mr ——, we wish you well and fine,
> For Summer is I-comen in today.
> You've a shilling in your pocket, and I wish it were in mine,
> In the merry morning of May.

There are many verses of this song, and not all of them are personal greetings. Two of them run:

> The young men of Padstow, they might if they would,
> For Summer is I-comen in today,
> They might have built a ship and gilded her with gold,
> In the merry morning of May.
> The young maids of Padstow, they might if they would,
> For Summer is I-comen in today,
> They might have made a garland of the white rose and the red,
> In the merry month of May.

In the morning, the Old Oss comes out of the Golden Lion Inn, which is his headquarters and the place where his accoutrements are kept during the year, accompanied by his Teaser. He sets off, capering and gambolling through the streets; he chases the girls, and sometimes corners one of them against a wall and covers her with his huge tarpaulin skirt. This is supposed to bring her a husband, if she has not got one already, or a baby within the year, if she has.

Once, the inside of the cloth was smeared with blacklead, which left a mark upon the girl's face or dress, as a sign of the good fortune to come, but this has not been done for many years now. Once also, the Oss and his followers went to Treator Pool, and he drank from it, after which the spectators were sprinkled with the water. This looks very much like a rain-making rite, and probably was originally, but like the smeared tarpaulin, it has dropped out of the programme, and has not been done since about 1930.

Every now and then, the Oss dies a magical death. The lively music of the Night Song changes to the slower and sadder Day Song (the two songs alternate all through the day), and the Mayers, and most of the onlookers, sing:

O, where is St. George? O, where is he, O?
He's out in his long-boat, all on the salt sea O.
Up flies the kite, down falls the lark, O.
Aunt Ursula Birdwood, she had an old ewe,
But it died in her own Park, O.

The Oss sinks to the ground as though he were dying, and lies there while the Teaser gently strokes his head with his club. He has gone, and the strange song, though its words have become quite incomprehensible by now, is plainly his dirge. And then, suddenly, the music changes once more, the Oss leaps up, high in the air, and off he goes again, as full of life as ever.

For the past fifty years or so, there has been a second Hobby Horse, almost a replica of the traditional one, who has his own Teaser and followers. This is the Temperance, or Blue Ribbon, or Peace Horse, who came into being at about the end of the First World War. Although they were once rivals, the two Horses now live amicably together, and do not encroach upon each other as they run through the town. They meet only in the late afternoon in the market square, where after an interval of some years, the Maypole once more proudly stands, too tall for ribbon streamers, but gaily decorated with garlands and flags, and bunches of fresh Spring flowers.

The Hobby Horse of Minehead differs in form from his brother of Padstow, but he is no less impressive. His body is formed by a frame covered by a horsecloth which has gaily coloured circles painted on it. On the flat top of this frame, there is a mass of short, brightly-hued streamers, like a great rag mat. He has a long rope tail, like that of a cow, but longer, a tall cap, and a painted mask of savage aspect over his face. Once he had a horse-head with napper jaws, but that appears to have been lost. He is known as the Sailors' Horse and lives on the Quayside. He comes out on Warning Night, which is May Eve, and again on May Day itself, when he and his attendants go to Dunster Castle, and all over the townships of Dunster and Minehead.

This Horse seems once to have been a great deal fiercer than the Padstow beast. He used to be accompanied by two masked men, known as Gullivers, who wore tall headdresses, and carried tongs and a whip, which they used to frighten people into free giving. A man truly ungenerous, or in some way tiresome, was liable to the penalty of booting, that is, of being bound round with the rope tail, and struck anything up to ten times with a boot carried for the purpose. The Gullivers have disappeared now, but booting has occurred occasionally within this century. Formerly, household doors were left open for Horse and Gullivers to enter and bring the luck of the Summer to the inmates, but now the Horse cavorts alone in the open street, and dances a few steps outside the houses that he visits.

May Horns. The noise of horns, loudly and continuously blown, was a very familiar sound on May-morning until almost the end of last century. 'Noise' is perhaps a more accurately descriptive word than 'music' for this traditional method of welcoming the Summer, since the performers were usually young and far from expert musicians, and their instruments were often unmelodious cow-horns, or tin trumpets specially sold by shopkeepers and stallholders for the occasion. Gangs of boys went about vigorously sounding them from daybreak onwards, and sometimes even earlier. 'At Oxford', wrote John Aubrey in the seventeenth century 'the boys do blow Cows horns and hollow Caxes all night'.[1] More than two hundred years

1. J. Aubrey, *Remaines of Gentilisme and Judaisme*, 1686–7, ed. J. Britten, 1881.

later, an elderly Oxonian recalled how, in his Victorian childhood, every boy in the city took care to provide himself with a suitable instrument some days before the festival, and to blow it constantly from then on until May Day was past.[1] Only while the traditional Latin Hymn was being sung on the top of Magdalen College Tower was there an interval of silence. Then, says Jewitt, writing in 1846, 'as soon as the singers cease . . . the boys, who have been impatiently waiting for the conclusion of the matins, now blow their trumpets lustily, and, performing such a chorus as few can imagine and none forget, start off in all directions, and scour the fields and lanes, and make the woods re-echo to their sounds.'[2]

In Penzance, little bands of five or six boys used to assemble before dawn on May 1st at convenient points in the town, and march through the streets blowing horns and conch-shells. They visited the larger houses and sounded a blast under the bedroom windows, to let the sleeping inmates know that Summer had returned. For this they expected to receive gifts of money, and when they had collected enough, they went gaily off to some nearby farmhouse for a May-morning breakfast of junket, clotted cream, and other good things.

In the Isle of Man, horns were blown on the night of May Eve, or at daybreak on May Day, during the ceremony of setting fire to the gorse in order to scare away fairies and witches, who were supposed to be especially powerful at that time. A. W. Moore says that horns were sounded at dawn, or soon after, 'to prevent the fairies enticing the children away.'[3] It is possible that the May Horn custom everywhere, though usually explained as a greeting to the incoming Summer, may originally have been intended to avert evil at a significant season, since violent and raucous noises were usually said to have that effect. At Gainsborough in Lincolnshire, horn-blowing took place on Oak Apple Day, after a great crown-shaped garland of flowers, gilded oak-apples, and birds' eggshells had been hoisted across the street. A writer in *Notes and Queries* (Vol. V., 1852), records that, once the garland was in position, all the boys of the town began, and kept up throughout the day, 'a most terrible blowing of horns, the doleful noise being ill in accordance with the festivity and rejoicing which the garlands are supposed to indicate.' He adds that he did not know why they did this, or what the origin of the custom might be. Clearly, he was not a folklorist, and perhaps none of the horn-blowers could give him a reason for their actions, except that 'it had always been done.'

1. Revd. E. Sherwood, *Oxford Yesterday*, 1927.
2. L. Jewitt, in *Literary Gazette*, May, 1847.
3. A. W. Moore, *Folk-Lore of the Isle of Man*, 1891.

May Queen. In most modern revivals of the old May Day celebrations the central figure is commonly the May Queen, usually a school-girl elected by her fellows, and crowned by her predecessor of the year before, or by some local notability. Formerly, she was not a child, but a young woman, the prettiest girl in the area or the most popular, and she was not usually alone, as she is now. There was often a May King who reigned with her, or a Lord and Lady of the May. In the Isle of Man, until about the end of the eighteenth century, May Day was marked by a battle between the Queen of May, and the Queen of Winter. The latter was a man dressed in women's clothes. Both Queens had followers dressed in a manner appropriate to summer or winter, and both had a captain to command their forces. Waldron, in his *Description of the Isle of Man*,[1] relates how on May morning, 'both companies march till they meet on a common, and then their trains engage in a mock battle. If the Queen of Winter's forces get the better, so far as to take the Queen of May prisoner, she is ransomed, for as much as pays for the expenses of the day. After this ceremony Winter and her company retire, and divert themselves in a barn, and the others remain on the green, where having danced a considerable time, they conclude the evening with a feast; the Queen at one table with her maids, the captain and his troops at another. There are seldom less than fifty or sixty people at each board. . . .' In the course of time, this elaborate custom died out, and the battle was forgotten. Only the Summer

1. George Waldron, 1726, quoted by C. I. Paton, *Manx Calendar Customs*, 1939.

procession remained, later known as the Mace-board, and composed of little girls who went from house to house selling small pieces of ribbon which were called 'the Queen's favour'.

The May King who was once the Queen's partner has vanished now from almost every place where he once reigned, but the Lord and Lady of the May still survive in some parts of the English Midlands. They were young people chosen to preside over the local celebrations by the people of the village, though occasionally the Lady was chosen directly by the Lord. They were not crowned, and in fact, it is only since Ruskin made the custom popular in the late nineteenth century that the coronation of a child-Queen has become so important a part of the ceremonies in so many districts. In Oxfordshire, an eye-witness describing a village May procession in 1951, remarks that the Lord and Lady followed the Garland, which led the way, and were themselves followed by boys carrying four decorated staves, known as Maypoles. Whenever any money was given at any of the houses the procession visited, the Lord kissed the Lady under the four Maypoles which were crossed over their heads. A little more than a hundred years before, Jewitt described an almost precisely similar custom, which he saw at Headington, near Oxford, in 1846.[1]

1. L. Jewitt, *Literary Gazette*, 1847.

May Singing. Every year, at six o'clock on May morning, the choristers of Magdalen College, Oxford, go to the top of the Tower and greet the sunrise with a Latin hymn. In spite of the early hour (before the introduction of Summer Time, it was still earlier, at five o'clock), there is always a large crowd gathered on the Bridge below, to hear the singing and the pealing of the Tower bells which follows it. Immediately afterwards, the Morris dancers from Oxford and Headington run through the streets, and dance at various fixed points in the City.

The origin of the custom is uncertain. It is often said that a Requiem Mass for Henry VII used to be sung on the Tower on May 1st, and that, when this practice ceased at the Reformation, the present custom was substituted for it. There is not, however, any real evidence for this story. Anthony Wood says that, in his day, the choristers 'do, according to an ancient custom, salute Flora every year on the first of May at four in the morning, with vocal music of several parts.'[1] He adds that this, being sometimes well performed, 'hath given great content to the neighbourhood, and auditors underneath.'

It still does, but what the 'auditors underneath' hear today is not a concert, as in Wood's time. The change came, more or less accidentally, in the late eighteenth century. On one very wet May Day, the choristers were an hour late in reaching the Tower top and hastily substituted *Te Deum Patrem colimus*, a hymn which they all knew very well, for whatever they ought to have been singing. This hymn, dating from the seventeenth century, written by Dr Thomas Smith and set to music by Benjamin Rogers, was part of the College grace, and therefore well-known to all the singers. It has been sung on May morning ever since that first emergency occasion. It has been suggsted that the custom of May singing on the Tower may have started as an inaugural ceremony in the form of a secular concert, connected with the completion of the Tower, in 1509.

Hymns are also sung on the top of Bargate, in Southampton, on May Day. The custom lapsed for some years when it became unsafe to ascend the old gate, but was revived in 1957 when the choirboys of King Edward VI School sang from the lawn adjoining the Bargate. Happily, the Bargate itself has now been restored, and they are once more able to sing on the top as before.

Maypole. The Maypole is an ancient fertility emblem belonging to the beginning of Summer, and it also represents a tree; indeed, at one time it was a tree, brought in from the woods with ceremony, and set up on the village green. In the darkness of the early morning, the young people went out on May Day and cut down a

1. Anthony Wood, *History and Antiquities of the Colleges and Halls in the University of Oxford*, 1674, ed. J. Gutch, 1886.

tall, young tree, lopped off most of its branches, leaving only a few at the top, and so brought it home, to be adorned with flowers and garlands, and to serve as a centre for their dances. Stubbes, who like most Puritans, hated the Maypole because he associated it with paganism and immorality, describes how, in some parishes, twenty or forty yoke of oxen were used to drag it in, 'every Ox having a sweet nose-gay of flowers tied on the tip of his horns, and these oxen draw home this Maypole (this stinking Idol, rather), which is covered all over with flowers and herbs';[1] and he goes on to tell us how, when it is set in place and ready, the villagers begin to 'leap and dance about it, as the Heathen people did at the dedication of their Idols, whereof this is the perfect pattern, or rather the thing itself.'

Sometimes the parish possessed a standing Maypole, a permanent shaft which remained in position all the year, and was freshly painted and adorned when May Day came round. A few still stand, or rather, their descendants do on the traditional site, for the average age of a maypole is not much more than fifteen years. After that, it begins to rot at the foot and has to be renewed. These permanent poles are usually very tall.[2] That at Welford-on-Avon, with its bright red, circular stripes, like a barber's pole, is seventy feet high, that at Barwick-in-Elmet, near Leeds, is even taller, rising to eighty or ninety feet. This pole is taken down every three years, on Easter Monday, and set up again on Whit Tuesday. The arrangements are in the hands of three elected Pole Men. While it is down, the Maypole is re-painted, and every so often, when it becomes necessary, replaced, and its four garlands renewed.

The Church of St Andrew Undershaft, in Leadenhall Street, was so named because the great Maypole which annually stood before its south door was taller than the church itself. John Stow records in his *Survey of London* that the pole was never used again after the 'evil May Day' of 1517, when the London apprentices attacked the alien traders, and the Maypole was pulled down in the course of the ensuing riot. It hung for many years upon hooks under the eaves of the houses on one side of Shaft Alley, until in 1552, a firebrand curate from St Katherine's Church, preaching at Paul's Cross, denounced it as an idol. His sermon stirred up the people who lived under it in Shaft Alley to pull it down and saw it into pieces, each householder taking for firewood the part that lay over his own door.

In 1644, Maypoles were forbidden throughout England and Wales. All the standing-poles came down, or nearly all; in some quiet places, a few may have remained in position, waiting for better times, but no one danced round them any more. Nevertheless, most of them came back with the King, to be the gay centre of the festivities either on May Day, or on that royal occasion, Oak Apple Day. On the first May Day after Charles II's return, an immense pole was set up in the Strand, on the site now occupied by the island-church of St Mary-le-Strand. It was 134 feet high, and was adorned with crowns and the Royal Arms, splendidly gilded, garlands and streamers and three lanterns which were lit at night. It was floated upriver as far as Scotland Yard, and thence carried in triumphal procession to the Strand, through streets filled with cheering spectators who had not seen such a thing for nine weary years of Commonwealth rule. It took twelve seamen, specially imported for the purpose, four hours to set it in position; but once up, it stood for about half a century, which is a long time for a Maypole.

If there are not as many Maypoles today as there were in the happy days after the Restoration, there are still a good many. Most schools have them, on May Day, or on some convenient day during the month, and some villages maintain the old tradition, especially in places where there are standing-poles. In *Folklore*, Vol. 71 (1960) M. M. Rix mentions a curious Maypole-ceremony kept up, apparently quite spontaneously, by the children of Shrewsbury. A pram-

1. Philip Stubbes, *The Anatomie of Abuses*, 1583.

2. The shorter poles, round which the children perform a plaited-ribbon dance, and which are often seen at school May Day celebrations today, do not belong to the English tradition. They come from southern Europe, and seem to have been introduced into this country (by Ruskin) in 1888.

wheel, decorated with coloured crêpe paper and streamers, is set on top of a short pole in such a manner that it will revolve. A band of young (often very young) children go round with it, usually in the evening. There is a Queen who wears a crown of some sort, and a number of little girls, dressed in bright, crêpe-paper garments, who dance and sing round her, as she sits on a stool, holding the Maypole. The second verse of the customary song is sung by the Queen alone, while the dancers stand still, and then, resume their dance for the remaining verses. A collection is subsequently made by a child who carries a tin for the purpose.

Midsummer Fires. Midsummer Day (June 24th) is the Feast of the Nativity of St John the Baptist, that great saint who was the herald of Our Lord, and whose festival, unlike those of other saints, commemorates his birth rather than his death and entry into Paradise. It falls only three days after the Summer Solstice, the day on which the sun reaches its highest glory, and thereafter begins to decline, and in the liturgical calendar, it is equated with it. Anciently, it was a fire-festival of great importance when, through countless centuries, the sun was ritually strengthened by bonfires burning everywhere on Midsummer Eve, by torchlight processions through the streets, by flaming tar-barrels, and in some districts, by wheels bound with straw and tow, set alight, and rolled down steep hillsides into the valley below.

All this was said in the Middle Ages to be done in honour of St John, but in fact, the fires were much older than he. If, in pre-Christian times, they were lit to give magical aid to the sun who now, in the full tide of summer, began to wane, they were also lit, then as later, to drive out evil, and to bring fertility and prosperity to men, crops, and herds. In the Isle of Man on St John's Eve, bonfires burnt on the windward side of fields so that the life-giving smoke might blow over the crops, and blazing gorse or furze was carried round the cattle in the fold to protect them from disease or misfortunes. People danced round the fires on the hills, or the village greens; young men leapt through the flames as a purifying and strengthening rite, and cattle were driven over the dying embers to preserve them from the murrain.

In Cornwall, up to about the middle of last century, all the hills and cairns of Mount's Bay were crowned with bonfires on Midsummer Eve. Old people used to count the fires they could see from any given point, and read the future from their number and appearance. In Penzance, tar-barrels set on the tops of long poles were burnt in different parts of the town, and young people from the quayside went through the streets, swinging large canvas torches round their heads on the end of chains or poles. Later on, when the torches had burned down, they began to dance in a long line through the roadways and alleys, shouting 'An eye! An eye!', until two of the dancers formed an arch (or an 'eye') by raising their joined hands for the rest to run under; and the company then fell to playing Thread the Needle until they were all exhausted.

Midsummer fires were known all over Europe, and some still survive. They blaze all over the Pyrenees, each district having its own special customs and dances, but always the fire, lit by the parish leaders, or sometimes by the inhabitants of a single town street, or by some private individual on his own land. In Hungary, these fires are supposed to drive out snakes, as well as protecting the young crops and purifying the air. Midsummer is one of the great occasions of the Swedish year, with its huge bonfires and its Maypoles which here as in some other northern countries, appear in high June instead of in May.

In Scotland, most of the Midsummer fires have vanished, but there is one place where the custom persisted until the middle of the present century, and may not be gone for ever even yet. This is Durris, in Kincardineshire, where, in the eighteenth century, Alexander Hogg tended cattle in his youth, and every year helped to prepare the St John's Day bonfire. When he died in England, as a wealthy merchant, he left money for the continuance of the Midsummer festival in his old parish, stipulating that there should be a great bonfire on Cairnshee,[1] the material for which had to be collected by the herd-boys of the nearby farms. Each boy received a silver sixpence, and in the latter years of the custom, the youngest among them had the privilege of lighting the fire. While it burnt, the people danced round it, to the music of pipes. This ceremony has not been held since 1945, and no one now knows when, or if, it will be revived.

Some of Cornwall's ancient bonfires have come to life again since the Federation of Old Cornwall Societies revived them between the two wars of this century, and now a chain of such fires is to be seen again on the Cornish hills at Midsummer. At Whalton, in Northumberland the change in the Calendar in 1752 has been ignored, and the local people hold their time-honoured ceremony on July 4th, Old Midsummer Eve. A huge fire is lit in the middle of the village, and those who come to see it dance round it as of old. It is said to have burnt without a break in the same place for more than two hundred years.

Midsummer Tithes. At Wishford Magna, in Wiltshire, a custom known as the sale of the Midsummer Tithes is observed on Rogation Monday. By a gift of which the date and the donor are both now unknown, the parish church owns the grazing rights of two pieces of water-meadow from that day until August 12th (Old Lammas Day), and these are customarily let at the beginning of the period by an old and curious form of auction which depends upon the setting of the sun.

The parish clerk, or a deputy, goes to the church just before sundown. He walks up and down between the porch and the churchyard gate, with the church door-key in his hand. While he does so, those present make their bids. Bidding goes on as long as the sun remains above the horizon. As soon as it disappears, the clerk strikes the gate with the key, and the maker of the last bid received before he does so then becomes the owner of the grazing rights until the end of the season.

1. The original site on the summit of this hill was needed for afforestation in the present century, and the fire was then built on a site near Cairnshee Farm.

Minden Roses. August 1st is the anniversary of the Battle of Minden, which was fought in 1759, during the Seven Years' War, and in which six famous British regiments played a conspicuous and very gallant part. One incident in the story of the battle, and the victory that followed is annually commemorated on Minden Day – August 1st – by the wearing of roses in the men's hats, and the decking of Colours and drums with roses in the six regiments concerned.

Ordered by Prince Ferdinand of Brunswick, then in command of the Allied forces locally, to get ready to advance upon the French position at Minden, they started off too soon, owing to an error in transmission of the command, and set off at a good pace across Minden Heath, to the sound of their own drums and the guns of the enemy. Minden Heath was then all abloom with wild roses, and as the men passed they snatched the flowers from the rose-briars and stuck them in their hats and coats, and in their equipment. Thus adorned, they faced the French cavalry sent out against them, and inflicted an unexpected defeat upon them, driving them from the field. The regiments concerned were the Royal Hampshire Regiment, the King's Own Scottish Borderers, the King's Own Yorkshire Light Infantry (now part of the new Light Infantry), the Lancashire Fusiliers (now part of the Royal Regiment of Fusiliers), the Royal Welsh Fusiliers, and the Suffolk Regiment (now part of the Royal Anglian Regiment).

The Lancashire Fusiliers celebrate Minden Day with a profusion of roses. Every man wears a red and a yellow rose, the drums are decorated with roses of the same colours, and the Regimental Colour bears a wreath of red and yellow roses. Various traditional customs are observed on this day, but perhaps one of the most interesting is the ceremony of Eating a Rose. After dinner in the Officer's Mess, every officer who has not already done so on a previous occasion stands to eat a rose, which is ceremonially handed to him in a silver finger-bowl containing champagne. Until he has performed this ritual, he is not considered to be a full member of the Lancashire Fusiliers.

Mischief Night. Guy Fawkes' Eve – November 4th – is Mischief Night in most parts of Yorkshire, and in some other districts of northern and midland England.[1] On this night, prudent householders look up whatever is easily portable in their gardens, yards, and outhouses, seal up their letter-boxes to prevent fireworks being pushed through them, and ignore all knocks on their front doors or tappings on their windows. Outside, in both towns and country villages, mischief and merriment reign supreme. Young people indulge in pranks of every sort. Fireworks are let off in the streets; paint or whitewash is slapped on to doors or windows; door-knobs are smeared with treacle, and drainpipes are stuffed with smouldering paper. Sometimes the door-handles of two adjacent houses are tied together so that neither door will open, or house-numbers may be unscrewed and set up again on the doors of other houses. Any dustbins, pails, tools, or garden-seats that have been carelessly left outside will vanish as if by magic, and so will any loose pieces of wood or other objects capable of serving as fuel for the following day's bonfires. Gates are taken off their hinges, hidden in ditches or odd corners, or thrown into ponds, often at a considerable distance from the field or garden to which they belong. Searching for these and other pieces of lost property is one of the customary tasks of householders on the morning after Mischief Night. In a letter to the present editor, written in 1956, a Craven correspondent remarked that, in the seven miles between Skipton and his home, there was not a single gate in its rightful position when November 5th dawned.

Yet tiresome as these pranks must be to sober citizens, few people really mind them. Some complaints there are, of course, but in general, and provided there is not too much damage, the whole affair is treated with cheerful tolerance on the grounds that November 4th is Mischief Night, and that high-spirited antics on the part of the young are sanctioned then by tradition and age-old custom.

In fact, it is only in comparatively recent years that Mischief Night has been celebrated on that date. Until well towards the end of the nineteenth century, Hallowe'en or May Eve was the customary anniversary so observed. No early writer mentions Guy Fawkes' Eve in this connection, and it seems clear that the modern custom represents a transference from the older Hallowtide festival. In her *History of Honley* (1914) Mary Jagger says that in her youth the Yorkshire Mischief Night fell on October 31st. In Scotland, boys went about then uprooting kail-stocks, turning horses loose, bombarding doors with cabbages and turnips, stopping chimneys with turf, puffing smoke through keyholes, and stealing and hiding any ploughs, carts, gates, and farming implements on which they could lay hands. Similar customs were observed in Ireland, and in neither country are they altogether extinct even yet. In Sutherland and Caithness, Hallowe'en is still the regular Mischief Night, as it is, or was until recently, on Exmoor, at the other end of Great Britain.

May Eve was formerly as great an occasion for mischief in some districts as Hallowe'en

1. Mainly in parts of Lancashire, Derbyshire, Nottinghamshire, north Cheshire and north Lincolnshire.

was in others. In places as far apart as the Scilly Isles and the English northern counties, the old Eve of Summer was celebrated with the same cheerful lawlessness as the old Eve of Winter was elsewhere. In the Calder Valley district of Yorkshire, young people still occasionally indulge in lively antics on that night, though not now with quite the same vigour as on November 4th.

On Nickanan Night (Shrove Monday) young men and boys in various parts of Cornwall used to prowl through the streets with short clubs in their hands, knocking loudly on the doors of all the houses they passed, and then running away before the doors could be opened. They also carried off any unguarded objects they could find and left them where they would be discovered on the following morning, 'displayed in some conspicuous place, to disclose the disgraceful want of vigilance supposed to characterize the owner.'[1] In Penzance, people in the streets were liable to be deluged with water on that night, or to have their faces blackened by the sooty hands of the revellers. If the door of any house or shop was left unlocked, shells and rubbish of all sorts were thrown inside. M. A. Courtney relates that at one time, when shops kept open very late 'boys were occasionally bribed by the assistants to throw something particularly disagreeable in on the floors, that the masters might be frightened and order the shops to be shut.'[2]

In North Devon also, when the children went shroving on Dappy-Door Night, that is, on Shrove Monday, the older boys seized the opportunity to play a few time-honoured tricks. In his *Wanderings in North Devon* (1887), George Chanter says that at Ilfracombe, doorbells were rung, knockers loudly banged, and handles tied with lengths of strong string with which the hidden Dappy-doorers could jerk the door violently from the hands of the harassed and startled householder as soon as he tried to open it. He does not, however, mention the wholesale purloining of objects which was so common a feature of Mischief Nights elsewhere.

1. T. Quiller Couch, *History of Polperro*, 1871.
2. M. A. Courtney, *Cornish Feasts and Folk-lore*, 1890.

Moseley's Dole. An ancient and unusual charity which did not survive the activities of the Charity Commissioners in the early nineteenth century was Moseley's Dole. This was the distribution on Epiphany Eve of one penny to every inhabitant of the town of Walsall and some of its adjacent hamlets, including not only permanent residents but also any chance-come visitor who might happen to be staying there at the time. According to a long-lived local tradition, Thomas Moseley, who in the fifteenth century was Lord of the Manor of Bascote in Warwickshire heard a child crying for bread in a Walsall street on the Eve of the Epiphany, and vowed that no person in that town should ever want bread on that day again. For this story there is no documentary evidence, but it is a fact that, whether for this reason or some other, he settled the Manor of Bascote in 1452 upon William Lyle and Thomas Magot 'in trust for the use of the Town of Walsall.'[1] Certain payments had to be made from the estate income for the maintenance of obits for the giver's soul and that of his wife in the parish church, and at Halesowen; but all the rest of the money went to the town, and from it the penny dole was annually paid until 1825.

How much this cost in the fifteenth century we do not know. Dr Plot tells us in his *Natural History of Staffordshire* (1686) that the sum distributed in 1545 was £7 10s. 9d. The Corporation accounts show that in 1632 it had risen to £14 9s. 4d., and to £60 in 1786. How much would be needed today in a large industrial town constantly visited by business men and travellers from elsewhere, it would be difficult to calculate. Even when Walsall was still a small place, it took two men several days to distribute the dole, and the work usually began on January 1st, so that it might be completed on Epiphany Eve. Although as time went on, the value of a single penny steadily declined, the townspeople fiercely resented any attempts to withhold payment, and when in the eighteenth century the Corporation tried to suppress the custom, they were met by such violent

1. Sir William Dugdale, *Antiquities of Warwickshire*, 1656.

opposition, culminating in a riot, that they were forced to continue it.

In the following century, however, the Charity Commissioners, after due enquiry, reported that, in their view, Moseley's Dole was 'at the present day a very useless mode of employing a large sum of money', and strongly recommended the Corporation to 'substitute for it some other mode of application, which might render the fund really beneficial.'[1] Their advice was taken. The annual distribution ceased in 1825, and eleven almshouses were built instead, so bringing to an end an unusual and interesting custom that had endured for nearly four centuries.

Mothering Sunday. Mid-Lent Sunday, the fourth in Lent, has more than one name, but for English people the best-known of these names is Mothering Sunday. For at least three centuries this anniversary has been a day of small family reunions, when absent sons and daughters return to their homes, and gifts are made to mothers by their children of all ages. The roots of this pleasant custom can be traced back to pre-Reformation times when, on Mid-Lent Sunday, devout parishioners went to the Mother Church of the parish, or to the Cathedral of the diocese, to make their offerings. Exactly when the day also became a festival of human motherhood is uncertain, but evidently family gatherings and 'going a-mothering' were already well established in the middle of the seventeenth century. 'Every Mid-Lent Sunday is a great day at Worcester', wrote Richard Symonds in 1644, 'when all the children and godchildren meet at the head and chief of the family and have a feast. They call it Mothering Day.'[2] Herrick refers to the custom in the well-known lines in *Hesperides* (1648):

> I'le to thee a Simnell bring
> 'Gainst thou go'st a mothering,
> So that, when she blesseth thee,
> Half that blessing thou'lt give me.

It was formerly usual for apprentices and servants to be given a holiday on Mothering Sunday, so that they might visit their mothers and take them a cake, and perhaps a posy of violets or primroses gathered in the hedgerows as they went along. Flowers and simnel cakes are still the traditional mothering-gifts (*see Simnel Sunday*), but nowadays other and more elaborate presents are often given as well. Sometimes the whole family went to church together in the morning, and then there would be a special dinner at which roast veal or roast lamb was usually the main dish, with suet- or rice-pudding, or a custard, and ale or home-made wines. In some northern districts, fig-pies or puddings were eaten, though in most places these did not appear until two weeks later, on Palm or Fig Sunday. *(See Fig Sunday.)*

'Going a-mothering' never quite vanished from the English scene, but in the late nineteenth and early twentieth centuries it gradually became less widespread. In 1912, Mrs Leather wrote of the custom in Herefordshire as 'now by no means forgotten, but declining',[1] and the same could have been said of it in many other regions. But during the last twenty years or so, it has blossomed anew, and today it is again well-known. Mothering Sunday has, indeed, become rather regrettably commercialized, as shopkeepers and manufacturers realized its value as yet another present-giving anniversary. The price of flowers rises almost automatically on the preceding Saturday, and for some time beforehand shop-windows everywhere are filled with every kind of article that can possibly be advertised as a suitable gift for 'Mother's Day'. Nevertheless, the revival seems to be a real one, of which commercialization is a result rather than a cause. It has once again become quite usual for children away from home to take or send a gift to their mother on that day, or for a family gathering to be held then. In some parishes, there is a special service in the church, to which young children bring their mothering-posies to be blessed. This last cannot be described as traditional, for it is an altogether modern practice; yet, even so, it is a recognition of the age-old connection of Mothering Sunday with both Church and family.

1. H. Edwards, *A Collection of Old English Customs*, 1842.
2. *Diary of the Marches of the Royal Army during the Great Civil War, kept by Richard Symonds*, Camden Society, 1909.

1. E. M. Leather, *The Folk-Lore of Herefordshire*, 1912.

This sudden re-flowering of an ancient custom is at least partly due to the American servicemen stationed in England during the Second World War. They confused our Mothering Sunday with their own Mother's Day, and by doing so helped to infuse new life into the former. In actual fact, the two festivals are quite unrelated, being totally different in origin and history, and falling on different dates. The English Mothering Sunday custom developed from a mediaeval ecclesiastical practice, and has never lost its connection with the Church's calendar. The American Mother's Day is a modern secular anniversary which began only in 1907.[1]

In that year, Miss Anna Jarvis, of Philadelphia, who had recently lost her own mother, conceived the idea that one day in the year ought to be set aside for the special honouring of all mothers. She began her campaign by arranging for a service to be held in one of the local churches on the anniversary of her mother's death, and asking all who attended to wear a white carnation. Within twelve months she had succeeded in persuading the people of Philadelphia to adopt this new custom; and after a few more years of earnest propaganda and unremitting hard work, she prevailed upon Congress to recognize it also. In 1914, the second Sunday in May was established as Mother's Day throughout the United States. From that time onwards, the anniversary, with its gifts to mothers and its red and white carnations worn in their honour – red for living mothers, white in memory of those already dead – has been enthusiastically observed in its country of origin, and to some extent also in Canada and parts of Latin America.

1. As an unfortunate result of the English passion for aping American ways, Mothering Sunday, though still always observed on the right date, is often called by the wrong name, and referred to as Mother's Day. This is most marked among tradesmen advertising mothering-gifts, and others who are unaware of the history of their own traditional customs, and of the fact that the real Mother's Day is celebrated in May, not during Lent.

Needle and Thread Ceremony. A rebus on the name of Robert de Eglesfield, founder of the Queen's College, Oxford, forms the basis of a little ceremony which takes place every year on New Year's Day in that College.

Eglesfield founded the College in 1341. He provided for a Provost and twelve Fellows, in honour of Our Lord and the twelve Apostles. They were to wear crimson mantles, typifying the Blood of Christ, and they were to dine in Hall seated on one side only of the High Table, with the Provost in the midst, in imitation of traditional pictures of the Last Supper. He also directed that on New Year's Day every member of the College should receive from the Bursar a needle filled with coloured thread. This made a rebus – *Aiguille et fil* – on his name, Eglesfield, and as such was to be a little memorial of a man for whom the existence of the company that shares in the ceremony and the building in which it takes place might seem memorial enough. As New Year's Day falls in vacation, not all the members of the College are in Oxford then, but to such as are, and to the Fellows and their guests, the Bursar hands the threaded needle, saying to each one as he does so, 'Take this and be thrifty.'

Neville's Cross Commemoration. On May 29th, the choristers of Durham Cathedral go to the top of the great central tower and there sing three anthems, facing towards the east, the north, and the south, but not towards the west. No one knows for certain why the western side is thus avoided, though there is a vague tradition that once, long ago, someone, (usually said to have been a chorister, but this too is uncertain), fell from thence and was killed.

Although this ceremony now takes place annually on Oak Apple Day, it has nothing to do with the Restoration of Charles II, nor was it always held on May 29th. It commemorates the battle of Neville's Cross, which was fought and won three centuries before King Charles' reign. During the absence of Edward III in France, the Scots under David I invaded England and penetrated as far south as Co. Durham. On October 17th, 1346, they were defeated by the English forces at a place on the

Red Hills where, long before, a member of the great house of Neville had set up a fine stone cross.[1] Round it much of the fiercest fighting raged, and from it the battle gained its name.

On the eve of the contest, John Fossor, Prior of Durham, was commanded in a dream, or vision, to go on the morrow to a certain hill near the cross, carrying with him as a banner one of the Abbey's treasured relics, the cloth which St Cuthbert used to cover the chalice when he said Mass. In later years, this became the battle standard of the Durham men, the famous Banner of St Cuthbert, which they carried to Flodden Field and during the Pilgrimage of Grace. On this October day, the Prior set it on the hill named in his vision, and he and a small company of monks stood round it, praying, close to the fighting, but unharmed. Meanwhile, in Durham, the rest of the monks assembled on the high Abbey Tower, to see or hear whatever they could of the distant battle and to pray for the success of the English army and the safety of their Prior. When victory was certain at last, they sang a joyous *Te Deum*, and so made the good news known to the anxious townsfolk.

From then onwards, thanksgiving for that deliverance was annually offered on the anniversary of the battle and in the same high place, first by the monks, and later by the choristers of the Cathedral who, with very few interruptions, have done so ever since. But in the seventeenth century this custom, like so many others, became absorbed in the spreading celebrations of Oak Apple Day, and now it is in May and not in October that it is observed. Nevertheless, in spite of the arbitrary change of date, the original meaning of the ceremony has never been forgotten. It remains, as every Durham man knows, what it always was – the commemoration of a fourteenth-century victory, with only a coincidental connection with Restoration festivities.

1. Neville's Cross was thrown down at the Reformation and broken, only a stump being left. There is a legend that if any one walks round that stump nine times and then puts his ear to the ground, he will hear the cries and noises of the mediaeval battle.

New Year Water. The first water drawn from any well, pond, or stream on New Year's morning formerly had a very special significance. It was known as the Flower of the Well, or the Cream of the Well, and whoever obtained it was certain of good luck in the coming year. If a young girl did so, she could expect to marry her true love before twelve months were out. Farmers in Scotland washed their dairy utensils with it, and gave it to the cows, to drink, in the belief that by so doing they would increase the supply of milk. If it was bottled and kept in the house, it never lost its original freshness and purity, and by its presence there, it protected the family from misfortune until the next New Year came round.

Since the Flower of the Well could only be drawn once, there was often keen competition to be the first on the spot, especially where one spring served several families. Many people used to sit up to see the New Year in, and then rush off to the well as soon as midnight had struck. Sometimes a specially eager person would go there before midnight and watch by the wellside until the right moment came. In Northumberland, the lucky first-comer, having filled his pail, threw a little grass or hay, or a few flowers into the water, both as an offering to the spring and as a notification to the next to arrive that he or she had come too late. On some Herefordshire farms, the servants raced to the well immediately after midnight, each hoping to be the one to ensure good luck by 'creaming the well'. If one of the maids succeeded in doing this, she carried the water to her mistress, who rewarded her with a present of money. This habit, however, seems to indicate a decline in the belief in the magical powers of the water; where it flourished really vigorously few girls would have been willing to barter a year's good luck and the likelihood of marriage for a small money-gift.

In the Scottish Highlands, water from 'the dead and living ford', that is, from a ford over which the living passed and the dead were carried, used to be brought indoors after sunset on the last day of the Old Year. This had to be done in complete silence by some person who could be trusted to go to the ford and return thence without uttering a word. The vessel in which the water was carried was not allowed to touch the ground. Early next morning, all in the house drank some of the water, and the head of the family then went into every room, sprinkling the water that remained over all the beds and any that lay in them. When this part of the ritual was ended, the doors and windows were closed and every crevice stopped up, and branches of juniper which, like the water, had been brought in after sunset on the previous evening, were set alight. A pungent smoke filled the house, causing everybody to cough and gasp for breath until, when they could bear it no longer, the windows were opened again, and the fumes were blown away. The byres and stables were then fumigated in the same way. Thus, by water and by fire, evil and disease were driven from the homestead at the beginning of the year.

A custom known as New Year's Water, or New Water, was kept up in South Wales until shortly before the beginning of this century. At about three or four o'clock on the morning of January 1st, boys went round the parish carrying a vessel full of freshly-drawn spring water and a twig of some evergreen plant. If they met any one on their way, they sprinkled the face and hands of that person with the luck-bringing water. They went from house to house, seeking admittance. If this was denied, they sprinkled the door and went on, but usually they were allowed to enter, and indeed, welcomed, since they brought good luck for the New Year. They went into every room, scattering their New Water over it, and over the occupants, who were often still in bed when they arrived. To each person they wished a happy New Year, and while they sprinkled the water, they sang, or recited, the following curious song:

> Here we bring new water from the well so clear,
> For to worship God with, this Happy New Year,
> Sing levy dew, sing levy dew, the water and the wine,
> With seven bright gold wires, the bugles that do
> shine;
> Sing reign of fair maid, with gold upon her toe,
> Open you the west door, and turn the old year go;
> Sing reign of fair maid, with gold upon her chin,
> Open you the east door, and let the new year in.

Exactly what these words mean is still a matter of debate among scholars, but the general intention is clearly one of well-wishing and New Year good fortune. Having performed their luck-bringing water-rite, the boys were rewarded with money, often quite generously, and then went on to the next house, and the next, until they had completed the round of the parish.

Oak Apple Day. Oak Apple Day, Royal Oak Day, Oak-and-Nettle Day, and in some places, Shick Shack Day, are all traditional names for May 29th, the anniversary of Charles II's triumphal entry into London after the Restoration of 1660. Of all his many and memorable adventures during his long span of misfortune and exile, it was his concealment in the oak at Boscobel which seems to have made the greatest impression upon his people. Hence the names of the festival. Oak Apple Day was for a long time an extremely popular holiday, and tended in some districts to overshadow even May Day itself, and to absorb some of its ceremonies. Towards the end of last century, its popularity waned somewhat, and some of its customary observances were forgotten; but a number of the customs of the day still survive, and nearly always have some connection with the oak.

Founder's Day at the Royal Hospital, Chelsea, is celebrated every year on or about May 29th. It was Charles who founded this 'hostel or guest-house for worthy veterans of the Army who are prevented by old age or disabilities from earning a livelihood' in 1682. Nell Gwynne is said to have suggested it to him, but there is no real proof that she did so, and whether it was her idea or his, he was ready enough to put it into practice. In the centre of the main court of Sir Christopher Wren's building, there is a statue of Charles, the work of Grinling Gibbons, and this on Founder's Day is entirely covered with oak boughs. In front of it some special visitor, a member of the Royal Family, or some famous general, stands to watch the march past of the veterans in their scarlet coats, all of them wearing sprigs of oak, as the visitor does himself (or herself). There are, of course, some who are too crippled or too infirm to take part in the parade, but they have their places reserved for them in the court, where they can see all that happens, and take part in the final cheers for the visitors, the Founder, and the Queen. They too wear the oak.

At Leycester Hospital, Warwick, which is also a soldiers' hospital, but much older than the Chelsea foundation, Oak Apple Day is celebrated by decorating the rooms and galleries with oaken greenery, and by the issue of a special ration of food and drink. At Worcester, where the last disastrous battle was fought in 1651, the Guild Hall gates are hung with oak-boughs, and a commemorative ceremony is held. In Northampton, the people remember the King with gratitude as well as loyalty, for in 1675, when a large part of the town was destroyed by fire, he gave them a thousand tons of timber from Whittlewood Forest to build new houses, and also forgave them the payment of Chimney-tax for seven years. Here, on May 29th, the Mayor and Corporation, carrying bunches of oak-apples and gilded leaves, lead a procession which includes school-children bearing the same emblems. The procession goes from the Town Hall through some of the main streets to All Saints' Church, where a service is held and a charity sermon preached. At this church, there is a statue of Charles II, which is decorated with oak-boughs for the occasion by the choristers.

These are all solemn occasions, but for nearly three centuries, the day has been celebrated with more jovial customs, and particularly by the wearing of oak-sprigs and the chastisement of those who do not. Formerly, almost everyone, old or young, wore oak-leaves and, if they could be had, oak-apples, and any person appearing without these loyal emblems was liable to be pelted with wild birds' eggs, or beaten with nettles. It was not for nothing that in some counties this day was known as Oak-and-Nettle Day. Another possible penalty was to be vigorously pinched or kicked. Usually, though not invariably, the danger of punishment ceased at noon. In Berkshire and Wiltshire, it was customary for oak-leaves to be worn until noon, and then to be replaced by even-ash leaves, which were kept in place until sunset. The oak-wearing custom was once very general, and it still survives among children in parts of the northern counties, and of the north midlands.

Not only people and statues, but also churches and houses used to be adorned with oak on May 29th. In a number of places, large boughs were set up on church towers. At Whitechurch Canonicorum, in Dorset, men went out at three o'clock in the morning to gather oak-branches, one of which was always put on the church tower, and another on a post in the centre of the village, on the site of the present War Memorial. The bells were rung, and the ringers then went round the village, setting branches over the doorways of the houses. These house-visits ceased eventually, but the bell-ringing and the hanging of the oak-boughs on the church continued until well within the present century. Elsewhere, until about seventy or eighty years ago, it was quite usual, in some districts, for tradesmen to trim their windows with oak, and for ordinary householders to hang oak-apples, sometimes gilded, on the latches or the knockers of their doors. Horses 'wore the oak' very often, and so, though more occasionally, did the engines on some railways, and the fishing-boats in some harbours. *(See also: Garland King Day: Groveley: Nevill's Cross Commemoration.)*

Oakham Horseshoes. When a peer of the realm comes for the first time to the Manor of Oakham, in Rutland, tradition requires that he should pay tribute to the Lord of the Manor in the form of a shoe from his horse or, failing that, a sum of money in lieu thereof. This custom is said to date from the reign of Henry II, and to have been instituted by Wakelin de Ferrers, who built Oakham Castle about the year 1180. Whether he then had the right, or the power, to enforce his demands upon travelling princes as well as upon lesser noblemen is not clear, but certainly Elizabeth I was willing to conform to what had already become 'immemorial custom' by her time, for she contributed a shoe in 1556. She was not, of course, Queen at that date; but since then several reigning monarchs and their near kinsmen have done as she did, including Queen Victoria, Edward VII, George VI, the Duke of Windsor (when he was Prince of Wales), the Duke of Edinburgh and, in 1967, Queen Elizabeth II.

Originally, the shoes thus presented, or if a real shoe was refused, substitutes bought with the compensation money, were nailed on the outside of the castle gate, where all could see them. They now hang indoors, round the walls of the Great Hall. Practically all the horseshoes there displayed are in fact substitutes, some of which are very large, or of fancy construction. One presented by the Prince Regent in 1814 is of immense size and made of bronze and ormolu. Many of the more recently presented shoes are gilded, ornamented, and surmounted by a coronet. Each one bears the name of the giver and the date on which he gave it.

Oranges and Lemons. Annually, on March 31st, or as near as possible to that date, the Oranges and Lemons ceremony is held in the Church of St Clement Danes, in London. The children of the nearby primary school come to the church for a short service of prayers and hymns, in which the lesson is read by a child, and the sermon and blessing are given by the Royal Air Force Chaplain, in whose charge the church now is. When the service is ended, the tune of the traditional nursery rhyme that begins:

> Oranges and Lemons,
> Say the bells of St Clemens.

is played upon handbells by members of the London County Association of Change Ringers. Then, as the children stream out of the building, each one is given an orange and a lemon by the Chaplain and his helpers.

This charming ceremony is not at all old, dating only from 1920, but it is nevertheless a continuation, in a new form of the centuries-old association of St Clement Danes parish with oranges and lemons. The present church was built in the seventeenth century, but another stood upon the site as early as the tenth century, and served the Danes who then lived in the neighbourhood. When oranges and lemons first came to England in the Middle Ages, they were brought up-river in barges from the Pool of London, and are traditionally said to have been landed close to the churchyard, which once ran right down to the shores of the Thames. They were carried thence by porters to Clare Market, passing through Clement's Inn, where a toll had to be paid for the right of passage. What appears to have been a relic of this old commercial usage was preserved in a custom that existed in Clement's Inn until almost within living memory. On New Year's Day, the attendants visited all the tenants of the Inn, to present each one with an orange and a lemon, and to receive from each half-a-crown in return.

The children's ceremony was started in 1920 by the Reverend William Pennington-Bickford, then Rector of the parish. In the previous year the bells, which had been silent since 1913 because their oak frame was unsafe, were restored and re-dedicated, and on March 31st, 1920, the nursery-rhyme tune rang out once more from the belfry. Oranges and lemons were given by London's Danish colony for distribution to the children, and from then on Oranges and Lemons Day was annually observed until the outbreak of the Second World War. The church and its famous bells were both seriously damaged in 1941, but after the war ended, the building was restored and became the Royal Air Force church. The bells were re-hung in 1957. Now the children's ceremony is again regularly held, and the oranges-and-lemons tune is played by the bells four times every day – at nine o'clock in the morning, at noon, at three o'clock in the afternoon, and at six in the evening.

Oyster Feast, Colchester. Colchester has owned the oyster-fisheries in the River Colne since Richard I gave them to the town in 1186, and this fact is annually celebrated in the ceremonial opening of the season on September 1st, and the splendid Oyster Feast in October, at which three or four hundred guests are usually present.

On the first day of the dredging season, the Mayor of Colchester in his robes of office, accompanied by members of the Town Council and of the Fishery Board, goes in a fishing-boat from Brightlingsea into Pyefleet Creek. The Town Clerk reads aloud an ancient Proclamation, dated 1256, which asserts that the fishery-rights in the River have belonged to Colchester 'from the time beyond which memory runneth not to the contrary'. The company then toast the Queen in gin and eat small pieces of gingerbread, after which the Mayor ceremonially opens the season by lowering the trawl and bringing up the first oysters.

The famous Oyster Feast is held in October, in the Moot Hall. This is the last of the many civic feasts for which Colchester was once renowned, all of which were held at the expense of the citizens of the town, and all of them swept away by the ruthless broom of the Municipal Reform Act of 1835. The Oyster Feast perished with the rest, but after some four hundred years of continuous life, it was too dear to the pride of the community to be allowed to vanish altogether. It was revived, and has since been held annually with much magnificence on or about October 20th. More than twelve thousand oysters are said to be consumed by the guests on this great occasion of the town's year.

Pace Egging. In the three or four days before, or after, Easter, or on the morning of Easter Day itself, the Pace-Eggers, or Jolly-Boys, still go on their rounds in many districts of the English northern counties.[1] Nowadays, it is mainly children who keep up the old custom, but eighty or ninety years ago it was young men and lads who paraded through the villages, begging for eggs and other gifts, and acting the Pace-Egg Play, the Easter version of the Mumming Play. They were disguised in various ways, as befitted their ancient character of ritual performers. Often they appeared with fluttering paper streamers sewn all over their ordinary garments, or in a variety of strange costumes dictated either by personal fancy, or by the parts they acted in the Pace-Egg Play. Usually, too, their faces were blackened with soot, or hidden by masks. In Lancashire, they frequently carried wooden swords, with which they sometimes fought any rival gangs of Jolly-Boys encountered on the way.

Their real business, apart from the practical matter of collecting eggs, was the acting of the Play. This was the essential ritual which, in earlier times, was probably never omitted; but when the pace-egging custom began to decline towards the end of last century, it was sometimes forgotten. The old disguises were still worn, and some of the character-names, like Old Tosspot, or Lord Nelson, or Betsy Brownbags, were retained, but the play to which they belonged was not always presented. The Pace-Eggers limited their performance to the singing of traditional songs, like that which begins:

We are a two-three jolly-boys, all of one mind,
We are come a-pace-egging, and we hope you'll prove kind.
We hope you'll prove kind with your eggs and strong beer,
And we'll come no more a-pace-egging until another year.

In the Calder Valley, in Yorkshire, the Midgley version of the Pace-Egg Play is still acted in full by the boys of the Calder High School, who wear curious stylized headdresses and beribboned costumes, and are the last of many such teams that once performed on Good Friday in the streets of the valley towns. In the two Westmorland villages of Far and Near Sawrey, another version is, or was until very recently, acted by the children of certain families. In an account printed in *Folk-Lore* in 1951, the writer says that these children had learnt the words by oral transmission from their parents, and regarded the presentation of the play as a sort of hereditary possession of their own small group. They ran the whole thing themselves, including the making of their dresses and the allotting of the parts. No outsider was allowed to act in the play without their invitation, and that invitation was rarely given except when there was an unusual vacancy to be filled. In 1951, when such a vacancy occurred, the part was given to a young visitor to the village rather than to a local child from some other family.

1. Pace-egging was best known in Yorkshire, Durham, Northumberland, Cumberland, Westmorland, Lancashire and Cheshire, and it is in these parts of England, especially in the north-western counties and Yorkshire, that traces of it can still be found.

That year, the six performers were all girls, a departure from normal custom that was probably due to a temporary shortage of boys of suitable age in the families concerned.[1]

Elsewhere, the children who now go Pace-egging on their own rarely act the old Play, and are probably unaware of its existence except in a few places where its words and actions are still remembered by parents or grandparents. Quite often, they dress up in some fantastic manner, or black their faces, but even this is not universal today. They do, however, usually remember one or more of the traditional begging-songs appropriate to the occasion, such as:

> Please, good mistress, an Easter egg,
> Or a flitch of bacon,
> Or a little trundle cheese
> Of your own making.

or the little verse used by Cheshire children which runs:

> Please, Mrs, Whiteleg,
> Please to give us an Easter Egg,
> If you won't give us an Easter Egg,
> Your hens will all lay addled eggs,
> And your cocks all lay stones.

and these they cheerfully sing or chant outside the doors of the houses they visit.

Anglesey children 'clap for eggs' at Eastertime, a custom that now seems to survive only in that county, though formerly it existed in many other parts of North Wales. They go round the farms and houses of the district carrying wooden clappers or, more usually now, two pieces of slate with which they make a noise like the rattle of castanets. They also sing a pathetic-sounding little ditty in Welsh, of which the English translation is 'Clap, clap, ask for an egg for little boys on the parish.' Their object is, of course, to collect eggs, either for eating or for use in games. Anything else, however, is equally acceptable, and here, as in other areas of Britain, the children are often given sweets, or cakes, or money by housewives who have not the time or the inclination to prepare the pace-eggs of tradition.

1. M. Danielli, 'Jollyboys, or Pace-Eggers, in Westmorland', *Folk-Lore*, Vol. 62, 1951.

Young lads, and sometimes poor adults, used to beg for 'peace' or 'paiss' eggs in Scotland, though this seems to have been done with less ceremony than in England. In the Highlands and the Western Isles, egg-collecting was sometimes practised in another manner. During Holy Week, boys stole as many eggs as they could lay their hands on and hid them in some secret place where they were safe from prying eyes. On Easter Sunday, they met together in a quiet and remote spot, a good long way from their homes, and made themselves a splendid feast of pancakes. All had to be done in strict secrecy, and only stolen eggs were considered worthy to be eaten on this occasion. Nevertheless, their elders usually knew, or guessed what was happening, if only because they had probably done the same when they were young themselves. The practice was sanctioned by custom, and was not regarded by any one as ordinary theft. *(See Easter Eggs: Easter Games.)*

Palming. On Palm Sunday the Christian Church remembers the triumphal entry of Our Lord into Jerusalem, and the green branches which the rejoicing people tore from the trees to strew in His path. From a very early period, this happening has been commemorated by solemn processions in which blessed palms are carried, and by the distribution of small palm-crosses to the congregations assembled in churches all over Europe. These ceremonies have never ceased in Roman Catholic and Orthodox countries, and today they are included in part or in full, in the Palm Sunday services of many Anglican churches and those of other communions. There was a time, soon after the Reformation, when they declined, or were abolished, in most Protestant lands. In England, they survived until the reign of Edward VI, but about 1548 they ceased to be part of the official rites of the Church of England. 'This yeere,' says Edmund Howes in his continuation of Stow's *Annals*, 'the ceremony of bearing of palmes on Palme Sunday was left off, and not used as before.'

Nevertheless, in Great Britain as elsewhere, the traditional association of this Springtime Sunday with palms and evergreens was never quite forgotten by ordinary people. 'Going a-palming' was a widespread custom until fairly recent times. In the three or four days before Palm Sunday, young people went into the woods and fields to collect green branches with which to adorn their houses and the parish church, and little sprigs of greenery to wear in their hats and buttonholes. Since there are no palms in Britain, they gathered willow or hazel, box or yew, and especially the sallow willow with its beautiful fluffy golden catkins, *Salix caprea*, which is often known as the English Palm. In Scotland, long after all memory of the old religious processions had faded, children in some areas held their own processions, marching along the roads with willow-boughs in their hands, though probably none could say exactly why he did so except that it was the custom. At Lanark, the boys of the Grammar School had a holiday on the Saturday before Palm Sunday, when they went in parade through the streets. The boy who had made the largest Candlemas offering to the master became their King for the day, and walked in the procession 'with his life-guards and sergeants. The palm, or its substitute, a large tree of the willow kind decked with a profusion of daffodils was carried before him; also a handsome embroidered flag, the gift of a lady residing in the town to the boys. The day finished off with a ball.'[1]

It was commonly believed that the branches gathered for the festival, if kept in the house, would protect it from evil in the following months. In northern England, they were often made into little crosses and hung upon the walls of houses. 'I can myself bear witness', wrote William Henderson in 1866, 'to their constant use in the city of Durham, about forty years ago. Many a time have I, when a boy, walked with my comrades to the river-bank, near Kepier Hospital, to gather palms; and many a cross have I made of them for Palm Sunday. We formed them like a St Andrew's Cross, with a tuft of catkins at each point, and bound them with knots and bows of ribbon.'[2]

1. E. J. Guthrie, *Old Scottish Customs, Local and General*, 1885.

2. William Henderson, *Notes on the Folk-Lore of the Northern Counties of England and the Borders*, 1866.

Sometimes other magical powers were attributed to the Palm Sunday greenery. Carew, in his *Survey of Cornwall* (1602), mentions 'idle-headed seekers' who used to go to Our Lady of Nant's Well at Little Colan and throw palm crosses into it for purposes of divination. If a cross sank, the person who threw it would die soon, but if it floated, he would live at least until next Palm Sunday. Near Morley, in Yorkshire, those who resorted on that day to the gathering on the Howley Hills which was known as Fieldkirk Fair brought green branches with them, and threw them into Lady Ann's Well.

The waters of this well were said to change colour on the festival anniversary and, though they had no healing properties at other times, they were believed to acquire them for that one day after the palms had been thrown into them.

A curious celebration of uncertain origin and meaning, known as Seeking the Golden Arrow, used to take place on Palm Sunday on Pontesford Hill in Shropshire. Large numbers of people went to the hill-top in the early morning, supposedly to search for the Golden Arrow, but actually to picnic, gather greenery, and make merry. Charlotte Burne, who recorded the custom as it was in the nineteenth century,[1] says that no one knew what the Golden Arrow was, or why it ought to be sought. Some great personage was vaguely believed to have dropped or lost it long ago. According to one legend, an estate would change hands when it was found, but only the rightful (and hitherto defrauded) heir could hope to find it. Another tradition said that a fairy had commanded the search to be made, and that when the Arrow was discovered, some ancient curse would be lifted, or a long-forgotten wrong righted: but to ensure success, the search must be made in the darkness of the very early morning, immediately after midnight, by a young girl who was less than twenty years of age, and who was also the seventh daughter of a seventh son.

Seeking the Golden Arrow was often called 'going a-palming' because gathering green branches was an essential part of the custom. The 'palms' gathered could be any kind of

1. C S. Burne, *Shropshire Folk-Lore*, 1883.

greenery, including sprigs from a solitary yew-tree, the only one of its kind on the hill-top. This tree was said to be haunted, presumably by a benevolent spirit, since it was thought lucky to be the first to gather a spray from it on Palm Sunday. Whoever did this would be fortunate throughout the year, provided that the sprig was carefully preserved. When the palming was over, and everyone had his or her green branch, young people of both sexes raced down the steep sides of the hill to a stream in a hollow known as Lyde Hole. If anyone could run the whole way down at full speed without falling (a feat which Miss Burne describes as practically impossible), and then dipped the fourth finger of the right hand into the water, he or she would be sure of marrying the first person of opposite sex afterwards encountered.

How or when this peculiar custom began does not seem to be known. 'Going a-palming' at this season was nothing out of the ordinary, and had its Christian explanation; but the festive gathering on a hill-top at an early hour, the luck attached to the haunted yew that may once have been a holy tree, and the mysterious Golden Arrow which only a specially qualified person can find, and which will cause changes when found, all suggest that the celebration is older than the Christian Palm Sunday. One explanation put forward in 1841 was that it commemorated a battle fought at Pontesbury in A.D. 661, but it seems more likely that it represented the fragmentary remains of a pagan Spring Festival rite associated with the sunrise.[1]

The custom gradually declined in popularity towards the end of the nineteenth century. In 1949, it was still kept up in a modified form, but a few years later it ceased, and has not since been revived.

Pancake Bell. Ringing the Pancake Bell on Shrove Tuesday is an old and once widespread custom which still survives in a number of parishes. Originally, this bell had nothing to do with pancakes. It was the Shriving Bell, which rang to summon the faithful to church, there to confess their sins to be shriven in preparation for the holy season of Lent. It was from this pious and once general practice of pre-Lent confession that the name of Shrovetide is derived. After the Reformation, the bell continued to be rung, although the religious reason for it had ceased, and came to be regarded as a signal for the holiday revels to begin. It was then that it acquired the name of Pancake Bell, or in some districts, Fritter, or Guttit Bell. Now that Shrove Tuesday has lost much of its festival character, it is often supposed to ring as a warning for housewives to start preparing their pancakes. Usually it is sounded at about eleven o'clock in the morning, but the hour varies in different parishes, and may be earlier or later. At Scarborough, where the old bell used for this purpose now hangs in the town's museum and not in the church, it rings at noon.

At Hedon in East Yorkshire, until about 1885, all the apprentices of the town whose indentures were due to end before the next Shrove Tuesday came round, used to assemble in the church tower at eleven o'clock and take turns to toll the Pancake Bell for an hour. A somewhat similar custom prevailed in York Minster until it was suppressed, with more than a little difficulty, by Dr Lake in the seventeenth century. In a tract written in 1690, and quoted in Brand's *Popular Antiquities* (Vol. I), it is stated that 'all the apprentices, journeymen, and other servants of the town, had the liberty to go into the cathedral, and ring the pancake bell (as we call it in the country) on Shrove Tuesday.' This was, adds the writer of the tract, 'thought a more innocent divertisement than being in the alehouse.' Nevertheless, Dr Lake, when he first came to York, disapproved of the custom very strongly and, in spite of violent opposition, he finally succeeded in suppressing it.

Pancake Greeze. The custom known as the Pancake Greeze is annually observed on Shrove Tuesday at Westminster School. At eleven o'clock in the morning, the cook, in his white jacket, cap, and apron, comes to the Great Schoolroom, where a crowd of boys and spectators awaits him. He is preceded by the verger, bearing a silver-topped mace, and he carries a frying-pan containing a pancake. This cake

1. Revd. C. H. Hartshorne, *Salopia Antiqua*, 1841.

he tosses expertly over the high iron bar which separates the old Upper and Lower Schools, and as it falls on the farther side, a wild scramble to catch it begins. At one time, all the boys in the school took part in this scrimmage, but now each form chooses one of its members to represent it. The boy who succeeds in securing the pancake, or the greater part of it, receives a guinea from the Dean. The cook also receives a fee, and this he certainly deserves, for tossing a pancake neatly over a bar sixteen feet from the ground is by no means an easy task. Yet only rarely has there been a failure. In 1934, the cake hit the bar, and most of it remained hanging there far above the heads of the boys and the onlookers. Another pancake was quickly produced and tossed, this time successfully, and the scramble then proceeded as usual.

Pancake Race. One of the main events of Shrove Tuesday at Olney in Buckinghamshire is the Pancake Race. This race is said to have been first run there in 1445, and to have continued intermittently ever since, with occasional lapses and revivals. One such lapse occurred, for obvious reason, during the Second World War, but in 1948 the custom was re-started and has not since suffered interruption.

The competitors are housewives who must be inhabitants of Olney, or the nearby Warrington. The rules also require them to wear aprons and to cover their heads with a hat or scarf. The course to be run is from the village square to the parish church, about four hundred and fifteen yards. A bell rings twice before the race, once to warn the women to make their pancakes, and again to bid them assemble in the square, each one carrying a frying-pan with the cooked cake in it. Finally, the Pancake Bell is rung to start them running.

The pancakes have to be tossed three times during the race, and some, inevitably, land in the road, but this does not disqualify the runner, who is allowed to pick it up and toss it again. At the church door, the Vicar waits to greet the breathless women, and to award the winner and the runner-up a prayer-book as prize. With him stands the verger who has the right to claim a kiss from the winner, and is usually given her pancake as well. Then all the pans are laid round the font in the church, and a short service of blessing is held.

Since 1950, a similar race has been run on the same day at Liberal, Kansas, and there is keen competition in running-times between these two widely-separated townships. Pancake races can now be seen in several other places in England, but these are mainly modern imitations, most of them having been organized within the last twenty years or so. That at Olney is the only one that can claim to be genuinely old.

Pax Cakes. The distribution of Pax Cakes on Palm Sunday at Sellack and Kings Caple in Herefordshire, and until recently, at Hentland in the same county, is a ceremony which certainly dates from the sixteenth century, and may be far older. About the year 1570, Lady Scudamore, a local landowner, charged the revenues of Baysham Court with three annual payments of five shillings and ninepence each to provide cake and ale every year on Palm Sunday for the parishioners of the three villages. From the money, five shillings was to pay for the cake and the odd ninepence was to be spent on ale. The food and drink were to be given at the morning service and consumed in the church.

The donor believed that in this way peace and friendship at the holy season of Easter would be ensured, since those who had shared a common meal in church would surely be readier to compose any quarrels that might exist between them, and to come together in amity to their Easter Communion a week later. Although there is no doubt that her benefaction was inspired by this pious intention, it is by no means certain that the custom itself was new in her day. It has a strong pre-Reformation flavour about it, and it is quite probable that, as in the case of some other endowed customs, her money was given to preserve an ancient ritual that was already in existence, rather than to inaugurate something quite new.

Originally, one large cake was provided and presented by the churchwardens to the Vicar, who cut the first slice. The rest was then carried round to the people in their seats. At one time it seems to have been usual for the clergyman to break his cake with some of his principal parishioners, and for others in the congregation to break theirs with their neighbours, saying 'Peace and good neighbourhood', or 'Peace and good will', as they did so. Glasses of ale were also distributed, but at some time in the nineteenth century the funds to pay for this were lost, perhaps owing to the fall in the value of money. For some years thereafter the deficiency was supplied by local farmers who brought their own ale or cider to the service; but eventually, with changing ideas of decorum, this ceased, and only the cake remained.

Later, the single large cake was replaced by small cakes, one for each person. An account in the *Herefordshire Journal* for March 20th 1907, speaks of baskets, covered by a white cloth and filled with buns, being carried round by the churchwardens immediately after the collection. The writer adds that these cakes 'well within living memory of the inhabitants of Sellack . . . have been the means of settling bitter feuds, notably between two sisters just before one of them passed away.'

Nowadays, the Pax Cakes are small flat wafers, stamped with the image of the Paschal Lamb. They are no longer distributed or eaten in the church, but are handed by the Vicar, standing outside the church door, to each person as he or she comes out of the building. As he does this, the clergyman says 'God and Good Neighbourhood' to every recipient, as a reminder of the intention of this ancient ceremony.

Peace and Good Neighbourhood Dinner. At some now uncertain date, usually believed to be about five hundred years ago, an unmarried woman, whose name has been forgotten, left forty shillings to the inhabitants of Church Street, Kidderminster, in order to provide, every year on Midsummer Eve, a farthing loaf for each child born in that street, or living in it. She also expressed a wish that the person acting as trustee for this money should, on the same day, invite to his house all the men of the street, so that they might meet together in friendship, and settle any differences that might have arisen between any of them in the year just passed. Because of this bequest, the anniversary was long known in the neighbourhood as Farthing Loaf Day.

The money was lost for a time, owing to a bad investment, but kindly local individuals replaced it, and in 1776 it was supplemented by the will of John Brecknell, himself a resident of Church Street. He left £150 to pay for a twopenny plum-cake to be given to every child or unmarried woman in the street, in addition to the farthing loaves already provided, and also for pipes, tobacco, and ale for the men who attend the Midsummer meeting. This latter gift was, as he says in his will, given to foster 'the better establishment and continuance of the said Friendly Meeting for Ever'. Any remaining money was to be given to the poor in sums not more than five shillings or less than two shillings for each person.

These two bequests were the foundation of the Peace and Good Neighbourhood Dinner, now held every year at Midsummer. The chairman asks at the beginning if any one in Church Street is at odds with his neighbour, and offers to try to reconcile them, if that is the case. The main toast at the Dinner is 'Peace and Good Neighbourhood', and these words are also said when the cakes and the loaves, and the money gifts to the poor, are distributed to the people of Church Street.

Plague Memorial, Eyam. In 1665, a box of infected cloth was sent from London, where the plague was then raging, to the village tailor at Eyam in Derbyshire. It arrived in Wakes week, at the end of August. Within a month, all in the tailor's house were dead of the plague, except the man himself, and the disease was spreading through the parish with appalling rapidity. The Rector, William Mompesson, realized that little could be done for Eyam itself, but that the surrounding district could still be saved if his parishioners would agree to abandon all ideas of flight, and to confine themselves, voluntarily, within their own boundaries for as long as the epidemic lasted. Helped by his nonconformist predecessor, Thomas Stanley, who had been ejected from the living after the Restoration, he persuaded them all to consent to this truly heroic course, from which, once agreed to, none deviated until the end came some thirteen months later.

No one was allowed to go more than half a mile from the village, and no outsider was permitted to approach or enter it. The Earl of Devonshire arranged to send food and other necessities, which were left on a stone far enough off to be safe for his messengers, and were afterwards fetched by Eyam men still well enough to carry them. The church was closed, but open-air services were held on Sundays in a hollow known as Cucklet Dell, where the Rector preached to his stricken people from a rock. The plague declined a little in the cold winter months, but it broke out again with renewed ferocity in the following May. Altogether, two hundred and fifty-nine people perished, out of a total population of three hundred and fifty. One of the victims was Catherine Mompesson, the Rector's wife. Out of two leading families, the Talbots and the Hancocks, only one person was left alive when the visitation ended.

There is no doubt that many who died could have saved themselves if they had fled from the village before the plague struck them, but no one did. Their sacrifice was not in vain. The infection did not spread, as it quite certainly would have done if that sacrifice had not been made. It is true that the hamlet of Foolow, two miles away, did suffer an outbreak of plague in October 1665, supposedly caused by a straying dog from Eyam, who brought the germs to a farmhouse there. But except for this, the neighbourhood went free.

Now, once a year, on Wakes Sunday, the last Sunday in August, this act of collective heroism is remembered at a memorial service for the men and women who died in the epidemic. A long procession of local people and visitors, led by Anglican and Nonconformist clergy, and headed by a band, winds its way out to Cucklet Dell, and there the service is celebrated, as once, long ago, so many others were in less happy circumstances. It includes a sermon, prayers and a lesson, and the singing of a special hymn known as the Plague Hymn.

Planting the Penny Hedge. The Penny Hedge, or Horngarth, is annually planted on the morning of Ascension Eve below high-tide mark on the river shore at Boyes Staith, Whitby. This is an ancient tenure-custom whereby certain lands were formerly held from the Abbots of Whitby by the service of erecting a stout fence, or hedge, made of stakes and interlaced osiers. It had to be strong enough to withstand the force of three tides, and to be in position by nine o'clock on the appointed morning, unless the state of the tide made this impossible. Certain other conditions had also to be fulfilled some of which are still in force today.

The age of this service is unknown, though it is certainly very old, and may possibly run back to Anglo-Saxon times. A local legend fixes its origin in the middle of the twelfth century, and connects it with a penance. According to this tale, William de Bruse (or Bruce), Ralph de Percy, and a freeholder named Allatson, went hunting on October 16th, 1159, in the woods of Eskdale-side. These woods were on the Abbot of Whitby's lands, and in them was a hermitage where one of the monks of the Abbey was then living. The three huntsmen started a wild boar which fled before their hounds and, when nearly exhausted, ran for shelter into the chapel of the hermitage. The hermit, either from a humane desire to protect the boar (which died almost immediately), or simply to save the chapel from being overrun, shut the door in the faces of the hounds, so that when their owners arrived, they found the frustrated pack milling about and baying outside. In their rage at this interruption of their sport, they beat the hermit so unmercifully that he died soon afterwards, though luckily for them, not before he was able to save them from their well-merited punishment. Not only did he forgive them freely for his sufferings and death, but he also persuaded the infuriated Abbot, who was demanding the full penalties for murder and sacrilege, to be satisfied with the penance which the hermit himself devised for the culprits.

This was that they and their descendants should henceforth hold their lands from the Abbot and his successors by the service of the Horngarth. They were required to go every year at sunrise on Ascension Eve to Stray-head Wood where the Abbot's bailiff awaited them, and there cut a prescribed number of stakes and osiers with a knife valued at one penny. They were then to carry these stakes upon their backs through Whitby to a point on the river-shore – once at the Town End, now a little farther along the estuary of the Esk, at Boyes Staith – which must be reached before nine o'clock in the morning. If it was then full tide, they need do no more; but if not, they were to set about building their strong hedge. At intervals during the proceedings, and when the work was completed, the Abbot's bailiff was to sound his horn and cry 'Out upon ye! Out upon ye!' as a reminder of their dreadful crime. If this service was refused at any time, the holding dependent upon it was forfeit.

Whether there is any truth in this explanatory legend, and if so, how much, it is now impossible to discover. Lionel Charlton, in his *History of Whitby and Whitby Abbey* (1779), says that 'the making-up of the Horngarth . . . was the tenure by which all the Abbey-land near Whitby was formerly held'. He adds that this tenure was locally so interwoven with the tale of the death of the hermit that 'it will require some trouble to clear up matters', and suggests that there may possibly have been an actual murder of a monk or priest at some period, of which the tradition had somehow become attached to the performance of an older tenure-service due to the Abbey.

That service is now rendered for part of the original lands to the Lord of the Manor of Whitby who, in this matter, has taken the place of the Abbey, long since dissolved and fallen into ruins. Annually, on the traditional day, the tenant, now usually surrounded by an admiring crowd, drives his stakes into the muddy ground and joins them with the osiers to make a stout, tide-resisting hedge of the age-old pattern. The Manor Bailiff stands by, and when the work is finished, be blows a blast upon an ancient horn and cries out 'Out upon ye! Out upon ye!' as his ecclesiastical predecessor did of old. It is his duty also to see that the tenant renders 'good service', and that the Horngarth he builds is strong enough to withstand three successive tides. It should be that at least, since in another sense it has withstood the passage of eight centuries, and possibly more.

Plough Monday. Plough Monday is the first Monday after January 6th, so called because it was formerly the day on which work on the farm was resumed after the Twelve Days of Christmas, and Spring ploughing began.

Plough Monday, next after that Twelfth tide is past,
Bids out with the plough, the worst husband is last.

wrote Thomas Tusser in 1580,[1] conjuring up a picture of industrious ploughmen hard at work on countless farms at the beginning of the season. But how much actual work was ever done on this anniversary is very uncertain because, in England at least, the principal feature of the day was not ploughing but the ritual dragging about of a decorated plough, called the Fool, or the White Plough, by bands of young men variously known as Plough Stots, Bullocks, Jacks, or Jags. In Northamptonshire and Huntingdonshire they were called Plough Witches. They wore fanciful costumes of various

1. Thomas Tusser, *Five Hundred Points of Good Husbandrie* ed. Dorothy Hartley, 1931.

kinds, usually adorned with ribbons, jewellery, and any sort of ornament available, including in some districts, horse-brasses. With them went a man dressed in women's clothes, who was called the Bessy and carried a collecting-box. There were also Sword-dancers in areas where the Sword-dancing tradition existed, and, in some counties,[1] the colourful characters of the Plough Play, the ancient folk-play which belongs to this season and was often acted on the Plough Monday festival.

The Fool Plough was drawn through the streets and up to the doors of houses, where gifts of money, or of food and drink, were demanded from the householders. If these were given, as almost invariably they were, the young men shouted 'largesse!' and danced round the plough; if they were refused, the ground in front of the house was roughly ploughed up by way of punishment for the tenant's want of generosity. Probably this happened only rarely, but the knowledge that it could happen may often have acted as a powerful stimulus to open-handed giving. 'I have a vivid recollection', wrote J. C. Cox in a fotnote to Joseph Strutt's *Sports and Pastimes of the People of England*,[2] 'of seeing the Plough Monday mummers with their plough, when a small boy at Parwich, near Ashbourne, in 1847–1848, and being taken in the latter year to see the havoc made by the plough in the small front garden of a well-to-do but niggardly resident.' The Plough Stots themselves were all convinced that they had an inalienable right, based upon an 'old charter' of which no details were ever given, to act thus when the occasion arose; and though it cannot be supposed that all their victims shared this belief, it is a curious fact that none ever seems to have attempted any retributive action beyond lively remonstrance.

In the Middle Ages, part of the money collected was used to support the Plough Light maintained by the Ploughmen's Guild in the parish church. This light burnt before the Guild altar, and was never allowed to go out. After the Reformation, the Plough Light disappeared, and the money once gathered for it was given to the Churchwardens to help with parochial expenses, or went with the rest to provide a convivial evening for the performers. Later still, it was asked, and given, quite simply for the last-named purpose alone.

The lively secular celebrations of Plough Monday died out gradually at the end of the nineteenth and the beginning of the twentieth century, though their memory still lingers on in many villages. But Ploughtide was one of the seasons of the Church's agricultural year, and an occasion for the blessing of tillage, and of that fact we are reminded today by the Plough Sunday services which have become increasingly popular in many agricultural districts since 1943. On the day before the old festival, a plough is brought into the church by farmers and ploughmen who come, in the words of the service, 'to offer the work of the countryside to the service of God.' Prayers are offered for a plentiful harvest, that the people may be fed, and finally the plough is blessed, and with it the ploughmen and all who work on the farms of the parish.

Plygain. *Plygain*, which literally means the 'crowing of the cock', is the Welsh name of an early morning service which was once held all

1. Chiefly Yorkshire, Lincolnshire, Leicestershire, Nottinghamshire, Rutland, Cambridgeshire and Norfolk.
2. 1903 edition, edited by J. Charles Cox.

over Wales on Christmas Day, and which still survives in a modified form in a few places. A shortened version of the morning service, with prayers, carols, and sometimes a brief sermon, was celebrated in the parish church at some time between three and six o'clock in the morning, and was followed by more carol-singing which often went on for a considerable time. Practically everyone in the parish came to it, even when it meant a long, cold journey in the darkness from remote outlying farms. In some counties the congregation included nonconformists as well as churchpeople, sectarian differences being forgotten for the occasion; in other regions, particularly in South Wales, the local chapels had their own, slightly different form of the *plygain*. Many householders who were too old or infirm to go to church rose at cock-crow with the rest of the family, and spent the hour of the service in prayer and carol-singing at home.

Quite often, however, it was not so much a case of rising early as of staying up all night. Young people used to pass the time of waiting in singing, dancing, and making merry at some chosen farmhouse or in running up and down the streets with lighted torches. In Tenby, cheerful and noisy crowds shouted and blew cow-horns through the night until the hour of the *plygain* drew near, and then the young men formed a procession and escorted the Rector to church with flaming torches. These were extinguished in the porch, and lighted again after the service, when the procession re-formed to take the Rector back to his house. In Llanfyllin, in Montgomeryshire, there was a similar procession in which candles were used instead of torches. Special candles were made and sold there for the occasion, large and thick, and with wide strong wicks designed to withstand the winter winds.

The soft and lovely light of candles was one of the memorable features of the *plygain* everywhere. It was usual for each person to bring a coloured candle to supplement the normally rather poor and sometimes non-existent lighting of the church, and these, set in chandeliers or in sockets fixed to the pews, gave an unexpectedly brilliant illumination. When the service was over, what remained of the candles was commonly given to the parish clerk or, in the case of nonconformist chapels, to the caretaker. In some Glamorganshire chapels, they were lighted again on each following Sunday until they finally burnt away.

Burning candles, both at home and in church, appears constantly in Christmas customs since, for all Christian men, they are obvious symbols of the birth of Christ, Who is the Light of the World. A Christmas Day service rather like the Welsh *plygain* and known as *Julotte* still takes place in some parts of Norway. Here the people assemble in the darkness of the very early morning, and the church is filled with light from innumerable candles fixed in rows on the backs of the benches. At Bethlehem in Pennsylvania, the Moravian Church has a candle-service on Christmas Eve, beginning in the evening and ending at midnight, in which everyone carries a lighted candle during the singing of carols. This ceremony is said to have begun in 1741 at Herrnhut in Austria, when Count von Zinzendorf, the leader of the European Moravians, took up a lighted candle and led his followers to the stables of the settlement, there to watch and wait, sing hymns and listen to readings from the Bible, until the hour of midnight struck.

The custom which most closely resembled the Welsh *plygain* was the *Oie'l Verrey* of the Isle of Man. The people came to church at midnight on Christmas Eve, each person bringing a candle which might be of the ordinary type or made with two or three branches. Here, after prayers, they sang endless carols, known as *carvals*. A. W. Moore records how 'after the prayers were read, and a hymn was sung, the parson usually went home, leaving the clerk in charge. Then each one who had a carol to sing would do so in turn, so that the proceedings were continued to a very late hour, and sometimes also unfortunately became of a rather riotous character, as it was the custom for the female part of the congregation to provide themselves with peas, which they flung at their bachelor friends . . .'[1] Since the *carvals* were often very long – C. I. Paton mentions two or

1. A. W. Moore, *Folk-Lore of the Isle of Man*, 1891.

three examples containing as many as three hundred and sixty lines[1] – and sometimes rather gloomy, the misbehaviour of the young women (and probably of the young men also, though this is not mentioned) is perhaps understandable even if inexcusable. However, Moore goes on to say that when he wrote in the 'nineties of last century, the *Oie'l Verrey* ceremonies had been 'entirely shorn of all their riotous accompaniments, while ordinary hymns or short carols sung by the choirs, have taken the place of the lengthy solos of the past.'

Preston Guild. Once in every twenty years, in the week following the Feast of St John the Baptist on August 29th,[2] the Borough of Preston in Lancashire. holds the splendid civic festival which is known as Preston Guild. This celebration is certainly six hundred years old, and may possibly be older, since it began as a customary meeting of the mediaeval Guild Merchant which appears to have existed by prescriptive right before the town received its first Charter. The most important ceremonies are still the meeting of the Guild Court, and the procession of the burgesses, Masters and Wardens of Companies and the Guild Mayor to the Parish Church, where a special sermon is preached. There are also other colourful processions through streets decorated with flags and banners and, during the week-long festivities, balls, receptions, concerts, a lively pleasure-fair, and numerous other entertainments and gaieties.

At the Court meeting, the charters granted to the Borough by various monarchs are recited, a roll-call is taken of the existing Free Burgesses, who answer to their names in person or by proxy, and new Freemen are admitted. Originally, this meeting was necessary for the transaction of the legal business of the Guild Merchant, and the renewal of the burgesses' privileges. In the Middle Ages, those privileges were very important and jealously guarded. The Guilds were extremely powerful fraternities, exercising authority over every aspect of the town's commerce, and providing strong protection and a virtual trading monopoly for their members. In the twelfth-century document called the Custumale of Preston, it is stated that 'the liberties of Preston in Amundrenesse' include the right to 'have a Guild Merchant, with Hanse and other customs' and that 'no one who is not of that Guild shall make any merchandise in the said town unless with the will of the burgesses.'[1] Here, as in other mediaeval guild-towns, no outsider could buy or sell goods without permission, except during the annual fairs, when the normal guild regulations were suspended for so long as 'the Glove was up.'[2] A clause in the oath sworn by burgesses in the seventeenth century required them to give warning immediately to the Mayor, or the Bailiffs, of any such illicit trading that came to their notice. Even the residence of strangers in the town seems to have been viewed with suspicious dislike. A by-law passed in 1616 ruled that, if any householder had admitted an outsider whom the authorities chose to consider 'noe fytt person to inhabite' their town, that outsider had to leave within a month of notice being served upon him, and his host had to see that he did so, or else pay a fine of 6s. 8d. a week for so long as his guest remained.

Before 1562, Preston Guild seems to have been held at irregular intervals. The earliest celebration of which we have a clear record was in 1329, and there were others in 1397, 1415, 1459, 1501, 1543, and 1562. It was then decided that the festival should take place at the end of every twenty years, and this has been the custom ever since. There was a moment of danger in 1842. The exclusive privileges of the Free Burgesses had already dwindled considerably by then, and the passing of the Municipal Reform Act in 1835 had swept away the last remaining traces of the Guild Merchant's old importance.

1. C. I. Paton, *Manx Calendar Customs*, 1939.

2. The principal feast of St John the Baptist is that of his Nativity, which is celebrated on June 24th, Midsummer Day; but he has a second festival on August 29th, when his death at the hands of Herod Antipas is commemorated.

1. Charles Hardwick, *History of the Borough of Preston*, 1858.

2. A glove or a wooden hand exposed in some prominent position where all could see it was a sign that a fair was in progress, and that outside merchants could safely enter the town and trade therein for as long as the fair lasted.

When, seven years after the passing of the new Act, Preston Guild fell due again in 1842, there was much debate as to whether it was worthwhile to hold it in that year, or ever again. Fortunately, the town authorities decided that it was, though as a concession to the abolitionists, its length was shortened from a fortnight to a week. Exactly a century later the 1942 celebrations had to be postponed on account of the war then in progress; but the belated Guild-festival was duly held in 1952, and again in 1972, and at the present time, there is no reason whatever to suppose that others will not follow in their normal twenty-year sequence.

Prize Besom Ceremony, Shaftesbury. Until about the middle of the nineteenth century, the inhabitants of Shaftesbury, in Dorset, living on the top of a high hill, and having no springs of their own, were dependent for their water supply upon the wells of Enmore Green, in the parish of Mottcomb, in the valley below. The water had to be laboriously carried up the steep hill, in carts or pails, or on horseback, and sold to the townspeople at so much a pailful. But first of all, since Mottcomb was not under Shaftesbury's jurisdiction, permission to draw from the Enmore Green wells had to be obtained anew every year, and for this purpose, a curious ceremony of uncertain age and origin had to be performed.

On some agreed date in May, a long procession set out from Shaftesbury and wound its way down the hill. First came a young couple, the two most lately married in the town, and after them a man carrying a large dish with a decorated calf's head upon it, having a purse of money in its mouth. Next came the Prize Besom, a staff or besom adorned with feathers, gold and jewels. The Mayor and Corporation followed, and after them a crowd of townspeople, all wearing their gayest clothes. On their way down the hill they danced, and on arrival at Mottcomb, they danced again for an hour on Enmore Green, 'with minstrelsy and mirth of game.' The Bailiff of Mottcomb was then presented with the Besom, the calf's head and the money purse, bread, ale, and a pair of laced gloves, after which the use of the water

by Shaftesbury was granted for another year. The Bailiff kept the food, the money, and the laced gloves, but the Besom, that treasure of the upland township, he returned. The visitors then went home again, and the rest of the day was spent in dancing and revelry, both in Shaftesbury and Mottcomb.

When or how this curious custom began is unknown. An indenture of 1527 mentions it as dating from 'time out of remembrance and mind'. That it was more than a mere May frolic is shown by the fact that if the full ceremony of procession, dances, and gifts was not performed, Mottcomb had the right to refuse the water-privileges, and is said to have done so once in the early nineteenth century. However, the custom ceased in 1830, and some time later, the town acquired a water-supply of its own through the sinking of an artesian well. All that now remains to remind the townsfolk of the ancient ceremony is the Prize Besom, now kept in the Town Hall.

Punkie Night. The last Thursday in October is Punkie Night at Hinton St George in Somerset. On this night a little festival of lights is held, for which the children make punkies, or candle-lanterns, from hollowed-out mangold-wurzels. These are similar in form to the lanterns made elsewhere for Hallowe'en, but they are more elaborate. Instead of the simple holes for eyes and nose of the usual Hallowtide 'face', quite intricate flower-, ship-, or animal-patterns are cut on the outer skin of the mangold. The inner pith is removed, except for the small amount needed to preserve the lantern-shape, and a short piece of candle is set inside. When the candle is lit, the result is a most effective and pleasing lantern, shedding a soft, glowing light. The finished punkies are carried on strings threaded through two holes near the top, and with them the childen parade the streets for about two hours in the evening, visiting the houses and singing,

> Its Punkie Night tonight.
> Give us a candle, give us a light,
> If you don't, you'll get a fright.
>
> Its Punkie Night tonight.
> Adam and Eve, they'd never believe
> Its Punkie Night tonight.

It is usual for the children to go round beforehand to beg the necessary candles from local householders. It is, or was, considered very unlucky to refuse the gift.[1] Shortly before the outbreak of the 1939 War, a newly-appointed constable, coming from another area and unfamiliar with the custom, tried to stop the parades. This action on the part of a 'foreigner' was hotly resented by the villagers. A complaint was made to the Chief Constable in Taunton, by whose orders the ban was lifted, and since then, the celebration has gone on without further disturbance.

Local tradition says that Punkie Night was once connected with the now extinct Chiselborough Fair, though no one seems to know exactly what the connection was. In fact, the custom, though now observed on the last Thursday of October, regardless of its date, really belongs to the Hallowtide Guisers' ritual, in which the strange lanterns and their bearers represented the returning dead. It is kept up in some other South Somerset villages also, where the punkies are carried about, not on a fixed day as at Hinton St George, but during the week in which Hallowe'en falls.

1. Information given to the Editor in 1939 by a resident of Hinton St George.

Ram Roasting. The Ram Roasting Fair at Kingsteignton in Devon takes place annually on Whit Monday. The decorated carcase of a ram-lamb is carried in procession through the streets, and is afterwards roasted on a spit before a great open-air fire by the side of Oakford Lawn. The roasting takes about four hours, during which time sports and maypole-dancing go on in the field. Then the cooked meat is cut up, and slices are distributed to the spectators. By tradition, everyone present should receive a slice, but in recent years the crowds attending the festival have become so large that this is no longer possible. The difficulty is overcome by the drawing of numbered programmes, certain numbers entitling the holder to a share of the luck-bringing meat.

This celebration is a modified form of a custom which formerly extended over both the Monday and Tuesday of Whit Week. On the Monday, a living lamb was adorned with flowers and ribbons, and drawn through the village in a garlanded and canopied cart. Like the lamb at Kirtlington (*see Lamb Ales*), it was the honoured centre of the festival, for it, too, was a sacrificial victim, due to die for the good of the people on the following day. On the Tuesday it was killed, and the dressed and decorated carcase was paraded on a handbarrow before being roasted and carved up for distribution. In a description of the ceremony as it was until about 1883, it is stated that the slices were sold for a penny or threepence, and the sports held during the cooking took place on the high road.[1] At about this time, the procession of the living lamb was abandoned, though the carcase was still carried through the village on the Tuesday. For many years the celebrations were confined to Whit Tuesday, but later they were transferred to the Monday, to give the Bank Holiday revellers a chance to take part.

During most of the 1939–45 War, the Ram Roasting Fair was in abeyance, but in 1946 it began again. Meat-rationing was still in force and the Ministry of Food would not allow the use of a lamb for the ceremony. Not to be daunted by this, the Kingsteignton people roasted various substitute animals, the most usual being a deer presented by Lord Clifford of Chudleigh, or by the Earl of Devon. In 1952, when no deer was available, a reindeer was procured from London. Two years later, the restrictions were lifted, and since then, the traditional ram has been annually roasted, as in the past. Legend connects the origin of the custom with a dearth of water. Until piped water came to the village in 1895, the main source of supply was the Fairwater, a stream which runs through the churchyard and is said never to run dry, even in the hottest weather. Tradition has it that it did so once, on some undated occasion in the pre-Christian past, and the people sacrificed a ram in the dry bed of the leat. As soon as they had done so, the water flowed again, and thereafter the same offering was made every year, in thanksgiving according to

1. *Transactions of the Devonshire Association*, Vol. 40, 1908.

some accounts, but more probably to ensure that the failure of the stream should never be repeated. Although for many years now the roasting has taken place on a piece of open ground, or in a field, it was apparently once performed in the bed of the leat itself. In the *Western Antiquary* (Vol. III, 1883) it is stated that the carcase used to be cooked there, the water being 'turned off on the previous Saturday in order that the bed might be cleaned and purified'.

Ram Roasting feasts were known in other parts of Devon, though that at Kingsteignton is the only one which has survived. One at Buckland-in-the-Moor was held on Midsummer Day. Another, at Holne, is said by a writer in *Notes and Queries* (1st Series, VII, 1853) to have taken place on May Day, though a later account gives Old Midsummer Day as the customary date. Both these feasts seem to have been associated with menhirs. At Buckland-in-the-Moor, the ram was apparently killed and roasted near an ancient stone in a field, at Holne by a now vanished pillar of granite in the centre of the Ploy Field. According to the *Notes and Queries* account already mentioned, the young men of the parish used to meet in this field before daybreak on May-morning and then go off to the Moor to find and run down a ram lamb. When caught, the animal was brought back in triumph and fastened to the standing-stone, where its throat was cut. It was then roasted, just as it was, in its wool and hide, and at noon, a lively struggle took place for slices of the cooked meat. The rest of the day was spent in dancing and a variety of vigorous sports.

This description of the Holne ceremonies, which was signed by 'An Old Holne Curate', has often been quoted as evidence for a late survival of stone-worship in Devonshire. In 1896, however, doubt was cast upon its accuracy by a writer in *Transactions of the Devonshire Association* (Vol. 28). At this date, the Ram Feast was still in existence, but it was held on Old Midsummer Day (July 6th), and when enquiry was made of some of the oldest parishioners, one and all stated that they had never known it held at any other time of the year. They also said that they had never seen, nor had they ever heard of, a standing-stone in the Ploy-Field. It would seem from this that if the May-date and the menhir ever existed, it must have been in a period that was already beyond living memory in 1896. In any case, the Holne festival and that at Buckland-in-the-Moor have both vanished now, neither of them having survived the turn of the century.

Riding the Black Lad. Riding the Black Lad (or the Black Knight) was a lively Easter Monday custom which survived at Ashton-under-Lyne in Lancashire until just before the outbreak of the 1939 War. The effigy of a knight in black armour and a black velvet cloak was paraded on horseback through the streets, accompanied by musicians and a company of young men, mounted or on foot, who represented the Knight's retainers. The procession went round the town, through streets densely packed with spectators, and then to an open space, where the effigy was dismounted, pelted with stones and any other handy missiles, and finally shot to pieces with guns. This cheerful and very noisy celebration was one of the highlights of Ashton's year until 1914, and thousands of visitors from the surrounding towns and villages came annually to see it. In the period between the two wars, it was less regularly observed, but it was still extremely popular, and in 1935 it was made the basis of an elaborate traders' pageant.

Local tradition explains it thus. The Black Lad represented Sir Ralph de Assheton, who lived in the fifteenth century and shared with his brother, Robin, the right of guld-riding in the district. This was a mediaeval method of enforcing good farming. Certain privileged individuals were empowered to inspect particular lands annually, and to fine or otherwise punish tenants who allowed carrgulds, or corn-marigolds, and other weeds to flourish upon them. Sir Ralph is said to have carried out this duty with great severity, and to have earned the hatred of the people thereby. Other tyrannies also have been ascribed to him, but these are probably later embroideries of the original tale. Eventually, according to legend he was killed in the streets of Ashton by some aggrieved person, and it is this event, and the subsequent abolition of the inspections, that the Riding is supposed to commemorate.

That this is the true explanation of the custom is very unlikely.[1] Sir Ralph de Assheton certainly existed, and he may have had guld-riding powers, for in the Manor Rental of 1422 it is stated that he and his brother 'have the sour guld rode and stane rynges for the term of their lives'. He may also have been a harsh and unmerciful inspector. The legend, however, goes on to say that after his death, his half-brother, who was his father's heir and successor,[2] not only abolished the guld-riding, but also gave money for an annual ceremony whereby the Black Lad's dreaded visits to the low-lying lands known as the Sour Carrs should be remembered for ever. Such an action on the part of a near kinsman seems hardly credible, unless the two men disliked each other very bitterly, and we have no evidence that they did so. Even if they did, it is difficult to believe that any man would go out of his way to perpetuate what amounted to a public display of hatred and derision directed against a member of his own family who had already perished by violence. Nor do Sir Ralph's own misdeeds really appear quite bad enough to have been remembered with so much rancour for five centuries.

It seems far more probable that, because he was disliked and feared while he lived, his name afterwards became attached to an already existing custom, and that the original effigy was not his, but that of some more ancient and universal figure associated with Winter and its evils. Riding the Black Lad may perhaps be a late form of the ritual 'driving out hunger', in which a real historical personage has taken the place of the older symbolic figure. There is nothing to show whether any such Springtime custom was known in Ashton in the fifteenth century; but if Sir Ralph's half-brother really did give money for an annual ceremony, it is more likely to have been for the support of some existing traditional rite than for a completely new celebration perpetuating his relative's unpopularity.

Riding the Lord. A custom not unlike the Riding of the Black Lad at Ashton-under-Lyne, but much more primitive in form, and with no explanatory legend, was kept up at Neston in Cheshire until about the middle of last century. It was called Riding the Lord and, like the Ashton Riding it took place on Easter Monday. On that day, a man was engaged to ride on a donkey from one end of the long village street to the other. As he did so, he was pelted with mud, rotten eggs, and other rubbish, to the accompaniment of jeers and catcalls from the large crowd assembled to see him go by. At the end of his ride, he dismounted and was paid for his services, and that, at least in the later years of the custom, was the end of the matter. Whether anything further once occurred, or

1. Another tradition, less often repeated and scarcely more likely, is that the Riding was instituted in the fourteenth century by Thomas Assheton to commemorate his own valour at the Battle of Neville's Cross in 1346. He captured the Scots royal standard during the fight, and was afterwards knighted for it by Edward III.

2. Sir Ralph de Assheton was a son of his father's second marriage. This fact is supposed to have been commemorated formerly by the custom of emblazoning upon the Black Lad's armour the initials, or some emblem of the occupation of the first couple 'linked together in the course of the year.' (J. Harland & T. Wilkinson, *Lancashire Folk-Lore*, 1867).

how anyone, however poor, was persuaded to play so unpleasant a part, is not remembered.

The origin and history of this peculiar ceremony has not been preserved, so far as is known, either in the written records of the parish or in any tradition handed down by word of mouth. The only explanation that nineteenth-century enquirers were ever given was that it was something 'that had always been done'. Clearly the rider was some sort of scapegoat originally. He may have represented the dying Winter, or the long Lenten fast that had just ended; but why he was called the Lord, or how long the custom had existed at Neston before it finally died out, no one knows.

Ringing the Devil's Knell. The Devil's Knell, or the Old Lad's Passing Bell, is rung every year on Christmas Eve in the parish church of Dewsbury, in Yorkshire. The tenor bell is tolled once for every year that has passed since the first Christmas Day; in 1976, there were one thousand nine hundred and seventy-six strokes, and one more will be added in every following year for as long as the custom continues. The whole solemn and lengthy ringing is timed to end exactly at midnight.

The Devil's Knell is said to be rung to proclaim Satan's defeat and death when Our Lord was born, or according to another form of the tradition, to protect Dewsbury people from the Devil in the coming twelve months. The precise age of the custom is uncertain, but it is known to have begun in the Middle Ages, and the late thirteenth or early fourteenth century has been suggested as the most likely period. It is usually believed to have been instituted by Sir Thomas de Soothill, who gave the tenor bell to the church. He is supposed to have done this, and to have required the bell to be tolled every Christmas Eve for ever, in expiation of a murder which he had committed. Little else seems to be known about him, except that he probably derived his name from Soothill, which was a small township within Dewsbury parish. Until very recently, the tenor bell he gave to the church was known as Black Tom of Soothill.

Ringing Night. One of the celebrations ordered by Parliament to be observed 'for ever' after the discovery of the Gunpowder Plot was the ringing of chuch bells on November 5th. This was so widespread a custom during the following two centuries that in many places the anniversary came to be known as Ringing Night, or Ringing Day. In countless churchwardens' accounts all over the country, there are entries for sums paid to the bellringers on this occasion. 'Paid to ye Ringers for ye 5th of November being ye powder plot, 6s. 8d.', says one entry in the Great Budworth (Cheshire) accounts for 1700; and forty-one years later, 'paid on gunpowder treason, 15s. od.' appears among other sums given to the ringers at Bampton-in-the-Bush in Oxfordshire. Evidently the bells were rung there for a longer time than at Great Budworth, or else the cost of the men's services had risen since 1700. At Spelsbury, also in Oxfordshire, a piece of land called Syndall still provides money for ringing on those two great occasions of English rejoicing – Guy Fawkes' Day and Oak Apple Day. In Cornwall, the bells used to be pealed on November 4th, and the name of Ringing Night was applied to this date, Guy Fawkes' Eve, instead of to the anniversary itself, as elsewhere.

In some places, the custom of 'shooting Old Guy', that is, running down the scale and clanging the bells together, is, or was until recently, observed after the peal is ended. Rippingale in Lincolnshire is one of the parishes where this is done. Harlington in Middlesex is another, and here the bellringers are given a supper of pork and ale afterwards. The money to pay for this is provided by a piece of land which was given for the purpose by some kindly individual whose name has been lost. It is usually thought that the giver was a woman, but the relevant papers are missing, and nothing is now known about her. One of the Rectors of the parish is said to have destroyed a number of old deeds, including this one, after a quarrel with his parishioners in 1805. Nevertheless, she (or perhaps, after all, he) is duly honoured at the annual supper, when a toast is drunk to 'the Unknown Donor'.

Rogationtide. Rogationtide falls in the fifth week after Easter, and consists of Rogation Sunday and the three days immediately following, the Monday, Tuesday, and Wednesday before Ascension Day. The name springs from *rogere*, to ask or beseech, and the object of the processions still held in many English parishes on those four days, or on Ascension Day itself, is to beseech God's blessing upon the newly-springing crops, or in coastal areas, upon the fisheries. They also serve to mark the parish boundaries, though this was always secondary in importance, being merely the secular side of a mainly religious ceremony.

Rogation rituals are very old. Their remote roots run far back into pre-Christian times, and they first appear as part of the Christian scene in the fifth century A.D. In 470, during a period of earthquakes, and plague, Mamertus, Bishop of Vienne, ordered litanies to be said in solemn procession through the fields on Ascension Day, or on the three days preceding it. Forty-nine years later, in A.D. 511, the first Council of Orleans extended the pious custom to the whole of Gaul, and by the early eighth century, it had spread to England. An old north-country name for Rogationtide was the Ganging Days, or Gang Days, from the Anglo-Saxon *gangen*, to go, because the people went about the parish then for the blessing of the crops.

After the Reformation, many time-honoured religious customs disappeared, but the Elizabethan clergy were enjoined – or at least, permitted – to beat their bounds, as of old, and to preach, or offer prayers, at certain fixed points along the route. George Herbert, in *The Country Parson* (1652), gives four clear reasons why they should do so. There are, he says, 'contained therein four manifold advantages. (1) a blessing of God for the fruits of the field: (2) Justice in the preservation of bounds: (3) Charitie, in living walking and neighbourly accompanying one another, with reconciling of differences at that time, if they be any: (4) Mercie, in relieving the poor by a liberal distribution of largess which at that time is or ought be made.' And he adds that the parson should require 'all to be present at the perambulation, and those that withdraw or sever themselves from it he mislikes and reproves as uncharitable and unneighbourly, and if they will not reform, presents them.'

'Justice in the preservation of bounds' is not so dependent upon beating the bounds as it used to be, but the old custom is still kept up in many parishes. When maps were scarce and hard to come by the simplest method of remembering how the parish limits ran was to walk round them at least once a year, and to ensure that everyone who took part in the perambulation had good reason to recollect where the boundary-marks lay. Young people, especially, had their situation impressed upon their memories by painful physical experience. They were bumped upon mere-stones, thrown into dividing streams or ponds, dragged through hedges or over walls, and forced to climb over roofs of houses built across the line. Afterwards, they were rewarded with money, or white willow wands, or some other gift. They were not likely to forget their experience, and for the rest of their lives, they would be able to state quite definitely where any boundary-mark was, should a dispute arise. It was not, in fact, very probable that their evidence would ever be needed, for the old line, carefully followed, year by year, for generations, was too well-known for that; but still, it would be available if necessary.

One of the surviving twenty-five marks of St Clement Danes parish, in London, is now below ground-level, and a choirboy has still to be suspended by his heels, head downwards, over it, to enable him to reach it. In Leicester, formerly, when any newly-appointed parish officer took part in the perambulation for the first time, he was liable to be seized, thrust head downwards in a hole in a bank at Redhill, and smitten with a shovel. He then had to pay a fine of five shillings, after which he was considered to be 'free' of the parish.

Leicester's bound-beating is a triennial ceremony, and so is that of the Tower of London. On Ascension Day, the Resident Governor in full dress, the Yeoman Warders in their scarlet and gold uniform, the Chaplain of the Tower, and the choirmen and boys in their red cassocks perambulate the limits of the Tower Liberty. When one of the thirty-one Crown Boundary Marks is reached, the Chaplain calls out loudly, 'Cursed is he who removeth his neighbour's land mark!', the Chief Warder gives the order, 'Whack it, boys, whack it!', and the choirboys enthusiastically beat the mark with their long willow wands. This ceremony is known to have been performed as far back as 1555, although at that time there was some uncertainty as to the actual limits of the Liberty. In 1687, however, they were clearly defined in a Charter granted by James II, which now hangs in the Constable's office.

In Oxford, the lines of St Mary-the-Virgin and of St Michael-in-the-Northgate parishes run through the quads of All Souls and Lincoln Colleges respectively, and when the boys have beaten the marks there, they scramble for hot pennies thrown to them by the Fellows. At Lichfield,[1] the clergy and choir of the Cathedral carry elm boughs as they go round, and halt along the route to read the Gospel and sing a psalm at eight points where formerly there were wells. When the perambulation is over, the company return to the Cathedral and gather round the font, and there the elm boughs are left. In a few coastal parishes, where the fisheries matter more than the fields, the nets, the boats, and all who sail in them, are blessed, and sometimes, the sea itself. At Brixham, on Rogation Sunday there is a waterside sevice for this purpose, as there is also on different days in Rogation Week in several Kent parishes. At Cullercoats, in Northumberland, clergy and choir sail out into the harbour among the boats they bless, and so they do at Mudeford, at the other end of England, and at North Shields. In the last-named place, they also sail for some way up the River Tyne, which here forms the boundary between North and South Shields.

Rope Pulling. Rope-Pulling was a lively Shrove Tuesday sport which flourished at Ludlow in Shropshire until 1851.[1] The inhabitants of Broad Street Ward and those of Corve Street Ward annually held a tug-of-war in the main streets of the town, using an immense rope, thirty-six yards long and three inches thick, with a large knob at each end. This rope was provided by the Corporation, and at four o'clock on Shrove Tuesday afternoon, the Mayor lowered it from the windows of the Market Hall to the crowd waiting below. A fierce struggle then began between two teams of indeterminate size, known as the Blue Knobs and the Red Knobs. Each side tried to drag the rope to its own boundary-point, the River Corve for the Blue Knobs, the River Teme for the Red Knobs, and having got it there, to dip it in the water. As soon as this had been successfully achieved by one team or the other, that round was over, and the rope was returned to the Market Hall. The losers then bought it back from the winners with money hastily collected from their supporters, or perhaps held in readiness beforehand, and a second struggle began. If the same side won, the fight was ended for that year; but if not, there was a third contest, and the winners of that were held to be final victors. The rope was afterwards sold, and the money spent upon beer.

Rope-Pulling Day, or the latter half of it, was a general holiday in Ludlow. Indeed, it could hardly be anything else, for long before the actual tug-of-war started, the streets were impassable, all the shops were closed, and business was at a standstill. Thousands of people shared in the fun as contestants or spectators, and the victory celebrations after the rope-money had been spent, were both lively and prolonged. Fights often broke out among the supporters of the two sides, as was perhaps to be expected on such an occasion of excitement and rivalry, and in the course of these scrimmages, windows and other things were sometimes broken as well as heads. A newspaper account

1. Not to be confused with the Sheriff's Ride on September 8th, which is a purely secular ceremony. See page 179.

1. A similar custom was once observed at Pontefract on the same day, and also at Presteign in Radnorshire. The Presteign contest outlived that at Ludlow, and survived at least into the 'eighties of last century. *The Shropshire Guardian* for March 1st, 1884, records that rope-pulling took place 'as usual' on Shrove Tuesday in that year.

of the 1846 contest, quoted in Brand's *Popular Antiquities* (Vol. I), ends with the pleasing statement that 'we are happy to add that not an accident occurred to mar the pleasures of the day'. But if this was true in 1846, it was by no means always so. Charlotte Burne[1] makes it quite clear that the victory celebrations often gave rise to a great deal of rowdiness, and that this frequently involved injuries to many people and much damage to property. It was for this reason, she tells us, that Ludlow's ancient Rope-Pulling was finally discontinued in 1851.

Royal Epiphany Gifts. The gifts which the Three Kings brought to the Holy Child on the first Epiphany are commemorated every year in London by a royal ceremony of mediaeval origin. On January 6th, during the Epiphany service in the Chapel Royal at St James' Palace, two Gentlemen Ushers offer gold, frankincense and myrrh on behalf of the Queen. Silk bags, or purses, containing the gifts are laid upon an alms dish and carried to the altar-rails during the offertory. The gold is now given in the form of twenty-five golden sovereigns, which are afterwards exchanged for £25 in ordinary notes, and the money is distributed to the aged poor.

Until the latter part of George III's reign, the Sovereign came in person to make his offerings before the altar. During the Regency, however, when the King's mental illness made it impossible for him to perform this or any other royal duty, the presentation had to be made by proxy, and this has been the custom ever since.

Royal Maundy. The distribution of the Royal Maundy takes place every year on Maundy Thursday, normally in Westminster Abbey in years of even date, and elsewhere in those of odd number. Purses of money are given to as many poor men and as many poor women as there are years in the Sovereign's age, the actual presentation being made either by the Queen herself or, if she is absent, by the Lord High Almoner acting on her behalf, or by a member of her family.

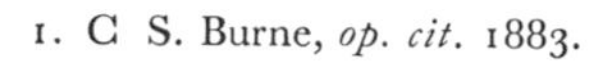

1. C S. Burne, *op. cit.* 1883.

This is a very old ceremony, which once included an even older rite that is now omitted. From a very early period in the history of the Church, it was a pious custom among priests and devout persons to wash the feet of twelve poor men on this day, following the example set by Christ on the eve of His death, when He washed the feet of the Apostles, and said to them: 'If I then, your Lord and Master, have washed your feet, ye also ought to wash one another's feet. For I have given you an example that ye should do as I have done to you.'[1] Exactly when it became a recognized ecclesiastical ritual is uncertain. It appears to have been known in Britain as early as A.D. 600, and perhaps earlier, and in the eighth century, St Alcuin set out a form for its celebration in his Book of Offices. In the course of time, the giving of food, money, or clothes to the poor people concerned was added to the feet-washing rite. During the Middle Ages, this symbolic act of humility and charity was performed by the reigning monarchs and high Church dignitaries of several European countries, and by some of the greater nobles also, with the perhaps inevitable result that what had

1. *John*, XIII, 14, 15.

originally been a very simple ceremony gradually developed into a solemn and splendid function, full of colour and beauty.

In Seville formerly, a magnificent feast was provided for twelve poor men who afterwards went in procession to the Cathedral, where the Archbishop received them and himself washed their feet. There were similar customs in France and, before the Revolution, in Russia. In Austria, until the fall of the monarchy, the Emperor, attended by Archdukes of the blood royal, waited upon his humble guests during a dinner of many courses, and then, upon his knees, washed their feet with water from a gold ewer and dried them with a lace-edged towel. Each man's place at table was laid with a dish emblazoned with the Imperial arms, a silver goblet, a wine jug, and the necessary cutlery, all of which he was allowed to take home with him. He also received from the Emperor's own hands a purse containing thirty pieces of silver which was hung round his neck on a green silk cord. In Rome still, the feet of thirteen priests are washed by the Pope, who then serves his guests with bread and wine and after blessing them, leaves them to finish their repast. Of this company, twelve are elderly men, representing the Apostles, but the thirteenth is always young, representing the Angel who, according to tradition, once came to the table when St Gregory the Great was serving it on Maundy Thursday.

The custom of varying the number of poor people according to the age of the person performing the ceremony seems to have begun in the Middle Ages. In 1212, King John, having reigned for thirteen complete years, gave thirteen pence each to thirteen poor men at Rochester. In 1361, Edward III, then aged fifty, washed the feet of fifty men and distributed fifty pairs of slippers. It appears to have been the custom at one time for the Sovereign to add the robe he had worn at the celebration to his other gifts. Presumably these were sold for the recipients' benefit, since they could hardly have worn them. Mary I evidently observed this custon, for we hear of her giving, in 1556, her Maundy robe of fine purple cloth lined with marten's fur; but after her time, the royal gowns were commonly redeemed by a special money payment. It was probably Elizabeth I who introduced this sensible reform, for in 1572 a leathern purse containing 20s. od. was given to each of the thirty-nine women whose feet she washed at Greenwich 'for the redemption of Her Majestie's gown'. This additional sum still forms part of the Royal Maundy today.

On the same occasion, Queen Elizabeth presented to every one of the women a miscellaneous collection of gifts including thirty-nine pence in a small white purse, she being thirty-nine years of age at the time, broadcloth to make clothes, a pair of sleeves, a wooden platter with half a side of salmon, the same quantity of ling, six red herrings, and six loaves upon it, a white wooden dish of claret, one of the aprons worn by her attendants, and a towel used by the Queen herself in the washing ceremony. The number and character of the 'maunds' varied with the generosity and fancy of different monarchs, but until the eighteenth century, food, drink, and either clothes or materials for their making, were customarily included. Then, in 1724, a money allowance was substituted for the women's garments, and in 1837, a similar change was made in respect of the provisions. Finally, in 1882, the cloth for the men vanished also, and now only money is given.

James II was the last English King known to have performed the washing rite in person.[1] In a small book entitled *Chapels Royal Register*, now in Somerset House, it is recorded that 'On Maundy Thursday, April 16th, 1685, our gracious King James ye 2nd wash'd, wip'd, and kiss'd the feet of 52 poor men with wonderful humility. And all the Service of the Church of of England usual on that occasion was per-

1. A quotation from *The Protestant Mercury*, April 1698 given in *British Calendar Customs: England* (Vol. 1, 1936) says that on the Maundy Thursday of that year, William III 'came to the Banqueting House from Kensington, and washed the feet of 12 poor men; and gave them money and cloth to make them garments'. There does not seem to be any other record of this event which seems unlikely in view of William III's known dislike of unusual ceremonies.

form'd, His Masjestie being present at the time.' After his time, a simplified version of the ceremony was performed, by the Lord High Almoner, or his deputy, acting on behalf of the King until about the middle of the eighteenth century, when it was discontinued. The last traces of the ancient custom are the towels and the nosegays of flowers carried by the Almonry officials and the Children of the Royal Almonry in the modern Maundy celebration. The giving of the Royal Maundy never ceased but from the end of the seventeenth century onwards, no reigning British monarch distributed his own gifts until 1932, when George V 'made his maunds' in Westminster Abbey. Both Edward VIII and George VI followed his example, as, normally, does the present Queen.

The modern celebration begins with the processional entry of the officiating clergy in splendid robes, and carrying bouquets of sweet herbs and flowers, preceded by the Beadle with the Mace, the bearer of the Westminster Cross in scarlet, gold and white, choristers in scarlet cassocks, and the Children and the Gentlemen of the Chapel Royal. Behind them come the Queen's Body-guard of the Yeomen of the Guard, two of whom bear the great dishes on which the purses are piled, the Children of the Royal Almonry, and the Almonry officials. After a service of prayers, hymns, and anthems, the Queen, or in her absence, the Archbishop of Canterbury, in his capacity of Lord High Almoner, distributes the three sets of purses. During this part of the ceremony, the clergy put off their robes and pass down the waiting lines of men and women, wearing simple white, and girt with linen towels.

There are two distributions. In the first, a white purse is given to each man and a green one to each woman. These contain the allowance in lieu of clothing. In the second, the redemption money for the royal robes and the allowance for provisions are given in a red purse with white thongs, and the specially minted Maundy Money in a white leather purse with red thongs. The Maundy Money, which was first struck for the occasion in Charles II's reign, consists of silver penny, twopenny, threepenny, and fourpenny pieces, corresponding in number to the Sovereign's age. The total sum is naturally small, but the rest of the gifts amount to £4 15s. od. for the men and £4 5s. od. for the women, a useful addition to an Old Age Pensioners' income. The Maundy coins are legal tender and can be spent like the rest, but usually they are treasured as mementoes, and only rarely do they pass into general circulation. When the distributions are over, the celebration ends with further prayers and hymns, the Blessing pronounced by the Dean of Westminster, and the singing of the National Anthem.

The name 'Maundy' as applied both to the day and to the ceremony has been explained in various ways. One theory is that it derives from 'maund', meaning a gift, or from a type of wicker basket, still called a maund in some districts, in which the traditional gifts were carried. The most widely accepted explanation is that it comes from *mandatum*, a command, commemorating the new commandment of love which Our Lord laid upon His disciples at the Last Supper.[1] Another old name for the anniversary was Chare, or Shere Thursday, which is usually thought to refer to the ceremonial cleansing of altars in the churches, and perhaps also to the cleaning of houses in preparation for Easter.

Running Auction, Bourne. In 1770, Richard Clay, of Bourne, in Lincolnshire, provided in his will for an annual gift of bread to the poor of Eastgate Ward, the cost of which was to be met by the rent of a certain piece of meadowland, now known as White Bread Meadow. This land has since been let every year at Easter by a form of auction in which bidding is only valid while two boys are running up and down a prescribed length of road.

How long they have to keep going depends upon the keenness of the competition and the number of offers. If a bid is made while they are on the

1. The antiphon *Mandatum novum do nobis* – 'A new commandment I give unto you, That ye love one another; as I have loved you, that ye also love one another' (*John* XIII, 34) – comes at the beginning of the Royal Maundy ceremony, and of the feet-washing ritual which still forms part of the Maundy Thursday service in Roman Catholic churches.

move and is not capped by another before they return to their starting point, that bid stands; but if another is made while they are still running, they have to race off again. The auction ends only when no bid has been received during the double run to a fixed point and back again. The successful bidder then becomes the lessee of White Bread Meadow for the following twelve months. The boys are rewarded for their quite strenuous labours, and by custom, all those concerned in the auction afterwards share in a supper of bread and cheese, spring onions, and beer.

Rushbearing. When the boarding of church floors was still comparatively unusual, rushes were often thickly strewn in the aisles and chapels as a protection against the penetrating cold and damp of stone-flagged or beaten-earth floors. This green carpet had to be renewed at least once a year, usually at the Wakes, when the ceremonial bringing-in of the new reeds was normally the principal event of the Patronal Festival. Every part of the parish contributed its quota of sweet-smelling rushes, sometimes carried in bundles by young women in white, but more often piled high in decorated harvest-wains, and held in place by flower-covered ropes and the high harvest-gearing. The best horses in the village were chosen to draw the carts; Morris dancers usually preceded them, and children and young people walked beside them, carrying garlands which were hung in the church after the new rushes had been laid down. Often the procession perambulated the parish in the morning, stopping outside the great houses of the district where the Morris-men danced; and then, the long round ended, the whole company came to the church, to the sound of pealing bells, and there strewed their rushes on the floor (and sometimes on the graves outside as well), and hung up their garlands in the appointed places. The rest of the day was spent in merrymaking of various kinds.

This custom died out slowly when, with the increase of wooden church-floors, rushes ceased to be needed for warmth and dryness. By the 'nineties of last century, ceremonial rushbearing had become fairly rare, but a modified form of it still persists in a few parishes today. At Barrowden, for instance, in Rutlandshire, rushes are cut from church land on St Peter's Eve, brought into the church, and left lying on the floor for a week. At Glenfield in Leicestershire, new-mown hay is similarly laid down on the Thursday after July 6th, as grass is at Shenington in Oxfordshire on Trinity Sunday and the Sunday following. Fresh hay is brought into church at Wingrave, near Aylesbury, on the Sunday after June 29th. It comes from a field left to the parish by an old lady who, according to tradition, once lost her way at night, and was guided to safety by the sound of the Wingrave bells. The revenues of this field are also used to provide new hassocks or carpets, when these are needed. On the Sunday nearest St Swithun's Day (July 15th), hay is scattered in Old Weston Church, in Huntingdonshire, the donor of the land on which it grows is said to have been a woman who left it to the parish in the hope of muffling (if only for one day in the year), the noise made by heavily-booted parishioners as they clumped up the aisle.

When the Lord Mayor of Bristol comes in procession to St Mary Redcliffe Church on Whitsunday, and is received there with ceremony by the Bishop of Bristol he enters (to a fanfare of trumpets), a church strewn with rushes, and having a bouquet of flowers on every seat. This pleasant custom springs from the will of William Spenser, once Mayor of Bristol, who, in 1493, left 'certain premises situate on the back of Bristol'[1] to pay for a sermon (originally three, but now reduced to one) to be annually preached in that church at Pentecost before the Mayor and commonalty of the town. Part of the money was allotted to the rush-strewing for the occasion, and the ringing of the bells, but the seat-posies appear to be a later addition.

Of Westmorland's remaining rushbearings, two – Warcop and Great Musgrave – have become garland-bearing festivals rather than straightforward rush-carryings. In both places, there is a procession of little girls, wearing flower-crowns on their heads, made of light

1. H. Edwards, *A Collection of Old English Customs*, 1842.

wood entirely covered with blossom. They are traditional; garland-headdresses of this kind were worn during last century, when the festival really was concerned with rush-strewing in the Church. There are no rushes now, except that about forty years ago, the Vicar of Warcop arranged for boys to carry rush-crosses in the procession on June 29th, to remind the people of the real meaning of the celebration.

At Ambleside, on the Saturday nearest St Anne's Day (usually the last Saturday in July), a procession of adults and children goes through the town, carrying garlands of flowers, and crosses, harps, and other devices made of rushes, including two great pillars of rush, ten feet high or more. They go into the Church, where a service is held, and afterwards the children are given a piece of gingerbread each. So they are at Grasmere where what is perhaps Westmorland's best-known rush-bearing takes place on the Saturday nearest St Oswald's Day (August 5th). The local people say the ceremony has never lapsed, though before 1885, it was held on the Saturday next July 20th. The church floor was boarded in 1841, but the old rush-bearing ceremony continued, and is still kept up today. Here there are rushes in plenty – some carried loose in a hand-woven linen sheet by six young girls, and others carried by villagers in a variety of traditional forms – harps, gates, maypoles, crosses, St Oswald's Crown, and his wonder-working Hand, and many more. They are all carried into the church at the end of a procession round the village, and laid along the walls while a service is held. There they are left until the following Monday, when they are fetched away by their owners, and another procession sets out for the School Field, for sports and tea.

St Andrew's Day. St Andrew the Apostle is the patron saint of Scotland, where his feast-day (November 30th) is variously known as Andermas, or Andrys Day, or Androiss Mess. It is now chiefly observed as a patriotic festival, especially by Scots away from their homeland. Before the Reformation, it was a holiday in both the religious and the popular sense, and even after that great change, it remained a day for feasting and rejoicing of a secular kind. It was customary for men and boys to go 'Andra-ing' in the morning, that is, to roam through the woods and fields catching rabbits and squirrels for their Andermas dinner, and then to spend the rest of the day eating and drinking and making merry with their families and friends. The Andermas, or St Andrew's Dinner, is still a main feature of the celebrations wherever Scots are gathered together. Traditional dishes are served, including haggis and a singed sheep's head, and toasts are drunk to the glory of Scotland and the honoured memory of her patron saint.

The Scottish veneration of St Andrew is of great antiquity. The Apostle had no personal connection with Scotland, as he is said to have had with Greece and Russia, the two other countries of which he is the patron. According to tradition, he preached the Gospel in Asia Minor, South Russia and Greece in the years immediately following the Ascension of Our Lord, and was crucified at Patras in Achaia in or about the year 64. There he was buried, but his remains were afterwards transferred to Constantinople. In 1210, they were removed again, to Amalfi in Southern Italy, where his reputed burial-place still is. There is, however, another legend which asserts that some of his bones were brought to Scotland in the fourth century by St Regulus (or Rule). Very little is known about this saint. He is said to have been a Greek abbot to whom an angel appeared, instructing him to sail towards the west with the relics, and to build a shrine for them in whatever place the hazards of winds and tides might bring him to land. This he did, and coming eventually to Muckross, now St Andrews, on the coast of Fife, he landed and set up the shrine on the site which is now covered by the Cathedral.

Another, and perhaps more probable story, is that the relics of St Andrew were brought to Scotland by Bishop Acca when he was banished from Hexham in A.D. 732, and sought refuge with Angus mac Fergus, King of the Picts. Some years later, that monarch is said to have seen, on the night before a battle a great X-shaped cross, the emblem of St Andrew, flaming across the sky. The subsequent victory of the Pictish forces was not unnaturally attributed to the saint's intervention, and thereafter he was venerated throughout Angus' kingdom. So, too, at Bannockburn in 1314, St Andrew came to the aid of Robert Bruce. These tales, if they are nothing more, are reflections of the strong devotion of the Scots to the fisherman-saint. All through the Middle Ages, his shrine in Fife was visited by countless pilgrims from every part of the country, and eventually, though at what precise date is uncertain, his cross, the

Saltire of heraldry, became the acknowledged national emblem of the Scottish people.

In England, St Andrew's Day was less highly regarded, although as a holy day of the Church's calendar and the festival governing the date of Advent Sunday, it was always an important anniversary.[1] In some parts of Kent and Sussex, it was once a traditional day for squirrel-hunting. Men and boys went out armed with sticks and clubs and sometimes with guns, shouting and hallowing to frighten their unhappy victims and, according to Hasted, often killing more valuable beasts than squirrels. 'The labourers and lower kind of people', remarks that historian bitterly, '. . . spend the greatest part of the day in parading through the woods and grounds, with loud shoutings; and, under the pretence of demolishing the squirrels, some few of which they kill, they destroy numbers of hares, pheasants, partridges, and in short, whatever comes in their way, breaking down hedges and doing much other mischief, and in the evening betaking themselves to the alehouses, finish their career there as is usual with such sort of gentry.'[2] It is possible, however, that the damage done was not quite so extensive as this account suggests, for hunts of this kind at particular seasons seem to have been permitted and tolerated customs in various parts of the country.[3]

Like the Feast of St Catherine five days earlier (*see Cattern Day*), St Andrew's Day was a lacemakers' holiday in Bedfordshire, Buckinghamshire, Hertfordshire and Northamptonshire. It was known in these districts as Tandering Day, or Tanders, or Tandry. Much the same jollifications were held on both occasions, though the Tandering holiday does not seem to have had quite the same festival importance as its predecessor, perhaps because the two dates came so close together. In Northamptonshire, however, where the feast was kept on Old St Andrew's Day, December 11th, the celebrations were very lively. Not only the lacemakers, but everyone else in the parish took part in them. Sternberg describes the holiday as a day of 'unbridled licence', when drinking and feasting prevailed 'to a riotous extent.'[1] The schoolchildren barred out their master, as they did in some other parts of Great Britain on this anniversary (*see Barring-out the Schoolmaster*). Men went about in women's clothes, and women in men's garments, visiting each other's houses, and consuming large quantities of hot elderberry wine, which was the traditional drink of this feast. In the evening, the Mumming Play was acted for the first time in that year.

The lacemakers' customs connected with Cattern Day and Tandering Day flourished until the last quarter of the nineteenth century, and then gradually died out as the handmade lace trade declined.

1. Advent Sunday the first day of the Church's liturgical year is the Sunday nearest St Andrew's Day.

2. E. Hasted, *The History and Topographical Survey of Kent*, 1782, Vol. 2.

3. Notably in the New Forest and in Suffolk on or about Christmas Day, and at Duffield Wakes on All Saints' Day, when the people claimed the right to hunt squirrels in Kedleston Park.

1. T. Sternberg, *The Dialect and Folk-Lore of Northamptonshire* 1851.

St Blaise's Day. The feast-day of St Blaise is celebrated on February 3rd, and was formerly kept as a holiday in the wool-manufacturing districts of several countries, including Great Britain. It was also, until fairly recently, the day on which Bavarian farmers brought their working-horses to be blessed by the parish priest; and in many English[2] and Continental Roman Catholic churches, it is the anniversary on which the ancient and beautiful ceremony of Blessing the Throat is still performed.

These customs stem from various legends concerning St Blaise which are recorded in the *Acts of St Blaise* and other early writings, or have been preserved by tradition. According to these legends, he was a physician who became Bishop of Sebastea in Armenia and suffered martyrdom there in or about A.D. 316. He is said to have had great power over animals of all kinds. When during Licinius' persecution of Armenian Christians, he retired to the mountains and lived for a time in a cave, wild beasts came to him to be blessed and healed of their wounds. On his way

2. Notably at the Church of St Etheldreda, Ely Place, London, once the chapel of the Bishops of Ely.

to prison, after he had been captured, he commanded a wolf which had stolen a poor woman's only pig to give up its prey, and to the amazement of all, it did so. On the same journey, he blessed the draught-horses encountered on the road. Another legend relates how he saved a child who was in danger of death by choking. This boy had swallowed a fishbone which stuck in his throat and could not be moved. When St Blaise touched him, the bone was instantly dislodged. These stories made him the patron saint of both wild and working animals, and also of sufferers from all kinds of throat-diseases, for the cure of which he has been invoked both at home and in church, for many centuries, right down to our own day.

In the ceremony of Blessing the Throat, two long candles are blessed, lighted, and tied together with ribbon in the form of a St Andrews Cross. The patients kneel before the altar, and the ribbon-cross is laid under their chins, while their throats are gently touched with the ends of the lighted candles. As he touches each person, the celebrant says 'May the Lord deliver you from the evil of the throat, and from every other evil.' One tradition says that these candles, as well as the many others that once burnt in the churches everywhere on this day, commemorate the gratitude of the woman whose pig was saved. When St Blaise was thrown into an unlighted and windowless prison and left there to starve, she secretly brought him food and candles, and so made his sufferings at least a little more endurable until they were finally ended by his execution.

His martyrdom took the horrible form of having his flesh torn with sharp iron combs, after which he was beheaded. Because these combs resemble the implements used in the preparation of wool-fibres for cloth-making, he was adopted by woolcombers everywhere as their patron saint,[1] and upon his feast day they kept holiday. Until the early years of last century, magnificent pageants and processions were held in the wool-towns of Yorkshire and East Anglia, in Aberdeen, Guildford, Northampton and elsewhere. Everyone connected with the industry took part in them, from shepherds and loom-makers to master-combers and wealthy merchants. St Blaise himself was represented by a man on horseback, dressed as a bishop, and carrying a comb in one hand and a book in the other. With him went a variety of colourful characters, including Jason, carrying the Golden Fleece, mounted Argonauts riding two by two, Hercules, Castor and Pollux and other mythological figures, famous heroes of the wool-trade like Jack of Newbury, and sometimes the simple source of all this splendour, a live lamb carried by a shepherdess riding in a carriage. Frequently also there were skilled orators who made speeches or recited verses in honour of the wool-trade and its patron saint at intervals along the route. 'Orations spoke in most of the principal Streets', wrote Parson Woodforde in his diary for 1783, describing the Norwich celebration of that year, with its twelve companies of combers, all in 'white ruffled shirts with Cross-Belts of Wool of divers Colours – with Mitred Caps on their heads', and Bishop Blaise, 'very superbly dressed', riding in a phaeton drawn by six horses. 'I never', he said, 'saw a Procession so grand and well conducted.'[1]

These lively festivals, which brought thousands of visitors into the towns in which they were held and were a great source of local pride, died out gradually in the first quarter of the nineteenth century. In Northampton, the last celebration took place in 1804. At Bradford, in Yorkshire, where the procession was held every seven years, there was a truly magnificent parade in 1825, but this was the last in that town, and

1. He was also the patron of wax-chandlers. In the Middle Ages, great quantities of votive candles were lit in churches on his feast-day to honour the saint and to secure his protection. In the *The Golden Legend* we read that he instructed the woman already mentioned to burn a candle in church every year; 'and she did all her life, and she had much great prosperity. And know thou that to thee, and to all them that so shall do, shall well happen to them.'

1. *The Diary of a Country Parson, 1758–1802*, ed. John Beresford. (One-volume edition, 1935). This particular procession, which took place on March 24th, 1783, instead of on the usual day, may have been grander than usual because it also celebrated the signing on January 20th of the same year of provisional articles of peace between England, France and Spain; but the records of the Blaise festival elsewhere, and in other years, show that it was always a colourful and splendid affair.

almost the last in England. A full-dress Blaise celebration was held in Norwich in 1836, but this was a revival connected with the laying of the foundation-stone of a new yarn factory. *Times's Telescope* for 1830 speaks of the festival at St Blazey in Cornwall as still in existence at that time, and perhaps it was, though if so, it was a late survival. In that parish an additional fillip was given to the custom by a local tradition that St Blaise came to England during his lifetime and landed at St Blazey. Unfortunately, there seems to be no foundation whatever for this interesting tale, which was probably evolved by lively imaginations from the dedication of the church.

In many parishes of Britain, bonfires used to be lit on the hill-tops on the night of February 3rd. This custom is sometimes said to have arisen from a punning association of the saint's name with the word 'blaze'. It is probable however, that the bonfires were simply another form of the candles that once flamed everywhere in honour of a saint whose legend connects him with lights, and whose feast-day is the 'morrow' of Candlemas, which is also a festival of fire and light. Another, and long since forgotten celebration, mentioned in Brand's *Popular Antiquities* (Vol. I), was a special holiday kept by women, 'when country women goe about and made good cheere, and if they find any of their neighbour women a spinning that day, they burne and make a blaze of the distaffe, and thereof, called St Blaze his day.'

St Clement's Day. St Clement, whose emblem is an anchor, is the patron saint of anchorsmiths and blacksmiths, and he is also one of the several saints who are invoked by seamen. This is because according to a rather uncertain tradition, he was martyred by drowning about A.D. 100, being thrown into the Black Sea with an anchor tied to his neck.[1] On his feast-day (November 23rd), smiths used to honour his memory by exploding gunpowder on their anvils, firing guns, and holding a feast at night which was known as the Clem Feast. In some districts, there were torchlight processions in which 'Old Clem' was represented either by one of the blacksmiths, who wore a long grey beard for the occasion and was carried through the streets in a chair, or by an effigy, similarly bearded, with a grey wig on its head and a pipe in its mouth. At Woolwich, until at least as late as the first half of last century, the blacksmiths' apprentices in the dockyard chose one of their number to act as Old Clem. He too wore a beard and a wig; his face was masked, and he carried a pair of tongs and a wooden hammer as emblems of his trade. A wooden anvil was borne before him in the procession, which consisted of young men carrying torches, banners, tomahawks and batle-axes, drum-and-fife players, and six strong men supporting the stout wooden chair in which Old Clem himself rode. A contemporary account of the festivities, printed in 1826, describes how the company went round the town, 'stopping and refreshing at nearly every public house, (which by the by, are pretty numerous), not forgetting to call on the blacksmiths and officers of the dockyard; there the money-box is pretty freely handed, after Old Clem and his mate have recited their speeches . . .'[1] The evening ended with a jovial supper and, doubtless, a good deal of hard drinking at one of the local inns.

In Cambridge, the bakers held an annual supper known as the Bakers' Clem on November 23rd, and at Tenby, the crews of the fishing-boats feasted then on roast goose and rice pudding provided by the boat-owners.

Dr Plot, writing in 1686, mentions 'the ancient custom of going about that night to beg drink to make merry with',[2] and long after his time, the same 'ancient custom' was still being enthusiastically kept up by the men of the English northern counties. Children and young people also went round Clementing in much the

1. In *The Book of Saints*, compiled by the Benedictine Monks of St Augustine's Abbey, Ramsgate (4th ed. 1947) it is stated that although St Clement is venerated as a martyr, the fact of his martyrdom cannot be proved, nor can any of the legends attached to it. He died about A.D. 100 after ruling the Western Church as Pope for about ten years, but the circumstances of his death are uncertain.

1. Hone's *Every-Day Book*, Vol. I, 1826. Contribution signed R.R.

2. Dr Robert Plot, *The Natural History of Staffordshire*, 1686.

same way as they, or others like them, went Catterning two days later on St Catherine's Day (*see Cattern Day*). They visited the houses of the parish, singing songs that began 'Clemeny Clemeny, year by year', or 'Clementsing Clementsing, apples and pears', or 'Cattern and Clement be here, be here', and demanding the usual largesse of apples, beer, and whatever else they could get. Sometimes the boys added colour to the proceedings by carrying lighted turnip-lanterns of the Hallowtide pattern. At Ripon, on or near the anniversary, the Cathedral choristers went round the church, offering to everyone present an apple with a sprig of box stuck in it, and were rewarded by small money-gifts. In his *History of Walsall* (1887), Frederick Willimore records how crowds used to gather on November 23rd outside the Guildhall of that town, waiting for the Town Crier to appear at one of the windows and scatter apples and hot pennies among them. Meanwhile, the boys of the Grammar School scrambled for apples inside the Sessions Court. This cheerful custom was abolished in 1860.

As a festival occasion, St Clement's Day, like St Catherine's is now almost entirely forgotten. Nothing remains of the trade celebrations that once enlivened the anniversary, and the Clementing custom did not survive the end of the nineteenth century.

At Enville, in south Staffordshire, it was revived in a modernized form in 1961 by the headmistress of a local school. The children go in procession to Enville Hall, where they sing the Clemeny-song of the district, and are then given an apple apiece, and scramble for a shower of hot pennies thrown to them. This pleasant and orderly little ceremony preserves a memory of old songs and old ways and the children enjoy it; but it is no more than a pale ghost of the noisy, lively and quite unorganized custom that our forefathers knew.

St. Giles' Day. *(See Wakes and Fairs.)*

St. Valentine's Day. *(See Valentine Gifts.)*

Searching the Houses of Parliament. The memory of the Gunpowder Plot of 1605 is

preserved by many cheerful customs in various parts of Great Britain (*see Guy Fawkes' Day*), and by one dignified ceremony that takes place in London before the Opening of Parliament.

This is the searching by a detachment of Yeomen of the Guard of the cellars under the Palace of Westminster, either on the evening before the Opening or, more usually, on the morning of the day itself. The Yeomen, in their scarlet and gold uniforms, come from the Tower of London to the Princes' Chamber in the House of Lords and there, in the presence of a number of the Palace officials, they are given old candle-lanterns for use during the ceremony. As soon as the order to search has been received, they set out on a prolonged tour of the basements, vaults, and cellars below the building. Carrying their lighted lanterns in their hands, and firmly ignoring the existence of the very efficient electric lighting, they search every cranny and crevice, every corner and conceivable hiding-place, to satisfy themselves that no gunpowder barrels, bombs, or infernal machines have been anywhere concealed with intent to blow up Sovereign, Lords, and Commons. When they have proved by personal and most careful inspection that all is well, a message is sent to the Queen, the Yeomen are given some well earned refreshment and return whence they came, and Parliament is then free to assemble without fear of disaster.

It need hardly be said that the safety of the reigning monarch, ministers, peers, and elected members of Parliament does not really depend upon this picturesque last-minute ceremony. Nevertheless, there was a night in 1605 when it did so depend upon a grimly earnest and quite unpicturesque search through the multifarious cellars that then underran the Palace of Westminster, and it is this event which the modern ceremony is traditionally supposed to commemorate. In fact, there does not seem to be any real evidence for the connection. Some authorities think that regular inspections of the cellars did not begin until the time of the Popish Plot scare in the latter half of the seventeenth century. However that may be, there is no doubt that the ceremonial search made by the Yeomen of the Guard before the State Opening of Parliament is as much a reminder of the Gunpowder Plot for most people as any bonfires blazing and rockets soaring heavenwards on the night of November 5th.

Notwithstanding the candles, the search now made is a real one, and certainly any secret enemy of the Queen and Parliament would find it hard to conceal any material evidence of evil intentions from the keen eyes of the Yeomen of the Guard.

Seeking the Golden Arrow. *(See Palming.)*

Sheriff's Ride, Lichfield. Once a year, on September 8th, the Feast of the Nativity of the Blessed Virgin Mary, the Sheriff of Lichfield, accompanied by some forty or fifty horsemen, rides round the city limits, halting at each of the surviving boundary-marks, or places where marks formerly existed, in the sixteen-mile circuit. This custom runs back to Tudor times, and was confirmed by a charter still in force, granted by Charles II in 1664. By this charter, the Bailiff and Brethren of Lichfield were required to choose annually, on July 25th, a Sheriff from among those citizens who were not themselves Brethren. The Sheriff in his turn, was required, amongst his other duties, to perambulate the city boundaries in the manner already mentioned, and this he still does.

On the morning of September 8th, the Sheriff's party start out from the Guildhall at about eleven o'clock and circuit the town, a ceremony which, with various stops for refreshments and the necessary formalities, takes up most of the day. On their return in the evening, they are met by the City Sword- and Mace-bearers, who conduct the Sheriff back to the Guildhall. This traditional perambulation is a purely civic custom, and has nothing at all to do with the ecclesiastical Beating of the Bounds, which takes place in Lichfield on Ascension Day. *(See Rogationtide.)*

Shrovetide Food. When Shrove Tuesday was really Fastern's E'en, in the sense that it was the eve of a seriously-kept fast, it was inevitably a day for feasting upon good things that would not be seen again, at least in pious households, on any day but Sundays for six long weeks. Lean times began on the morrow; but this was Pancake Day, or Guttit Tuesday, or Bannock Night, or Doughnut Day, according to local usage, when, for the last time, meat, butter and other luxuries could still be, and were, enjoyed in as large quantities as possible.

Of all the traditional foods of Shrove Tuesday, pancakes and bannocks have proved the longest-lived in Great Britain. Pancakes are still tossed and eaten then in very many homes, and they are the centre of such surviving customs as the Olney Pancake Race and the Westminster Pancake Greeze. Like hot cross buns, they have a long ancestry and are probably descendants of the small wheaten cakes that were once made at pre-Christian festivals of early Spring. Before the Reformation, they were useful as well as much-liked items of the feast because they enabled the housewife to empty her larder of the butter and fats that could not be eaten in the days that followed. Later on, when Lent was less rigidly observed, custom filled the gap that had been left by a waning piety. Pancakes continued to be made for pleasure and for luck in all but the poorest households; and when children from such poor homes went round Lent-crocking, and begging for gifts of food of various kinds (*see Shroving*), it was pancakes which they most often demanded and received.

Mrs Bray tells us how, at Tavistock about 1833, 'the farmers considered it (Shrove Tuesday) a great holiday, and every person who was in their employ feasted on pancakes. The great sport of the day was to assemble round the fire and each person to toss a cake before he had it for his supper. The awkwardness of the tossers, who were compelled to eat their share, even if it fell into the fire itself, afforded great diversion.'[1] On some north-country farms, anyone who could not finish his pancake by the time the next one was ready was hustled outside and thrown into a gooseberry bush or on to the midden. The first pancake made was often given to the cock in the poultry-yard, by the cook if she was unmarried, and if not, by some other girl who watched to see how many hens would come to share it with him. As many as came, so many years would she have to wait before her wedding-day.

In Scotland, beef, brose and bannocks were the essential foods of Fastern's E'en, and the day itself was often called Brose Day, or Bannock Tuesday. Everyone who could had beef for his dinner; farmers certainly did so, because tradition said that if they did not, their cattle would not thrive. Another customary dish was a kind of boiled dumpling made of oatmeal and suet and roughly shaped like a bird, which was known as the Fitness or Fastyn Cock. Brose was a rich, savoury broth, well known at other times of the year, but dignified on this day by the name of Matrimonial Brose. It was served in a large bowl into which a wedding-ring had been dropped for purposes of divination. Young people thrust their spoons into the thick liquid, hoping to find the ring. Whoever did so would be the first to marry among those present; but custom required that he (or she) should conceal the lucky find until the bowl was quite empty. Other charms were often hidden in the brose as well as the ring, including a small coin, which meant money in the coming year, and a thimble or a button, which meant that the finder would remain unwed, at least until next Brose Day came round.

In the evening, the bannocks were baked. They were usually made of oatmeal, eggs and salt, mixed with milk or broth, but sometimes a more pancake-like mixture of flour, eggs and sugar was used. They were baked upon a girdle in the presence of a lively company which consisted of the householder's family and servants, and of invited friends and neighbours, especially young people. Each unmarried person was supposed to take some share in the work, one carrying the batter to the fire, another turning the cake, a third removing it when ready, and so on.

When as many bannocks as possible had been eaten, hot from the girdle, it was time to prepare the last and most important. This was variously known as the sauty bannock, the dreaming-bannock, the dumb-cake, or in some areas where a little soot was added to the mixture for luck the sooty skone. It was bigger and thicker than the rest of the cakes, and like the brose, it usually contained a ring and a variety of other small objects foretelling the finder's future. It had to be cooked in complete silence, otherwise its magical properties would be lost. Part of the fun of the evening consisted in trying to provoke the cook to speech or laughter; if she broke her ritual silence, someone else had to take her place.

As soon as the dreaming-bannock was ready, it was cut into as many pieces as there were unmarried people present. The cook put the pieces into her apron, and went round the room asking each person to choose his own portion; or else, following another tradition, she was blindfolded and, standing by the door, she held up each piece separately, saying 'who owns this?' The first to answer had it, along with whatever prophecies for the future might be indicated by the article he found in it, or by the discouraging fact that he found nothing at all. The portion of bannock obtained by either of these methods – or by a third, rather less usual, in which each individual silently baked a small dreaming-bannock for himself – was not eaten then and there, like the other cakes. It was saved until bedtime, when it was

1. Mrs A. E. Bray, *The Borders of the Tamar and the Tavy*, 1879 2nd ed.

wrapped in a left-foot stocking and placed under the owner's pillow, in order that he or she might see the future wife or husband in a dream.

Other traditional foods are, or were, associated with Shrove Tuesday, and with the other days of the short Shrovetide season.[1] All over Europe, cakes of various kinds were made, and in some places there were special soups and broths. Vienna had its doughnuts for Carnival, still known there today; and at Baldock in Hertfordshire, doughnuts fried in hog's lard used to be eaten on Shrove Tuesday, which was known there as Doughnut Day. In Norwich small currant loaves, or buns, shaped like shells and called coquilles, were sold in the streets and in most bakers' shops on the same day. On Brusting, or Bursting Saturday (an old Lincolnshire name for Quinquagesima Eve), frying-pan pudding, a kind of thick and very crumbly pancake was popular. Shrove Monday was Peasen or Paisen Monday in Cornwall because pea-soup was the customary dish there, but in northern England it was Collop Monday. Eggs and fried collops of bacon, or mutton, or any other meat, fresh or salted, that was in the house, were eaten for dinner. Originally, of course, this was done to clear the larder of forbidden foods before Lent began, but like the making of pancakes, it continued as an accepted custom long after the earlier religious urgency in this matter had ceased to be felt.

Shrovetide Football. Football of the old, wild type, with no definite rules and teams of indeterminate size, was one of the traditional sports of Shrovetide. It was, of course, played at other times, not only at high festivals like Christmas and Easter, but also, quite commonly, on Sundays and local holidays. At Workington, in Cumberland, it still exists as a vigorous street game played out between teams known as 'Uppies' and 'Downies' on Good Friday, Easter Tuesday, and the Saturday following, and so it does at Kirkwall in the Orkneys on Christmas and New Year's Day. There was formerly a Christmas Day match at Kirkham, in Lancashire, and, until the beginning of last century, in more than one South Cardiganshire parish where, apparently the game was played with 'such vigour that it became little short of a serious fight.'[1] At Llanwennog, near Lampeter, after the Christmas morning service, two teams, called the Blaenaus and the Paddy Bros assembled on the turnpike road and began a game which raged all over the parish, and sometimes went on until darkness fell. The Paddy Bros were men from the highland part of the parish, so called because they were supposed to be descended from Irish immigrants in the past. The Blaenaus lived in the lowland region, and claimed to be of pure Brython descent. The game continued until one side or the other managed to get the ball into its own goal, that of the Blaenaus being at New Court, and that of the Bros being up the hill to the highland hamlet of Rhyddlan. Not a few of the players were injured by kicks on the shins, and sometimes two of them would break off during the game to indulge in a private bout of fisticuffs but the fierce zest for victory never failed. An old inmate of Lampeter Workshouse, describing the custom long after it had ceased, said that any Bros or Blaenau 'would as soon lose a cow from his cowhouse, as the football from his portion of the parish.'[2]

Football was played at Shrovetide in Chester until 1539. It was an old custom of that city, 'time out of memory of man', for the Shoemakers' Company to provide annually a football valued at three shillings and fourpence, and to present it ceremonially to the Drapers' Company on Shrove Tuesday, in the presence of the Mayor, at the Cross on the Roodee. Thereafter followed a boisterous game between the Cross and the Common Hall, in the course of which many people were often injured, 'Some having their bodies brused or crushed; some their arms, heades, or legges broken, and some otherwise

1. These are: Quinquagesima Eve, known as Shrove, or Egg Saturday; Quinquagesima Sunday; and Shrove, or Collop Monday. In some northern districts, the day after Ash Wednesday was Fruttors Thursday, when a special kind of fritter with currants in it was eaten. In Ireland, the whole season was often called Shraft, and Shrove Tuesday itself was known as 'the last day of Shraft'.

1. *Oswestry Observer*, March 2nd, 1887. Quoted by G. L. Gomme in *The Village Community*, 1890.

2. Ibid.

maimed or in peril of their lives.[1] In 1539, partly 'to avoid the said inconveniences', the Shoemakers' football was replaced by six silver gleaves and the street-game by foot-races, for which the gleaves were awarded as prizes. Apparently, this change in the annual pastime was accepted without undue local opposition; but three hundred years later, it proved rather less easy to suppress Derby's traditional Shrovetide game.

There a very violent form of football was played by the men of All Saint's and St Peter's parishes, with so much enthusiasm and strong party feeling that the contest, especially towards the end, was more like a fight between the two sections of the town than an ordinary game. The ball was thrown at noon, or near it, from the Town Hall to an immense crowd waiting in the Market Place. There were two goals, at opposite ends of the town, and the object of both sides was to get the ball into their own goal. Victory for either was announced by the pealing of the church bells in the parish concerned. When, finally, in 1846, this immensely popular game was banned by the authorities, soldiers and special constables had to be brought in, and the Riot Act read, before the prohibition could be enforced. Games almost as wild were played at Dorking and Kingston-on-Thames. At Chester-le-Street, Co. Durham, a fierce contest between the Up-streeters and the Down-streeters raged every year through the centre of the town, between shops and houses with barricaded windows, until it was suppressed, with some difficulty, in 1932.

Shrovetide football still flourishes at Sedgefield, Co Durham, Alnwick in Northumberland, Ashbourne in Derbyshire, and Atherstone in Warwickshire. At Ashbourne, it is played on Ash Wednesday as well as on Shrove Tuesday, beginning at two o'clock in the afternoon of both days, and once (but no longer[2]) continuing until midnight. The two goals are the mills at Clifton and at Sturston, which are three miles apart, and separated by the quite sizeable Henmore brook and some lesser streams, across or through which the players have to make their strenuous way. The teams, which like some country-dances are for 'as many as will', are known as Up'ards and Down'ards, according to whether the men who compose them come from north or south of the Henmore.

At Atherstone, the Shrove Tuesday game lasts only for three hours, from two o'clock until five, and is played along that part of Watling Street which is also the main street of the town. The football used is decorated with red, white and blue ribbons, and is filled with water, to prevent its being kicked more than a few yards at a time. There are no goals, and no recognized sides, although formerly, two teams took part, one composed of Warwickshire men, and the other of men from the neighbouring county of Leicestershire. But during the present century, this inter-county aspect was lost sight of, and now each man plays as an individual, and does his energetic best to capture the ball for himself at the end of the game. If he succeeds in doing this, in spite of the determined efforts of all his fellow-players to stop him, he is the winner of the game, and is allowed to keep the ball.

The Alnwick game was formerly a street contest, like the rest, but for many years now it has been played on a field called The Pasture, between goals decorated with greenery, and standing about a quarter of a mile apart. The rival teams are men from the parishes of St Michael and St Paul. The ball is fetched from Alnwick Castle by a committee in charge of the proceedings, and is ceremonially piped to the field by the Duke of Northumberland's piper.

The game continues until three goals have been won, after which there is a wild scramble to get the ball off the field and back across the Duke's boundaries.

In the Cornish towns at St Ives and St Columb Major, hurling takes the place of football at Shrovetide. This is an ancient Cornish game, once very popular, in which the ball used is about the size of a cricket-ball, made of cork or light wood, and thinly covered with silver. It is thrown up at the beginning of a match, and then tossed, hurled, or carried over

1. *Certayne Collection of Anchiante Times concerning the Ancient and Famous Citie of Chester*, published in Lyson's *Magna Britannia*, 1810.

2. By amicable arrangement with the police, made in 1966 the game now ends at 10 p.m.

the ground, but never kicked. At St Columb Major the game is played on Shrove Tuesday through the streets of the town. At St Ives, it takes place on the previous day, on Quinquagesima Monday which is also Feasten Monday. Tradition says that on Quinquagesima Sunday, the patronal festival, St Ia, the town's patron saint, landed in Cornwall after her flight from Ireland on a leaf. This game also was originally played all through the town, but was later transferred to the beach. The Mayor stood on the West Pier and threw the silver ball to the waiting crowd below. In 1939, it was moved again, this time to a public park, where it is still played.

Shroving. Shroving, or Lent-crocking, at Shrovetide was a widespread children's custom until fairly recently, and in some parts of Great Britain it is not yet quite extinct. Like some other customs kept up then, it has added special names to the season, such as Lentsherd (or Lansherd) Night, Dappy-door Night, Lincrook Day, or Sharp Tuesday. On Shrove Tuesday, or on the day before, little bands of Shrovers visited the various houses of the parish to ask for pancakes, eggs, cheese, or anything else that the householder could be induced to give them. In some districts, this was done by the poor genuinely seeking alms. 'Pray, mistress, can you give me any aumus?'[1] was a request often heard in the North Riding of Yorkshire during the nineteenth century and it was answered by the generous with gifts of flour, milk, bacon, or other foods wherewith to make a little Shrovetide feast. In Wales, too, it was usual to give flour and fats to poor mothers, to enable them to make pancakes for their families. But Shroving was also a custom of young people and children, and in their hands it was not so much a way of asking for charity as part of the traditional licence of merrymaking of the season.

Small groups went about, knocking on every door, and singing,

1. C. Clough Robinson, *A Glossary of Words pertaining to the Dialect of Mid-Yorkshire, with others peculiar to Lower Nidderdale*, 1876.

A-shroving, a-shroving,
We be come a-shroving;
A piece of bread, a piece of cheese,
A bit of your fat bacon,
Doughnuts and pancakes,
All of your own making.

or

Snick, snack, the pan's hot,
We're come a-shroving.
Strike while the iron's hot,
Something's better than nothing
Flour's cheap and land's dear[1]
And that's why we come shroving here,

or some other version of this song which varied from county to county, and frequently from one district to another in the same county.

Polite requests for gifts were sometimes reinforced by more direct methods of persuasion, especially in the West of England, where the Shrovers often went out armed with stones or pieces of broken crockery, and used them as weapons to enforce generosity or punish refusals. In this *Natural and Historical Account of the Isle of Scilly* (1750), Robert Heath says that 'the boys of this island have a custom of throwing stones in the evening against the doors of the dwellers' houses; a privilege they claim from time immemorial, and put into practice without control. . . . The terms demanded by the boys are pancakes or money to capitulate.'

The idea that stone- or shard-throwing was an inalienable right on Shrove, or Sharp Tuesday was not confined to the Scilly Isles. In Cornwall, the clubs used on Nickanan Night (*see Mischief Night*) were used again next day to pound upon the house-doors in time with the chanted lines,

Nicka, nicka, nan,
Give me some pancake, and I'll be gone;
But if you give me none,
I'll throw a great stone,
And down your door shall come.

At St Ives, the boys demanded 'a pancake, now, now, now', with a somewhat similar threat, the shouted verse being punctuated by bangs on the door with stones tied to the ends

1. Sung at Drayton in Berkshire. In another Berkshire variant of the song, the fifth line runs 'Flour's scarce and lard's dear', which sounds rather more likely.

of cords. In some Dorset villages, until about 1890, little gangs of children sang,

> Here I come, I never came before,
> If you don't give me a pancake,
> I'll break down your door.

and then, without further delay, they joyfully hurled broken bits of crockery against the door. 'The owner of the house,' says a Sherborne correspondent, 'was supposed to come out and toss a pancake for the children to catch.'[1] Round South Molton, in Devon, where Lent-crocking took place on Shrove Monday, it served as a kind of preliminary notice for the morrow. As the young people threw their missiles, they chanted:

> Once, twice, thrice,
> I give thee warning,
> Please to make pancakes
> 'Gin tomorrow morning.

Like many old customs that involve asking and receiving, Shroving has been somewhat frowned upon in recent years by those who regard it as a form of begging. Where it survives, it is usually in its gentler form, without the lively bombard ment of doors which must formerly have been, at least for the children, three parts of the fun. Here and there, traces of the old exuberance are still visible. At Clovelly, boys race down the steep High Street on Lansherd Night, dragging or kicking tin cans of every kind over the stones as they run, and making as much noise as possible. On Exmoor, and in the West Somerset hills, children sometimes come round, as of old, singing

> Tipety, tipety, tin,
> Give me a pancake and I will come in.
> Tipety, tipety, toe,
> Give me a pancake and I will go,

and throwing broken crockery against the door, or if the door stands open, into the house itself. When they have done this, they make off as fast as they can pursued in most cases by some agile member of the family visited who, if he can catch them, blackens their faces with soot and brings them back to the house to receive the desired pancake or some other gift.

In some places, Shroving has acquired adult patronage, and consequently tends to be a more or less organized affair. At Gittisham in Devon, the version of the custom known as Tip-toeing is kept up thus. The children march round the village in orderly fashion after school-hours, stopping outside the houses to sing

> Tip, tip, toe,
> Please to give us a penny,
> And away we'll go,

and receiving small gifts of money in return. Here they carry no missiles, and perhaps they never did; but elsewhere in the country, the Tip-toers used to come armed with shards and ready to use their weapons upon the doors of the ungenerous. In such places, their song sounded a more threatening note, with

> Please to give me a pancake,
> Or I'll let go,

and let go they did, with the greatest enthusiasm, often without waiting to see whether their demands would be refused or not.

At East Hendred in Berkshire, a somewhat limited form of the old custom is kept up on Shrove Tuesday. The children no longer go round the parish, as their predecessors once did, but punctually at noon they march up to Hendred House, singing a local variant of the Berkshire Shroving-song which ends with the lines

> With the butcher up my back,
> A halfpenny's better than nothing!

On arrival at the house, each child is given a halfpenny, and also a bun, and then they all march away again, singing the same song, with its rather grudging suggestion of gratitude.

In one Dorset village, an attempt has been made to secure the continuance of Shroving by means of a bequest. In 1925, Mr Valentine Rickman, of Durweston, left a sum of £50, vested in the Rector and churchwardens, of which the interest was to be annually divided among legitimate scholars of the parish who

1. *Dorset Up Along and Down Along*, ed. M. Dacombe, n.d.

go a-shroving on the right date to at least three houses.[1]

Shuttlecock Day. Shuttlecock Day was one of the names given to Shrove Tuesday in Leicester and in some other places in the same county because it was formerly the custom for adults and children alike to play Battledore and Shuttlecock in the streets then. The *Leicester Chronicle* for February 12th, 1842, remarks that 'Shrove Tuesday is celebrated in Hinckley by a general game of shuttlecock and battledore, which is a very novel and amusing sight to a stranger.' If, however, that stranger had come from the West Riding of Yorkshire, the spectacle, though it might have amused him, would not have been new to him because he would probably have seen it at home many times before on the same anniversary. 'In the villages of the West Riding', wrote William Henderson in his *Folk-Lore of the Northern Counties* (1879), 'the streets may be seen on this day full of grown-up men and women playing "battledore and shuttle-feathers".' In York also, this was one of the games that were played then by people of all ages on Baile Hill.

Shuttlecock, or Shuttlefeather, is a very old game, which was sometimes used by young people in a form of divination. Lady Gomme suggests that this was the true origin of the game.[2] A question concerning the number of months before marriage, or years before death, or the initials of the future wife's or husband's name, was asked at the beginning, and answered by the number of successful strokes made before the player missed, and the shuttlecock fell to the ground. The same type of enquiry was, and perhaps still is, made when tossing a cowslip ball, or counting how many times in succession the cuckoo calls.

Simnel Sunday. The fourth Sunday in Lent is sometimes called Simnel Sunday because it was, and still is, the traditional day for eating simnel cakes. These cakes are eaten at other seasons also, but from mediaeval times onwards, they have been specially associated with Mid-Lent Sunday. When it became usual for gifts to be made to mothers on that day (*see Mothering Sunday*), simnel cakes were often given, and today they are still sold in large quantities round about that time, and sometimes, though less correctly at Eastertide also.

Simnel cakes are of three main types, named after the towns which first produced them. The Shrewsbury simnel, which is the most widely known, is rich and dark, with a thick hard crust of almond paste, and decorations of candied fruits and marzipan flowers. The Devizes simnel is star-shaped, without a crust; the Bury cake is flattish, usually round and thickest in the middle, and full of currants, spices, almonds and candied peel. Enormous quantities of Devizes and Bury Simnels are made every year in their name-towns, not only for mothering-gifts, but as customary Mid-Lent fare for all. In both places, baking begins soon after Christmas, so that the cakes may be sent to people living abroad in time for the festival. Some bakers have standing orders on their books that were first given seventy or eighty years ago by some local man who emigrated to the Dominions or the United States, and have been regularly renewed by their sons and grandsons ever since.

The name 'simnel' is almost certainly derived from the Latin word *simila,* meaning the fine wheaten flour of which such cakes are made. There are, however, two popular and quite unreliable legends which attempt to explain it otherwise. One is that a man named Simon and his wife, Nell, quarrelled at some unknown date about the cooking of a cake. One said the mixture should be boiled, the other that it should be baked. As a compromise, it was both boiled and baked, and the resulting confection was named 'simnel' after both cooks.

The other story is that Lambert Simnel, one of the false pretenders to the throne in Henry VII's reign, was the son of a baker, and that when his rebellion failed, some of his father's cakes were derisively nicknamed 'simnels' after him. But Lambert Simnel's father appears to have been a joiner, not a baker, and in any

1. *Dorset Up Along and Down Along,* ed. M. Dacombe, n.d.

2. A. B. Gomme, *The Traditional Games of England, Scotland, and Ireland,* Vol. II. 1898.

case, simnels were known long before his day. They are mentioned in the *Annals of the Church of Winchester* for the year 1042. There is it recorded that Edward the Confessor ordered, and confirmed by charter that, so often as he, or any of his successors, should wear his crown at Winchester, Worcester or Westminster, the precentor of the place should receive half a mark from the royal purse, and that a hundred simnels and a measure of wine should be given to the convent.

In Hampshire formerly, Mid-Lent wafers sometimes took the place of simnels. Thin, crisp wafers, always stamped with an ecclesiastical pattern, were made by pressing batter between the two circular iron plates of specially marked wafering-irons. These were often used as Mothering-gifts in later years, but it seems probable that they had real religious significance in pre-Reformation times. At Chilbolton, where they were still being made about thirty years ago, there is a tradition that during the Middle Ages they were manufactured in a nearby monastery for distribution to the faithful after Mass on Mid-Lent Sunday.[1] Chilbolton, was the last stronghold of the centuries-old custom. The Baverstock family, long resident in that parish, owned a secret recipe which was never written down, but was passsed on by word of mouth to one person in each generation, and also an ancient pair of wafering-irons locally believed to be of fifteenth-century date. These irons werc used for the last time by Mrs Baverstock in 1936. After that date, she found the work of making large quantities of wafers every year too heavy, and the custom was given up. It is not likely to be revived now, although the secret recipe is still known to her daughter, and will in due course be passed on to another member of the family.

Singing on the Bargate, and on Magdalen Tower. *(See May Singing.)*

Skipping. On Shrove Tuesday afternoon, the people of Scarborough – men, women and children – go down to the foreshore to skip. At noon on this day, the Pancake Bell (which now hangs in the Museum) is rung, and between two o'clock and half-past two, the people begin to drift down to the beach, and stay there, skipping, until about tea-time. This is an entirely spontaneous gathering; the police, it is true, do recognize it by closing the foreshore to all but the most essential traffic, but otherwise there is nothing whatever organized about it.

At Brighton formerly, skipping took place at the other end of Lent, on Long Rope Day, which was the local name for Good Friday. The fishermen and their families skipped on the beach and in the forecourt of the Fish Market, and sometimes overflowed, skipping, into the streets of the town. At one time, this was an immensely popular custom, but it ceased, neccessarily, when the beaches were closed during the Second World War, and was not revived at that war's end. However, Good Friday skipping still exists at Alciston in Sussex and, since 1954, at South Heighton, near Newhaven. At Alciston, it takes place outside the Rose Cottage Inn, where as many as two hundred skippers sometimes assemble.

Until very recently, it was customary for young lads to skip on Parker's Piece, in Cambridge, on Good Friday morning; girls were not allowed to join in until the afternoon. Within the last twenty years, this custom has died out, for no very obvious reason, as towards the end of last century, a similar one did in the Bartlow Hills. These so-called Hills, seven in number, are in fact burial-barrows, standing on the borders between Essex and Cambridgeshire; and there, on Good Friday, the people of Linton and Hildersham used to meet, to take part in the old ritual known as 'skipping at the Hills'.

Skipping, besides being an ancient magical game associated with the sowing and upspringing of the seed in Springtime, seems to be one of those mentioned by E. C. Curwen[1] as having been played on barrows on Palm Sunday and Good Friday during the Middle Ages. Such games, including skipping, used to

1. *It Happened in Hampshire,* W.I. Publication, 1937, ed. W. G. Beddington and E. B. Christy.

1. E. C. Curwen, *Prehistoric Sussex,* 1930.

be played on a large barrow near Hove until the middle of last century. This barrow was then just outside the town, though the spread of building has since swallowed up the site. It was destroyed in 1856. There are barrows near Alciston, where the Good Friday skipping still occurs, and so there are on Haughmond Hill, near Shrewsbury, where it is said to have flourished some seventy or eighty years ago.

Souling. On All Souls' Day, or on its Eve, little bands of children in some country districts of Cheshire and Shropshire still go Souling, or Soul-caking, from house to house, singing traditional songs and receiving gifts of money, sweets, fruit, or cake. This practice is all that now remains of a once well-known custom in which, until at least as late as the 'sixties of last century grown men and young lads, and poor people of all ages used to take part.

Like the children today, they made their rounds, singing some version of the ancient Souling-song, and hoping for the charity of their richer neighbours. Alms of any kind might be given to them, but one traditional gift was a specially-made cake or loaf, usually called a Soul-cake but sometimes known by other names. In Aberdeenshire, a particular type of cake was baked for this anniversary and called a Dirge-loaf. Large quantities had to be prepared, since it was the practice to give one or more to every person who came to the house, regardless of whether he came begging for it or not. Aubrey records much the same custom as existing in his day in Shropshire, where great piles of Soul-cakes, 'about the bignesse of 2d. cakes', were set upon a board or table, and 'n'ly all the visitants that day took one.'[1] In Carmarthenshire, the name Dole-cake was sometimes used, and in Yorkshire, Saumas- or Soulmas-cake.

Ingredients and form varied also in different districts. The Yorkshire Saumas-cake was a small fruit-cake; the Northamptonshire Soul-cake was made with caraway seeds. Elsewhere, a kind of light, flat bun, well spiced and sweetened, was very usual. In some areas, small round loaves of bread, made of wheat or barley flour, were given instead of cakes, and one of these would often be kept for luck during the coming year. In his *History of Whitby* (1817) George Young mentions a woman of that town who possessed a Saumas-loaf that had been preserved in her family for about a hundred years. Nowadays, no one troubles to make these special cakes or loaves, but the term 'Soul-caking' still survives, and in some districts, the children often refer to any sort of present received on their rounds as a 'Soul-cake'.

In his account of the Shropshire custom already mentioned, Aubrey tells us that 'there is an old Rhythm or saying:

> A Soule-cake, a Soule-cake,
> Have mercy on all Christen soules for a
> Soule-cake.'

This 'rhythm' was probably a line from the Souling-song is use there. Of this song there are a number of variants. One well-known version runs:

> Soul! Soul! for a soul-cake!
> I pray you, good missis, a soul-cake!
> An apple, a pear, a plum or a cherry,
> Or any good thing to make us all merry.
> One for Peter, two for Paul
> Three for Them who made us all.
> Up with the kettle and down with the pan.
> Give us good alms, and we'll be gone.

The last line of this ditty varies in different places. Sometimes it is ale that is demanded instead of alms, sometimes an apple, and in one instance, simply an answer, as though the singers knew it should be something beginning with an A, and settled for a word that might be considered to cover every possibility. In any case, it is a more or less straightforward begging-song, akin to others used at other seasons, and to a Yorkshire variant which asks for 'a copper or two', and then obligingly adds,

> If you have no coppers, silver will do;
> If you have no silver, then God Bless you.

There are, however, other versions which come closer to the religious origin of the Souling custom. One, from Staffordshire, has a verse which says:

1. John Aubrey, *Remaines of Gentilisme and Judaisme*, 1686–7 ed. James Britten, 1881.

Soul Day! Soul Day!
We've been praying for the souls departed;
So pray, good people, give us a cake,
For we are all poor people, well known to you before,
So give us a cake for charity's sake,
And our blessing we'll leave at your door.

So too, in a letter written to Charlotte Burne, in 1913, the writer recalls a song he heard in 1857, when he was a boy at Bilston in Staffordshire. It was sung by a group of old women, and contained the lines,

Remember the departed for holy Mary's sake,[1]
And of your charity, pray gi' us a big soul-cake.

Remembering the departed was, in fact, the essence of the matter, In pre-Reformation times, alms were solicited at this season to provide Masses for the souls in Purgatory, and men paraded the streets to remind the faithful of their duty of prayer and charity. Centuries before the feasts of All Saints and All Souls were instituted to commemorate the Christian dead, the pagan dead were ritually remembered at the great Celtic and Teutonic festivals in early November and were believed to return from the grave then to their earthly haunts. This conception of an annual return survived into Christian times, and coloured many of the customs of Hallowtide. A widespread European tradition held that all the souls in Purgatory were released for forty-eight hours on All Hallows' Eve, and visited their homes in the following two days. All over Europe, candles were, and often still are, lit for them, indoors or on the graves in the churchyard, and household fires were kept burning for those who came from the cold tomb. In Ireland, lighted candles were placed in the windows to guide them home, and food, drink, and tobacco were put out for them in the living-room. In Brittany also, the fire in the houseplace was carefully made up, and a little feast was set out on a table covered with a white cloth. The family then retired to bed, and if they heard strange sounds during the night they took no notice, for they knew these were made by their departed kinsfolk moving about below. Soul-cakes appear to have been originally an offering to the dead on this night of their return, and the giving of such cakes as a charity was generally believed to benefit them in some way. In Flanders, children used to build little altars in the streets on All Souls' Eve, and beg for money to buy cakes 'for the souls in Purgatory'. On the following morning, small loaves of Soul-bread were baked in most Flemish households and were eaten, piping hot, while the eater said a prayer for the departed. It was believed that for every loaf thus eaten, one poor soul would be freed from the pains of Purgatory.

After the Reformation, the English Soulers forgot that their ritual had once been concerned with prayers for those in Purgatory, and so equally did the householders who annually made Soul-cakes to give them on their rounds. The reformed faith refused belief in the need for such prayers; but it could not altogether destroy the deep-seated notion that the charity of the living somehow benefits, or is acceptable to, the dead. The words of some Souling-songs suggest that the expected gifts are made in the name of the departed, and if in the course of time the connection became more and more dimly realized, the fact that it had once existed may account for the long persistence of the Souling custom. It may also be noted that in some Scottish districts, where Souling in its usual form was unknown, it was nevertheless customary to give alms on November 2nd to any poor person asking for them.

In Cheshire, the Soul-Caking Play was acted on All Souls' Night, and was closely associated with the Souling rite. It is a version of the St George play, always given in that county at Hallowtide instead of at Christmas or at Easter, as elsewhere, and includes in its cast a character unknown in other versions, Wild Horse, or Dick, a man wearing a horse's skull. *(See Hodening.)* Until the 1914 War, it was regularly acted in several villages, and it continued annually at Comberbach until shortly before the Second World War. It is performed now at Antrobus, where the old custom has been revived after a long lapse.

1. Quoted in *British Calendar Customs*: *England*, ed. A. R. Wright and T. E. Lones, Vol. III, 1940.

Spanish Sunday. Spanish Sunday is an old name for Palm Sunday in the English Midland counties, and in parts of the West Riding of Yorkshire. It is derived from a children's custom that flourished there as recently as the first twenty years of this century, and of which traces still remain in a few districts. A sweet drink was made for the festival from broken pieces of Spanish liquorice, peppermint or lemon sweets, brown sugar, and well-water. The solid ingredients were put into glass bottles on the previous evening, and a little water was added to make a thick rich, sediment. On Palm Sunday morning, the children went to some local holy or wishing-well, walked round it once, or in some places three times, and then filled their bottles with its water. Almost every region had some particular spring which was visited for this purpose, and to it children came from surrounding parishes in quite considerable numbers.[1] When the bottles were filled, they were vigorously shaken, and as soon as the sweet sediment was sufficiently dissolved to flavour the water, the 'Spanish' drink was ready to use.

In some Derbyshire parishes, the ceremonies were slightly different. At Castleton and Bradwell, the bottles were called Easter Monday bottles because they were filled on Easter (or Shakkin') Monday; but on the previous Palm Sunday, the children went to the Lady Wells at Great Hucklow and Castleton and dropped straight new pins into them. They believed that if they did not do this, the 'Lady of the Well' would not let them have clean water during the year, and that their bottles would break when they returned to fill them on Shakkin' Monday. At Belper, the children carried mugs or porringers instead of the twelve-ounce bottles that were usual elsewhere. They did not use liquorice, but made what must surely have been a rather inspid drink out of oatmeal mixed with sugar and water. According to one account, their visits to the Lady Well for this purpose were not restricted to a particular festival day,but could be made at any time.[1] Tideswell children took a cup to the Dropping Tor on Easter Day, filled it from the slowly falling drops, and then dissolved a quarter of a pound of sugar in it to make a sweet but unflavoured drink. This practice was known as Sugar-Cupping.

Although the 'Spanish' drink itself was doubtless the most interesting feature of the occasion from the children's point of view, the fact that certain rules had to be observed in its preparation suggests that the original intention of the Spanish Sunday custom may have been to honour or draw benefit from some holy or magical spring. A personal visit to a particular well, not necessarily the nearest, was essential. In two of the Derbyshire parishes mentioned above, a preliminary offering was required. The spring visited was almost always a Lady-Well, if one existed in the district, and if not, a saint's well or a wishing-well. It had to be circuited a prescribed number of times before the bottles were filled. Only its water could be used in the making of the drink, the single exception to this rule being that a very small quantity of tap-water was permitted for the overnight softening of the ingredients. All these regulations were strictly observed as late as Edward VII's reign. In the period between the two Wars, they seem to have been gradually forgotten, but by that time the Spanish Sunday custom itself was already falling into decay.

1. An informant from Stonesfield (Oxon) said that when she was a child, about 1905, she went to the Lady Well at Wilcote to fill her Palm Sunday bottle, and found about a hundred children gathered there. (*Information give to the Editor by a member of the Oxfordshire Folklore Society.*)

1. R. C. Hope, *The Legendary Lore of the Holy Wells of England*, 1893.

Straw Bear Tuesday. The day after Plough Monday was known as Straw Bear Tuesday, or Strawbower Day, in the fenland area on the borders of Huntingdonshire and Cambridgeshire, though not in other parts of either county nor, so far as can be traced, elsewhere in England. On that day, within living memory, the Straw Bear appeared. This was a man, or a boy, completely swathed in straw; his face was covered as well as his body, so that he could hardly see as he went along, and was quite unrecognizable. According to a description given by a man from Ramsey Mereside who had often taken part in the ceremony, tightly twisted straw-bands were wound round the Bear's body, with separate bands for his arms and legs. He wore a tail, and a peculiar head-dress formed by two sticks fastened to his shoulders, which met in a point above his head, and were covered by straw drawn up to make a kind of cone. In this guise, he lumbered about the streets with a band of companions, one of whom led him by a strong chain fastened under his armpits. On arriving at a house, he went down on his hands and knees, groaning and growling as the door was opened, while his attendants pretended to restrain his dangerous ferocity by pulling on his chain and beating him with a stick. The householders were expected to reward him with money-gifts.[1]

A contributor to *Folk-Lore* (Vol. 20, 1909) says that the Bear used to dance before the houses, like the real dancing-bears that were once so common in England. He adds that he saw a Straw Bear at Whittlesea in 1909, and except for the fact that there was no dance, the ceremony was exactly as he remembered it in the same town forty years before. Another form of the custom is recorded in F. W. Bird's *Memorials of Godmanchester*, where it is stated that on Strawbower Day in some areas (though not in Godmanchester itself), the men who had acted as Plough Witches on the previous day (*see Plough Monday*) went through the streets dressed from head to foot in straw, and demanded alms from the passers-by.

The Straw Bear was, of course, only one of that large company of mysterious beasts which, as bringers of fertility or as scapegoat-symbols, appeared in due season all over Europe; but in England at least, his bear-form was unusual. Violet Alford has described in her *Pyranean Festivals* (1937) the ritual hunting on December 26th, or at Carnival, of a straw-clad man-bear in Andorra, and other hunts of the same kind in Catalonia and the Basque country, where the bears are truly terrifying creatures dressed in skins and masks. In Germany also, when the *Schimmel*, the German equivalent of our Hoden-ing Horse, appeared at Christmas, he was sometimes accompanied by a boy swathed in straw who was supposed to be a bear. In England however, the ritual beasts were usually horses, or bulls, or deer. How this alien creature found his way into one small corner of the country we do not know, unless, perhaps, some ancient fertility figure associated with the start of the Spring ploughing once had another name there, and came to be called a bear in the days when bear-baiting was a favourite sport.[1] He has gone now, whatever his origins, though he survived long enough to be remembered by some elderly people. It is said that the police frowned upon the ceremony because they regarded it as a form of begging, and it may be partly for that reason that this ancient and interesting custom has now disappeared.

1. C. F. Tebbutt, 'Huntingdonshire Folk and Their Folklore', *Transactions of the Cambridgeshire and Huntingdonshire Archeological Society*, Vol. VI, Part V.

Street Football. *(See Shrovetide Football.)*

Swan Upping. Swan Upping on the River Thames takes place annually towards the end of July, when the young swans of the river between London and Henley are rounded up, caught, and marked with the swan-marks of their different owners. This process, which takes several days, is carried through by the Royal Swanherd and the Swan Wardens of the Dyers' and the Vintners' Companies of the City of London, with their attendants, and is now all that actively remains of the once-elaborate ritual connected with the ownership of swans in England.

The Mute Swan was, and is, a Royal bird, and seems to have been so since at least as early as the twelfth century, and possibly earlier. All swans, therefore, belonged to the Crown, and no subject might own any unless the privilege of doing so had been specially bestowed upon him by the Sovereign. From time to time, such grants were made by the reigning king to

1. The existence in England of numerous bears for baiting up to the beginning of the nineteenth century probably accounts for tales of spectral bears still remembered in some districts.

favoured individuals or corporate bodies, and with them a distinctive swan-mark whereby ownership of the birds could be clearly recognized. By an Act of 1482, possession of a 'Game of Swans' was restricted to holders of freehold land and tenements to the yearly value of five marks, or more. Anyone may now keep captive birds on his own private waters, but unmarked swans at large on open waters are still automatically the property of the Queen.

Although various secular landowners and monastic houses once enjoyed swan-rights on the River Thames, there are now only two non-royal swan-owners on that river. These are the two great City Livery Companies, the Dyers, to whom rights were granted in 1473 and later confirmed by Queen Anne, and the Vintners, who received theirs at some time between 1472 and 1483, though the first documentary record of their use appears only in the accounts of 1509. On the first day of the Upping, the Swan Wardens maintained by the two Companies, with their uniformed assistants, meet the Royal Swanherd, with his, at Southwark Bridge, from whence all travel together up the river as far as Henley, in six rowing-boats. The Royal Swanherd's boat leads the way, flying two flags, one of which has the Queen's initials and a crown upon it, and the other a swan with raised wings. The other royal boat, and the two provided by each of the Companies, fly only one flag apiece, those of the Companies displaying their arms as well as swans.

As the boats make their slow way upriver, the Uppers catch and examine some six hundred birds, a task that calls for considerable skill, and does not lack excitement, since swans are not particularly docile creatures, and they are very strong. The existing markings of the adult birds are examined to determine ownership, and the cygnets of each family are similarly marked, with nicks cut in their beaks – one nick for the Dyers' birds and two for those of the Vintners. The well-known inn-sign, the Swan with Two Necks, is said to be a corrupt version of the Vintners' mark; it should be, and doubtless once was, the Swan with Two Nicks. If the cygnets are of mixed parentage, the cob belonging to one owner and the pen to another, half the brood receive their father's markings and the other half those of their mother. If the numbers are uneven, the odd cygnet is marked like the cob.

The Queen's swans are rounded up and examined like the rest, but they are not marked. It is not necessary that they should be since all unmarked swans on the Thames are hers by prerogative, including any which may happen to stray there on their own from other waters.

Tar Barrel Ceremony. *(See Burning the Old Year Out.)*

Teddy Rowe's Band. Teddy Rowe's Band is the name of a lively and noisy parade which, until 1964, regularly ushered in Pack Monday Fair at Sherborne in Dorset. This fair is held on the Monday following Old Michaelmas Day (October 10th); it is really St Michael's Fair, but it is far better known by its secondary name of Pack Monday Fair. In the very early hours of the morning, soon after midnight, young people of both sexes marched through the sleeping town, blowing horns, bugles and whistles, banging upon tin trays and frying-pans, and generally making as much discordant noise as possible. This was Teddy Rowe's Band, which is locally believed to have heralded the Fair thus for nearly five centuries.

Tradition says that the custom began in 1490 when, after the completion of the great fan vault in the nave of the Abbey Church, Abbot Peter Ramsam gave his masons a well-earned holiday, telling them to pack their tools and then go out and enjoy themselves. This they did with enthusiasm. Led by their foreman whose name was Teddy Rowe (or Roe), they marched in triumph through the streets, blowing horns, and giving vent to their high spirits by shouting and making cheerful noises of all kinds. In the years that followed, the townspeople are said to have repeated the lively performance annually on the morning of Pack Monday Fair. The Fair itself is supposed to have gained this name from the packing of the masons' goods after the completion of their work, and their subsequent departure from the town.

Whether this is the true explanation of the custom or not, it seems clear that Teddy Rowe's Band existed for several centuries, and survived more than one attempt to suppress it. Now, however, its future is extremely uncertain. The parade was held as usual in 1963, but because of hooliganism and malicious damage on that occasion, it was banned by the police in 1964, and this ban has since been annually repeated. Only time will show whether, as now seems very likely, Sherborne has seen the last of Teddy Rowe and his followers, or whether, like some other tough old customs elsewhere, this one will reappear in due course perhaps in a modified form.

Thomassing. 'Going a-Thomassing' on the Feast of St Thomas the Apostle (December 21st) was a customary practice in most parts of England until well towards the end of the nineteenth century. In some areas it was called 'going a-gooding', or 'mumping', or 'curning', and the festival itself was variously styled Mumping or Gooding or Doleing Day. Poor women went from house to house to ask for gifts from their richer neighbours. They rarely if ever, came away empty-handed, though what they received naturally varied with the generosity of the giver, and also with the custom of the district. An account of the custom in the Grimsby area of Lincolnshire says that well-to-do people normally gave a shilling to each applicant, and 'the village shop perhaps gives them a candle apiece; one farmer gives each family a stone of flour; another a piece of meat. . . .'[1] A writer in *Notes & Queries* (1857) records that in Staffordshire, 'the clergyman is expected to give one shilling to each person, and consequently the celebration of the day is attended with no small expense.' In addition, the parishioners gave alms in kind or in money, either directly to the women, or to a fund known as St Thomas' Dole, which was distributed by the clergy and churchwardens on the Sunday nearest December 21st.

A very usual gift at this time was a quart or a pint of wheat with which to make loaves and puddings for the Christmas feast. The millers' contribution was made by grinding it into it flour without charge. In Herefordshire a sack of corn was put outside each farmhouse, and from it a quartern measure of grain was ladled out to every woman who came for it, with extra allowances for those who had large families.[2] Sometimes the more generous householders provided hot spiced ale for the Thomassers on their rounds, which must have made a very comforting addition to the customary gifts on a cold winter's morning. For all this, acknowledgement was made by loudly expressed good wishes for Christmas and, in some districts, the presentation of a luck-bringing sprig of holly or mistletoe.

When wages were very low and poverty often extreme, the fruits of 'going a Thomassing' must frequently have made all the difference to a poor family's enjoyment of Christmas. It was not, however, only the very poor who followed the custom. In some regions, women who would never dream of asking for charity at other times went 'a-Thomassing' without any sense of shame. F. T. Elworthy remarks that in Somerset, when he wrote in 1886, 'it is thought no disgrace for quite well-to-do people to go round begging'[3] on St Thomas' Day. That no one denied even such apparently undeserving applicants suggests that the custom was widely regarded as an expression of Christmas goodwill to all, rather than straightforward almsgiving. Nevertheless, almsgiving it was; and with the coming of better times it became less necessary, and has now died out completely. A number of fixed charities are still however, distributed on St Thomas' Day in various places.

1. *The Antiquary*, Vol. 14, 1886: quoted in *Folk-Lore concerning Lincolnshire*, ed. Mrs Gutch & Mabel Peacock, 1908.

2. E. M. Leather, *op. cit.*

3. F. T. Elworthy, *West Somerset Word-Book*, 1886.

Tichborne Dole. The Tichborne Dole, which is annually distributed on Lady Day to the parishioners of Tichborne, Cheriton and Lane End in Hampshire, is one of the oldest charities in England. According to the tradition handed down in the Tichborne family, it was founded in the twelfth century by Lady Maybella, wife of Sir Roger de Tichborne. In her lifetime she was extremely generous to the local poor, and when she was dying, she tried to ensure that they would not suffer by her death. She asked her husband to provide an annual dole of bread on Lady Day, and he, taking a burning brand from the fire, told her that he would give as much land for this purpose as she could walk round before the flame went out. This practically amounted to a refusal in view of her weak state, and no doubt it was so intended. But Lady Mabella was not to be thus easily defeated. She ordered her women to carry her outside and then, finding she could not walk, she began to crawl over the ground as rapidly as she could. In this way she managed to cover twenty-three acres of land, still known as The Crawls, before the torch flickered out.

Before she died, she made her husband promise to honour his bargain; and in addition, she warned him that if he or any of his descendants stopped the dole thus hardly won, a curse would fall upon the family. Their fortunes would fail, their name would be changed, the house would fall down, and the ancient line would die out. As a sign of this, there would be a generation of seven sons, followed by one of seven daughters, and then the end would come.

The dole was duly given without interruption until 1796, when it was stopped, and the revenues of the Crawls were diverted by Sir Henry Tichborne, then head of the family, to the Church. In due course, Sir Henry had seven sons, and his heir had seven daughters, and part of the house collapsed. These rather alarming coincidences gave the family pause. The dole was restored by Sir Edward Doughty-Tichborne, Sir Henry's third son, and since then it has been distributed with unfailing regularity on March 25th every year.

In 1948, however, it was seriously endangered through no fault of the Tichbornes. Bread-rationing was still in operation and the Ministry of Food, after agreeing to issue the necessary bread-coupons for the dole, suddenly went back on its word. This was reported in almost every newspaper, with full accounts of the legend and the curse that threatened the family if they were forced to fail in their centuries-old duty. An appeal for the gift of bread-units was made, and as a result, more than five thousand of these were received from people all over the country. Strictly speaking, this was illegal, as the Ministry of Food hastened to point out, and for a time the issue was still in doubt. Public opinion, however, was strongly on the family's side, and finally the Ministry gave way. Coupons were issued to enable the dole to be distributed as usual, and those sent by individuals were gratefully returned to the givers.

In its present form, the dole consists, not of loaves as in earlier times, but of a ton and a half of flour made from wheat grown on The Crawls. An open-air service is held, to which the public are admitted. The Tichbornes being Catholics, this is conducted by their Chaplain, or sometimes by the Roman Catholic Bishop of Portsmouth. Prayers are offered for the repose of Lady Mabella's soul, the flour is blessed, and at the end of the service, it is distributed to the villagers, who bring bags and pillow-cases to hold it. A gallon is given to every male applicant, and half a gallon to each woman and child.

Travice Dole. *(See Graveside Doles.)*

Turning The Devil's Boulder. A curious ceremony of uncertain age and origin is annually performed at Shebbear in north Devon on the night of November 5th. Just outside the east gateway of the churchyard stands an ancient oak-tree, said to be a thousand years old, and under it lies a large stone known as the Devil's Boulder. This stone is turned every year by the bellringers, who first go to the belfry and ring a loud, jangled peal on the bells, and then go out to the stone where, armed with crowbars, they perform their ritual task. Local tradition says that if this is not done, serious misfortune will overtake the parish during the following year.[1]

When this ceremony was first performed, or why, is not known. It has nothing to do with the Gunpowder Plot, in spite of the fact that it takes place on Guy Fawkes' Night, and it is almost certainly older than that comparatively recent historical conspiracy. The boulder itself is apparently an erratic, one of those alien rocks of a geological type foreign to the locality that were left behind by the retreating ice at the end of the Ice Age. Such intruders are found in numerous places, and usually they are associated in legend with Satan, or with giants. This one is supposed to have been dropped on to its present site by the Devil, whose power to harm the village can only be averted by the annual turning and by the discordant peal rung beforehand. One of the few good things that tradition tells us about demons and their kin is that they do not, apparently, like loud noises, and in many parts of the world it is customary to avert evil at significant seasons by jangling bells, firing guns, and creating as much din and uproar as possible in a variety of other ways.

Another local legend says that the Devil's Boulder was quarried at Henscott, a village about a mile and a half from Shebbear across the River Torridge, for use as the foundation-stone of a new church. During the night it vanished, and was found next day at Shebbear. Its owners retrieved it, but on the following night the same thing happened, and so it went on for a long time. Finally, the Henscott people grew tired of rolling an irregularly-shaped boulder of

1. In 'Some Notes on Shebbear and Durpley Castle' (*Transactions of the Devonshire Association, Vol. LXX*, 1948), Mrs B. W. Olliver remarks: 'In 1940 it was decided not to continue the old custom, but that was a year of such desperate war news that the inhabitants agreed that they must leave no stone unturned, and the ceremony was duly carried out a week later. The result, though not immediate, was at least satisfactory.'

considerable weight over a mile and a half of rough ground every day, and decided to give up the unequal struggle against an obviously supernatural opponent. When, therefore, the stone was once again miraculously transported to Shebbear on the night of November 5th, it was left lying where it was found and, except for the ritual turning on the anniversary, it has not since then been moved by either man or spirit.[1]

Legends of church materials moved by fairies or demons, or, as in this case, by the Devil, are very numerous. Some are, perhaps, no more than attempts made by local people to explain something peculiar in the siting or construction of their church; but there are others which may possibly preserve dim memories of a time when the struggle between Christianity and native paganism was still sharp and bitter. It is not at all unlikely that the work of erecting Christian churches was sometimes hindered by angry pagans who stole materials left by the builders, and damaged or destroyed by night what had been accomplished during the day; nor need it surprise us if, during the course of centuries, these ordinary beings have been transformed in legend into fairies and demons. Most of these stories end in a kind of 'draw' between the contending forces. The transported stones are put to their intended use and the new church is duly built, but not on the site originally chosen by the builders. At Shebbear, however, this part of the tale is absent. The boulder lies outside the churchyard, and the traditions that surround it suggest that it remains the property of the Devil.

1. J. A. R. Bickford, 'Boulder outside Shebbear Church', *Devon & Cornwall Notes & Queries*, Vol. XXIV. (1950–1).

Twelfth Day Revels. The Vigil and Feast of the Epiphany (January 5th and 6th) are known as Twelfth Night and Twelfth Day respectively because they come at the end of the Twelve Days of Christmas. These are the days that link the two great feasts of Christ's Nativity and His Manifestation to the Gentiles, and form the heart and centre of the long ecclesiastical Christmas season which runs from Advent to Candlemas Eve. All of them still have a festival significance for most people, in spite of the modern tendency to limit Christmas and New Year celebrations to a few days only, and once they had much more. Ephraim Syrus, one of the Fathers of the Eastern Church, knew them as a festal tide in the religious sense as far back as the end of the fourth century, and in A.D. 567 they were declared to be so by the Council of Tours.[1] For ordinary people during many centuries, they were a bright medley of splendid Church ceremonies and secular revelry, and an almost continuous holiday, when work was reduced to a mere necessary minimum, and many customary restrictions were relaxed.

They had also a darker side. Notwithstanding its immense sanctity for all Christian people the Christmas season, and especially the Twelve Days, was an uncanny and perilous time. Shakespeare says that then:

> . . . no spirit dare stir abroad;
> The nights are wholesome; then no planets strike,
> No fairy takes, nor witch hath power to charm,
> So hallow'd, and so gracious is the time,[2]

1. Sir E. K. Chambers, *The Mediaeval Stage*, 1903, Vol. I.

2. *Hamlet*, Act 1, Scene 1.

and it may be that in the sixteenth century there were some, perhaps many, devout persons who felt that this was true. But the folk-traditions of almost every European country are against him. It seems to have been widely believed that in this dark midwinter period, spirits of many kinds did stir abroad, and not all of them were friendly to mankind. The Wild Hunt raged across northern skies, led by Woden or the Devil, or whatever unhappy human soul was locally thought to be condemned to take their place. Werewolves ran through the woods and trolls appeared in large numbers on the Scandinavian hills. The dead also returned then, fairies and the Will o' the Wisp were active, and in some regions it was considered safer to stay indoors at night, lest by venturing out in the darkness a man might encounter mysterious entities that it was better not to encounter. A faint trace of these once widespread beliefs lingers, perhaps, in the many stories that are still told of ghosts and phantoms which appear at this season and are nearly always ominous of death or misfortune to those who see them.

Nevertheless, if superstitious terrors were part of the pattern of the Twelve Days, so also were feasting and merriment and all the joys of holiday. On Epiphany, or Twelfth Day,[1] that holiday ended with a variety of lively celebrations, some of which still survive in a number of European lands today. In Great Britain, most of the traditional revelries have vanished now, though some old customs are kept up in particular localities, and it is a favourite time for parties everywhere. Formerly, however, it was a high festival occasion here, as elsewhere, both because of the religious importance of the Epiphany itself, and because Twelfth Day provided a kind of 'last fling' before the world resumed its workaday aspect on Plough Monday.

1. The Twelve Days are not reckoned everywhere in the same way. In some regions, Christmas Day is counted as one of their number, in others it is not. If it is, Epiphany is really Thirteenth Day, and in some parts of Europe it is so named. In England it is usually called Twelfth Day, and its Eve is variously known as Twelfth Day Eve, or Twelfth Night, the latter designation springing from the ancient Teutonic custom of reckoning time by nights instead of by days.

It is true that the full Christmas season extended beyond it to Candlemas Eve, and that there were still some festive days to come in the interval, but for most people the real Yuletide ended with Epiphany. On that anniversary, therefore, or on the previous day, a splendid revel and feast was customarily held, of which, in several countries and especially in France, the distinctive feature was the election of the Epiphany King, or King of the Bean.

He was a Mock King with a long ancestry running back to the Roman Saturnalia, and farther still, who was chosen, by the finding of a hidden bean in a cake, or some other appeal to chance, to rule over the festivities in private houses, monasteries, royal palaces, universities, and the English Inns of Court. In Brittany, the monks of Mont St Michel are recorded as choosing their Epiphany King in the thirteenth century by means of a number of small cakes, in one of which a bean was hidden. There is an English reference to the King of the Bean in Edward II's accounts for 1316. At the University of St Andrews, a minute dated 1432 mentions the robes to be worn by the 'Rex ffabe' and his attendants 'on the Feast of Kings'.[1] Agnes Strickland in her *Lives of the Queens of Scotland* (1850–59), describes a Twelfth Day feast at Holyrood in 1563, at which Mary, Queen of Scots, was present. On this occasion there was no King, but Mary Fleming was chosen as Queen of the Bean and, splendidly attired in cloth-of-silver and a wealth of jewels, presided over the company which included her royal mistress. This, however, was not a very common practice. The Twelfth Day Queen, where she existed (and some early accounts do not mention her at all), was rarely ruler of the feast in her own right, but was the consort of a male monarch whose traditional lineage appears to be much longer than hers.

The choice of the King and Queen depended upon the discovery of a bean and a pea concealed in a great cake known as the Twelfth Cake in Great Britain, as the *gateau des Rois* in France. If a man found the bean in his portion, he became the King, and crowned and royally

1. A. J. Mill, *Mediaeval Plays in Scotland.*

robed, reigned as master of the revels for as long as the feast lasted. If a girl found the bean, she had the right to name the King. The Twelfth Day Queen was she who received the slice containing the pea, though sometimes the King chose his own consort, or if a man found the pea, he could name the girl of his choice as Queen. Occasionally, silver coins were substituted for the bean and pea, and in some districts, lots were cast for the Kingship, or marked slips of paper were drawn from a hat.

In sixteenth-century France, the choice sometimes depended upon the random words of a small child sitting under a table. The *gâteau des Rois* was cut into as many slices as there were people present. The master of the house lifted each piece in its turn, and asked the hidden child to whom it should be given. He answered as he thought fit, and according to his nominations, the slices were distributed. This went on until someone received the portion in which the bean was hidden. That individual then became the Epiphany King and ruler of the feast, even though, as Étienne Pasquier puts it, 'he may be a person of the least importance.'[1] In some French districts it was customary, until well into the nineteenth century, to set aside the first two slices cut from the cake, one for *le bon Dieu* and one for the Blessed Virgin, and to give them to the first poor person who afterwards came to the house.

In England, the King of the Bean ceremony began to decline during the eighteenth century, though feasting and revelry on January 6th continued for much longer, especially in those regions where many people obstinately ignored the calendar reform of 1752, and continued to celebrate their Christmas on Old Christmas Day rather than on the New Style date. The last relic of the old Twelfthtide banquet was the Twelfth Cake itself. Until about a hundred years ago, such cakes were sold in enormous quantities every year in London and other towns. They were masterpieces of the confectioners' art – rich, dark, iced, and lavishly decorated with coloured flowers, gold and silver stars, crowns, dragons, and little figures of the Three Kings. But they lacked the bean and pea which had once given them a meaning above that of other cakes, and except in a few households where they were made at home, there was no ceremony attached to their cutting and distribution. By the middle of the nineteenth century, their popularity was already waning, and now, with the fading of the Twelfth Day holiday and the rise in importance of the Christmas cake, they are very rarely seen.

1. Étienne Pasquier, *Les Recherches de la France*, 1621; quoted by C. A. Miles in *Christmas in Ritual and Tradition*, 1912.

One still does make an annual appearance at the Theatre Royal, Drury Lane, in London, This is the Baddeley Cake which commemorates Robert Baddeley, who was once a chef and afterwards became a successful actor. When he died in 1794, he left £100 to provide wine and a Twelfth Cake to be shared every year on Twelfth Day by the members of the Company then playing at Drury Lane. After the performance has ended on January 6th, the cake is carried into the Green Room by the theatre attendants in their eighteenth-century liveries and powderded wigs. There it is ceremonially cut up and distributed to the assembled actors, and a toast is drunk in wine to the memory of the man who was once an actor too, and desired to be remembered in the theatre in which he played.

Twelfth Night Fires. On Twelfth Night, the Eve of Epiphany, fires used to be lit in the fields on many farms in the West Midland counties of England.[1] Until about the middle of last century, it was customary on that night for the farmer, with his servants and a number of his friends, to go to one of the sown wheatfields and there, on the highest part of the ground, to light twelve small bonfires and one larger one. In some areas, these fires were arranged in a straight line, in others, in a circle, but invariably one was bigger than the rest. The men stood round it in a wide ring, and toasted their master, each other, and the coming harvest in cider. Then followed an outburst of

1. The custom has been recorded in Herefordshire, Worcestershire, Gloucestershire and Staffordshire.

shouting and hallowing, which was often answered by similar shouts from other farms nearby, where the same ceremony was being performed. When the fires had burned down, all concerned returned to the farmhouse where a good supper had been prepared for them.

In Herefordshire and south-west Worcestershire, there was a further ceremony after the supper had been eaten. The company went to the cattle-byre to wassail the oxen, taking with them a large plum-cake with a hole in the centre. The master, standing before the finest ox, toasted him by name in a flagon of strong ale, after which the other men toasted the rest of the oxen, each one separately and by name. This was done in a set form of words, varying a little in different regions. A version given in the *Gentleman's Magazine* for 1820 runs:

> Here's to thee, Benbow,[1] and to thy white horn,
> God send thy master a good crop of corn,
> Of wheat, rye and barley, and all sorts of grain,
> You eat your oats, I'll drink my beer
> May the Lord send us a happy new year.

The plum-cake was then hung on the horns of the first ox, who was tickled, touched with a goad, or doused with cider to make him toss his head and throw it off. If he did so of his own accord, without being touched, it was an omen of very good luck to the farm. If the cake fell behind the ox, it was customary for the mistress to claim it; if in front, the bailiff had it. According to one account quoted by Mrs Leather, 'if it fell forward, it was a good omen for the harvest; if backward, the reverse.'[2] The ox-wassailling and the cake-tossing being over, the company returned to the house, finding their way in darkness because at least on some farms, tradition forbade the carrying of lanterns or candles on that journey. In the meantime, those left at home had locked the house-doors against them, and no one was suffered to enter until several songs had been sung outside. Eventually, however, all were admitted and the rest of the evening was spent in merriment, often lasting until a very late hour.

1. Or whatever the ox's name was.
2. E. M. Leather, *The Folk-Lore of Herefordshire*, 1912.

In Ireland, a rather similar fire-custom was observed on Epiphany Eve, but with candles instead of bonfires. Twelve lighted candles were set in a sieve of oats, with a larger one burning in the centre. Sir Henry Piers, who wrote in the seventeenth century, says that this was done 'in memory of Our Saviour and his Apostles, lights of the world.'[1] A contributor to *Folk-Lore* (Vol. 5, 1894) describes a custom apparently still extant in Co. Leitrim when he, wrote, which seems to be akin to that mentioned by Sir Henry Piers. 'A piece of board', he tells us,

> 'is covered with cow-dung, and twelve rush-lights are stuck therein. These are sprinkled with ash at the top, to make them light easily, and then set alight, each being named for some one present, and as each dies, so will the life of the owner. A ball is then made of the dung, and it is placed over the door of the cow-house for an increase of cattle. Sometimes mud is used, and the ball placed over the door of the dwelling-house.'

The English bonfires, like the Irish candles, were usually given a Christian explanation as symbols of Our Lord and the twelve Apostles. In Staffordshire, they were said to represent the Star which guided the Three Kings to Bethlehem. Where they were named for Christ and His Apostles, the one representing Judas Iscariot was kicked out after a brief burning, and its ashes scattered. The rest were allowed to burn away, and omens were often read from the manner in which they did so, and the time they took to die out. Sometimes, however, the central fire was said to typify the Virgin Mary, or a somewhat ill-defined character known as Old Meg. The latter may perhaps be connected with another tradition in which the large fire was lit 'to burn the old witch'. The general belief seems to have been that the lighting of the fires was necessary for the welfare of the corn. 'Without this festival', says a writer in *Notes & Queries* (Second Series, Vol. VIII), 'they think they should have no crop.' Like many other customs associated with corn-growing or the increase of cattle, this one may well be older

1. Sir Henry Piers, *Description of the County of Westmeath*, 1682, quoted by T. Thistleton Dyer, *British Calendar Customs*, 1876.

than the Christian festival on which it was celebrated.

A Twelfth Night fire-ceremony of a quite different character was held at Brough-under-Stainmore in Westmorland, until at least as late as 1886. Epiphany Eve was there called Holling or Holly Night, because the Carrying of the Holling took place then. A tree with flaming torches tied to its upper branches was carried in procession through the streets, followed by the town band and a company of torch-bearers. Originally this was a holly-tree, as the name of the ceremony denotes, but in later years an ash was substituted. The two principal inns of the town took it in turn to provide the tree. At the end of the procession, what was left of the Holling was fought for by the supporters of the rival houses, the victors carrying the remnant in triumph to the inn of their choice. This odd custom, which does not seem to have been recorded elsewhere in Britain, was said to commemorate the Star of Bethlehem.

Tynwald Ceremony. One of the most important days in the Isle of Man Calendar is Tynwald Day, which falls on July 5th, Old Midsummer Day. On that anniversary, every law which has been passed by the Manx Parliament during the preceding year has to be promulgated from the Tynwald Hill in Manx and in English. Formerly, each one was read in full in both languages, but since 1865, only the titles and abstracts are given. Until this has been done, no new law has any legal force in the Island.

Tynwald Hill is an artificial mound built upon an open space at St John's, and said to have been constructed of earth taken from all the seventeen parishes of the Isle of Man. It is twelve feet in height, circular in form, and has four terraces round it, at three-foot intervals. The word Tynwald is devised from the Norse *thing-vellir*, which means a place where a Thing, or public assembly, was held. The Scandinavian Thing was a democratic gathering, usually held in an open space, away from houses or villages, to which the people came from all over the region affected by it, and lived in temporary booths. Here new laws were enacted, disputes settled, and judgement pronounced upon criminals. The Isle of Man was subject to Viking rule once, and one of the relics of that time is the Tynwald Ceremony still held at Midsummer.

Exactly how old it is in its present form is not quite certain, but the earliest known description of it differs only a little from the present-day proceedings. In his *Statutes and Ordinances of the Isle of Man* . . . (1792), T. G. Stowell quotes a document of 1417, which runs as follows:

'This is the Constitution of old Time how the Lord should be governed on the Tynwald Day: First he is to come thither in his royal Array, as a King ought to do, by the Prerogatives and Royalties of the Land of Man, and upon the Tynwald Hill sit in a Chair covered with a royal Cloth and Cushions, and his Visage to the East, and his Sword before him, holden with the Point upwards, his Barons in the third Degree sitting beside him, and his beneficed Men and Deemsters before him, and his Clerk, Knights, Esquires, and Yeomen about him, and the worthies of the Land to be called in before the Deemsters, if the Lord will ask any Thing of them, and to hear the Government of the Land and the Lord's Will, and the Commons to stand without the Circle of the Hill with three Clerks in their surplices. . . .

. . . Then the chief Coroner, that is the Coroner of Glenfaba, shall make a Fence upon Pain of Life and Limb, that no Man shall make any Disturbance, or stir, in the Time of Tynwald, or any Murmer, or rising in the King's Presence, upon Pain of hanging and drawing; and all the Barons, worthiest Men and Commons, to make Faith and Fealty to the Lord: and then to proceed in whatsoever Matters are there to do in Felony and Treason, or other Matters that touch the Governance of the Island.'

Today the ceremonies are very much the same as they were when this document was written. The Lieutenant-Governor, representing the Queen, attends a service in St John's Church, and then goes in procession to the Tynwald Hill. The thirteenth-century Sword of State is carried before him, point upwards. He mounts to the highest of the four platforms on the Hill, and sits in a red velvet chair, facing eastwards, as 'the Constitution of old Time' dictates. The Bishop of Sodor and Man, the last of the Island Barons, sits beside him, and round them stand the two Deemsters and the other members of the Council. The members of the House of Keys – the elected house of the Manx Parliament – assemble on the platform below; on the third platform are the clergy, the High Bailiffs, and members of the Bar, and on the fourth, minor officials of various kinds. The ordinary people of the Island stand on the grass all round the Hill.

The Court is 'fenced', as of old by the Coroner of Glenfaba, who calls upon all present to refrain from brawls, quarrels, and every kind of disturbance for so long as it is sitting. When this has been done, the Coroners are sworn in, and the main business of the day – the reading of the titles and abstracts in Manx and English of all laws passed during the year – takes place. The people signify their consent to what has been done in their name by giving three cheers for the Queen. The procession then reforms, and the Court returns to St John's Church, where the bills are signed by the Lieutenant-Governor, and the ceremonies of Tynwald Day come to an end.

It should be noted that although new laws are promulgated once a year on Tynwald Hill, the normal work of the Manx Legislature is done on other days in Douglas. Acts passed by the House of Keys and by the Council are sent to the Queen for her consent and are then proclaimed on the following Tynwald Day.

Up-Helly-Aa. The splendid fire-festival of Up-Helly-Aa is held annually at Lerwick, in the Shetland Isles, traditionally on Twenty-Fourth Night (January 29th), but now always on the last Tuesday in January. Twenty-Fourth Night is, or was, so called because it marked the end of the festivities of Yule (Old Style) which, in this northern region, lasted for twenty-four days.

Up-Helly-Aa has a long history, of which, perhaps, not the least interesting detail is the manner in which the celebrations have blossomed and expanded during the last hundred years. Until as late as the 'seventies of last century, the principal features of the day were not, as now, a torchlight procession and a burning ship, but blazing tar-barrels dragged by young men through the streets on wooden sledges. Each sledge contained from four to eight barrels, and was drawn by chains, of which the rattling made a fine din to which the young men added by horn-blowing. This lively business continued through most of the night; and when it was over, the Guizers, clad in exotic costumes, went round the town, visiting the houses of their friends and being warmly welcomed as Luck-bringers, until morning came.

These were time-honoured customs which can be traced a long way back. Fire and the visits of Guizers are still essentials of the festival in its modern form, but the tar-barrels have gone. In 1874, the town authorities banned them because of the danger of fire, and also because housewives complained that tar spilt on the roads and brought in on the boots of their menfolk fouled their houses for days afterwards. But this prohibition did not bring the old Yule-end rejoicings to an end. The Guizers remained, and when a short time later, a festival committee was formed, its leader was their elected chief, the Worthy Chief Guizer, now known as the Guizer Jarl. A torchlight procession was introduced in place of the tar-barrels; and in 1889, that procession was led for the first time by the dragon-headed model of a Norse galley which has been the main glory of the celebrations ever since.

Preparations for Up-Helly-Aa go on for months beforehand. The 31-foot galley, with

its oars and heraldic shields, has to be built and decorated, and some seven or eight hundred torches made from wood and sacking. The Guizers split up into squads, or teams, each squad representing a special theme of its members' own choosing, and designing costumes to correspond. Themes and costumes are both kept strictly secret from all but the Guizer Jarl until the actual day of the festival. There is also 'the Bill', or Guizer Jarl's Proclamation which appears on Up-Helly-Aa morning, displayed upon a ten-foot-high decorated board set up at the Mercat Cross. 'The Bill' is a lively document, full of satirical references to local institutions and personages, and humorous accounts of the events of the past year. It is quite modern, having been introduced only in 1931, but it is extremely popular, and people from all over Lerwick flock to read and enjoy it as soon as it is visible.

At a little before seven o'clock in the evening, the Norse galley is brought to the starting-point of the procession and the torch-bearers take up their appointed places along the route behind it. The Guizer Jarl, in full Viking armour and flowing cloak, takes his place at the helm, with his own squad of Guizers, also dressed as Vikings, lined up alongside the ship. At half-past seven, the double ranks of paraffin-soaked torches are lit by flares, and the procession moves briskly off to the singing of the *Up-Helly-Aa Song*. Bands play, the different squads of Guizers march in their order through the streets bright with torch-fire, and ahead of all goes the Norse longship carrying its memories of the six hundred years when the Shetlands and the Orkneys were both subject to the Norse crown. When the Burning Site is finally reached, the torch-bearers form a huge fiery ring round the galley, the Guizer Jarl leaves it, and, at the sound of a bugle, all the torches are flung together into the ship, which at once bursts into flames. While it burns *The Norseman's Home* is sung, ships in the harbour sound their sirens, and a great noise of cheering goes up from the watching crowds. In less than an hour, the galley is totally consumed and nothing remains but ashes.

This is not, however, the end of the proceedings. After the burning, the Guizers go round the town, as of old, though they no longer visit private houses. Instead, each squad, in turn and in strict order, visits every one of the thirteen halls of Lerwick, where refreshments and entertainment are organized for them by local hostesses, and where they dance and make merry, and usually give some sort of performance based upon their own special theme. As there are about fifty of these squads, this takes time, but nobody minds. Revelry and general merriment continue unabated all through the night, and not until daylight pallidly appears at about six or seven o'clock is Up-Helly-Aa, and with it the final festivities of Yule (old Style) truly ended for that year.

Valentine Gifts. St Valentine's Day, February 14th, has been a customary day for choosing sweethearts and exchanging love-tokens from time immemorial. Countless generations of young people have acknowledged St Valentine as the friend and patron of lovers, and, according to a country tradition which was known at least as early as the fourteenth century, so have the birds. In *The Parlement of Foules*, Chaucer refers to a once common belief that all birds choose their mates on February 14th, a pleasant, if slightly inaccurate notion which still survives in some districts as a tale told to children. It is true that nothing whatever is known about St Valentine that would suggest such a patronage. He is, indeed, rather a misty figure altogether. In the Roman Martyrology there are two martyrs of that name, one a Roman priest who perished in A.D. 269, the other an Umbrian bishop who was executed in A.D. 273. It is not clear which of the two is really the lovers' saint and so far as we know, there is no historical reason why either of them should be so regarded.

It is their death-date, rather than any incident of their lives, which probably accounts for the tradition. Both are said to have died for their religion on February 14th, the Eve of the Roman Lupercalia. This was partly a fertility festival, on which, after goats and a dog had been sacrificed for the protection of flocks and herds, two young men of high rank ran about with thongs of goat-skin, striking all the women they met to make them fruitful. Other fertility rituals seem to have been performed also, including the choice of partners by lot. In due course, this pagan Spring festival was superseded by the Christian Feast of Candlemas, but some of its ancient traditions lingered on, attaching themselves quite naturally to the rather nebulous saint whose martyrdom was honoured on the day that had once been Lupercalia Eve.

The method of choosing sweethearts on St Valentine's Day varied in different times and places. It could be a serious matter, leading to matrimony, or it could be a kind of game. When Margery Brews' marriage to John Paston was being arranged in 1477, she wrote to him as her 'right well beloved Valentine'.

In another letter, wherein her dowry was mentioned, she said, 'If ye could be content with that good and my poor person, I would be the merriest maiden on ground; a good true and loving Valentine . . . as I may be your true lover and bedewoman during my life.'[1] This was the serious Valentine, the sweetheart deliberately chosen for love, who was later to be wife or husband. But quite as often, the selection was made in a much more haphazard manner. 'It is a ceremony, never omitted among the Vulgar', wrote Bourne in 1725, 'to draw lots which they term Valentines. The names of a select number of one sex are by an equal number of the other put into some vessel; and after that, everyone draws a name, which for the present is called their Valentine, and is also look'd upon as a good omen of their being man and wife afterwards.'[2]

Gifts were usually exchanged after the lot-drawing and for some days afterwards the pair went about together, each wearing a billet or paper with the other's name on it in their dress. In some parts of Scotland, the name-paper had to be carried to the sweetheart's house, where an apple or some other small thing was given in return for it. Another Scottish custom, particularly in the southern counties, was for the lots to be drawn three times, the slips being returned to the vessel after the first and second drawing. If any one drew the same name three times running, it was a certain omen of marriage. In Derbyshire, if a girl already had a sweetheart, and he failed to visit or kiss her on St Valentine's Day, she was said to be 'dusty', and had to submit to being swept by her companions with a broom or a wisp of straw. She then had to cast lots with the other girls in the usual way.

Sometimes pure chance was the deciding factor. There was a common belief that the first man seen by any woman on February 14th must be her Valentine, whether she liked him or not. Great care was therefore needed to ensure that the first man encountered was the right one. In their *Lore and Language of Schoolchildren* (1959), Iona and Peter Opie say that modern schoolgirls still believe this, or pretend to do so, and some have been known to go about with their eyes closed until they know it is safe to open them. Mrs Pepys did much the same in 1662, keeping her hands over her eyes all the morning for fear of seeing one of the painters who were gilding the chimney-piece in her house. Eventually Will Bowyer came to be her Valentine, and all was well.

In her time, it was apparently usual for married as well as unmarried women to have and to be Valentines, either by direct choice or by the drawing of name-papers, and for handsome presents varying from gloves, silk stockings and garters to valuable jewellery to be given to the women. In Samuel Pepy's *Diary* there are several entries concerning his expenditure on Valentine gifts. In 1661, for instance, a pair of embroidered gloves and six pairs of plain ones for Martha Batten cost him 40s. od; in 1669, he spent 28s. od. on green silk stockings, garters, shoe-strings, 'and two pairs of Jessamy gloves' for his Cousin Turner. These were not inconsiderable sums in those days, when the value of money was far greater than it is now, but they were small indeed in comparison with the amounts sometimes spent by wealthier men. On April 26th, 1667, Pepys noted that 'The Duke of York having once been Mrs Stewart's Valentine, did give her a jewel of about £800, and my Lord Mandeville, her Valentine this year, a ring of about £300.'[1]

Present-giving on this day was not confined to sweethearts. Until very recently, children used to go about singing.

> Good morrow, Valentine,
> First 'tis yours, then 'tis mine,
> Please to give me a Valentine.

or some other version of this nation-wide ditty. They were given money, fruit, or in some districts, specially-made cakes known as Valentine Buns or Plum Shittles. Like many similar customs, this was a morning activity, the earlier the better. Norfolk children were supposed to

1. *The Paston Letters, 1422–1509*, ed. James Gairdner, 1900.
2. H. Bourne, *Antiquitates Vulgares*, 1725.

1. *The Diary of Samuel Pepys*, ed. H. B. Wheatley, 1893–9.

go out before sunrise, and any demand for largesse after the sun had risen could be refused on the grounds that the asker was 'sunburnt'. In Norwich, and elsewhere in the county, until towards the end of last century, St Valentine's Eve was a great present-giving anniversary for adults as well as children. Anonymous gifts of all kinds, ranging from mere trifles to quite expensive objects, were laid upon the doorsteps of houses. A bang on the knocker and the sound of hastily retreating footsteps warned the inmates of the house that one of these secret packages had arrived, but the giver, or his messenger, took care to be out of sight before the door could be opened. Nothing in or on the parcel indicated whence it had come, for secrecy was considered essential, and a great part of the fun of St Valentine's Eve consisted in trying to identify the unknown giver. At one time, the presents bought and given on this anniversary were more numerous, and often more valuable, than those given at Christmas.[1]

The Valentine card that we know today came into being during the eighteenth century when the expensive gifts of earlier years had gone out of fashion. At first it was hand-made, with little paintings of hearts and flowers, and a short verse composed by the sender. Such pleasant proofs of devotion are not yet quite extinct, and the hand-written and hand-painted Valentine can still be seen occasionally though its verses are now rarely original. The commercial card appeared in the nineteenth century, complete with ready-made sentiments and decorations, embossed, brightly coloured and gilded, and later on, lace-edged, perfumed and packed in a neat box. Since it saved much mental effort and careful handwork, its popularity was immediate and lasting. Thousands of these cards were sent through the post every year, and the steadily increasing flood did not fail until almost the end of Queen Victoria's reign.

Eventually, however, a decline set in, partly, no doubt, because customs do naturally decay as ideas and fashions change, but partly also because of a growing dislike for the so-called humorous Valentine. This, which had grown up under the shadow of the sentimental original, was sometimes really humorous, but usually, it was extremely vulgar and often definitely cruel in intention. Both types fell into disfavour together, and it was not until the 'thirties of the present century that the romantic Valentine came back into fashion. Today it is once more quite well-known and used by many young people all over the country, though it has not yet recovered (and probably never will) the enormous popularity of its Victorian hey-day.

1. 'Cutlery, silver pencil-holders, magnificent books' are mentioned by a contributor to *Notes and Queries* in 1850 (1st Series, Vol. 1) in a list of gifts likely to be deposited in this secret manner, and he adds: 'Indeed, I have known a great library chair come in this way.'

Wakes and Feasts. The Patronal Festival of any parish church is primarily a religious occasion, but in many villages it is, and has been for centuries, a local secular holiday as well, celebrated with sports and games, and sometimes an unofficial 'fair' to which travelling showmen come with their swings and roundabouts. In northern and midland England, this holiday is usually known as the Wake, or Wakes; elsewhere, it is the Feast, or in the West-country, the Revel. The word 'wake' in this connection really means a vigil, and springs from the ancient custom, now obsolete, of 'waking', or watching in the church during all or part of the night before a holy day.[1] This devotional practice disappeared long ago, but the old word still survives as a name for the parish anniversary and its festivities.

Since the date of any particular Wake or Feast depends upon the dedication of the church, there is no fixed season for the celebrations, which may occur at any time of the year. In 1536, an Act of Convocation ordered that every parish should keep its Wake on the first Sunday in October, without reference to the date of its Patronal Festival or Dedication anniversary, but this order was a dead letter from the start. Local people clung tenaciously to their own Saint's Day, or in some cases, to a customary day at the end of hay or corn-harvest. They continued to hold their festivities then, whatever the authorities might say, and today it is still usual to keep the holiday either on the Patronal Festival itself, or on some convenient day near it.

1. The same idea appears in the Lykewakes, or watches, formerly kept after a death had occurred. Between the death and the funeral, friends and neighbours watched by the corpse, often whiling away the time with drinking, story-telling, and even games, which no one considered irreverent. The more people who came to the Lykewake, the greater the honour paid to the dead man and his family.

Modern Wakes and Feasts are cheerful and lively anniversaries in many districts, but they are but a shadow of their predecessors. Until about the end of the nineteenth century, or a little later, Wakes-day was the highlight of the village year. It began with the pealing of bells and a morning service in the church, and continued with sports, racing, dancing, feasting, entertaining friends, and every kind of merry-making. In some places the jollifications went on for two or three days, or even a full week, after the actual festival-date. Very often there was a ceremonial rushbearing, when great piles of rushes were brought to the church in decorated harvest-wains and strewn upon the floor, and sometimes on the graves in the churchyard also. This custom slowly declined as the boarding-over of church floors became more usual and the rushes ceased to be necessary; but for so long as it was observed in any parish, it was always the principal event of the feast. *(See Rushbearing.)*

Bull- or bear-baiting was an almost invariable feature of the occasion until it was made illegal in 1835. Even after that date, it persisted for some time, the bait being held in some secluded spot, with the constable turning a blind eye upon the proceedings. Itinerant musicians and entertainers came to add to the general gaiety and earn money for themselves, in much the same way as the travelling fairmen come today with their roundabouts and sideshows. Among them were the wandering bearwards, whose dancing bears many old people can still remember from their childhood days. In late Victorian and in Edwardian times, music was often provided by the German bands which, right up to the outbreak of the First World War, came to England every year in early summer and travelled all over the country until towards the end of October, playing at Wakes, Club-days, and any other rural festivities where their services were needed.

Pedlars and salesmen came as well, and in most places, the village street was lined with stalls from which gingerbread and ribbon 'fairings', and sometimes more substantial wares, could be bought. Occasionally these unofficial temporary markets assumed quite large proportions, and some, in the course of time, developed slowly into customary 'fairs', which, though they had no charter, nevertheless flourished without that safeguard, and sometimes outlived the true charter fairs of the district. St Giles' Fair in Oxford is an example of this process. It is held annually on the Monday and Tuesday after the first Sunday after St Giles' Day (September 1st) in the two or three streets nearest to the ancient church of that saint. Thousands of people come to it every year without realizing that they are actually attending the old Wakes of Walton.

When the parish comprising the Manor of Walton lay outside the boundaries of Oxford, it had its Wake, like other parishes, and no doubt this was originally quite a humble affair. By 1573, however, it had grown into a 'fair' of considerable size, at which large quantities of cloth, ironmongery, crockery, and agricultural produce were sold. Today, only a few trading-stalls remain as a reminder of past commercial glories; but St Giles' Fair is still well known as one of the principal pleasure-fairs of the south Midlands, and has cheerfully outlived the five real fairs once held in the city, all of which have now vanished.

In the industrial towns of Lancashire and Yorkshire, Wakes Week is the name given to the annual holiday when the mills and factories are closed, and many hundreds of workers go away to the seaside or elsewhere. There are, however, local celebrations also, and even in these days of holidays-with-pay, this week is still the great event of the year for the majority of the townsfolk. The industrial Wakes have travelled a long way from their religious and communal beginnings, but the old name preserves the connection, and in some towns at least, their starting-date is still governed by the Patronal Festival from which they originally sprang.

Wassailling. The word 'wassail' is derived from the Anglo-Saxon *wes hál*, meaning 'be whole', or 'be of good health'. To wassail a man was to drink to his health and prosperity with more than usual ceremony, especially at Christmas-time, when the wassail bowl was passed round with toasts and singing, during the feasting of that season. A large bowl was filled with some kind of hot drink, usually Lambs Wool, which is a mixture of hot ale spices, sugar and roasted apples, to which eggs and thick cream are sometimes added. The bowl was circulated among the assembled company like a loving-cup, or if it was too large to be

moved easily,[1] individual drinking-vessels were filled from it. Everything was done according to a customary pattern, the master of the house drinking first, then the mistress, and so on through the rest of the family and the guests. In some districts, each person came in turn to the table, took a roasted apple from the bowl and ate it, and then drank to the health of all present. A Scottish form of this ceremony was the drinking of the Het Pint on New Year's morning. This was a heady compound of hot spiced ale, sugar, and whisky, which was shared by everyone in the house, again in due order, as soon as the clocks had ceased striking midnight.

A kindred custom was the carrying round of the wassail bowl from house to house. During the Twelve Days of Christmas, and often in the last weeks of Advent also, bands of young people went about after dark, carrying a good-sized bowl which was decorated with coloured ribbons, streamers, and evergreens. In some areas, they were led by a man known as the King or Captain of the Wassaillers, in whose charge the bowl remained during the rest of the year. It was normally made of wood, though earthenware bowls were not unknown. In the decay of the custom, humbler vessels occasionally made their appearance, such as tin basins, or buckets.

The Wassaillers sang on their rounds some version of the Wassail Song, which is a cheerful mixture of good wishes and requests for gifts. It has many variants:

> Wassail, Wassail, all over the town!
> Our toast it is white, and our ale it is brown,
> Our bowl it is made of the white maple tree;
> With the wassailling bowl we'll drink to thee,

run the first lines of the Gloucestershire carol. The Somerset song begins rather similarly, except that there the bowl is 'made of the good ashen tree', and there is a genial chorus:

> For its your wassail, and its our wassail,
> And its joy be to you, and a jolly wassail!

The lovely north-country version begins:

> Here we come a-wassailling
> Among the leaves so green,
> Here we come a-wandering
> So fair to be seen.
>
> Love and joy come to you,
> And to your wassail too,
> And God bless you, and send you
> A happy new year.

But all these toasts and blessings were not entirely altruistic. In every variant of the carol, there is some form of direct request – for 'a good loaf and cheese', or 'a good piece of beef', or some other seasonable food, in one version for money to fill 'a little stretching leather skin', and in almost all, for something to drink. 'A drop or two of cider will do us no harm' comes from the Somerset carol, and from northern England, a more dignified request:

> Call up the butler of this house,
> Put on his golden ring;
> Let him bring us a glass of beer,
> And better we shall sing.

Some early accounts of Wassailling, as well as the words of the carols, indicate that originally the bowl was full when it was carried round. Probably the householders visited were invited to drink from it in return for their largesse, or at least, were toasted in drink of the Wassaillers' own providing.[1] In later years, this was not so. The bowl was taken round empty, and hopefully presented at each house for filling with ale, or a mixture or hot cider and gin, or some other exhilarating liquid. Eventually even the bowl was forgotten in some areas, and either the Wassaillers went round empty-handed to sing their songs and receive money and other gifts, or else they carried a green branch trimmed with ribbons and oranges, which was known as the Wassail Bough.

A custom often confused with Wassailling, though its origin seems to have been different, was that of the Vessel Cup. In Advent, and during the Twelve Days of Christmas, women

1. A magnificent silver-gilt wassail bowl, owned by Jesus College, Oxford, holds ten gallons, and has a ladle holding half-a-pint.

1. In Glasgow and Edinburgh, kettles full of Het Pint were formerly carried through the streets on New Year's Eve. Any one encountered by the bearers was invited to drink a little from a cup carried by one of the party, and to share in toasting the New Year.

and children in northern England used to go round with a decorated box containing two dolls (or sometimes only one), surrounded by silver papers stars, apples, oranges, evergreens and flowers. The box was covered by a clean white cloth which hid the dolls from view until the moment came to display them. The carriers went from house to house, singing carols like *The Seven Joys of Mary*, or *God Rest Ye Merry, Gentlemen*, or one of the Wassail songs, especially 'here we come a-wassailling among the leaves so green.' They were rewarded with gifts of food or money, and when these had beens received, the white cloth was removed, and the little figures, which represented the Infant Jesus and His Mother, were shown to the giver.

The box was variously called the Vessel Cup, or the Wassail-bob, or the Wesley-bob, all of which names were corruptions of Wassail Cup, or the Milly-box, which was originally My Lady's Box. In some areas the figures of Our Lord and Our Lady which it contained were known as Advent Images because they were taken round in that season, as a promise of the coming Nativity. Indeed, they were often carried about long before Advent began, sometimes from Martinmas onwards, or even earlier. It was usually considered unlucky for any householder to refuse alms to the first band of singers to arrive on the doorstep; and if any house was left unvisited, without sight of the Advent Images, as late as Christmas morning, it was a bad omen for the family in the following year.

Those who went round with the Vessel Cup were often called Wassaillers, and some of the songs they sang, as well as the most usual names for their box, suggest that they thought of themselves thus. Nevertheless, in spite of similarities of detail and season, there was a difference between their custom and Wassailling. Both took place round about Christmas, but they were not usually found together in the same region. The true Wassaillers, with their beribboned drinking-bowl, and their jovial songs represented a kind of pagan luck-bringing that would have been equally appropriate at the pre-Christian Yule or Winter Solstice festivals. The Vessel Cup custom was more definitely Christian in origin and intention; and the unveiling of the images was meant – even though the performers may not always have remembered this very clearly – to bestow upon those who saw them the blessings and spiritual graces of Christmas as well as its secular joys.

Wassailling Orchards. In the fruit-growing districts of southern and western England, the apple-orchards used to be wassailed with cider and songs and the firing of guns during the Christmas season, sometimes on Christmas Day itself, sometimes at New Year, but most usually on Twelfth Night, or Old Twelfth Night.[1] This is still done in a few West-country parishes, either because the custom has never been abandoned there, or because it has recently been revived. Like many ancient rituals that have outlived the beliefs from which they originally sprang, apple-wassailling today is largely a cheerful frolic, vaguely associated with good luck; but not so very long ago its old magical meaning was still remembered, and the ceremony was regularly performed to protect the trees from evil, and to make them bear a plentiful fruit-crop in the coming season.

The farmworkers and their families went to the orchard after dark, carrying shot-guns and horns, and a large pail full of cider. One tree, the best in the orchard for preference, was usually chosen to represent them all. Cider was poured round its roots; a piece of toast, or cake, soaked in cider, was laid in its fork; sometimes the tips of the lowest branches were drawn down and dipped in the cider pail. The tree was toasted as though it were a living person, and a traditional song that was at once an admonition and a blessing (or a charm) was sung to it. One widespread version of this song ran:

> Here's to thee, old apple tree,
> Whence thou may'st bud and whence thou
> may'st blow,
> And whence thou may'st bear apples enow.
> Hats full, caps full, bushel, bushel sacks full,
> And my pockets full too! Hurrah!

1. The custom has been recorded in Cornwall, Devon, Somerset, Kent, Surrey, Sussex, Gloucestershire, Worcestershire, Herefordshire, Wiltshire, and Monmouthshire, and in some Irish districts.

In Sussex they sang:

> Stand fast root, bear well top,
> Pray God send us a good howling crop,
> Every twig, apples big,
> Every bough, apples enow.
> Hats full, caps full, full quarter sacks full,
> Holla, boys, holla!
> Huzza!

In some orchards, the men showed the tree what was required of it by bowing down to the ground before it three times, and rising up slowly, miming the actions of one burdened by a heavy sack of apples. A ceremony recorded in Devon, but not, apparently, elsewhere, was to lift a little boy on to one of the branches, where he sat crying 'Tit, tit, more to eat' and was given bread, cheese, and cider.[1] He was said to represent a tom-tit, but probably he really stood for the spirit of the tree, which was propitiated in that form.

When the toasts and the singing were over, the shot-guns, some of which were very old and noisy, were fired through the topmost boughs, while those who had no guns shouted and beat upon trays and buckets, or blew long blasts upon cow-horns. The object of this clamour was to drive away evil spirits, and to arouse the sleeping trees; and if in the later years of the custom, the noise-makers did not always realize just what they were doing, it was nevertheless felt by all that it would be unlucky to omit this part of the ritual.

In some parts of Worcestershire, the apple-wassailling ceremonies were combined with the lighting of bonfires on Twelfth Night to protect the wheat-crop. *(See Twelfth Night Fires.)* The men went first to the wheatfield to kindle the fires there, and when this was done, before going back to the farmhouse for supper, they went to the orchard and wassailled the trees.

In Normandy, bands of men, women and children used to visit the orchards on Epiphany Eve, or in some places on the first Sunday in Lent, to throw lighted torches against the apple-trees, and sometimes to make little bonfires of dry hay or straw under their branches. These fires had to be lit by children who were not yet twelve years old. Aubrey mentioned an English Midsummer custom connected with fruit which seems to be quite forgotten now. 'In Herefordshire', he says, 'and also in Somersetshire, on Midsommer-eve, they make fires in the fields in the waies; sc. to Blesse the Apples. I have seen the same custome in Somerset, 1685, but there they doe it only for custome-sake.'[1] Midsummer was then, and still is in many regions, one of the principal seasons for lighting bonfires, but usually the reasons given for doing so have more to do with ancient solar ritual and the driving out of evil than with the prosperity of orchards. *(See Midsummer Fires.)*

Other fruit-bearing trees used to be wassailled as well as apples. Herrick says in his *Hesperides*,

> Wassail the trees that they may bear
> You many a plum and many a pear;
> For more or less fruits will they bring,
> As you do give them wassailling.

An account written in 1907 describes how the custom was then kept up at Camberley in Surrey. Boys came to the writer's garden on Christmas Eve and, standing before the apple-trees, repeated a verse very similar to the Sussex song given above. They began in a low mumbling tone, gradually rising in pitch until they were shouting and then they sounded a blast on a large cow-horn. Not content with thus rousing the apple-trees to a sense of their duty, they went round to every other fruit-tree in the garden, varying the words of their verse by substituting for 'apple' the word 'mulberry', or 'fig', or 'currant', or 'nut', as circumstances required. 'When I told them our fig trees did not bear', says the writer, 'they said they would take care it didn't happen again'.[2]

Apple-orchards are still wassailled, though probably 'only for custome-sake', at Carhampton and Roadwater, in Somerset on Old Twelfth Night, at Trusham in Devon, and occasionally elsewhere. A curious sequel to the Roadwater custom is that, when the ceremony

1. *Transactions of the Devonshire Association*, Vol. 8, 1876.

1. J. Aubrey, *Remaines of Gentilisme and Judaisme*, 1686–7 ed. James Britten, 1881.

2. *British Calendar Customs: England*, ed. A. R. Wright and T. E. Lones, Vol. II, 1938. Information given by A. M. Spoer, of Camberley.

is over, the men return to the local inn, enter by the back door, and after they have drunk to the health of the house, leave again by the front door. Tradition says that if this manner of entry and exit were to be reversed, it would bring bad luck to the inn.

Watch Night. On December 31st, in many places, Watch Night services are held in the local Anglican or Nonconformist churches, where the congregations assemble to watch the old year die, and the new year come in. This is not an ancient custom, stemming, as might perhaps be supposed, from pre-Reformation practice. On the contrary, it dates only from the eighteenth century, when Watch Night services were first introduced by the Methodist Society, and slowly spread from them to other communions. 'This eve', says J. Timbs, writing of New Year, 'is called by the Wesleyan Methodists *Watch Night* because at their principal chapels the ministers and congregations hold a service to watch out the old year, i.e. they pray until about five minutes to twelve o'clock, and then observe a profound silence until the clock strikes, when they exultantly burst forth with a hymn of praise and joy. Latterly, this service has been very generally observed by evangelical churchmen.'[1] In some towered churches, the short ceremony is followed by the singing of a hymn on top of the tower, and wherever bells exist, by the pealing of the bells.

Wayfarers' Charities. In the days when any lengthy journey was a slow, difficult and often hazardous undertaking, even for the rich, the provision of food and shelter for poor travellers was a common form of Christian charity. Before the Reformation, this was mainly the task of the monastic houses; but both then and later, kindly individuals shared in it, either by personal hospitality, or by leaving money to pay for doles of food, or for the maintenance of houses wherein the benighted could find shelter without cost. One such benefactor was Richard Watts, of Rochester, who in 1579 provided in his will for 'six poor travellers not being rogues or proctors' to be fed and housed for one night, and to be given fourpence each when they left in the morning. This charity still exists, though the sum given on departure has been raised in accordance with the change in the value of money. The bread-dole at Ellington, in Huntingdonshire, distributed in the church at Eastertide, is thought to have been a travellers' charity originally, since one of the conditions is that the recipient must have slept the previous night in the parish. This proviso would hardly be necessary if the dole was intended for the ordinary untravelled inhabitants of the village.

The Wayfarers' Dole which is given daily at the Hospital of St Cross, near Winchester, is far older than either of these charities. In one form or another, it has been in existence since the twelfth century, when, in 1136, Henry de Blois founded the Hospital as an abiding place for thirteen poor men. In 1446, Cardinal Beaufort added another almshouse, that of 'Noble Poverty' for men of higher rank who had fallen on evil days through no fault of their own. Both these foundations exist today as separate institutions under one head. The two sets of beneficiaries are distinguished by their gowns, the Blois Brethren, the original poor men, wearing black gowns, and the silver cross of the Knights Hospitallers of St John, and the Beaufort Brethren wearing dark red and the Cardinal's hat-badge. All enjoy free housing allowances for food, and pocket-money.

In Henry de Blois' time, the Hospital provided free meals for a hundred poor people, every day, and later the number was increased to two hundred. This open-handed hospitality declined at one period, during which incompetent or corrupt Masters of the Hospital allowed the revenues to be deflected, but matters were put right in the fifteenth century by William of Wykeham. Nevertheless, in good or in evil times, charity never ceased to be dispensed here in some measure. The Wayfarers' Dole is still given every day to the first thirty-two persons who come to the Porter's Lodge to ask for it. It consists of a piece of white bread which is handed to the traveller on an old carved wooden platter, and a draught of ale served in a horn bearing the arms of the Order. No questions are

1. J. Timbs, *Something for Everybody*, 1861.

asked, and no conditions have to be fulfilled by the applicant, the only distinction ever made being that those who are really in need receive much larger portions.

Another form of aid to travellers was the endowment of a bell to be rung at night during the winter months, usually at eight or nine o'clock, for the guidance of those who might have lost their way in the surrounding countryside. 'Lost i' the Dark' is the homely name often given to such bells, which are still rung in some parishes though the true need for them has gone. Once, they served a really useful purpose. To be benighted and astray, perhaps in snowy or foggy weather, coming across some desolate moor or through thick woods, along ill-kept roads full of potholes and devoid of signposts, could be an extremely alarming experience, all the more so because of the ever-present danger of attack by lurking footpads. The sound of a distant church-bell might and frequently did, restore a lost sense of direction, and set the bemused wanderer on his right road again. It is not surprising that some who had been thus saved from peril should wish to ensure that others in the same plight should be similarly helped, and many left money for this purpose.

In 1691, John Carey, of Woodstock in Oxfordshire, amongst other benefactions to the town, provided for the ringing of what is still locally called the 'Lost in the Dark Bell' at eight o'clock each night between Michaelmas and Lady Day 'for the guidance and direction of travellers'. Until the outbreak of war in 1939, the Curfew continued to be rung regularly at Charlton-on-Otmoor, in the same county between October 11th and March 25th for the same admirable purpose because a man named Thomas Tryte, lost on the moor, had once been saved by its sound. Another such bell at Barton in Lincolnshire is said to have been endowed by a woman whose name is not now remembered. Tradition says that she missed her way in darkness when out on the wolds, and was guided home by hearing the Curfew ringing in St Peter's Church. In gratitude, she gave a piece of land to the parish clerk and his successors on condition that one of the church-bells should be rung from seven until eight o'clock every weekday night from 'the day of the carrying of the first load of barley in every year till Shrove Tuesday next ensuing inclusive.'[1]

The annual feast given to the bellringers on October 7th at Twyford in Hampshire commemorates the narrow escape of a rider who heard the church-bells ringing and changed direction just in time to save himself from falling into a deep chalk-pit. In his will, he provided for the annual pealing of the bells on the anniversary of this adventure, and for a subsequent feast for the ringers. At Kidderminster also, a bell in St Mary's Church was similarly endowed by a man named Pecket who, astray in the mist on his way back from Bridgenorth Fair, was halted by its sound, and found himself on the extreme edge of a precipitous rock in Habberley Valley, now known as Pecket's Rock.

A horn is still blown at nine o'clock on every night between Michaelmas Eve and Shrove Tuesday at Bainbridge in Yorkshire, for the benefit of travellers coming across the moors. This is not a wayfarers' charity, but a communal custom which is certainly centuries old, and is said by some to run back to the time of the Romans.

Well-Dressing. Springs and wells have always been venerated, from exceedingly remote times onwards, because water is a basic necessity of life, and to our forefathers it seemed a mysterious and spirit-haunted thing. A lively spring which brought fertility to the land where it flowed, and to the men and beasts who depended upon that land, was once almost universally supposed to be the dwelling place of some powerful spirit to whom prayer and sacrifice were due. Wells were honoured with religious ceremonies and dances, and decorated with flowers and green branches at the greater festivals. When Christianity came, water-worship, as such, was strictly forbidden, but most of the ancient and well-loved springs were purged of their pagan associations, purified, and rededicated to the Blessed Virgin Mary or to one of the Saints. The wells were still dressed with flowers and honoured with processions and

1. H. Edwards, *A Collection of Old English Customs*, 1842.

similar rites on great feast-days; but now it was done for the glory of God, and in thanksgiving for the gift of water, and not any longer in praise of, or to placate any indwelling spirit.

Well-dressing in Derbyshire is a relic of this ancient form of worship, though it is hardly necessary to say that in no part of that county has it continued uninterrupted since pagan times. On the contrary, it has always been a very intermittent custom, and even the most famous of all the dressings, that at Tissington, is only supposed to run back as far as 1350. It comes and it goes, like the land-springs in the chalk hills of southern England, but a lapse is frequently followed by a revival, and no one can safely predict in what village the ritual will suddenly re-start after a very long pause. In form, it has changed considerably in the last hundred and fifty years, and it has now become an intricate and beautiful craft which does not appear to be known elsewhere.

Until the beginning of the nineteenth century, the wells seem to have been decorated with simple garlands, but by about 1818, boards 'cut to the figure intended to be represented, and covered with moist clay'[1] began to appear. The modern 'well-dressing' consists normally of a large picture, usually religious in subject, and made from a mosaic of overlapping flower-petals (or in some villages, flower-heads tightly packed together), leaves, berries, tree-cones, bark, mosses, and lichens, pressed upon a wooden background covered with soft clay. Everything used in the picture has to be of natural origin. Pebbles, or fine fluor spar, sand or small shells may be included, but not pieces of glass or tin, or any other manufactured material. The clay has to be dampened with water and salt, kneaded, rolled. and well worked by hand, and then laid, thickly and very smoothly upon the wooden screen. The chosen design is transferred to it either by being drawn directly on it, if there is a capable artist available, with a sharp-pointed implement, or, more usually, by making a full-size copy on paper, laying it upon the clay surface, and pricking it through with a skewer. All this, together with the arduous task of collecting the necessary flowers and other materials, the making of the picture itself, and finally, the careful erection of the finished product behind the well for which it was designed, is in the hands of local men, many of whom have been well-dressing for years, and some of whom can claim to have had a father or a grandfather who was himself an experienced worker in this beautiful rural craft.

Of the various places in Derbyshire where well-dressing is, or was, customary, Tissington has the longest tradition. One account says the custom began there in 1615, after a prolonged and very severe drought, lasting from March until September. Alone in the district, Tissington's five wells continued to flow without ceasing throughout that dreadful time, supplying not only their own people, but also many men and animals who came from all round-about. Thereafter, the well-dressing was observed as a form of thanksgiving. Another story, however, says it began in 1350 because, during the Black Death of 1348–9, when hundreds of Derbyshire people perished from the plague, Tissington remained untouched, owing, it was said, to the purity of its water. It is possible that both these tales are true, and that in 1615, all that was done was to revive an ancient ceremony that had been allowed to lapse. It now takes place every year on Ascension Day, beginning with a service of thanksgiving in the Church, and afterwards, a procession of clergy, choir and congregation to bless each of the five dressed wells in turn.

At Buxton, well-dressing takes place on the Thursday nearest Midsummer Day, and is often said to have begun there in 1840. It is, however, possible that during the Middle Ages, and perhaps even earlier, well-rituals may have been performed by St Anne's Well, which was a healing spring in mediaeval times. It was Roman in origin, and Roman relics have been found in or near it. No legend connecting it with St Anne in person is known but at some time in the Middle Ages a statue was discovered in its depths, and was believed by the people of the time to represent St Anne. It may, quite possibly have been a Roman statue, perhaps of a pagan water-spirit, but it was piously

1. Edward Rhodes, quoted by Crichton Porteous in *Beauty and Mystery of Well-Dressing*, 1949.

enshrined in a chapel near the well, and many miracles were ascribed to it. In 1538, it was swept away by Sir William Bassett, one of Thomas Cromwell's agents, together with all those 'crutches, shirts and shifts, with wax offered', which had been left as votive offerings by grateful pilgrims. The chapel was forcibly closed and eventually destroyed and although, within the next forty years, Buxton had become a noted spa, the cures achieved there were altogether medical, and had no religious significance. The modern well-celebration includes the blessing of two dressed wells, and a festival for the whole town, over which a Wells Festival Queen presides.

In some places, it is not open-air wells that are dressed, but the taps which appeared when the village first had water laid on. At Wirksworth, this happened in 1840. Today the taps have all disappeared, and there are no visible wells, but the town's very fine well-dressings are set up in Whit Week on traditional but now waterless sites. Here, as at Buxton, there is a Queen of the Wells, and a festival which is one of the highlights of the town's year. Youlgreave still has five old public taps which are annually dressed on the Saturday nearest St John the Baptists' Day (June 24th). At Barlow, a pump with a round stone basin, erected in 1840, is dressed on the Wednesday after St Lawrence's Day (August 10th), with large floral pictures arranged in triptych form. This village claims the distinction of having kept up the custom without a break since 1840, the war years not excepted.

Whipping Toms. Until 1847, a singular custom known as Whipping Toms was annually kept up on Shrove Tuesday in a part of the precincts of Leicester Castle called the Newarke. Boisterous games of various sorts, including a wild kind of hockey or shinney, were played there from the time that the Pancake Bell was rung until one o'clock. At that hour, a number of burly men appeared, dressed in blue smocks and armed with long whips. These were the Whipping Toms, each of whom had an attendant carrying a bell. As soon as the latter sounded their bells, the Whipping Toms began

to drive everyone out of the Newarke with vigorous strokes of their whips, lashing out freely on all sides, and sometimes bringing their victims to their knees by curling the thongs round their legs.

By custom the Whipping Toms were not allowed to strike above the knee, and consequently a kneeling man was safe as long as he remained in that position. Nor could they strike at all unless the bells were ringing, so that if their opponents could surround a bellman and silence him, that particular Whipping Tom was temporarily helpless unless, as usually happened, some other Tom and his bellman rushed to his rescue. It was possible to purchase immunity by paying a small sum to any of the aggressors who demanded it, but otherwise there was no safety for any one except by immediate flight to one of the recognized 'bounds', where no one might be attacked. These were the Magazine Gateway and the Turret Gateway, the lane leading to Rupert's Tower, and a narrow passage on the edge of the Newarke known as Little London. But if the prudent paid or fled, many young men preferred to defy the Whipping Toms and try to parry the whipstrokes with long sticks. This was called 'having a pennyworth of whipping', because those who failed to ward off the blows of the whips had to pay a fine. Most, however, were extremely skilful in the use of their sticks, and the contest often developed into a very exciting 'fencing-match', round which a ring of spectators would quickly form until the sudden sound of yet more bells warned them that other Whipping Toms were approaching to take them in the rear. These boisterous proceedings continued, with much shouting and laughter, until five o'clock in the afternoon, after which peace descended on the Newarke for another year.

When, or why, this curious custom was instituted is unknown. It seems to have been peculiar to Leicester, but even the citizens of that town were uncertain about its origin and meaning. One traditional explanation was that it commemorated the massacre of the Danes in 1002. *(See Hocktide.)* Another theory was that it was connected with certain privileges granted by John of Gaunt, and that it was a tenure-custom by which those privileges were maintained. However that may be, it was certainly old and very popular, and it was generally believed by the townsfolk that it could not be legally abolished. Nevertheless, it was suppressed in 1846 by a clause in the Leicester Improvement Act of that year, to the furious indignation of its supporters. On the following Shrove Tuesday, the Whipping Toms and a large crowd of angry people gathered in the Newarke as usual, determined to uphold what they regarded as their traditional rights. A serious clash with the police followed, during which many hard blows were struck by both sides, and several arrests were made. That, however, was the end; and since that tumultuous day in 1847, no further attempt has been made to revive the custom.

Whitsun Ales. At Whitsuntide formerly, it was the custom in most parishes to hold a Church Ale in order to raise money, and also to provide a lively social gathering for the parishioners. This was not the only occasion in the year when such ales were held; they often occurred at Easter, or May Day, or at the Patronal Festival, but the one which took place at Whitsun was usually the most important.

'There were no rates for the poor in my grandfather's days,' wrote John Aubrey in his account of Wiltshire, 'but for Kingston St Michael (no small parish) the Church Ale of Whitsuntide did the business. In every parish is (or was) a church-house to which belonged spits, crocks, etc, utensils for dressing provisions. Here the housekeepers met, and were merry and gave their charity. The young people were there too, and had dancing, bowling, shooting at butts, etc, the ancients sitting gravely by, and looking on. All things were civil and without scandal.'[1]

Normally, a Lord and Lady of the Ale, or a Whitsun King and Queen were elected to preside over the festivities, sometimes attended by a steward and a sword-bearer, and other officers. Richard Carew, in his *Survey of Cornwall* (1602) says that 'two young men of the parish were yearly chosen by their last fore-runners to be Wardens', and in that capacity, to be responsible for collecting money or provisions from the parishioners, and for the general success of the Church Ale. The churchwardens' accounts for Mere, in Wiltshire, record the appointment in 1568 of John Watts 'to be Cuckowe King this next year, because he was the Prince last year', and in 1606 of Henry Foster as 'Lord of the church ale, and John Forward Prince.'

There was a Lord and a Lady at Woodstock in Oxfordshire, where a very famous Whitsun Ale was held every seven years. It began on Ascension Eve with the erection of a Maypole, and went on until the end of Whit Week. The Lord and Lady went round the town in procession, carrying maces,[2] in the centre of which there was a Whit Cake which was offered to people to taste in exchange for a small money payment. Other Whit cakes, all rather like small Banbury cakes, were sold to all and sundry by a man who took them round in a large basket. Included in the procession were the attendants of the Lord and the Lady, the Morris dancers, and two men carrying a painted wooden horse. This horse, and a stuffed owl and a stuffed hawk hung up outside a long shed, decorated with evergreens and called the

1. John Aubrey *Introduction to the Survey and Natural History of the North Division of the County of Wiltshire.*
2. cf. *Lamb Ales*, p. 118.

Bowery, were given fancy names, and any one calling them anything else was fined; if he refused to pay the forfeit, he was liable to be set astride the wooden horse and carried thus, shoulder-high round the maypole. The maypole itself came to a hilarious end when the Woodstock Ale ceased about the middle of last century. The last pole was erected about 1843, and was left in place after the festivities were over. A Mr Holloway of Woodstock bought it, to keep as a relic of former happy times, but he never enjoyed any advantage from this nostalgic purchase. Before he could remove it, the Yeomanry, being then in the town, pulled it down one night in an excess of high spirits and destroyed it.

Woodstock's Whitsun Ale lasted rather longer than most of the Ales that once flourished in villages up and down the country. At least in its later days, it seems to have lost its early character as a practical money-raising event for the parish needs, and to have become far more of a boisterous festival. In most places, the Church Ales died out in the eighteenth century, or even earlier, for two main reasons. One was that the average Ale was a lively and cheerful gathering, and so earned the disapproval of the puritanically-minded. This was true of them all, but especially of the Whitsun Ale. The people danced and sang, ate, drank, and sometimes got drunk, set up their Summer Bower in the churchyard, played games, and loudly welcomed the Morris dancers in their ribbons and bells. All this seems, and probably was, innocent enough, but there were some who did not think so, and did their best to suppress these merry occasions wherever they could. The other reason for the decline was financial. Changes in the system of parish rating, charging rents for church pews, and various other ways of raising money slowly made the Ales no longer necessary. One by one, they ceased. The Church Houses mentioned by Aubrey, in which they used to be held, were put to other uses, or disappeared altogether. By the nineteenth century, with only a few exceptions, the whole custom had gone, and was no more than a fading memory.

Whuppity Stourie. Whuppity Stourie (or Scoorie) is an old Springtime custom which is peculiar to the Royal Burgh of Lanark. It takes place on the first day of March, and begins with the ringing of the town bell in the parish church. Between the beginning of October and the end of February, this bell is not rung at six o'clock every evening, as it is during the rest of the year, but on March 1st the nightly ringing begins again. Crowds of children come to the Cross and wait outside the church, together with many adult spectators, and the Provost and other town officials who watch the proceedings from a platform erected for their use. Each child carries a home-made weapon consisting of a tightly-rolled ball of paper tied to the end of a long string. As soon as the bell's note is heard, they all rush off round the church, whirling their paper balls round their heads, and beating each other with them as they run. They circuit the church thus three times, and then there is a wild scramble for pennies thrown to them from the platform[1]. £10 is allotted annually for this purpose from one of the town funds. When the scramble is over, the Provost addresses the assembled people, children and adults alike, and so the brief and lively celebration comes to its end for that year.

This is the modern form of Whuppity Stourie. The runners are now all children, but until at least as late as the first decade of the present century, the youths of the town also took part. The customary weapons then were not paper balls, but the caps, or bonnets, of the runners attached to cords. With these the lads not only beat each other, but also attempted to strike the bellringer as they ran, a proceeding known as 'buffing the bell-man'. As soon as the church had been circuited thrice, they all dashed away to the Wellgate Head to meet the youths of New Lanark, and a stand-up fight with the

1. In 1964, the children were too impatient to wait for the bell to be rung, and started running as soon as the clock struck six. It was impossible to stop them in their wild flight, but when they had completed their unauthorized rounds, they were made to repeat the three-fold run before the pennies were thrown for the scramble. (*Hamilton Advertiser*, March 6th, 1964.)

stringed bonnets followed. Afterwards, the victors, paraded the streets, their leader carrying a flag made from a handkerchief fixed on a pole, and all loudly singing:

> Hooray, boys, hooray!
> For we have won the day
> We've met the bold New (Old) Lanark boys
> And chased them doun the brae![1]

There is no fight now, for this part of the proceedings was suppressed by the magistrates but hearty blows with the paper balls are still exchanged as the children run round the church.

Various theories have been put forward to account for the whole curious ritual, of which the origin is very uncertain. One is that it is intended to herald, or welcome the Spring. Another explains it as a commemoration of a former custom of whipping penitents round the church. The latter theory would not cover the fight, which was probably the most important part of the whole affair for those who took part in it. It seems probable, in view of the Springtime date, the ringing of bells and general noise, the former battle, and the emphasis even now upon blows given and received, that here we have the remains of that ancient magical rite, found in various forms in many northern countries, whereby Winter and all its attendant evils was fought, defeated, and finally driven away from the land.

Wichnor Flitch. *(See Dunmow Flitch.)*

Woodmen of Arden's Meetings. At Meriden, the Warwickshire village which claims to be the true geographical centre of England, and was once very near to the centre of the then wide-spread Forest of Arden, the archery company known as the Woodmen of Arden meets every year, to hold its Wardmotes in June and July, and its Grand Wardmote in August. As far as its records show, this company is not yet quite two hundred years old, having been formed in 1785; but it is probable that Meriden, or its immediate surroundings, have seen the meetings of many earlier companies in the Middle Ages, when archery was of the first importance,

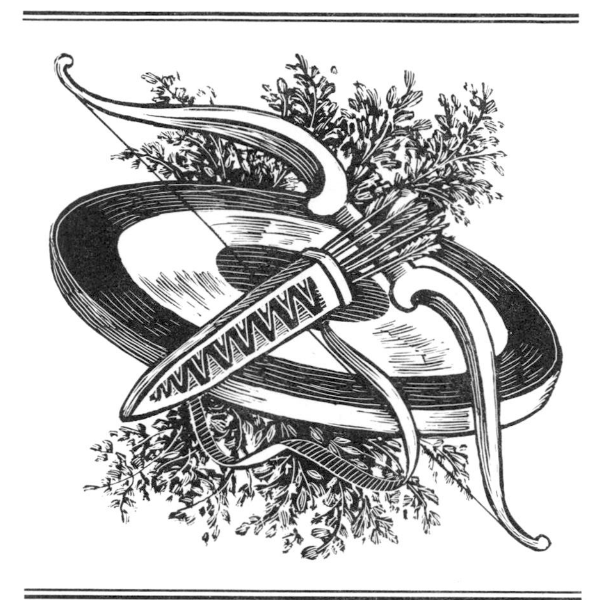

and the foresters settled their affairs at open-air gatherings in the Forest's centre.

The present company of Woodmen is limited to eighty members. They wear a uniform consisting of a green coat with gilt buttons, a green hat, buff waistcoat, and white trousers. They use a six-foot yew bow of the type known at Crécy and Agincourt, and arrows stamped according to their weight in silver, as was usual in mediaeval times. Archery competitions take place at the June and July Wardmotes, and most especially, at the Grand Wardmote, which lasts for four days at the beginning of August.

Wroth Silver. Wroth Silver is money annually due from various parishes of Knightlow Hundred, in Warwickshire, to the Duke of Buccleuch, who is Lord of that Hundred. Very strict and obviously ancient rules govern its collection. It has to be paid before sunrise on St Martin's Day, November 11th, at Knightlow Cross, which stands in a roadside field not far from Dunchurch. Here the representatives of the parishes concerned meet to hear the Duke's agent read the Charter of Assembly and, as he calls upon them severally to do so, to drop their coins into a hollow in the large stone which is all that now remains of the Cross. Each man,

1. F. Marian McNeill, *The Silver Bough*, Vol. IV, 1968.

as he makes his payment, says 'Wroth Silver'; formerly, as Sir William Dugdale records in his *Antiquities of Warwickshire,* he was also required to walk round the stone three times before laying his money in the hollow. The sums due vary from one penny to two shillings and threepence. When all the payments have been made, the entire company, led by the agent, goes to the Dun Cow Inn at Stretton-on-Dunsmore, where they have breakfast at the Duke's expense, and drink his health in rum and milk.

The payment of Wroth Silver is a very old custom which is said to run back to Anglo-Saxon times. It has been variously explained as money originally given for exemption from military service, or as a form of wayleave-payment to secure the right of driving cattle over Dunsmore Heath. The total sum collected each year does not exceed nine shillings and fourpence, which certainly cannot cover the cost of the breakfast given by the Duke after the ceremony. Nevertheless, payment is rigidly enforced, and the penalties for default are not of a kind to encourage evasion. For every penny left unpaid, a fine of £1, or alternatively, of a white bull with red ears and a red nose, can be imposed. Such an animal would be exceedingly difficult to find today, and probably has been so for a very long time, for the description suggests the old wild cattle of England, which are now virtually extinct. It is therefore interesting to read in *Notes and Queries* (December 16th 1893) that the fine in this form was imposed at least once during the nineteenth century, 'a white bull having been demanded by the Steward of the late Lord John Scott, then Lord of the Hundred'.

Yule Candle. The Yule, or Christmas Candle was an ornamental candle of great size which was once very widely used at Christmas in Great Britain, Ireland, and the Scandinavian countries. It was often coloured red, or green, or blue, and was sometimes decorated with sprigs of holly and other evergreens. It was lit either on Christmas Eve to shed its light on the festival supper and afterwards to burn all through the night, or early on Christmas morning, to burn until bed-time. It was then ceremonially extinguished, and in some districts, that was the end of the matter. More usually, however, it was re-kindled on each successive night of the Twelve-day festival, and was not finally put out until Twelfth Night.

So long as the Yule Candle burnt steadily, it was believed to shed a blessing on the household, but if it went out too soon, or was accidentally blown out, it was an omen of misfortune or death in the coming year. In some houses, only the head of the family, or its oldest member, was allowed to light or extinguish it, and it was generally considered unlucky for any one else to touch it once it was alight. While it burnt, it was unlucky to snuff it, or move it from the place originally chosen for it. When the time came to extinguish it, this was usually done by pressing the wick carefully with a pair of tongs. The flame was never blown out, for that brought bad luck.

Occasionally the candle was allowed to burn itself out on the last night, but this was not very usual because the unconsumed remnant was widely believed to have protective or fertilizing powers. It was normally kept in the house during the following twelve months as a charm against evil. In Denmark, it was often hastily relit during thunderstorms, to save the house from being struck by lightning. Swedish farmers used it for smearing the plough with tallow at the start of the Spring ploughing, in order to hallow the soil and make the seed prosper. In some parts of Scotland, what remained of the Yule Candle was put into a locked chest and kept for use at the owner's wake after his death.

Until about the middle of last century, chandlers used to present their regular customers with Yule Candles as a mark of respect. Candles of various sizes were then a usual gift at Christmas-time. 'The poor', wrote R. T. Hampson in 1841, 'were wont to present the rich with wax tapers and yule candles are still in the north of Scotland given by merchants to their customers. At one time children at the village schools in Lancashire were required to bring a mould candle before the *parting* or separation of the Christmas holidays.'[1] As late as just before the outbreak of the 1914 War, it was still a common practice for English grocers to send their customers boxes of coloured candles at Christmas though these, being of ordinary size, could not supply the place of the older, long-burning Yule Candle. A curious and apparently unique custom connected with candles, though not with gifts, was recorded by a contributor to *Notes and Queries* in 1873. He said that when he was a child, the colliers of Llwynymaen, near

1. R. T. Hampson, *Medii Aevi Kalendarium*, 1841.

Oswestry, used to go round from house to house on the evenings of Christmas week, carrying boards covered with clay into which lighted candles were set. Only the miners took part in this ceremony, which does not seem to have been recorded elsewhere.

The true Yule Candle is now rarely seen, but a host of smaller candles, real or electric, still burn on the Christmas Tree or the Kissing Bough, or before the small models of the Crib which some families set up in their houses every year. Another lovely and very old custom still observed in some homes is that of putting lighted candles in the window during the Christmas season. An ancient tradition says that this was first done to guide the homeless Christ-Child through the darkness and lead Him to shelter in the warm and lighted house.

Yule Log. The Yule Log was formerly one of the most important features of the Christmas festivities in Great Britain, France, parts of Italy, and Germany, and some East European countries, At dusk on Christmas Eve, a large log of oak, or ash, or fruit-tree wood was ceremonially brought into the house and laid upon the open hearth. It was kindled with a fragment of last year's log that had been especially saved for the purpose, and once alight, it was essential that it should burn steadily until the time came for it to be deliberately extinguished. How long that was varied in different regions. Almost everywhere the log was expected to burn for at least twelve hours; in many districts it was kept alight throughout the Twelve Days of Christmas. It was never allowed to burn away completely, but was quenched at the end of the customary period.

While it burnt, the greatest care had to be taken to prevent its flames from going out untimely, for that would have been a very bad omen for the coming year. 'The embers were raked up to it every night', a Shropshire informant told Miss Burne in the 'eighties of last century, 'and it was carefully tended that it might not go out during the whole season, during which time no light might either be struck, given, or borrowed.'[1] In most parts of

England, it was extinguished at the end of the Twelve Days. Often, it was relit at Candlemas, when it was allowed to burn all through the day, and was finally put out at the close of the festival. Herrick tells us in his *Hesperides* how, in his time, it was customary on February 2nd to:

> Kindle the Christmas Brand, and then
> Till sunne-set let it burne;
> Which quencht, then lay it up agen
> Till Christmas next returne.
>
> Part must be kept wherewith to teend
> The Christmas Log next yeare;
> And where 'tis safely kept, the Fiend
> Can do no mischiefe there.

The Yule Log was the domestic counterpart of the great communal fires of the midwinter and midsummer festivals, and like them, it was associated with fertility and continuing life, and with preservation from evil. It had also a more intimate significance, in that its flames gave light and warmth to the family dead who, in many areas, were believed to return to their homes at Christmas. Time-honoured rituals surrounded its bringing home and kindling. In England, it was thought to be very unlucky for the Yule Log to be bought. If a man had

1. C. S. Burne, *Shropshire Folk-Lore*, 1883.

trees of his own, he cut it from them, if he had none, he fetched a log from someone else's woods. Very often it was a gift from the local landowners, or the village carpenter, or it might be 'found' in the soldiers' sense of that word, but money must not be exchanged for it.

For its home-bringing, it was often decorated with evergreens and dragged to the door by cart-horses or oxen. In some districts, corn was thrown over it and cider or ale sprinkled upon it just before it was set alight. In Cornwall,[1] the figure of a man was sometimes roughly chalked on the surface of the Christmas Mock, or Block, there to blacken and fade slowly in the fire and smoke as the great log smouldered through the Twelve Days. This custom, with its faint suggestion of sacrifice, does not seem to have been recorded in any other English county, and its origin is unknown.

Elsewhere in Europe, the ceremonies were often far more elaborate, In Jugoslavia, a young tree was felled before sunrise on Christmas Eve and sawn into logs, of which several were frequently carried into the same house, though one somewhat larger than the rest seems to have been the essential Christmas Brand. Women and girls adorned it with flowers and leaves, red silk and gold wire. At twilight, it was brought indoors through a door lit by candles held on either side, and corn and wine were thrown over it as the threshold was crossed. The oldest man of the family laid it on the fire, and prayers were said for the welfare of the homestead and the farm, and all living things within them. On the following morning, when the *polaznik* (an East European equivalent of the British Lucky Bird, or First Foot) arrived with his luck-bringing greetings, he threw wheat over the assembled family, saying 'Christ is born', to which all present answered 'He is born indeed'. Then someone, usually the mother, threw wheat over the *polaznik*, after which he went to the hearth, struck the Yule Log and, as the sparks flew from it, wished prosperity and happiness to everyone in the house and all their animals.

1. M. A. Courtney, *Cornish Feasts and Folk-Lore, 1890.*

In Provence, where the Yule Log was called the *tréfoire*, the whole family went to fetch it home, and a carol was sung invoking blessings upon the women that they might bear children, and upon the crops, herds, and flocks that they might increase. Here, too, wine was thrown over the log, either by the master of the house, or by the youngest child. Frédéric Mistral recalls in his *Memoirs* how, when he was lad, he helped to bring in the *tréfoire*, walking in a single-file procession, 'headed by the oldest at one end, and I, the last-born, bringing up the rear.' The kitchen was circuited three times and then, the log being laid upon the hearth, his father poured wine over it, calling down God's blessing upon them all as he did so. After that, the wood was kindled and, says Mistral, 'as the first flame leapt up, my father would cross himself saying, "Burn the log, O fire", and with that we all sat down to the table.'[1]

The ashes and charcoal from the Yule Log were used in many regions as protecting, or healing, or fertilizing charms. Sometimes the ashes were scattered over the fields. In Brittany, they were thrown into wells to keep the water pure; in Italy, they were used as a charm against hailstorms or, more recently, to protect silk-worms from harm. Ashes from the German *Christbrand*, or *Christlotz*, freed cattle from vermin and fruit-trees from insects, and the log itself, which here normally burnt only for one night before being taken off the hearth, was kept in the house as protection against lightning, and was sometimes re-kindled during severe storms. Almost everywhere, an unburnt portion was carefully preserved, for the double purpose of averting fire and misfortune, and ensuring continuity by its use in the kindling of next year's Yule Log.

In some parts of the Scottish Highlands, a curious variant of the customary log ceremony used to be observed. Early on Christmas Eve, the head of the household went to the woods and searched for a withered tree-stump, which he then carved into a roughly made figure of an old woman. This was the *Cailleach Nollaich*, or Christmas Old Wife, a sinister being represent-

1. *Memoirs of Mistral*, trans. C. E. Maud, 1907.

ing, not fertility and life, but the evils of winter and death. At dusk, the figure was brought indoors and laid upon the burning peats of the house-fire. All the family sat round the hearth to watch it blaze and perish in the flames, and when it was finally reduced to ashes, the rest of the evening was spent in boisterous games and merriment. Here there was no question of saving a remnant of the log for next year's ceremonies; the Old Wife had to be totally consumed if death and misfortune were to be averted in the coming year. It was generally believed that if the *Cailleach Nollaich* was duly burnt at the proper time, death would not come to the house throughout the following twelve months. *(See Ashen Faggot.)*

SELECT BIBLIOGRAPHY

Addison, William. *English Fairs and Markets*, 1953.

Addy, S. O. *Household Tales and Other Traditional Remains collected in the Counties of York, Lincoln, Derby and Nottingham*, 1895.

Alford, Violet. *Introduction to English Folklore*, 1952. 'The Abbots Bromley Horn Dance', *Antiquity*, June, 1933.

Andrews, W. *Church History, Customs and Folk Lore*, 1881. *Curious Church Customs*, 1895.

Armstrong, E. A. *The Folklore of Birds*, 1958.

Atkinson, J. C. *Forty Years in a Moorland Parish*, 1891.

Aubrey, J. *Remains of Gentilisme and Judaisme, 1686–7*, ed. J. Britten, 1881.
Miscellanies upon Various Subjects, 1857, 4th ed.

Axon, W. E. *Cheshire Gleanings*, 1894.

Baker, A. E. *Glossary of Northamptonshire Words and Phrases*, 1854.

Balfour, M. C. and Thomas, N. W. *Northumberland, County Folk-Lore*, Vol. IV, 1904.

Bankes, M. M. *British Calendar Customs: Scotland, 1937–41*, 3 Vols., *Orkney & Shetland*, 1946.

Baring-Gould, S. *A Book of Folklore*, n.d. *Curious Myths of the Middle Ages*, 1869. *Strange Survivals*, 1892. *Yorkshire Oddities, Incidents, and Strange Events*, 1890.

Beamont, William. *An Account of the Cheshire Township of Appleton*, 1877.

Beddington, W., and Christy, E. *It Happened in Hampshire*, n.d.

Berkeley, M. and Jenkins, C. E. *A Worcestershire Book*, n.d.

Berkshire Book, The. Berkshire Federation of Women's Institutes, 1950.

Biddenden Local History Society. *The Story of Biddendon*, 1953.

Billson, C. J. *Leicestershire and Rutland. County Folk-Lore*, Vol. 1. 1985.

Bloom, J. Harvey. *Folk Lore, Old Customs and Superstitions in Shakespeareland*, 1929.

Blount, Thomas. *Fragmenta Antiquitates: or Ancient Tenures of Land and Jocular Customs*, ed. Jos. Beckwith, 1784.

Blundell, M. *Blundell's Diary and Letter-Book, 1702–1728*, 1952.

Bogg, Edmund. *From Eden Vale to the Plains of York*, n.d.

Borlase, W. *Antiquities of Cornwall*, 1784.

Bourne, N. *Antiquitates Vulgares*, 1725.

Brand, J. *Observations on the Popular Antiquities of Great Britain*, ed. Sir Henry Ellis, 1849.

Bray, Mrs A. E. *The Borders of the Tamar and the Tavy*, 1879, 2nd ed.

Brockie, J. *Legends and Superstitions of Durham*, 1886.

Burne, C. S. *Shropshire Folk-Lore*, 1883.

Burrows, Montagu. *Worthies of All Souls*, 1874.

Burton, A. *Rush-Bearing*, 1891.

Carew, R. *Survey of Cornwall*, 1602.

Carkeet-James, E. H. *His Majesty's Tower of London*, 1950.

Carmichael, A. *Carmina Gaedelica*, 1900.

Cashen, W. *Manx Folklore*, 1912.

Caudwell, I. *Ceremonies of Holy Church*, 1948

Chambers, E. K. *The Mediaeval Stage*, 1903, 2 vols.

Chambers, R. *The Book of Days*, 1864.

Chanter, G. *Wanderings in North Devon*, 1887.

Charlton, Lionel. *History of Whitby and Whitby Abbey*, 1779.

Cheshire Notes & Queries.

Cheshire Sheaf', 'The. Reprinted from the *Chester Courant*.

Courtney, M. A. *Cornish Feasts and Folk-Lore*, 1890.

Cox, M. R. *Introduction to the Study of Folk-Lore*, 1893.

Coxhead, J. W. R. *Old Devon Customs*, 1957.

Dacombe, M. R. *Dorset Up Along and Down Along*, n.d.

Davies, J. Ceredig. *Folklore of West and Mid-Wales*, 1911.

Denham, M. A. *The Denham Tracts*, ed. J. Hardy, 1892, 2 vols.

Derbyshire Notes and Queries.

Devon and Cornwall Notes and Queries.

Devonshire Association Transactions.

Ditchfield, P. H. *Old English Customs*, 1896.

Dugdale, Sir William. *Antiquities of Warwickshire*, 1656.

Dyer, T. Thistleton. *British Popular Customs*, 1876. *English Folk-Lore*, 1880.

Edwards, H. *A Collection of Old English Customs and Curious Bequests and Charities*, 1842.

Edwards, T. J. *Military Customs*, 1954.

Elworthy, F. T. *West Somerset Word-Book*, 1886.

Emden, A. B. *An Oxford Hall in Mediaeval Times*, 1923.

Farrer, J. A. *Primitive Manners and Customs*, 1879.

Folklore. Journal of the Folklore Society.

Folk-Lore Record, The, 1878–82.

Forby, R. *The Vocabulary of East Anglia*, 1830.
Frazer, Sir J. G. *The Golden Bough*, 1913–15.

Gairdner, James (ed.). *The Paston Letters, 1422–1509*, 1900.
Gentleman's Magazine Library, The.
Gloucestershire Notes and Queries.
Gomme, A. B. *The Traditional Games of England, Scotland, and Ireland*, 1894 and 1898, 2 vols.
Gomme, G. L. *Ethnology in Folk Lore*, 1892.
The Village Community, 1890.
Gregor, Walter. *Notes on the Folk-Lore of the North-East of Scotland*, 1881.
Greville, Charles. *The Greville Memoirs*, ed. Roger Fulford, 1963.
Gurdon, E. C. *Suffolk, County Folk-Lore*, Vol. 1, 1893.
Gutch, M. *The East Riding of Yorkshire, County Folk-Lore*, Vol. VI, 1912.
The North Riding of Yorkshire, York and the Ainsty, County Folk-Lore, Vol. II, 1899.
Gutch, M. and Peacock, M. *Folk-Lore concerning Lincolnshire, County Folk-Lore*, Vol. V, 1908.
Guthrie, E. J. *Old Scottish Customs, Local and General*, 1885.

Halliday, W. J. and Umpleby, A. S. *The White Rose Garland*, 1949.
Hampson, R. T. *Medii Aevi Kalendarium*, 1841.
Hardwick, Charles. *History of the Borough of Preston*, 1857.
Traditions, Superstitions and Folk-Lore, 1872.
Harland, J. and Wilkinson, T. *Lancashire Folk-Lore* 1867. *Lancashire Legends*, 1873.
Harman, H. *Sketches of the Buckinghamshire Countryside*, 1934.
Harrison, F. *Mediaeval Man and His Notions*, 1947.
Harrison, Jane. *Ancient Art and Ritual*, n.d.
Hartland, E. S. *The Science of Fairy-Tales*, 1891.
Gloucestershire, County Folk-Lore, Vol. 1, 1895.
Hasted, Edward. *History and Topographical Survey of the County of Kent*, 1790.
Havergal, F. T. *Herefordshire Words and Phrases*, 1887.
Henderson, William. *Notes on the Folk-Lore of the Northern Counties of England and the Borders*, 1866, 2nd ed., 1879.
Hinchcliffe, W. *Bartholmley*, 1856.
Hodgkin, R. H. *Six Centuries of an Oxford College*, 1949.
Hole, Christina. *Traditions and Customs of Cheshire*, 1937. *English Custom and Usage*, 1941. *Christmas and Its Customs*, 1957. *Easter and Its Customs*, 1961.
Hone, William. *The Everyday Book*, 1826. *The Table Book*, 1827. *The Year Book*, 1829.
Hope, R. C. *The Legendary Lore of the Holy Wells of England*, 1893.
Howitt, William. *The Rural Life of England*, 1840, 2nd ed.
Hughes, Thomas. *The Scourging of the White Horse*, 1859.
Hull, Eleanor. *Folklore of the British Isles*, 1928.
Hunt, R. *Popular Romances of the West of England*, 1881.

Jagger, Mary. *History of Honley*, 1914.
James, E. O. *Seasonal Feasts and Festivals*, 1961.
Jenkin, A. Hamilton. *Cornwall and the Cornish*, 1932.
Jones, F. *The Holy Wells of Wales*, 1955.
Jones, T. Gwyn. *Welsh Folklore and Folk-Custom*, 1930.
Johnson, W. *Folk-Memory*, 1908.

Kempe, A. J. (ed.). *Losely Manuscripts and Other Rare Documents, The*, 1830.

Leather, E. M. *The Folk Lore of Herefordshire*, 1912.
Lincolnshire Notes and Queries.
Long, George. *The Folklore Calendar*, 1930.

Macquoid, T. & K. *About Yorkshire*, 1883.
Marples, Morris. *White Horse and Other Hill Figures*, 1949.
Mason, M. H. *Tales and Traditions of Tenby*, 1858.
McNeill, E. N. *The Silver Bough*, 1957–1968, 4 vols.
Miles, C. A. *Christmas in Ritual and Tradition*, 1912.
Misson de Valbourg, J. *Memoirs and Observations of M. Misson in his Travels over England*, trans. J. Ozell, 1719, from the original French of 1697.
Mitchell, A. *The Past in the Present*, 1880.
Money, Walter. *An Historical Sketch of the Town of Hungerford*, 1894.
Morant, Philip. *History and Antiquities of the County of Essex*, 1768.
Moor, E. *Suffolk Words and Phrases*, 1823.
Moore, A. W. *Folk Lore of the Isle of Man*, 1891.
Morris, M. C. *Yorkshire Folk-Talk*, 1892.

Neville, C. A. *A Corner of the North*, 1911.
Newall, V. *An Egg at Easter*, 1971.
Nicolson, J. *The Folk-Lore of East Yorkshire*, 1890.
Noake, J. *Worcester in Olden Times*, 1840.
Notes & Queries.

Olivier, E. *Moonrakings*, n.d.
Opie, Iona and Peter. *The Lore and Language of Schoolchildren*, 1959.
Owen, M. Trefor. *Welsh Folk Customs*, 1959.

Parkinson, T. *Yorkshire Legends and Traditions*, 1891.
Paton, C. I. *Manx Calendar Customs*, 1939.
Plot, Robert. *The Natural History of Oxfordshire*, 1677. *The Natural History of Staffordshire*, 1686.

Polson, Alexander. *Our Highland Folklore Heritage*, 1926.
Poole, C. H. *Customs, Superstitions, and Legends of the County of Somerset*, 1877.
Porteous, Crichton. *The Beauty and Mystery of Well-Dressing*, 1949.

Quiller Couch, M. & L. *Ancient and Holy Wells of Cornwall*, 1894.
Quiller Couch, T. *History of Polperro*, 1871.

Records of Buckinghamshire.
Roberts, P. *Cambrian Popular Antiquities*, 1815.
Rudkin, E. *Lincolnshire Folklore*, 1936.

Scottish Notes and Queries.
Sherwood, Revd. E. *Oxford Yesterday*, 1927.
Shropshire Notes and Queries.
Simpkins, J. E. *Fife, County Folk-Lore*, Vol. VII, 1914.
Simpson, E. B. *Folklore in Scotland*, 1908.
Somerset and Dorset Notes and Queries.
Steer, F. W. *The History of the Dunmow Flitch Ceremony*, 1951.
Sternberg, T. *Dialect and Folk-Lore of Northamptonshire*, 1851.
Stow, J. *Survey of London and Westminster*, 1598.
Strutt, Joseph. *The Sports and Pastimes of the People of England*, 1801, ed. J. C. Cox, 1903.
Suffolk Garland, The.
Suffolk Notes and Queries.
Sussex Archeological Collections.
Sussex Notes and Queries.

Taunt, H. W. *History of Kirklington.*
Tebbutt, C. F. *Huntingdonshire Folk and Their Folklore*, 1951.
Thorsby, J. *History of Leicester*, 1791.
Tongue, R. L. *Somerset Folklore*, 1965, ed. K. M. Briggs.
Trevelyan, M. *Folk-Lore and Folk-Stories of Wales*, 1909.
Tusser, Thomas. *Five Hundred Points of Good Husbandrie*, ed. Dorothy Hartley.
Tyler, E. B. *Primitive Culture*, 1903, 2 vols., 4th ed.

Udall, L. S. *Dorsetshire Folk Lore*, 1922.
Urlin, E. *Festivals, Holy Days and Saints' Days*, n.d.

Vaux, J. E. *Church Folk Lore*, 1902.

Walford, C. *Fairs, Past and Present*, 1883.
Whistler, Lawrence. *The English Festivals*, 1947.
Whitcombe, Mrs H. F. *Bygone Days in Devon and Cornwall*, 1874.
Willimore, Frederick. *History of Walsall*, 1887.
Worcestershire Notes and Queries.
Wright, A. R. *English Folklore*, 1928.
Wright, A. R. & Lones, T. E. *British Calendar Customs: England*, 1936–9, 3 vols.
Wright, E. M. *Rustic Speech and Folk Lore*, 1913.

Yorkshire Notes and Queries.

INDEX